Learning from Words

CW00554340

Testimony is an invaluable source of knowle of those around us for everything from the ingredients in our food and medicine to the identity of our family members. Recent years have seen an explosion of interest in the epistemology of testimony. Despite the multitude of views offered, a single thesis is nearly universally accepted: testimonial knowledge is acquired through the process of *transmission* from speaker to hearer. In this book, Jennifer Lackey shows that this thesis is false and, hence, that the literature on testimony has been shaped at its core by a view that is fundamentally misguided. A detailed alternative to this conception of testimony is then defended: whereas the views currently dominant focus on the epistemic status of what speakers *believe*, Lackey advances a theory that instead centers on what speakers *say*. The upshot is that, strictly speaking, we do not learn from one another's beliefs—we *learn from one another's words*. Once this shift in focus is in place, Lackey goes on to argue that, though positive reasons are necessary for testimonial knowledge, testimony itself is an irreducible epistemic source. This leads to the development of a theory that gives proper credence to testimony's epistemologically *dual* nature: *both* the speaker and the hearer must make a positive epistemic contribution to testimonial knowledge. The resulting view not only reveals that testimony has the capacity to generate knowledge, but it also gives appropriate weight to our nature as both socially indebted and individually rational creatures. The approach found in this book will, then, represent a radical departure from the views currently dominating the epistemology of testimony, and thus is intended to reshape our understanding of the deep and ubiquitous reliance we have on the testimony of those around us.

Jennifer Lackey is an Associate Professor of Philosophy at Northwestern University.

To Mom, my strength,
Baron, my love,
and
Isabella and Catherine, my angels.
I have learned endless riches from your words.

Learning from Words

Testimony as a Source of Knowledge

Jennifer Lackey

OXFORD
UNIVERSITY PRESS

OXFORD

UNIVERSITY PRESS

Great Clarendon Street, Oxford OX2 6DP

Oxford University Press is a department of the University of Oxford.
It furthers the University's objective of excellence in research, scholarship,
and education by publishing worldwide in

Oxford New York

Auckland Cape Town Dar es Salaam Hong Kong Karachi
Kuala Lumpur Madrid Melbourne Mexico City Nairobi
New Delhi Shanghai Taipei Toronto

With offices in

Argentina Austria Brazil Chile Czech Republic France Greece
Guatemala Hungary Italy Japan Poland Portugal Singapore
South Korea Switzerland Thailand Turkey Ukraine Vietnam

Oxford is a registered trade mark of Oxford University Press
in the UK and in certain other countries

Published in the United States
by Oxford University Press Inc., New York

British Library Cataloguing in Publication Data

Data available

Library of Congress Cataloging in Publication Data

Data available

Typeset by Laserwords Private Limited, Chennai, India
Printed in Great Britain
on acid-free paper by the
MPG Books Group, King's Lynn, Norfolk

ISBN 978-0-19-921916-2 (hbk)
     978-0-19-957561-9 (pbk)

10 9 8 7 6 5 4 3 2 1

Contents

Preface

I have been working on themes surrounding the epistemology of testimony since my graduate school days, and so there are many who deserve thanks for their assistance in making this book possible. I have been fortunate to be a part of four institutions, Brown University, Pomona College, Northern Illinois University, and Northwestern University, that have created ideal environments for me to flourish in, both professionally and personally—my thanks to my teachers, friends, and colleagues at all of these places. I am also very grateful to the National Endowment for the Humanities for supporting my research during the summer of 2002; to Downing College at the University of Cambridge for providing exceptional work conditions while I was a Faculty Fellow in the summer of 2003; to Northern Illinois University for Research and Artistry Awards during the summers of 2004 and 2005; and to the American Council of Learned Societies for a generously funded Charles A. Ryskamp Fellowship in 2007 that enabled me to complete this book.

Portions of this manuscript have appeared in a variety of forms in previously published material. Chapter 1 is based on "The Nature of Testimony," *Pacific Philosophical Quarterly* 87 (2006); Chapter 2 and section 3.1 from Chapter 3 rely on "Testimonial Knowledge and Transmission," *The Philosophical Quarterly* 49 (1999) and "Learning from Words," *Philosophy and Phenomenological Research* 73 (2006); Chapter 4 is based on "Norms of Assertion," *Noûs* 41 (2007); and section 5.3 from Chapter 5 is based on "A Minimal Expression of Non-Reductionism in the Epistemology of Testimony," *Noûs* 37 (2003). I am grateful to Blackwell Publishing for their kind permission to use this material. Half of section 5.2 and Chapter 6 rely on "It Takes Two to Tango: Beyond Reductionism and Non-Reductionism in the Epistemology of Testimony," in Jennifer Lackey and Ernest Sosa (eds.), *The Epistemology of Testimony* (Oxford: Oxford University Press, 2006). For permission to use this material, I am grateful to Oxford University Press. Sections 7.1–6 of Chapter 7 are based on "Testimony and the Infant/Child Objection," *Philosophical Studies* 126 (2005), with kind permission of Springer Science and Business Media. Note 38 of Chapter 2 is based on a section of my review of Martin Kusch's *Knowledge by Agreement: The Programme of Communitarian Epistemology*, which appeared in *Philosophy and Phenomenological Research* 72 (2006). And the Appendix is based on "Memory as a Generative Epistemic Source," *Philosophy and Phenomenological Research* 70 (2005), and "Why Memory Really *Is* a Generative Epistemic Source: A Reply to Senor," *Philosophy and Phenomenological Research* 74 (2007). I am grateful to *Philosophy and Phenomenological Research* for their kind permission to use this material. It should be noted that, though I have drawn on some of my previously published work during the process of writing this book, much of this material has been rewritten, supplemented, or substantially revised.

I have presented parts of this book at various conferences, workshops, and colloquia over the years. My thanks to audience members at the University of Texas at Austin; Pomona College; Southern Illinois University at Edwardsville; the 2001 Southern California Philosophy Conference; the 2002 Pacific Division of the APA in Seattle, WA; the 2003 Pacific Division of the APA in San Francisco, CA; Northern Illinois University; the 2003 Bellingham Summer Philosophy Conference; the 2004 Pacific Division of the APA in Pasadena, CA; the University of Iowa; the 2005 Central Division of the APA in Chicago, IL; the 2005 Rutgers Epistemology Conference; the 2005 Bellingham Summer Philosophy Conference; the University of Kentucky; the 2005 meeting of the Central States Philosophical Association in Lexington, KY; the University of Wisconsin, Milwaukee; the 2006 Pacific Division of the APA in Portland, OR; the 2006 International Conference on Philosophy in Athens, Greece; Wheaton College; Northwestern University; Purdue University; the 2007 Pacific Division of the APA in San Francisco, CA; and Yale University.

I have also received insightful comments and invaluable encouragement from many people in a variety of ways while working on this project. Some offered penetrating objections or helpful conversations at critical junctures, others offered written comments on portions of the manuscript or formal comments at conferences, and still others provided support when it was needed the most. I am grateful to Jonathan Adler, Robert Almeder, Robert Audi, Kent Bach, Jason Baehr, Mike Bishop, Larry BonJour, David Buller, Liz Camp, Stew Cohen, Juan Comesaña, Marian David, Fred Dretske, Mylan Engel, Jeremy Fantl, Lizzie Fricker, Richard Fumerton, Tamar

Szabó Gendler, Cody Gilmore, Michael Glanzberg, Alvin Goldman, Peter Graham, John Greco, Liz Harman, John Hawthorne, Mark Heller, Ted Hinchman, Daniel Howard-Snyder, Paul Hurley, Tom Kapitan, Peter Klein, Jon Kvanvig, William Lycan, Matt McGrath, Brian McLaughlin, Ishani Maitra, Elijah Millgram, Ram Neta, Duncan Pritchard, Gurpreet Rattan, Wayne Riggs, Fred Schmitt, Dion Scott-Kakures, Tom Senor, Joe Shieber, Ted Sider, David Sosa, Ernie Sosa, Bill Tolhurst, Jim Van Cleve, Matt Weiner, Timothy Williamson, Charles Young, Linda Zagzebski, and Dean Zimmerman.

Three people deserve special thanks for their help with this book. Jason Kawall has been discussing the ideas in these pages with me since graduate school at Brown and read several chapters of the manuscript, offering his typically unique and penetrating comments. More than this, he has been the dearest of friends and has made the writing of this book much happier because of this. My warmest thanks to him. Sandy Goldberg and I have been meeting up at conferences and writing back and forth about testimony for years. His input never fails to make me think hard about my views, and his obvious passion for philosophy is a constant source of inspiration. And I am grateful to Blake Roeber, an exceptionally talented student of mine, who offered incisive and thorough comments on the entire manuscript, and provided invaluable assistance with the index.

My thanks also go to my teachers, Patti Sayre, who ignited my love of philosophy, and Marian David, who first inspired my passion for epistemology. Most of all, I am deeply indebted to Ernie Sosa, for being a superb mentor, an exemplary philosopher, and a treasured friend.

It has been an enormous pleasure to work with Oxford University Press. My thanks to Peter Momtchiloff for being an exceptional editor, and to Kate Walker, who has been invaluable in seeing the project through to completion. Finally, I wish to thank two anonymous readers for excellent feedback, especially one who provided 33 single-spaced pages of insightful input!

I am also grateful to my siblings and their families. My brother, Michael, has been discussing philosophical issues with me since I was a child, and sparked much of my early intellectual curiosity and excitement. Were it not for all of the books he gave me while growing up and the guidance he offered in choosing my college courses, my road to finding philosophy might have been much longer. My sister, Cathy, is a constant source of warmth and encouragement, and provides a familial haven that never fails to give me strength. And their spouses and children make my life, and my family's, much, much richer. My thanks to all of them.

Finally, my greatest intellectual debt is to my husband, Baron Reed— words cannot even begin to properly convey my gratitude to him for his help with this book. Every word has been painstakingly read by him numerous times, every argument has been evaluated and critiqued by him for hours, and every view has been discussed together for years. Where my thoughts end and his begin is impossible to say, and so I long ago stopped inserting individual acknowledgments to him, as they are woefully inadequate. My deepest and most profound thanks to you, my love.

This book is dedicated to my love, my joy, my life: to my mother, Janice Lackey, for unparalleled wisdom and devotion, and an awe-inspiring strength; to my husband, Baron Reed, for a love and a partnership that reaches depths I thought impossible; and to my beautiful and brilliant daughters, Isabella and Catherine Reed, for making every moment of every day overflow with the deepest meaning and the most sublime happiness.

JL

Introduction

0.1 Overview

Testimony is an invaluable source of knowledge. We rely on the reports of those around us for everything from the ingredients in our food and medicine to the identity of our family members, from the history of our civilization to the limits and contents of our planet. If we refrained from accepting what others told us, our lives, both practically and intellectually, would be unrecognizable.

The explosion of interest in the epistemology of testimony in recent years, then, is certainly well-deserved, and much of this interest has been shaped and guided by a thesis that is nearly universally accepted; namely, that knowledge is acquired through testimony when speakers *transmit* their *beliefs*, along with the *epistemic properties* such beliefs possess, to their corresponding hearers. According to a central component of this *transmission thesis*, hearers can acquire knowledge on the basis of the testimony of speakers only if the speakers themselves possess the knowledge in question. The widespread acceptance of this thesis is undoubtedly connected to its enormous intuitive appeal. For testimonial chains of speakers and hearers are often pictured as being much like bucket brigades: each person in a bucket brigade must have a bucket of water in order to pass it to the next person and, moreover, there must be at least one person who ultimately acquires the water from another source. Similarly, each speaker in the chain of transmitting knowledge must have the knowledge in question in order to pass it to the next person, and moreover, there must be at least one speaker in the chain who ultimately acquires the knowledge from another source, such as through sense perception or reason.

In this book, however, I argue that there are various ways in which hearers *can* acquire testimonial knowledge from speakers who do not themselves possess the knowledge in question, thereby showing that the transmission thesis is fundamentally misguided. In particular, I show that *unreliable believers* may nonetheless be *reliable testifiers*, and thus the testimony of speakers who do not possess knowledge of a given fact can nonetheless be the source of knowledge that hearers acquire of this very fact. Contrary to what is regarded as received wisdom in epistemology, then, I show that testimony is not merely a transmissive epistemic source but instead can *generate* new knowledge in its own right.

While the views dominant in the literature on testimony focus on the epistemic status of internal states of speakers—such as states of *believing* and *knowing*—I advance an entirely new theory that instead focuses on the linguistic or communicative items in testimonial exchanges—such as *statements* and other *acts of communication*. This view explains how knowledge can be acquired through the testimony of speakers, despite the fact that such speakers fail to possess the knowledge in question. The upshot of my view is that, strictly speaking, we do not learn from one another's *states of believing* or *knowing*—we *learn from one another's words*. In order to make genuine progress in the epistemology of testimony, then, we need to stop looking at what speakers *believe* or *know* and focus, instead, on what speakers *say*.

Once this shift in focus regarding the nature of the speaker's epistemic contribution is in place, I turn to the specific role played by the hearer in testimonial exchanges: in order to acquire knowledge from a speaker's testimony, is it sufficient, as *non-reductionists* maintain, for the hearer to merely lack *negative* reasons for trusting a speaker's reliable report, or must the hearer also possess *positive* reasons for trusting the speaker, as *reductionists* hold? Accordingly, is testimony an *irreducible* source of knowledge, as the former claim, or is it ultimately *reducible* to more basic sources of knowledge, as the latter hold? I argue in this book that both of these answers are inadequate: positive reasons are necessary for testimonial knowledge, but testimony itself is an irreducible source of knowledge. This leads to the development of my *dualist* view, which gives proper credence to testimony's epistemologically *dual* nature: in order to acquire testimonial knowledge, *both* the speaker and the hearer must make a positive epistemic contribution to the knowledge in question, the former through the reliability of her statement and the latter through her positive reasons.

The dualist view that I develop avoids many of the standard debates in the literature on testimony, which are often fueled by the assumption that

non-reductionism and reductionism exhaust our options for explaining testimonial knowledge. On the one hand, because non-reductionism endorses
the epistemic independence of testimony from other sources of knowledge,
such a view is often attacked for sanctioning gullibility and intellectual irresponsibility. On the other hand, because reductionism holds that testimony
is reducible to other sources of knowledge, such a view is often attacked for
underestimating or devaluing the importance of testimony. The dualist view
advanced in this book, however, avoids both of these objections: hearers
need positive reasons in order to acquire testimonial knowledge, thereby
avoiding the charge of gullibility and intellectual irresponsibility, and testimony is construed as an irreducible source of knowledge, thereby avoiding
the charge of underestimating or devaluing the importance of testimony.

The approach found in this book will, then, represent a radical departure
from the views of testimonial knowledge dominating the epistemology
of testimony. The transmission thesis and the debate between non-
reductionism and reductionism establish the terms of the debate in this area
of philosophy. By virtue of rejecting these views and advancing detailed
alternatives, this book is intended to reshape our understanding of the deep
and invaluable reliance each of us has on the testimony of those around
us. The resulting view not only reveals that testimony has the capacity to
generate knowledge, but it also gives proper weight to our dual nature as
both socially indebted and individually rational creatures.

0.2 Chapter Summaries

I begin, in Chapter 1, by discussing various views of the nature of testimony
found in the philosophical literature and I show how each of these views
has importantly different problems. I then offer a diagnosis of why the
disagreement over the nature of testimony is so deep—specifically, I argue
that our concept of testimony has two distinct and often independent aspects
to it. On the one hand, testimony is often thought of as an *intentional act
on the part of the speaker* and, on the other hand, testimony is often thought
of as simply a *source of belief or knowledge for the hearer*. Inadequate views of
testimony, I claim, result either from collapsing these two aspects into a
single account or from a failure to recognize one of them. Finally, I offer
an alternative, *disjunctive* view of the nature of testimony that adequately

captures these two independent aspects, and that provides the basis for an illuminating theory of testimony's epistemological significance.

With an adequate definition of testimony in place, I turn, in Chapter 2, to its epistemic status. A view dominating discussion in the current epistemology of testimony—which I call the *Belief View of Testimony*—holds that a testimonial exchange involves a *speaker's belief, along with the epistemic properties it possesses*, being *transmitted* to a hearer. There are two dimensions to this thesis; one is a necessity claim and the other is a sufficiency claim. According to the former, a hearer knows (believes with justification/warrant) that *p* on the basis of a speaker's testimony that *p* only if the speaker herself knows (believes with justification/warrant) that *p*. According to the latter, if a speaker knows (believes with justification/warrant) that *p*, and a hearer comes to believe that *p* on the basis of the content of this speaker's testimony that *p* without possessing any relevant defeaters, then the hearer also knows (believes with justification/warrant) that *p*. Support for this view derives from a purported analogy between testimony and memory. While memory is thought to be capable of only *preserving* epistemic properties from one time to another—and cannot therefore *generate* new epistemic properties—testimony is said to be capable of only *transmitting* epistemic properties from one person to another. In this chapter, I argue that this entire picture of the epistemology of testimony is fundamentally incorrect. In particular, I show, first, that *unreliable believers* can nonetheless be *reliable testifiers,* thereby showing that the necessity claim is false and, second, that *reliable believers* can nonetheless be *unreliable testifiers*, thereby showing that the sufficiency claim is false.

I then develop an alternative picture of the epistemology of testimony in Chapter 3—which I call the *Statement View of Testimony*—that focuses on the epistemic status of the *statements* of speakers, not of their beliefs. This new conception of testimonial knowledge shows that, strictly speaking, we do not learn from one another's *beliefs*; we learn from one another's *words*. I then devote the remainder of this chapter to defending my view from three different kinds of objections that have been raised in the recent literature: one that focuses on my counterexamples to the Belief View of Testimony, one that targets my positive Statement View of Testimony, and one that attacks my overall approach to theorizing about the epistemic status of testimony. I show that all three objections fail to pose a problem for my view of the epistemology of testimony.

In Chapter 4, I turn to a further objection that has been raised to my view, one that is grounded in a widely accepted thesis about the norm governing proper assertion. According to the *Knowledge Norm of Assertion*, or the KNA, a speaker should assert that *p* only if she knows that *p*. Given that my counterexamples to the Belief View of Testimony in Chapter 2 rely on speakers who offer assertions in the absence of knowledge, it has been argued by proponents of this view that such examples fail because the speakers in question violate the KNA. I argue, however, that the KNA is false. In particular, I show that there are cases in which a speaker asserts that *p* in the absence of believing and hence knowing that *p* without being subject to criticism in any relevant sense, thereby showing that knowledge cannot be what is required for proper assertion. The upshot of these considerations is that *it is a mistake to require proper assertion to originate in the relevant doxastic states of the asserter.* I then develop and defend an alternative norm of assertion—what I call the *Reasonable to Believe Norm of Assertion*, or the RTBNA—that not only avoids the problems afflicting the KNA, but also more fully and coherently accommodates our general intuitions about both asserters and their assertions. I conclude, then, that support for the Belief View of Testimony cannot be derived from considerations about proper assertion, both because the KNA is false and because the speakers in some of the relevant counterexamples in fact satisfy the RTBNA.

I then turn, in Chapter 5, to the topic of testimonial justification or warrant, where I critique the two central views found on this topic in the literature: reductionism and non-reductionism. According to reductionism, hearers *must possess non-testimonial positive reasons* in order to accept the testimony of speakers with justification or warrant and, thus, such justification or warrant is said to *reduce* to that provided by more basic epistemic sources, such as sense perception, memory, and reason. I argue, however, that while non-testimonial positive reasons are necessary for testimonial justification or warrant, this does not entail, as reductionists suggest, that the epistemic status of testimonial beliefs is reducible to the epistemic status of beliefs from other sources. More precisely, I show that there can be an asymmetry between the epistemic status of the testimonial beliefs purportedly being reduced and that of the non-testimonial beliefs that are said to be doing the reducing, thereby precluding precisely such a reduction. I then examine non-reductionism, which holds that hearers *need not possess appropriate positive reasons* for testimonial justification or warrant, thereby rendering testimony *just as basic* an epistemic source as sense perception, memory, and reason. I show, however, that accepting the testimony of speakers about whom hearers know nothing at all is epistemically irrational in ways that even non-reductionists are committed to finding objectionable. This reveals that at least minimal positive reasons are necessary for testimonial justification or warrant. Moreover, since there would be vicious circularity if these reasons were themselves ultimately acquired via testimony, direct input is needed from other epistemic sources. I conclude, then, that testimony is neither just as basic as, nor ultimately reducible to, other epistemic sources, such as sense perception, memory, and reason. Thus, both non-reductionism and reductionism in the epistemology of testimony are false.

I begin Chapter 6 by offering a diagnosis of the problem afflicting both reductionism and non-reductionism: in a testimonial exchange, information is typically communicated between two central participants, the speaker and the hearer. Reductionists and non-reductionists alike have attempted to place all of the epistemic work on only one or the other of these participants and, in so doing, have ignored the positive epistemic contribution that needs to be made by the other. Reductionists, on the one hand, focus entirely on the *hearer* in a testimonial exchange. For, in order for testimonial justification or warrant to be reduced to the justification or warrant of sense perception, memory, and reason, all of the epistemic work needs to be shouldered by the hearer since it is precisely her positive reasons that are supposed to provide the reductive base. Non-reductionists, on the other hand, capture the work that needs to be done by the *speaker* in a testimonial exchange, but neglect the positive contribution that a hearer needs to make. Specifically, they correctly require the truth-conduciveness of the speaker's testimony, but then mistakenly assume that the hearer need not have any relevant positive reasons about this testimony. In contrast to both of these views, I argue that we need to look toward a view of testimonial justification or warrant—which I call *dualism*—that gives proper credence to its *dual* nature by requiring both the truth-conduciveness of the speaker's testimony and the possession of appropriate positive reasons by the hearer. I then devote the remainder of this chapter to explicating the specific conditions of dualism and defending them from various objections found in the literature on testimony.

In Chapter 7, I defend dualism from an objection that is often regarded by non-reductionists as decisive against requiring positive reasons for testimonial justification or warrant: namely, the apparent fact that infants and young children are not cognitively capable of having such positive reasons, yet clearly possess testimonial knowledge. Since non-reductionism does not impose a requirement of this sort, it is thought to avoid this problem and is therefore taken to have a significant advantage over both dualism and reductionism. In this chapter, I show that if this "Infant/Child Objection" indeed undermines dualism and reductionism, then a variant of it similarly undermines non-reductionism. Thus, considerations about the cognitive capacities of infants and young children do not effectively discriminate between these three competing theories of testimonial justification or warrant.

In Chapter 8, I turn to a family of theories that has emerged in recent work in the epistemology of testimony. Though there are points of disagreement among some of the members of this family, they are united in their commitment to at least three central theses. First, and perhaps most important, the *interpersonal relationship* between the two parties in a testimonial exchange should be the central focus of the epistemology of testimony. Second, and closely related, certain features of this interpersonal relationship—such as the speaker *offering her assurance* to the hearer that her testimony is true, or the speaker *inviting the hearer to trust* her—are actually *responsible for conferring epistemic value* on the testimonial beliefs acquired. Third, the epistemic justification or warrant provided by testimony is *non-evidential* in nature. I call the general conception of testimony characterized by these theses the *Interpersonal View of Testimony*, or the IVT. The IVT has emerged in response to views of testimony, such as the one that I develop in the earlier chapters of this book, that purportedly neglect the epistemic significance of the interpersonal relationship between the speaker and the hearer. In this chapter, I argue against the IVT by showing that its proponents face a dilemma: either the view of testimony in question is genuinely interpersonal but not properly epistemological, or it is properly epistemological but not genuinely interpersonal. Either way, I conclude that the IVT fails to provide a compelling alternative to existing theories in the epistemology of testimony.

The book closes with an appendix, where I show that arguments similar in spirit to those found in Chapter 2 also show that a widely accepted view of the epistemology of memory, one that purportedly provides additional support for the Belief View of Testimony, is false. Memory, it is often said, is strikingly similar to testimony in some crucial epistemic respects. Most importantly, neither is regarded as a *generative* epistemic source: while memory *preserves* knowledge (justification, warrant) from one time to another, testimony *transmits* knowledge (justification, warrant) from one person to another. In this way, it is said to be true for both memorial knowledge (justification, warrant), on the one hand, and testimonial knowledge (justification, warrant), on the other hand, that the proposition in question must be *known* (justified, warranted) when it was originally acquired and, accordingly, that *a source other than memory and testimony, respectively,* must be responsible for its original acquisition. The standard view, then—which I call the *Preservation View of Memory*, or the PVM—is that memory cannot make a proposition acquire an epistemic status different than the one it had at the time it was originally acquired. In this appendix, I argue that the PVM is false. Specifically, I claim that it is not necessary for memorial knowledge (justification, warrant) that the belief in question be known (believed with justification, warrant) when it was originally acquired and, accordingly, that it need not be known (believed with justification, warrant) in a non-memorial way at this time. Hence, contrary to received wisdom in epistemology, memory can indeed play a generative epistemic role. This conclusion, in turn, undermines the purported analogy employed by proponents of the Belief View of Testimony, linking memory as a merely preservative source with testimony as a merely transmissive source.

0.3 Use of Terms

There is one final preliminary point that I should like to make: the central focus of this book is, first and foremost, testimonial or testimonially based *knowledge*. This focus is something that I share with all of those working in the epistemology of testimony. At various points in my discussion, however, it will be necessary to turn my attention more narrowly toward testimonial or testimonially based *justification* or *warrant*, terms that are used with far more variation in the epistemological literature. So let me be as precise as possible about my usage of these terms.

I will use "testimonially based justification" and "testimonially based warrant" interchangeably in this book.[1] Both concepts are technical notions that will be used to pick out the property that is necessary and, when added to true belief, close to being sufficient for testimonially based knowledge. Though this use of "justification" and "warrant" as epistemically equivalent is not universally accepted, it is certainly not without precedent. For instance, in his recent exchange with Ernest Sosa, Laurence BonJour writes: "the opposition between [internalism and externalism] is sometimes thought to pertain to the correct specification of the concept of *knowledge*: is the third condition for knowledge, the justification or warrant condition that goes beyond the requirements of belief or assent and truth, properly understood or formulated in an internalist or externalist way?" (BonJour and Sosa 2003: 35). Here, BonJour is carving up the relevant terms in much the same way as I am in this book.[2] In particular, knowledge is understood as follows:

S knows that *p* if and only if: (1) it is true that *p*

(2) S believes that *p*

(3) S is justified or warranted in believing that *p*

(4) S's belief that *p* is not Gettierized.

Following this general characterization, I will understand testimonial knowledge as roughly testimonially justified or warranted, un-Gettierized, true belief.

But, one might ask, why not just choose either "justification" or "warrant" for use in this book? Why continue to use both terms? If I were to choose one term, it would be "justification." But discussions in epistemology surrounding this concept have become increasingly obscure, with some relegating "justification" to epistemic corners that are, at best, only indirectly connected to knowledge. Indeed, in the wake of the new evil demon problem, it often seems as though internalists have won the

---

[1] I shall follow standard practice and also use "testimonially based justification" and "testimonial justification" interchangeably in this book. Similar considerations apply to "testimonially based warrant/knowledge" and "testimonial warrant/knowledge."

[2] BonJour, however, also says in his book that "the concept of knowledge is, in my judgment, a seriously problematic concept in more than one way. So much so that it is, I believe, best avoided as far as possible in sober epistemological discussion—as paradoxical as that may sound" (BonJour and Sosa 2003: 21). He later adds: "I will largely concern myself here with justification rather than knowledge" (BonJour and Sosa 2003: 23). Obviously, I am not sympathetic to BonJour's move here.

battle over the term "justification," but externalists have won the war over "knowledge." More precisely, it is frequently granted that my twin in an evil demon world may very well be equally justified in holding her beliefs as I am in the actual world, but then justification's connection with knowledge—if indeed it has one—is regarded as far less intimate than was traditionally thought. This leads some epistemologists to use "justification" as akin to "epistemic entitlement," "epistemic rationality," or "epistemic blamelessness" and "warrant" for the property that bears a necessary connection with knowledge. Given this, if I were to use only "testimonial justification" in this book, some readers may be inclined to misunderstand my conclusions by construing them in strictly internalist or overly subjective terms. If, however, I use "justification" and "warrant" interchangeably, it should serve as a reminder that I am interested in these concepts only insofar as they bear an intimate connection with knowledge.

It is also worth mentioning that there are independent virtues of carving up the terms and concepts in the way suggested here. For instance, on this reading of justification, internalists and externalists are engaged in a *genuine* debate about the *same* condition for knowledge. Moreover, it is clear why justification has epistemic value: it converts, with some help from a Gettier-condition, true belief into knowledge. In contrast, when internalists are granted the term "justification," which is then disconnected from knowledge, and externalists are granted "warrant," which is then construed as necessary for knowledge, not only does the internalism/externalism debate turn out to be quibbling over entirely different concepts, but the precise epistemic value of justification also becomes unclear.

What, then, do I say about the new evil demon problem? While a detailed discussion of this issue must await another occasion, here is my rough response: justification, when it is understood as the property that is necessary and, when added to true belief, close to sufficient for knowledge, has two general components. First, it has a *reliability*, or objective, component and, second, it has a *rationality*, or subjective, component.[3] There will obviously be disagreement regarding the details of these two components: for instance, some may argue that reliability requires truth-tracking while others may contend that proper functioning or virtuous formation is needed. Similarly,

---

[3] I argue for this kind of view of testimonial justification in Chapter 6.

some may argue that rationality requires merely the absence of negative reasons or defeaters for holding a belief, while others may say that the presence of positive reasons is needed. My point here is not to settle these details but, rather, to draw attention to these two dimensions of justification. Given these dimensions, I would say that even though my twin's beliefs in an evil demon world fail the reliability constraint and, hence, are neither justified nor known, they are nevertheless *rational*. Indeed, such beliefs possess many other positive epistemic properties, such as being held in an epistemically blameless way, being responsibly formed, and so on. This enables us to explain the intuition that the beliefs of my twin both *possess* and *lack* something epistemically important: they possess subjective rationality, but lack objective reliable formation and, hence, justification.[4]

As we shall see, both of these dimensions of justification play a crucial role in the account of testimonial knowledge developed in this book.

---

[4] Alternatively, one might argue that while my twin's beliefs are *subjectively justified,* they are not *objectively justified.* For more on the distinction between subjective and objective justification, see BonJour and Sosa (2003: 153–5).

1

The Nature of Testimony

1.1 Preliminary Remarks

Is testimony a reliable source of belief? When are we justified in accepting the testimony of a speaker? Is testimony just as basic a source of knowledge as sense perception, memory, and reason? These sorts of questions pervade the literature in the epistemology of testimony, and yet it is seldom recognized that there is substantive disagreement about what testimony even is, with theories being offered about what conditions need to be met for a person to testify that scarcely resemble one another. Even more importantly, when attempts are made at answering these questions, the epistemological consequences of competing views of the nature of testimony are often ignored.

In this chapter, I plan to remedy this by, first, clearing up much of the current confusion about the nature of testimony and by, second, offering an account of what it is to testify that is suitable for the epistemology of testimony. I shall proceed as follows: I shall first discuss various substantively different views of testimony and show how each proposal has importantly different problems. I shall then provide a diagnosis of why the disagreement over the nature of testimony is so deep; specifically, I shall argue that our concept of testimony has two different aspects to it. Inadequate views of testimony, I claim, result either from collapsing these two aspects into a single account or from a failure to recognize one of them. Finally, I shall develop an alternative, *disjunctive* view of the nature of testimony that adequately captures these two independent aspects, and thereby provides the basis for an illuminating theory of testimony's epistemological significance.

To begin, I should like to make several remarks about the topic with which I shall be concerned in this chapter. First, my central focus will be on what C. A. J. Coady calls *natural testimony*. Unlike *formal testimony*, the paradigm of which is a statement offered under oath in a courtroom or commission of inquiry, natural testimony "is to be encountered in such everyday circumstances as exhibit the 'social operations of mind': giving someone directions to the post office, reporting what happened in an accident, saying that, yes, you have seen a child answering to that description, telling someone the result of the last race or the last cricket score" (Coady 1992: 38).

Second, and related, I am not here specifically interested in characterizing the *speech act of testifying* but, rather, in carving out the *domain of testimony as a source of belief*. Otherwise put, in addition to sense perception, memory, reason, and introspection, "natural testimony" picks out the other traditionally recognized epistemic source, the source whereby hearers acquire information from either the spoken or written word of others.[1] Moreover, this is the same project that all of the authors considered in this chapter are engaged in—they all wish to capture what it is to testify for the purposes of theorizing in the epistemology of testimony.

Third, my purpose in this chapter is not to directly address how we acquire justified belief or knowledge via the testimony of speakers. These are extremely important questions—indeed, ones at which the remainder of this book ultimately aims. But here I am interested in the prior question of what precisely testimony is. Moreover, it will become increasingly clear throughout the discussion that lasting progress in the epistemology of testimony can be made only after we have settled upon a satisfactory account of the nature of testimony.

1.2 The Narrow View

With these points in mind, let us turn to the account of natural testimony put forth by C. A. J. Coady, whose seminal book on testimony sparked

---

[1] Henceforth, "testimony" should be understood as referring to natural testimony. It should be noted, however, that while my focus is on natural testimony, the account that I later offer will be general enough to subsume formal testimony (though a full account of the latter will most likely include even further conditions). I should also mention that I later argue that testimony need not involve any words at all. But for present purposes, this rough characterization of testimony is sufficient.

much of the recent interest in this topic. For reasons that will become apparent later, I shall refer to his account as the *Narrow View of the Nature of Testimony* (hereafter, the NVNT), according to which:

> NVNT: S testifies by making some statement that *p* if and only if:
>
> N1. S's stating that *p* is evidence that *p* and is offered as evidence that *p*.
>
> N2. S has the relevant competence, authority, or credentials to state truly that *p*.
>
> N3. S's statement that *p* is relevant to some disputed or unresolved question (which may or may not be whether *p*) and is directed to those who are in need of evidence on the matter. (Coady 1992: 42)

Now, according to Coady, the notion of evidence figuring in N1 is similar to what Peter Achinstein (1978, 1983) calls *potential evidence*. Evidence in this sense requires the truth of *e* and an objective connection between *e* and *h*, where *e* is the putative piece of evidence and *h* is that for which it is evidence. However, *e* can be evidence for *h* even if *h* is false, since all that is required is that there generally be an objective connection or association between *e* and *h*. Furthermore, though *e* must be true in order to be potential evidence, it cannot entail *h*: entailment is simply too good to be evidence.[2]

So, let us now consider a case in which a speaker makes a statement but it fails to satisfy all three conditions of the NVNT: suppose that Alice sincerely believes that she is a clairvoyant and tells Rita that she can see that Elvis Presley is not dead, but rather, that he is currently living in San Diego. Suppose further that there is no disputed or unresolved question in this context since Rita in fact knows that Elvis is dead and is therefore not in need of evidence on the matter. Such a statement, according to the NVNT, is not a case of testimony since it fails all three conditions. With respect to N1, Alice's statement, though offered as evidence to Rita, is not potential evidence since there is no objective connection between Alice's statement that Elvis is living in San Diego and the obtaining of this state of affairs. Indeed, there is no such connection between anything that

---

[2] It should be noted that this has the consequence that no one could testify about necessary truths, given that everything entails propositions that are necessarily true.

Alice says on the basis of her purported powers of clairvoyance and that for which it is offered as evidence. In this way, Alice's statement also fails N2 since she does not have the relevant competence, authority, or credentials to state truly that Elvis is living in San Diego.[3] Finally, Alice's statement fails both conjuncts of N3 given that, *ex hypothesi*, Rita *knows* that Elvis is dead—hence, her statement is not relevant to some disputed or unresolved question and is not directed at a hearer who is in need of evidence on the matter.[4]

In spite of Alice's failure to satisfy all three of the conditions for testifying found in the NVNT, I shall argue that her statement that Elvis is currently living in San Diego is nonetheless an instance of testimony. To this end, I shall raise three central problems with this account of testimony. The first is that Coady has confused the *metaphysics of testimony* with the *epistemology of testimony*. To see this, let us first consider N1. As will be recalled, in addition to requiring that the speaker offer her statement that *p* as evidence, Coady argues that her statement that *p* must be potential evidence in the sense specified above. This, however, conflates two distinct aspects of testimony: on the one hand, there is the question, "What is testimony, i.e., what are the conditions required for S to testify that *p*?" and, on the other hand, there is the question, "What is the difference between good and bad testimony, i.e., what is required for testimony to serve as an

---

[3] I am here assuming that clairvoyance is not a reliable belief-producing source and hence that a speaker who offers a statement that *p* as evidence that *p* on the basis of her purported powers of clairvoyance will invariably fail N2. If there are or could be reliable clairvoyants (!), then we can simply modify our example such that Alice, as a matter of fact, does not have such powers and thus does not have the relevant qualifications to state truly that Elvis Presley is currently living in San Diego.

[4] Is the mere fact that it seems to Alice that her statement regarding Elvis is relevant to some disputed or unresolved question and that it is directed to someone who Alice believes is in need of evidence on the matter enough for her statement to satisfy N3? (I am grateful to an anonymous referee for raising this point.) No. For notice that there is a difference between the following two conditions:

N3:   S's statement that *p* is relevant to some disputed or unresolved question (which may or may not be whether *p*) and is directed to those who are in need of evidence on the matter.

N3*   S believes that her statement that *p* is relevant to some disputed or unresolved question (which may or may not be whether *p*) and is directed to those whom S believes are in need of evidence on the matter.

While Alice's believing that Elvis is dead is sufficient to satisfy the subjective N3*, the objective N3 requires that there in fact is a disputed or unresolved question regarding Elvis's death and that Rita in fact needs evidence on this matter. Since, *ex hypothesi*, Rita knows that Elvis is dead, neither of these conjuncts is true. Hence, Alice's statement fails N3. (More will be said about the distinction between N3 and N3* when Peter Graham's view of testimony, which replaces N3 with a condition like N3*, is discussed in Section 1.4.)

epistemically adequate source of belief?"[5] According to Coady's NVNT, we need only ask the former question since a statement will not count as a case of testimony unless it is potential evidence. Thus, it is impossible to have an unreliable testifier on Coady's model: a speaker would simply fail to testify if there weren't an objective connection between the statement that *p* and that for which it is evidence.

This has the consequence that the work for epistemology is no longer to show that testimony is an epistemically acceptable source of justified or warranted belief but, rather, to *inquire as to whether we do in fact have an institution of testimony*. For if testimony is, as Coady suggests, a reliable source of knowledge by definition, then we need not give an account of the justification or warrant of testimonial beliefs. Instead, we need to show that we *do* have an institution of testimony or that when speakers are making statements, they are *really* testifying. Since this consequence is so unattractive, it should be clear that such a requirement is not necessary for a speaker to testify. Surely, the interesting epistemological question is how we are justified or warranted in accepting the testimony of others rather than whether we really do have an institution of testimony.[6] Furthermore, there is a natural sense in which we say that speakers can testify about UFO sightings, alien encounters, spontaneous human combustion, and the like. Certainly, we might not and should not accept their statements as a source of our beliefs, but why should this prevent the speakers themselves from testifying?

Similar remarks can be made regarding N2. For a speaker who states that *p* in the absence of the relevant competence, authority, or credentials to state truly that *p* may not be a *reliable* testifier, and her testimony may not be an *epistemically good source of belief*. But surely such a speaker is a testifier nonetheless. N2 is a distinctively epistemic condition that may be necessary for epistemically reliable or good testimony but not for testimony *simpliciter*.[7]

---

[5] Fricker (1995) raises a similar objection to Coady's view of testimony.

[6] A similar point is made in Chapter 2 and in Lackey (1999), though Coady is not my target in these works.

[7] A different sort of problem case for N2 is where a speaker knows that she does not have the relevant qualifications to state truly that *p* but intends to deceive her hearer, i.e., cases of lying or false testimony. Regarding this type of case, a proponent of N2 may argue that since we often think of testimony as requiring the intention on the part of the speaker to convey evidence, lying does not qualify as testimony since the speaker intends to deceive. But notice that it makes perfect sense to speak of a witness testifying in a courtroom to something that she herself does not believe—it is called perjury. Moreover, it is uncontentious that we have a concept of false testimony in the same way that we have concepts of valid and invalid deduction, veridical and non-veridical perception, and the like.

The second problem with the NVNT is that Coady fails to recognize the sense in which *testimony can be a source of belief or knowledge for a hearer, regardless of the speaker's intention to be an epistemic source*. For notice that many posthumous publications, especially of journals and diaries, will fail the second conjuncts of both N1 and N3.[8] For instance, if a private diary in which it is clear that the author was writing only for herself is posthumously published, then, according to Coady, we must deny that the thoughts expressed in the diary are instances of testimony. However, consider a case in which you learn from Sylvia Plath's posthumously published diary that she was deeply depressed, and then someone asks you what the epistemic source of this knowledge is. Isn't the natural answer to this question testimony? For, since you didn't acquire this information from sense perception, memory, reason, introspection, or combinations thereof and, moreover, since you acquired this knowledge from an expression of someone's thoughts, the intuitive conclusion to draw is that the source of your knowledge is testimony. Or consider a case in which you are talking on the phone and I overhear you say that you were in a car accident. Wouldn't we say that the source of my information is your testimony, despite the fact that you did not direct your statement to me (and thus failed the second conjunct of N3)?

The third problem with the NVNT is that Coady fails to recognize the sense in which *a speaker can testify, regardless of the epistemic needs of her hearers*. To see this, recall the case of Alice and her statement about Elvis currently living in San Diego. The mere fact that Rita rightly knows that Elvis is dead, and the context is therefore such that there is no disputed or unresolved question about him (thus Alice's statement fails the first conjunct of N3), should not necessarily prevent Alice from testifying. For

---

[8] It should be noted that Coady thinks that his account of testimony can be extended to capture some of these cases. So, for example, he claims: "Confidential documents such as diplomatic communications or the private record of conversations, or even private diaries which were never intended for communication to anyone, are perhaps more difficult to subsume under our definition but where we can legitimately create an author-reader situation it would seem natural to extend the notion of testimony to cover such cases as well, particularly where the document in question was concerned, for whatever reason, to set the record straight" (Coady 1992: 50). This response, however, will not do. Either the second conjuncts of N1 and N3 are necessary for S to testify that *p* or they aren't. If they are, then, e.g., posthumous publications of private journals will fail to be instances of testimony. If they aren't, then only the first conjuncts of N1 and N3 are necessary, along with N2, for S to testify that *p*. Thus, Coady cannot consistently remain committed to these conditions and simply claim that his definition can be extended.

a central aspect of our concept of testimony is that its purpose is, at least quite often, for speakers to communicate their beliefs to others, whether or not there is an open question about that which is being communicated. For instance, consider a dinner party of devoutly committed atheists. Here, there simply is no disputed or unresolved question since these atheists are as certain as one can be that there is not a God. But shouldn't it be at least possible for a theist to sit down and communicate, via her *testimony*, that there is a God? Couldn't her statement, "There is a God," be an instance of testimony, despite the epistemic needs or desires of her hearers?[9]

What these problems point to is that there are at least two aspects to our concept of testimony. On the one hand, we often think of testimony as a source of belief or knowledge for hearers, regardless of the speaker's intention to be such a source. On the other hand, we often think of testimony as involving the intention to communicate information to other people, regardless of the needs or interests of the hearers. One of the fundamental problems with the NVNT is that Coady requires the *conjunction* of these features (i.e., the speaker's intentions *and* the hearer's needs) rather than their *disjunction*.

It seems, then, that we need a broader notion of testimony than the NVNT, one that, first, doesn't confuse the metaphysics and epistemology of testimony and, second, adequately captures the dual nature of our concept of testimony. In what follows, we shall turn to several proposals that attempt to do just this and thus appear to provide more satisfying accounts of the nature of testimony.

1.3 The Broad View

One of the main questions in the epistemology of testimony is how we are justified or warranted in forming beliefs on the basis of what people say. This, rather than the nature of testimony, is often taken to be the issue

---

[9] One might say here that what the theist is testifying to is her *belief* that God exists, not that God exists. There are two points I would make by way of response. First, we could, of course, envisage a case in which all of the atheists in the room also know this state of affairs to be true, i.e., that the speaker is a theist. Nevertheless, I would still like to say that the theist could testify that she believes that God exists. Second, if we are inclined to say that the theist is merely testifying that she believes that God exists when she states that God exists, then why wouldn't we say the same thing about all (or most) statements? What makes this sort of statement relevantly different?

of central import from an epistemological point of view. As we saw in the previous section, Coady's NVNT has the unattractive consequence of reversing the priority of these questions which, in turn, makes the important epistemological question whether we do, in fact, have an institution of testimony. It is precisely to avoid these sorts of consequences that those who are interested in the epistemology of testimony often embrace a very broad notion of what it is to testify.

So, for instance, Elizabeth Fricker holds that the domain of testimony that is of epistemological interest is that of "tellings generally" with "no restrictions either on subject matter, or on the speaker's epistemic relation to it" (Fricker 1995: 396–7). Following this view, Robert Audi claims that in accounting for testimonial justification and knowledge, we must understand testimony as "people's telling us things" (Audi 1997: 406).[10] In a similar spirit, Ernest Sosa embraces "a broad sense of testimony that counts posthumous publications as examples... [It] requires only that it be a statement of someone's thoughts or beliefs, which they might direct to the world at large and to no one in particular" (Sosa 1991: 219).

In order to assess this broad approach to the nature of testimony, it will be helpful to abstract away from some of the inessential differences between these individual characterizations of testimony and focus on what they all have in common. Since it is most natural to understand a "telling" as an expression of one's thought, let us say that the *Broad View of the Nature of Testimony* (hereafter, the BVNT) is roughly:

> BVNT: S testifies that *p* if and only if S's statement that *p* is an expression of S's thought that *p*.

As should be clear, such a broad view of testimony avoids the problems afflicting the NVNT. First, since a speaker can surely state her thought,

---

[10] Elsewhere in the same article, Audi claims that "Testimony of the wide sort that concerns me — roughly, saying or affirming something in an apparent attempt to convey (correct) information — is what raises the question of how testimony is important for knowledge and justification" (Audi 1997: 405). There are, however, several questions that might be asked about this formulation. For instance, from whose perspective does the statement need to be apparently conveying information — the speaker's, the hearer's, or both? And, does the information need to seem correct to the speaker, the hearer, or both? In a similar spirit, Catherine Elgin characterizes testimony as "... utterances and inscriptions that purport to convey information and transmit warrant for the information they convey" (Elgin 2002: 292). Again, from whose perspective does the utterance or inscription need to purportedly convey information — the speaker's, the hearer's, or both? As will become clear in the discussion that follows, I think that there are difficulties with all of these responses.

both without it being potential evidence and in the absence of the relevant competence to state truly that p, such a view properly leaves the distinguishing feature between good and bad testimony a matter for epistemology to determine. Second, such a view allows for testimony to be a source of belief or knowledge for a hearer, regardless of the speaker's intention to be such an epistemic source. For, as Sosa makes explicit above, one can state one's thought and thereby testify even if one's statement is neither offered as evidence nor directed at those who are in need of evidence. Third, this account of the nature of testimony admits that a speaker can testify, regardless of the needs or interests of her hearers. For, again, one can state one's thought and thus testify, even if there is no unresolved or disputed question.

Despite the significant advantages of this broad account of the nature of testimony, however, there is reason to think that it is too broad. Specifically, the fundamental problem with the BVNT is that it fails to recognize the distinction between entirely *non-informational expressions of thought* and *testimony*. For instance, suppose that we are walking down the street and I say, "Ah, it is indeed a beautiful day." Suppose further that such a statement, though it expresses my thought that it is indeed a beautiful day, is neither offered nor taken as conveying information; it is simply a conversational filler, comparable to a sigh of contentedness.[11] Or consider a case in which Ned tells a joke among a group of our friends and I casually say, "He sure has a great sense of humor." Again, though I am stating my thought that Ned has a great sense of humor, the context is such that we all know Ned and we all know that he has a great sense of humor; thus, my statement is simply a polite response to a friend's joke. It should be emphasized, however, that my claim here is *not* that such conversational fillers and polite responses should *never* qualify as instances of testimony but, rather, that they should not *always* qualify as testimony. For instance, if I say in the presence of a blind companion, "It is a beautiful day today," such a remark may qualify as testimony in this context since its function may be to convey information, not to merely fill a gap in the conversation.[12]

---

[11] Similarly, Peter Graham says, "it should be noted that mere statements are not testimony. Saying 'It is a nice day' is not usually taken as testimony about the weather (though it is when said by the weatherman). Repeating what you have already said over and over does not count as testimony either, unless you have forgotten each previous utterance" (Graham 1997: 231).

[12] The positive view that I develop later in this chapter will be able to accommodate this feature of testimony since, on my account, sometimes these kinds of remarks qualify as testimony and other times they do not.

The upshot of these considerations, then, is that our concept of testimony is intimately connected with the notion of conveying information, and thus those statements that function as *mere* conversational fillers and polite responses should fail to qualify as instances of testimony.

Another type of case that poses a problem for the BVNT is this: in my young daughter's copy of *The Secret Garden*, Mary tells Colin as he attempts to stand for the first time, "You can do it! You can do it...I tell you, you can!"[13] While Mary's "telling" is surely an expression of her thought that Colin indeed has the capacity to stand, its function in this context is merely to encourage her friend to accomplish a task that is quite difficult for him, similar to clapping or cheering. There is no intention on Mary's part to convey information, nor is Colin apt to acquire information, from her words of encouragement. Hence, once again, this type of statement should not be regarded as testimony.

But perhaps the most decisive counterexample to the BVNT is the following type of case: suppose that in the middle of a dramatic theatrical performance on stage, Edgar, an actor, delivers his line, "Life no longer has any meaning for me." Surely, Edgar's line should not qualify as testimony, despite being an expression of his thought. Now, the response most likely to be offered here by the proponent of the BVNT is to deny that Edgar's delivering his line is truly an expression of his thought. In particular, since there is no sense in which Edgar believes that life no longer has meaning for him, such a statement, the objection goes, fails to express *Edgar's* thought. There are, however, at least two reasons why this response will not do. First, this criterion for expression of thought results in paradigmatic instances of testimony failing the BVNT: suppose, for instance, that Clare testifies under oath that she saw the defendant in a capital murder case at a local gas station on the date in question. Suppose further, however, that she committed perjury on the stand. Despite the fact that Clare does not in any sense believe what she is reporting to the jury, it is widely agreed that she can nonetheless offer her *testimony* on the stand. Hence, it is unclear how a proponent of the BVNT could exclude Edgar's statement as testimony while, at the same time, countenancing Clare's as such. Second, it is surely possible and, indeed, even likely that there are times when an

---

[13] Burnett, Frances Hodgson. Retold by Janet Allison Brown, (2001), *The Secret Garden* (New York: Penguin Putnam Books for Young Readers).

actor becomes so temporarily immersed in his character that the delivering of lines in fact expresses the actor's thoughts at that moment. But even if an actor achieves this kind of character immersion, it would still be quite odd to regard such lines as instances of testimony in any reasonable sense of the word.

In all of the above cases, proponents of the BVNT lack the resources to exclude such non-informational expressions of thought from qualifying as testimony. The upshot of these considerations is that if we embrace the BVNT, then *any* expression of thought, from conversational fillers and polite responses to encouraging cheers and the reciting of acting lines, turns out to be an instance of testimony. This is clearly an unacceptable result. Hence, we need an account of testimony that is broader than the NVNT but more restrictive than the BVNT.[14]

1.4 The Moderate View

Peter Graham (1997) offers an account of testimony that adequately represents a moderate view of testimony. For it is broad enough to avoid many of the problems afflicting Coady's account and yet it places restrictions on statements so that non-informational remarks are ruled out as instances of testimony. In particular, according to Graham's *Moderate View of the Nature of Testimony* (hereafter, the MVNT):

MVNT: S testifies by making some statement that *p* if and only if:

M1. S's stating that *p* is offered as evidence that *p*.

M2. S intends that his audience believe that he has the relevant competence, authority, or credentials to state truly that *p*.

M3. S's statement that *p* is believed by S to be relevant to some question that he believes is disputed or unresolved (which may or may not be whether *p*) and is directed at those whom he believes to be in need of evidence on the matter. (Graham 1997: 227)[15]

---

[14] I should mention that providing an account of the nature of testimony does not seem to be the central goal for proponents of the BVNT. Such an account is provided by these theorists primarily for the purpose of assisting with the epistemology of testimony.

[15] James Ross offers a definition of testimony that bears some similarities to Graham's account. According to Ross, testimony is "any verbalized reporting of a purported state of affairs where the

By amending Coady's proposal so that the conditions for testimony are subjective rather than objective, Graham avoids many of the problems that were raised against the NVNT. For instance, since Graham, first, does not require that the statement in question be potential evidence and, second, requires merely that S *intends* that her audience believe that she has the relevant credentials to state truly that *p* (rather than that she actually have such credentials), the MVNT does not confuse the metaphysics and the epistemology of testimony. Moreover, since he requires only that S *believes* that there is an unresolved question (rather than that there actually be an unresolved question), the MVNT also enables speakers to testify, regardless of the needs of the hearers. And, finally, since Graham places restrictions on the kind of statements being offered, non-informational remarks are distinguished from testimony. For the speaker must offer her statement that *p* as evidence that *p*, she must at least believe that *p* is relevant to a question that she believes is unresolved, and she must direct her statement to those whom she believes to be in need of evidence on the matter. In this way, my casual statement that "Ah, it is indeed a beautiful day," my polite response that "Ned sure has a great sense of humor," Mary's words of encouragement to Colin, and Edgar's reciting of his acting lines all fail M3 and thus do not qualify as instances of testimony.

However, although the MVNT avoids these problems, it should be clear that, by virtue of requiring various intentions and beliefs on the part of the speaker, Graham's account fails to capture the sense in which *testimony can be a source of belief or knowledge for a hearer, regardless of the speaker's intention to be such a source*. For instance, like Coady, Graham will have to deny that many posthumous publications are instances of testimony, e.g., private journals where the author did not offer her reflections as evidence. Similarly, consider a case in which Frank believes that I already know the confidential piece of information that the president of our university is resigning. Now, suppose that he casually makes a statement about this fact, though he does not offer this statement as evidence, does not believe that his statement is relevant to some disputed question, and does not direct his

reporter intends that the hearer (reader, viewer, etc.) will take it on his report that the state of affairs is *as* reported" (Ross 1975: 3). Thus, like Graham, he emphasizes the speaker's intention to convey information rather than the hearer's need for it. Though I shall not discuss Ross's specific account of testimony in any detail, the problems discussed in this section apply, *mutatis mutandis,* to his proposal.

statement to someone whom he believes to be in need of evidence on the matter. Frank's statement, therefore, fails M1 and M3 and is not a case of testimony according to Graham.

This, however, is an unwelcome consequence. For it is precisely because we often acquire knowledge from speakers, regardless of their intentions, that proponents of the BVNT urge the necessity of placing "no restrictions either on subject matter, or on the speaker's epistemic relation to it" (Fricker 1995: 396–7). If we are to have an account of the nature of testimony that is epistemically acceptable, it simply has to be acknowledged that we learn things from the testimony of others even when they don't intend for us to do so.

1.5 General Problems

Before turning to my account of testimony, I would like to briefly discuss two general problems afflicting all of the views that have been discussed thus far. First, notice that, in one form or another, all of the above proposals flesh out the notion of testimony in terms of *statements*. For instance, Coady and Graham both explicitly say that "a speaker testifies by making some *statement p*" and Sosa claims that his account of testimony "requires only that it be a *statement* of someone's thoughts or beliefs." Similarly, Audi maintains that testimony is "saying or affirming something" and Fricker holds that the domain of testimony is that of "tellings generally." The thought underlying these views is that an instance of testimony is fundamentally a *statement*, either verbal or in writing, of a speaker's thoughts.

But consider a case where Randall asks me whether there is any coffee left in the kitchen and I respond with a nod of my head. It is rather counterintuitive to say that a nod qualifies as a *statement*. In this context, however, it is an expression of a person's thought that is intended to, and successfully does, communicate information. Because of this, my nod does indeed seem to be a case of testimony. Or consider a case where Natasha asks me where the nearest coffee shop is and I, with a mouth filled with biscotti, point to the north. Again, it is doubtful that we would regard pointing as a *statement*, but, in this context, it does seem to qualify as testimony precisely because I intend to, and successfully do, convey information to another person. Other cases abound: winking, clapping, snapping, and so on. It is at least arguable that, in certain contexts, people can testify about countless things of varying degrees of importance without making statements. Thus, it seems that an adequate account of testimony needs to be fleshed out in terms broader than those imposed by statements.

Another problem shared by many of the aforementioned proposals is the assumption that there is always a one-to-one correspondence between the explicit content of one's testimony and that which is being testified to.[16] For instance, both Coady and Graham claim that "S testifies by making some statement p if and only if S's stating that p is offered as evidence that p" and Sosa holds that "one 'testifies' that p if and only if one states one's belief [or thought] that p." However, it is not uncommon for one to state one's belief that p as conveying the information that p *and* the information that q, and so on. For instance, suppose you ask me, "Is it raining outside?" and I say "There is an umbrella in the closet." In this context, my statement that there is an umbrella in the closet is meant to convey the information *both* that there is an umbrella in the closet *and* that it is raining outside.[17] I am, therefore, testifying to both propositions, despite the fact that the content of my testimony explicitly corresponds to only one of these propositions.[18]

In what follows, then, I shall offer an account of testimony that accommodates these features and avoids the problems afflicting Coady's NVNT, the BVNT endorsed by Fricker, Audi, and Sosa, and Graham's MVNT.

---

[16] A similar conclusion, though via different argumentation, can be found in Buenting (2006).

[17] Indeed, my testimony in this case is primarily meant to convey the information I do not explicitly state.

[18] I should note that there may be responses that can be offered to both of these problems. With respect to the first point, it may be argued that though I do not explicitly state that there is coffee left in the kitchen, there is a clear sense in which the non-verbal testimony provided by my nod has this as its content. For, just as my responding "Yes" in this context amounts to "There is coffee left in the kitchen," so too does my nodding in this context amount to testifying to this proposition. Regarding the second point, one might argue that your belief that it is raining outside relies too heavily on memory and inference to qualify as testimonial. In particular, one might claim that you must rely on background information stored in memory about the relationship between rain and umbrellas and explicitly infer that it is raining outside from my testimony that there is an umbrella in the closet. And, even though memory and inference arguably play a role in the acquisition of all testimonial beliefs, one might claim that here the role of memory and inference is simply too significant for the resulting belief to properly be regarded as testimonial.

Though I do not find either of these responses particularly compelling, I shall not here try to resolve these issues. I shall merely point out that the view that I develop in the next section has the advantage of being able to clearly and explicitly accommodate these types of cases.

1.6 The Disjunctive View

The diagnosis that emerges from the previous sections is that our concept of testimony has a dual nature since there seem to be two distinct and often independent aspects to such a notion.[19] On the one hand, testimony is often thought of as an intentional act on the part of the speaker. This is captured by the NVNT and, to a greater extent, by the MVNT. So, for example, both Coady and Graham require that the speaker offer her statement[20] as evidence that p and, in this way, non-informational remarks fail to qualify as instances of testimony. The thought underlying these conditions seems to be that a speaker cannot testify unless there is some intention on the part of the speaker to convey information. On the other hand, however, testimony is often thought of simply as a source of belief or knowledge for the hearer or audience. For instance, even if a speaker does not intend to convey information, as in the case of the posthumous publication of a private journal, we often think of the speaker's statement as testimony in the sense that it provides the hearer with information. In this sense, testimony does not depend on the intentions of the speaker but, rather, on the needs of the hearer or the receiver of the information in question. Indeed, it is my contention that inadequate accounts of testimony result from a failure to recognize this distinction between *testimony as an intentional act on the part of the speaker* and *testimony as a source of belief or knowledge for the hearer.*

To begin, let me make some remarks on behalf of the concept on which I shall be relying in order to flesh out the nature of testimony. I shall then discuss how I wish to apply the distinction between what we may call *speaker testimony* and *hearer testimony* (henceforth, s-testimony and h-testimony, respectively). Finally, I shall show how both notions fall under the general rubric of testimony and how such a distinction fares with respect to the problems afflicting the rival views.

---

[19] The dual nature that I discuss here should not be confused with the dualist view that I develop in Chapter 6. Here my thesis concerns the *metaphysics* of testimony, i.e., the nature of testimony has two different and often independent aspects. In Chapter 6, the dualist view that I defend concerns the *epistemology* of testimony, i.e., testimonial justification or warrant has two central components or dimensions.

[20] For the sake of ease of exposition, I shall often use the term "statement" when discussing a speaker's testimony, despite my earlier argument that the class of testimony is broader than statements. When offering my account of the nature of testimony, however, I shall be explicit that we cannot flesh out testimony in terms of statements alone.

In my proposal, I shall focus on the notions of an *act of communication,* a, *conveying the information that* p. There are, however, some points of clarification that are needed about how I am understanding these crucial notions. Let us begin with the concept of an act of communication. In the previous section, I argued against views that use the notion of a statement in order to flesh out the concept of testimony. In order to avoid the difficulties with this approach, I am construing the concept of an act of communication broadly so that it does not require that the speaker *intend to communicate to others;* instead, it requires merely that the speaker *intend to express communicable content.* A couple of examples should make this distinction clear. Consider a case in which, unbeknownst to me, Chloe has headphones on and is bopping her head to the beat of the music. I walk into the room, ask her if there is any cake left, and, seeing her bop her head, think that she has intended to communicate to me that there is cake left in the kitchen. To my mind, this sort of case may be an example of *ostensible testimony,* but it should not qualify as genuine testimony in any sense of the word. To use my terminology, I would say that Chloe's head-bopping *is not an act of communication since she did not intend to express communicable content.*[21] The same is true of cases in which a speaker babbles gibberish that just happens to sound like words or sentences in a foreign language, or has a cognitive condition that results in her involuntarily blurting out words or sentences in a way similar to the moving of her leg from the knee-jerk reflex,[22] or knocks over a tree while stranded on a deserted island whose branches just happen to fall such that they read "HELP ME" to a pilot flying overhead.[23] In all of these cases, there is not only the absence of the intention to communicate on the part of the speaker, but there is also the lack of her intention to express communicable content. Accordingly, none of these cases involve acts of communication on my view.

On the other hand, consider a case in which Davis is engaged in a soliloquy in his room and, unbeknownst to him, someone in the next room overhears what he is saying. Such a soliloquy, on my view, is an

---

[21] Even if one retains statements as the central items involved in testimony, a similar distinction will be necessary to distinguish genuine statements from spurious ones. For instance, if someone just happens to make sounds that mean "I like apples" in Japanese, we would be reluctant to regard this as a genuine statement.

[22] Thus, those tics stemming from Tourette Syndrome that work merely like reflexes fail to qualify as acts of communication on my view.

[23] I am grateful to Nathan Ballantyne for raising a case similar to this last one involving tree branches.

example in which a speaker intends to express communicable content but does not intend to communicate; accordingly, I would say that Davis's soliloquy qualifies as an act of communication. Similar considerations apply to posthumous publications of journals, private diaries, and so on. Such cases qualify as acts of communication since the speaker in question intends to express thoughts with communicable content, despite the fact that she does not intend to communicate them to anyone else.

There are also cases in which a speaker intends to express communicable content, and thereby offers an act of communication, despite the fact that the intention itself is involuntarily caused. For instance, suppose that Agent 86 intends to keep his secrets, but inadvertently slips truth serum into his own glass of wine rather than into his adversary's. After finishing his wine, the influence of the truth serum leads Agent 86 to disclose his secrets to his adversary.[24] Now, "truth serum…is a fast-acting barbituate that makes a person talkative, uninhibited, and extremely open to suggestion. It does not make a person 'tell the truth,' but [he or she] can be coaxed into saying things the interviewer wants [him or her] to say. The effect of this drug is similar to acute alcohol intoxication."[25] Given the way that truth serum works, Agent 86 clearly intends to express communicable content when he discloses his secrets to his adversary, though such an intention is one that he wouldn't have had were he not under the influence of the truth serum. Thus, on my account, Agent 86's statements qualify as acts of communication.

Let us now turn to the concept of conveying information. What does it mean for an act of communication, a, to convey the information that p? Here are at least three clear instances in which this is the case:

1. Where a is the utterance of a declarative sentence such that it expresses the proposition that p, a conveys the information that p.
2. Where $<p>$ is an obvious (uncancelled) pragmatic implication of a, a conveys the information that p.
3. Where an act of communication a expresses the proposition that q, and it is obvious (either to everyone in the exchange or to a normal competent speaker) that $<q>$ entails $<p>$, a conveys the information both that q and that p.[26]

---

[24] I owe this example to Nathan Ballantyne.

[25] See <http://www.answerbag.com/q_view.php/19856>.

[26] A further qualification may be required here. Because necessary truths are entailed by every proposition, but are surely not conveyed by every act of communication, we should say that an act

While I shall not defend 1–3 as an exhaustive list of ways that acts of communication convey information, they do represent paradigmatic instances of such a process. This will suffice for introducing the crucial distinction between speaker testimony and hearer testimony in what follows.

With these points in mind, let us now turn to the concept of speaker testimony. My account of s-testimony requires that a speaker intend to convey information to her hearer and, in this sense, it requires that the act of communication be offered as conveying such information. Since it is possible for one to offer one's act of communication as conveying the information comprising multiple propositions, let us say that s-testimony requires only that the act of communication be offered as conveying the information comprising *some* proposition(s).[27] So, let us propose the following:

> *Speaker Testimony*: S s-testifies that *p* by performing an act of communication *a* if and only if, in performing *a*, S reasonably intends to convey the information that *p* (in part) in virtue of *a*'s communicable content.

Two points should be noted about this account of s-testimony. First, notice that while there need not be a direct correspondence between the content of the proffered act of communication and the content of the proposition testified to—my saying that there are umbrellas in the closet, for instance, may be offered as conveying the information *both* that it is raining outside and that there are umbrellas in the closet—a *reasonably obvious* connection must exist between such contents. Roughly, the connection between the proffered act of communication *a* and the information that *p* must be such that a normal speaker who offered *a* in similar circumstances would intend to convey the information that *p* (in part) in virtue of *a*'s communicable content. For instance, my intending to convey the information that corn on the cob is yellow by virtue of saying that grass is green fails to qualify

of communication conveys the obvious and relevant entailments of the expressed proposition. More could be said about relevance, but that is tangential to the concerns I am pursuing here.

[27] Of course, not *every* proposition that a hearer could come to know through a speaker's act of communication qualifies as *testimonial* knowledge. For instance, if I come to know that you are feeling nostalgic from your testimony that looking at old photos made you cry earlier today, the resulting knowledge, though in part due to testimony, is primarily *inferential*. Although more might be said about distinguishing between knowledge that is testimonial and that which is inferential, I suspect that the boundary between these two kinds of knowledge is ultimately quite vague.

as s-testimony since, in the absence of rather unusual circumstances, there fails to be a reasonably obvious connection between the contents of these two propositions.[28] Second, notice that I have included the clause "(in part) in virtue of *a*'s communicable content." This clause is intended to rule out cases such as the following: suppose that I sing "I have a soprano voice" in a soprano voice and I intend to convey the information that I have a soprano voice in virtue of the perceptual content of this assertion.[29] Such an act of communication does not qualify as s-testimony, on my view, because it was not offered as conveying information (in part) in virtue of its communicable content; rather, it was offered as conveying information entirely in virtue of its perceptual content.[30] S-testimony, therefore, captures the sense in which testifying requires some intention on the part of the speaker to convey information. If, for instance, I make a casual remark, it will fail to be an instance of s-testimony because I am not offering such an act of communication as conveying information.

H-testimony, on the other hand, does not require any such intention on the part of the speaker.[31] For this notion captures the sense in which testimony can serve as a source of belief or knowledge for others, regardless of the testifier's intention to be such an epistemic source. In this way, posthumous publications of private journals and Frank's statement about the president of our university resigning will both qualify as h-testimony so long as someone takes the acts of communication in question as conveying information. Indeed, a speaker may h-testify even if she positively intends for her statement or thought never to be taken as conveying information to anyone. For example, suppose Lucy's private journal is found by the police. Suppose further that she wrote down that her husband had committed the crime for which he is suspected, though she intended such thoughts only for herself—in fact, she even encrypted the entries in what she (mistakenly) thought was an unbreakable code and, thus, in no way offered such thoughts as conveying information regarding

---

[28] A pre-established arrangement made between two parties to use language in a non-standard way, such as an agreement to use a code language, is a paradigmatic case of unusual circumstances.

[29] This is a variation of an example found in Audi (1997).

[30] The "in part" clause is included since an act of communication can, for instance, be offered as conveying information in virtue of *both* its perceptual and its communicable content and yet still qualify as s-testimony, e.g., I intend to convey the information that I have a soprano voice in virtue of both the perceptual and the communicative content of my saying, in a soprano voice, that I do.

[31] All that is required is what is necessary for there to be an act of communication.

her husband's guilt. Nonetheless, according to the current proposal, Lucy's journal will qualify as h-testimony since it is taken as conveying information by the police. Furthermore, just as in s-testimony a speaker's act of communication may be offered as conveying the information comprising multiple propositions, so in the case of h-testimony a hearer may take a speaker's act of communication as conveying the information comprising multiple propositions. So, let us propose the following condition for h-testimony:

> *Hearer Testimony*: S h-testifies that *p* by making an act of communication *a* if and only if H, S's hearer, reasonably takes *a* as conveying the information that *p* (in part) in virtue of *a*'s communicable content.

Notice that I have again included the clauses "reasonably" and "(in part) in virtue of *a*'s communicable content." The former clause is included to ensure that there is a relevant connection between the content of a proffered act of communication and that of the belief formed by a hearer. Roughly, reasonably taking *a* as conveying the information that *p* requires that a normal hearer in similar circumstances would take *a* as conveying the information that *p* (in part) in virtue of *a*'s communicable content. For instance, while it would be reasonable for a normal hearer to take the statement that there are umbrellas in the closet as conveying the information that it is raining outside, it would not be reasonable for a normal hearer to take a speaker's statement that bananas are yellow as conveying the information that grass is green. Hence, adding "reasonably" prevents such disconnected contents from qualifying as h-testimony.[32] The addition of the latter clause is intended to rule out cases such as the following: suppose that I say that ten people have spoken in this room today and you, having counted the previous nine, come to believe that ten people have spoken in this room today.[33] Here, my statement may certainly be causally relevant with respect to your forming this belief, but your belief is based on your having heard and counted the speakers in the room today, thereby rendering it perceptual in nature. Since you did not take my statement

---

[32] Of course, a consequence of my view is that a single statement may qualify as h-testimony for one person but not for another. But this is a virtue of the account, since surely, e.g., a statement in English is properly regarded as h-testimony for me but not for someone who speaks only Arabic.

[33] This type of example is found in Sosa (1991).

as conveying the information that ten people have spoken in this room today in virtue of its communicable content, then, it does not qualify as an instance of h-testimony.[34]

Now, notice that while the views of testimony considered earlier in this paper—notably, the NVNT and the MVNT—focus on the notion of offering evidence, I instead rely on the concept of conveying information. This is an important substitution. For with respect to both s-testimony and h-testimony, there is a crucial difference between an act of communication either being reasonably offered or taken as *conveying the information* that *p* and an act of communication being reasonably offered or taken as *evidence* that *p*. In particular, there are clear instances of an act of communication intuitively failing to qualify as testimony in which the latter is true of such an act even though the former is not. To see this, consider the following:

A. S reasonably offers an act of communication *a*, where the content is extremely complex and such as only someone intelligent could communicate, as evidence that she is intelligent.

B. H reasonably takes S's act of communication *a* as evidence that S had witnessed a certain episode, or had been at a certain locale, where *a* has communicable content that would be unlikely to occur to anyone who had not witnessed such an episode or visited such a locale.

C. H reasonably takes S's act of communication *a* as evidence that S can communicate such a content.

D. H reasonably takes *a* as evidence that people of a certain sort—to which S belongs—are prone to affirm things with that content.[35]

In each of the cases found in A-D, the following three things are true: (i) intuitively, S is not testifying to the proposition in question; (ii) the act of communication is either reasonably offered or taken as evidence for the proposition in question; but (iii) the act of communication is neither reasonably offered nor taken as conveying the information of the proposition in question. Let us begin with A: S is clearly not trying to convey the information that she is intelligent, nor could her act reasonably be taken

---

[34] Though, of course, such a case may qualify as s-testimony if the speaker reasonably offers her statement as conveying information (in part) in virtue of its communicable content.

[35] I am very grateful to Ernie Sosa for pressing these objections to an earlier version of this chapter.

to be conveying this information, even though she could reasonably offer it, and one could reasonably take it, *as evidence* that she is intelligent. Similarly, in B, S is not trying to convey, nor could reasonably be taken to be conveying, the information that she was in a certain place,[36] despite the fact that one could reasonably take her act as evidence that she was in a certain place. For notice that in both cases A and B, the propositions in question are unlike any of the three instances of conveying information discussed earlier, i.e., *a* is not the utterance of a declarative sentence such that it expresses the proposition that *p*, $<p>$ is not an obvious (uncancelled) pragmatic implication of *a*, and *a* does not express the proposition that *q*, where it is obvious (either to everyone in the exchange or to a normal competent speaker) that $<q>$ entails $<p>$. The same is true of C and D: in the former, a hearer could not reasonably take S's act of communication to convey the information that S is capable of performing such an act and, in the latter, a hearer could not reasonably take S's act of communication to convey the information that she belongs to a type of creature that can perform an act with that content. For, again, in both cases C and D, the acts of communication express propositions unlike those found in the three ways of conveying information discussed earlier. Nevertheless, in both cases, such acts could be taken as evidence for the propositions in question. This shows not only that an act's conveying information is importantly different than its being evidence, but also that the former, unlike the latter, corresponds with our intuitions regarding acts of communication that qualify as testimony and those that do not.

Both s-testimony and h-testimony seem to fall under the general concept of testimony. For, as mentioned earlier, testimony is thought of not only as an intentional act on the part of the speaker, but also as a source of belief or knowledge for the hearer. Many of the problems that we saw in the previous sections result from conflating these two aspects of testimony's dual nature. Once this distinction is made, however, and we see that a speaker can s-testify without h-testifying and vice versa, all of the desiderata for an adequate account of testimony can be captured.

To see this, recall that the NVNT includes restrictions on the speaker, the hearer, and the nature of the statement being offered. In doing so,

---

[36] Unless, of course, that S was at a certain place is an obvious pragmatic implication of what she says—e.g., S says, "Pavarotti's voice sounded great tonight, much better than on a recording."

Coady is conflating s-testimony and h-testimony.[37] Consequently, he fails to adequately capture either notion since he must rule out both (i) cases in which a speaker intends to convey information but her hearer is not in need of it and (ii) cases in which a hearer takes an act of communication as conveying information but the speaker does not offer it as such.

The MVNT, on the other hand, shifts the emphasis away from the hearer and focuses exclusively on the intentions and beliefs of the speaker. In this way, though Graham is more successful than Coady in capturing s-testimony, his account cannot sufficiently accommodate h-testimony. So, for example, he must claim that Lucy did not testify about her husband's guilt in her private journal since she did not direct her thoughts to those whom she believes to be in need of evidence on the matter. But there is a clear sense in which Lucy's journal writings *are* testimony, namely, the sense in which they serve as a source of information for the police. According to the above distinction, Lucy's journal writings are a case of h-testimony but not s-testimony.

Finally, if we endorse a view of testimony that relies on the distinction between s-testimony and h-testimony, we can also provide a more restrictive account than the one put forth by proponents of the BVNT. For recall that the only condition needed for a speaker to testify on this view is that she express her thought. This conception of testimony is too broad, however, since there is nothing that distinguishes non-informational remarks from genuine cases of testimony. The above distinction avoids such a problem since, if the speaker does not reasonably intend to convey information through her act of communication and if the hearer does not reasonably take the act of communication as conveying information, then it will fail to be a case of either s-testimony or h-testimony. Instead, it is simply a casual remark, conversational filler, or some other non-informational remark.

Thus, I propose the following *Disjunctive View of the Nature of Testimony* (hereafter, the DVNT):

DVNT: S testifies that *p* by making an act of communication *a* if and only if (in part) in virtue of *a*'s communicable content, (1) S reasonably

---

[37] This is not entirely accurate. For since neither s-testimony nor h-testimony requires that the proffered information be potential evidence, Coady is including a further requirement. As mentioned earlier, however, *a*'s being potential evidence is not necessary for a speaker to either s-testify or h-testify. Instead, it may be a helpful epistemic criterion for distinguishing between good and bad testimony.

intends to convey the information that p or[38] (2) a is reasonably taken as conveying the information that p.[39]

According to the DVNT, then, testimony is afforded with certain features that distinguish it from everyday chatter. I take this to be a significant advantage for the present account since not all expressions of thought are cases of testimony. Moreover, a further virtue of the DVNT is that it properly leaves the distinction between good and bad testimony for epistemology to delineate. For a speaker can surely reasonably intend to convey the information that p through offering an epistemically inadequate act of communication and, accordingly, a hearer can undoubtedly reasonably take an epistemically unacceptable act of communication as conveying the information that p. In this way, the DVNT allows for an illuminating theory of the epistemology of testimony.

In the remainder of this book, all of the statements (or other acts of communication) considered will, unless otherwise noted, qualify as s-testimony, h-testimony, or both and, hence, will clearly satisfy the DVNT. In what follows, then, I will leave it largely implicit that a given statement is an instance of testimony, and will not specify which disjunct(s) of the DVNT is satisfied, so that full attention can be devoted to issues surrounding the epistemic status of testimonial beliefs.

---

[38] This, of course, is not an exclusive "or"; both (1) and (2) could be satisfied simultaneously.

[39] Clause (2) of the DVNT may need to be modified in something like the following way:

(2*) a is *or should be* reasonably taken as conveying the information that p.

This modification would allow for the following type of case to qualify as testimony: Thelma, while engaged in a soliloquy, confesses to murdering her husband. Although I overhear her make this confession, I do not take her act of communication as conveying any information since I think it is far too outlandish a possibility. Nevertheless, we may still wish to regard Thelma's statement as an instance of testimony because I *should have* reasonably taken it as conveying the information that she murdered her husband. If this is correct, then (2*) can be substituted for (2) in the DVNT.

2

Rejecting Transmission

2.1 The Belief View of Testimony

There is a widely accepted family of views in the epistemology of testimony centering around the claim that *belief* is the central item involved in a testimonial exchange.[1] For instance, in describing the process of learning via testimony, Elizabeth Fricker provides the following: "one language-user has a *belief*, which gives rise to an utterance by him; as a result of observing this utterance another user of the same language, his audience, *comes to share that belief*" (Fricker 1987: 68, emphasis added).[2] In a similar spirit, Alvin Plantinga says that "a *belief on the part of the testifiee* has warrant only if *that belief has warrant for the testifier*" (Plantinga 1993b: 86, emphasis added). In both of these passages, we find strands of what I shall call the *Belief View of Testimony* (hereafter, the BVT).[3]

There are several different yet related components of the BVT. First, while statements are necessary for the process of communication, they are merely vehicles for expressing *beliefs*—they enable us to make public what would otherwise remain private. Strictly speaking, then, we do not learn

---

[1] As Michael Welbourne says, "it is more or less standard to describe the whole testimonial process in the vocabulary of belief" (Welbourne 1994: 305).

[2] In a more precise formulation, Fricker says: "A *speaker*, believing that *P*, and wishing to communicate this belief, makes an utterance which constitutes his asserting that *P*; his audience, a *hearer*, observing and understanding it ... as a result comes also to believe that *P*" (1987: 68–9).

[3] Proponents of different strands of the BVT include Austin (1979), Welbourne (1979, 1981, 1986, and 1994), Evans (1982), Hardwig (1985 and 1991), Fricker (1987, 1994, 1995, 2006b, and 2007), Ross (1986), Coady (1992 and 1994), Burge (1993 and 1997), Reid (1983), Plantinga (1993b), Dummett (1994), McDowell (1994), Williamson (1996 and 2000), Audi (1997, 1998, 2004, and 2006), Faulkner (2000 and 2006), Owens (2000 and 2006), Reynolds (2002), Adler (2002 and 2006), Pritchard (2004), and Schmitt (2006). It is of interest to note that the BVT cuts across the so-called reductionist/non-reductionist debate in the epistemology of testimony. For instance, Fricker (1987, 1994, 1995, forthcoming*a*, and forthcoming*b*) is a reductionist, Plantinga (1993b) is a non-reductionist, and Faulkner (2000) endorses a hybrid reductionist/non-reductionist view, yet all three espouse strands of the BVT.

from one another's *words*—we learn from one another's *beliefs*.[4] This is one of the reasons why nearly everyone takes sincerity on the part of the speaker to be a necessary condition for testimonial knowledge.[5] In order to properly learn from a speaker's belief, there needs to *be* a belief present from which to learn. Thus, if a speaker is insincere and expresses what she herself does not believe, there is nothing for her to pass on to a hearer.

Second, the process of communicating via testimony involves a speaker *transmitting* her belief to a hearer, *along with the epistemic properties it possesses*. For instance, following Fricker's talk of sharing beliefs and Plantinga's characterization of the transmission of warrant, David Owens claims that "a sincere assertion reflects the rationality (good or bad) of the belief it expresses and it *transmits* a belief *with those epistemic credentials* to an audience who are convinced by it" (Owens 2006: 123, emphasis added). And elsewhere he writes: "testimony transmits knowledge of *p* by transmitting the probative force of reasons for belief in *p* from one party to another" (Owens 2000: 169). Testimony, therefore, is said to be incapable of generating new epistemic properties—it merely has the capacity to transmit from one person to another beliefs that have already been rendered justified, warranted, or instances of knowledge via another source.[6]

---

[4] For instance, Robert Audi says that "if one takes it (as Thomas Reid may have) that the recipient of testimony is (characteristically) responding to the attester's *belief* —or at least a presumption thereof—and not just to a linguistic or other symbolic act, one may find it plausible to argue that testimony is a conditionally basic source of justification and perhaps of knowledge as well" (Audi 2004: 21). Similarly, Duncan Pritchard claims that the paradigm case of testimony is "the *intentional transfer of a belief from one agent to another*, whether in the usual way via a verbal assertion made by the one agent to the other, or by some other means, such as through a note" (Pritchard 2004: 326, emphasis added). And Ernest Sosa writes, "On the default assumption … which must be that of sincerity … the speaker's utterance does give to understand *what the speaker thinks*. So, the utterance carries a deliverance as to the *speaker's mind* … If we are to know a speaker's mind through his utterances, the speaker must have a reliable competence to *state his mind*. He must be able through his utterances to deliver safe deliverances about what he thinks on the topic at hand" (Sosa 2006: 121, emphasis added).

[5] For discussions specifically about the role of sincerity in testimony, see, for instance, Welbourne (1979, 1981, 1986, and 1994), Hardwig (1985 and 1991), Ross (1986), Fricker (1987, 1994, 1995, and forthcoming*a*), Plantinga (1993*b*), McDowell (1994), Audi (1997, 1998, and 2006), Owens (2000 and 2006), Root (2001), Adler (2002 and 2006), Moran (2005), Faulkner (2006), and Sosa (2006). For indirect endorsements of sincerity as a necessary condition for testimonial knowledge (justified/warranted belief)—e.g., via the stronger requirement that the speaker have the knowledge (justified/warranted belief) in question—see Burge (1993 and 1997), Williamson (1996 and 2000), Dummett (1994), Reynolds (2002), and Schmitt (2006).

[6] As discussed in the Introduction of this book, when I speak of *justification* and *warrant*, I am interested in these concepts only insofar as they have a necessary connection with knowledge. Thus, there may be some subjective notions of these concepts that escape some of the arguments I give in this chapter. My interest here, however, is in the *epistemology* of testimony.

Third, and closely related, *statements themselves are not the bearers of epistemic significance*—beliefs are. Notice, for instance, that Plantinga does not say that a belief on the part of the testifiee has warrant only if the testifier's *statement* has warrant; instead, he focuses entirely on the epistemic status of the speaker's belief. This is a natural consequence of the previous two points: if statements are merely vehicles for transmitting beliefs that already possess epistemic properties, then the statements themselves simply drop out of the epistemic picture.

While there is much that is intuitively plausible about the BVT, in this chapter I shall argue that this entire picture of the epistemology of testimony is fundamentally incorrect. In particular, I shall show that, both causally and epistemically, *statements*, not beliefs, are the crucial items in a testimonial exchange.[7] Hence, each of the components that constitute the BVT is false.

2.2 The Transmission of Epistemic Properties

Let us begin by focusing on the fundamental thesis of the BVT, which I shall call the *Transmission of Epistemic Properties* (hereafter, TEP). Roughly, the thought expressed by TEP is that a testimonial exchange involves a speaker's belief, along with the epistemic properties it possesses, being *transmitted* to a hearer. There are two dimensions to TEP; one is a necessity thesis and the other is a sufficiency thesis. More precisely:

TEP-N: For every speaker, A, and hearer, B, B knows (believes with justification/warrant) that p on the basis of A's testimony that p only if A knows (believes with justification/warrant) that p.[8]

TEP-S: For every speaker, A, and hearer, B, if (1) A knows (believes with justification/warrant) that p, (2) B comes to believe that p on the basis of the content of A's testimony that p, and (3) B

---

[7] For ease of expression, I shall focus on the role of a speaker's *statement* in a testimonial exchange. However, as we saw in Chapter 1, a belief may be acquired on the basis of a speaker's testimony that is not in the form of a statement—by a physical gesture, for instance. Thus, a more precise characterization of the arguments in this chapter would be in terms of a speaker's *act of communication*.

[8] Proponents of the necessity thesis (TEP-N) include Welbourne (1979, 1981, 1986, and 1994), Hardwig (1985 and 1991), Ross (1986), Burge (1993 and 1997), Plantinga (1993b), McDowell (1994), Williamson (1996 and 2000), Audi (1997, 1998, and 2006), Owens (2000 and 2006), Reynolds (2002), Adler (2006), Faulkner (2006), and Schmitt (2006).

has no undefeated defeaters for believing that p, then B knows (believes with justification/warrant) that p.[9]

Let us first focus on TEP-N. On behalf of this thesis, Robert Audi writes: "*I* cannot (testimonially) give you knowledge that p without knowing that p … . Testimonially based knowledge is received by transmission and so depends on the attester's knowing that p" (Audi 1997: 410). In a similar spirit, Tyler Burge says: "If the recipient depends on interlocution for knowledge, the recipient's knowledge depends on the source's having knowledge as well. For if the source does not believe the proposition, or

---

[9] Proponents of different versions of the sufficiency thesis (TEP-S) include Austin (1979), Welbourne (1979, 1981, 1986, and 1994), Evans (1982), Fricker (1987), Coady (1992), McDowell (1994), Adler (1996 and 2006), and Owens (2000 and 2006). Burge (1993), Williamson (1996 and 2000), and Audi (1997) endorse qualified versions of this thesis. For instance, Burge claims that "[i]f one has acquired one's belief from others in a *normal way*, and if the others know the proposition, one acquires knowledge" (Burge 1992: 477, fn. 16, emphasis added). Timothy Williamson writes that "[i]n *normal circumstances*, a speaker who asserts that P thereby puts a hearer in a position to know that P if (and only if) the speaker knows that P" (Williamson 1996: 520, emphasis added). Similarly, Audi writes, "Concerning knowledge, we might say that at least *normally*, a belief that p based on testimony thereby constitutes knowledge … provided that the attester knows that p and the believer has no reason to doubt either p or the attester's credibility concerning it" (Audi 1997: 412, emphasis added). It should be noted, however, that the arguments offered in Section 2.4 against TEP-S subsume even these three qualified versions of the sufficiency thesis.

It is of further interest to note that there is a version of the sufficiency thesis that is even stronger than TEP-S. With respect to justification and warrant, it can be expressed as follows:

TEP-S′: For every speaker, A, and hearer, B, if (1) A's belief that p has x amount of justification/warrant, (2) B comes to believe that p on the basis of the content of A's testimony that p, and (3) B has no undefeated defeaters for believing that p, then B's belief that p has x amount of justification/warrant.

A similar principle for knowledge can be formulated by substituting "has x amount of justification/warrant" with "is known with degree x of certainty" both in condition (1) and in the consequent of the conditional. In Section 2.4, I shall frame my arguments against the weaker TEP-S since they will apply just as well to the stronger TEP-S′. For instance, if A's belief that p is not justified and B acquires a justified belief that p on the basis of A's testimony that p, then obviously A and B do not share the epistemic property in question to the same degree. Nevertheless, I should mention that, given the picture of testimony painted by proponents of the BVT—in which a speaker's belief along with its epistemic properties is *transmitted* to a hearer—it is not entirely clear what would justify endorsing only the weaker TEP-S.

One final point: Fricker, who is a self-avowed reductionist, is included as a proponent of TEP-S. But if, *qua* reductionist, Fricker requires positive reasons for testimonial justification/warrant, how can she maintain that the satisfaction of conditions (1)–(3) of TEP-S is sufficient for testimonial beliefs to be justified or warranted? Given some of Fricker's other commitments, the most plausible interpretation of her view is that she endorses a restricted version of this thesis: satisfying (1)–(3) of TEP-S is sufficient for testimonial justification/warrant during the *developmental phase* of a person's life, which is the period during which an individual is learning her native language, and when the testimony is about *mundane topics*, such as testimony about what one had for breakfast, the time of day, and so on. These issues shall be discussed in much more detail in Chapters 5, 6, and 7.

if the proposition is not true, or if the source is not justified, the recipient cannot know the proposition" (Burge 1993: 486). And Steven Reynolds claims that "if you tell me that p, I can thereby come to know that p only if you already know it" (Reynolds 2002: 142). These quotations are characteristic of TEP-N, and it is this view of testimony that dominates the current epistemological literature.

This thesis, however, should be distinguished from one that is entailed by TEP-N but is a much weaker view of the transmission of epistemic properties via testimony. To see this, compare with the above quotations what Michael Dummett says about testimony in the following passage:

> If remembering something is to count as retaining a knowledge of it, it must have been known when originally witnessed or experienced; if it was derived from a misperception or misapprehension, the memory cannot of course rank as knowledge. The same naturally applies to taking something to be so, having been told it: the original purveyor of the information—*the first link in the chain of transmission*—must himself have known it, and therefore have been in a position to know it, or it cannot be knowledge for any of those who derived it ultimately from him. (Dummett 1994: 264, emphasis added)

The difference between this claim and the one put forth by proponents of TEP-N is that, on Dummett's view, at least the first link in the chain of testimonial transmission must know that p (via some non-testimonial means), whereas according to TEP-N, every link in the chain must know that p (via either non-testimonial or testimonial means). Let us characterize Dummett's weaker thesis as follows:

TEP-N*: For every testimonial chain, $A_1, \ldots, A_n$, speaker, A_n, and hearer, B, B knows (believes with justification/warrant) that p on the basis of A_n's testimony that p only if the first speaker, A_1, knows (believes with justification/warrant) that p in some non-testimonial way.[10]

So proponents of TEP-N*, unlike those who endorse TEP-N, can countenance testimonial chains that include some speakers who know (believe with justification/warrant) that p and some who do not. The crucial point of TEP-N* is that the original source of the knowledge (justification/warrant) that p, that is, the speaker who first testified that p in the

---

[10] Faulkner (2000) and Fricker (2006a and 2006b) also endorse TEP-N*.

relevant chain, must know (believe with justification/warrant) that *p* via some non-testimonial means.

Let us now turn to TEP-S. On behalf of this thesis, J. L. Austin claims that "where someone has said to me 'I know,' I am entitled to say I know too, at second-hand. The right to say 'I know' is transmissible, in the sort of way that other authority is transmissible" (Austin 1979: 100). Similarly, Jonathan Adler writes: "If S knows that *p* and S asserts that *p* to H, and H accepts *p* on the basis of S's testimony, then H knows that *p*" (Adler 2006).[11] And C. A. J. Coady accepts the following principle: "if *S* knows that *P* then (given the satisfaction of certain conditions relating to *S*'s sincerity, the willingness of *S*'s audience to accept what *S* says as an honest expression of what he knows, etc.) *S* can bring his listeners to know that *P* ... by telling them that *P*" (Coady 1992: 224).[12] Now, while simple endorsements of TEP-S of this sort are widespread in the literature, several points of clarification are in order regarding the specific conditions of this thesis.

Since TEP-S expresses the conditions required for *testimonial knowledge* (justification/warrant), condition (2) specifies that the hearer must form the belief in question on the basis of the *content* of the speaker's testimony. This precludes cases where a belief is formed, either entirely or primarily, on the basis of features *about* the speaker's testimony from qualifying as instances of testimonial knowledge (justification/warrant). For instance, suppose that you hear me say, "ten people have spoken in this room today" and, having counted the previous nine, you thereby come to know that ten people have spoken in this room today.[13] Or suppose that you say, in a soprano voice, that you have a soprano voice and I come to believe this entirely on the basis of hearing your soprano voice.[14] In both cases, the knowledge (justification/warrant) in question is perceptual, not testimonial: it is based on perceptual features about where or how the assertion is offered rather than on the content of the testimony in question. Condition (2), therefore, prevents cases of this sort from qualifying as instances of *testimonial* knowledge (justification/warrant).

Notice, however, that such a condition does not require that the hearer's belief be formed *entirely* on the basis of the content of the

---

[11] See Adler (1996) for a refined version of this thesis.
[12] This principle is quoted by Coady from Dretske (1982).
[13] This type of example is found in Sosa (1991).
[14] This example is a slight variation of one found in Audi (1997).

speaker's testimony. This is to allow cases where a given belief is formed on the basis of both the content of a speaker's testimony and, say, perception, but where, both causally and epistemically, the testimony is *sufficient* for the subject to hold the knowledge (justified/warranted belief) in question. In such cases, though perception plays both a causal and an epistemic role, it may be argued that the sufficiency of testimony renders the belief in question genuinely *testimonial*. In contrast, cases in which a hearer has relevant background information and uses it to derive knowledge (justified/warranted belief) from the statement of a speaker do not satisfy condition (2) of TEP-S. For example, suppose that you know from past experience that I report that there is no milk in the refrigerator only when there is some. Now when I report to you that there is no milk in the refrigerator, you may supplement my testimony with your background information and hence derive knowledge that there is milk in the refrigerator. Because the epistemic status of beliefs formed in these types of cases relies so heavily on memory and inference, the resulting knowledge (justification/warrant) is only partially testimonially based. Thus, in my discussion in this chapter, I shall focus only on cases in which the testimonial knowledge (justification/warrant) in question is based on the content of the speaker's testimony and thus clearly satisfies condition (2) of TEP-S.

It should also be noted that, in light of some of the considerations from Chapter 1, there is a weaker version of (2) (hereafter (2′)) that requires only that the hearer come to believe that *p* on the basis of the content of the speaker's *testimony*, not that such a belief be based on the content of the speaker's testimony *that* p. More precisely:

(2′) B comes to believe that *p* on the basis of the content of A's testimony. There is also a correspondingly weaker version of TEP-N:

TEP-N′: For every speaker, A, and hearer, B, B knows (believes with justification/warrant) that *p* on the basis of A's testimony only if (i) A's belief is known (justified/warranted), and (ii) B's belief that *p* is appropriately connected with the content of A's testimony.

Condition (ii) is included to prevent beliefs formed entirely on the basis of features disconnected from the content of the testimony in question, such as the one above about your having a soprano voice, from qualifying as *testimonial*.[15] Now, there are at least two different kinds of cases that might support including both (2′) rather than (2) and TEP-N′ rather than TEP-N. For instance, suppose that Virginia asks me whether it is cold outside and I respond by saying, "Your hat and gloves are in the closet." Here, one might say that, given the context, Virginia acquires knowledge (justified/warranted belief) that it is cold outside on the basis of my testimony that her hat and gloves are in the closet. Thus, one might claim that both (2) of TEP-S and TEP-N are, in fact, too strong since one can acquire testimonial knowledge (testimonially justified/warranted belief) that *p* on the basis of the content of a speaker's testimony that *q*. The second type of case that may pose a problem for both of these theses can be seen by considering the following: suppose that Edna asks me whether I see any bald eagles through my binoculars and I respond with a nod. Here, it might be argued that Edna acquires knowledge (justified/warranted belief) that I see bald eagles through my binoculars on the basis of the non-verbal testimony provided by my nod. In this way, one might claim that while knowledge (justified/warranted belief) that *p* is acquired on the basis of the content of my testimony, it is not based on the content of my testimony *that* p.

Although I think both types of examples provide convincing evidence for including the weaker versions found in (2′) and TEP-N′, I am leaving the stronger (2) and TEP-N in my characterizations of the relevant theses since these are the versions suggested by proponents of the BVT.[16] For those convinced by the cases discussed above, such theses can easily be substituted with the weaker (2′) and TEP-N′.

Let us now turn to condition (3) of TEP-S. There are two central kinds of defeaters that are typically taken to be relevant here. First, there are what we might call *psychological defeaters*. A psychological defeater is a doubt or belief that is had by S and that indicates that S's belief that *p* is either false or unreliably formed or sustained.[17] Defeaters in this sense function

---

[15] Of course, if TEP-N is substituted with TEP-N′, more will need to be said about what the appropriate connection in (ii) amounts to. See Chapter 1, Section 1.7.

[16] I say "suggested" because most proponents of TEP-N and TEP-S do not even explicitly require that the hearer's testimonial belief in question be based on the *content* of the speaker's testimony.

[17] To be even more precise, there are two different kinds of psychological defeaters: *rebutting defeaters* are those that indicate the target belief is *false* while *undercutting defeaters* are those that indicate the target belief is *unreliably formed or sustained*. See Pollock (1986) for further development of the distinction between rebutting and undercutting defeaters.

by virtue of being *had* by S, regardless of their truth-value or epistemic status.[18] For instance, suppose that Miranda learns that the textbook from which she acquired a certain belief about the Civil War was written by an incompetent scholar or a pathological liar. In this case, Miranda acquires a belief that indicates that the source of her historical belief is unreliable. Now, even if her original belief was produced by a reliable process, and even if the defeating belief in question fails to be true, the fact that a subject holds the defeating belief is often taken to be sufficient for preventing the target belief—or *defeatee*—from being known (justified/warranted).

Second, there are what we might call *normative defeaters*. A normative defeater is a doubt or belief that S ought to have and that indicates that S's belief that p is either false or unreliably formed or sustained.[19] Defeaters in this sense function by virtue of being doubts or beliefs that S *should have* (whether or not S does have them) given the presence of certain available evidence.[20] For example, suppose that Bill believes that the President is currently in Chicago, but then reads in *The New York Times* that the President is currently in China. If Bill continues to hold his original belief with no reason for doubting the report in the newspaper, it may be argued that even if the President is in fact in Chicago, Bill does not know this because there is evidence available to him that defeats his knowledge (justification/warrant). The underlying thought here is that certain kinds of doubts and beliefs—either that one has or should have—contribute epistemically unacceptable *irrationality* to doxastic systems and, accordingly, knowledge (justification/warrant) can be defeated or undermined by their presence.[21]

---

[18] For various views of what I call psychological defeaters see, for example, BonJour (1980 and 1985), Nozick (1981), Pollock (1986), Goldman (1986), Plantinga (1993*b* and 2000), Lackey (1999), Bergmann (1997, 2004, and 2006), and Reed (2006).

[19] Following the distinction in note 17, there are rebutting and undercutting normative defeaters. The central difference is that while psychological defeaters are doubts or beliefs had by the subject, their normative counterparts are doubts or beliefs that the subject *should* have. For more on this, see Lackey (1999) and Reed (2006).

[20] For discussions involving what I call normative defeaters, approached in a number of different ways, see BonJour (1980 and 1985), Goldman (1986), Fricker (1987 and 1994), Chisholm (1989), Burge (1993 and 1997), McDowell (1994), Audi (1997 and 1998), Williams (1999), Lackey (1999), BonJour and Sosa (2003), Hawthorne (2004), Bergmann (2006), and Reed (2006). What all of these discussions have in common is simply the idea that evidence can defeat knowledge (justification/warrant) even when the subject does not form any corresponding doubts or beliefs from the evidence in question.

[21] In addition to psychological and normative defeaters, there are what we might call *factual defeaters*. A factual defeater is a true proposition such that if it were added to S's belief system, then S would

The final point about condition (3) of TEP-S is that a defeater may itself be either defeated or undefeated. Suppose, for instance, that Holly believes that there is a hawk nesting in her backyard because she saw it there this afternoon, but Dominick tells her, and she thereby comes to believe, that the bird is instead a falcon. Now, the justification Holly had for believing that there is a hawk in her backyard has been defeated by her belief that the bird is a falcon. But, since psychological defeaters can themselves be beliefs, they too are candidates for defeat. For instance, suppose that Holly consults a bird guidebook to check whether the bird in her backyard is a falcon and she discovers that it is in fact a Cooper's hawk. In this case, the belief that she acquires from the bird book provides her with a psychological defeater for the belief that she acquired via Dominick's testimony, and hence it provides her with a *defeater-defeater* for her original belief that there is a hawk nesting in her backyard. And, as should be suspected, defeater-defeaters can also be defeated by further doubts and beliefs, which, in turn, can be defeated by further doubts and beliefs, and so on. Similar considerations involving reasons, rather than doubts and beliefs, apply in the case of normative defeaters. Now, when one has a defeater for one's belief that *p* that is not itself defeated, one has what is called an *undefeated defeater* for one's belief that *p*. It is the presence of undefeated defeaters, not merely defeaters, that is incompatible with testimonial knowledge (justification/warrant) and thus relevant to TEP-S.

Now, the view of testimony found in both TEP-N and TEP-S is, in large part, motivated by the striking similarities that testimony purportedly bears to memory. For instance, it is often assumed that neither memory nor testimony is, strictly speaking, a *generative* epistemic source: while the latter *transmits* knowledge (justification/warrant) from one speaker to

---

no longer be justified in believing that *p*. Defeaters in this sense function by virtue of being *true*. For instance, you may correctly believe that you saw a coyote in Joshua Tree National Park and yet the fact that there are dogs that you would not be able to distinguish from coyotes that frequently visit this park may nonetheless prevent such a belief from being an instance of knowledge. In particular, *that there are dogs indistinguishable to you from coyotes that frequent the park in which you saw the coyote* is a true proposition which, if added to your belief system, would result in your belief being unjustified. For discussions of factual defeaters, see Lehrer (1965 and 1974), Lehrer and Paxson (1969), Klein (1971, 1976, 1979, and 1980), Sosa (1974 and 1979), and Swain (1981). In this chapter, I shall focus on psychological and normative defeaters since these are the kinds of defeaters generally taken by proponents of the BVT to be incompatible with testimonial knowledge (justification/warrant). In contrast, the attempt to rule out Gettier-type cases via defeasibility accounts of knowledge involving the absence of factual defeaters is not typically endorsed by proponents of the BVT.

another, the former *preserves* knowledge (justification/warrant) from one time to another. Thus, just as subjects cannot remember that p unless they have something to remember, the thought underlying TEP is that speakers cannot give knowledge (justification/warrant) that p unless they have something to give.[22] In this way, the picture we have of testimony seems to be much like a bucket brigade: in order to give you a full bucket of water, I must have a full bucket of water to pass to you. Moreover, if I give you a full bucket of water, then—spills aside—the bucket of water you now possess as a result of our exchange will also be full. Similarly, in order to transmit to you a warranted belief, I must have a warranted belief to pass to you.[23] Moreover, if I transmit to you a warranted belief, then—defeaters aside—the belief that you now possess as a result of our exchange will also be warranted.

Despite both their intuitive plausibility and their nearly universal acceptance, I shall, in what follows, argue that TEP-N, TEP-N*, and TEP-S are all false. In so doing, I shall show not only that each of the components of the BVT is false, but also that testimony can function as a generative, rather than as a merely transmissive, epistemic source.

2.3 The Necessity Thesis

I shall now argue against TEP. In this section, I focus on the necessity thesis (TEP-N), leaving the sufficiency thesis (TEP-S) for Section 2.4. I shall present three different kinds of counterexamples to TEP-N: the first two involve speakers who fail to have knowledge (justified/warranted belief) that p because they fail to believe that p (i.e., they fail the belief condition of knowledge), but hearers who nonetheless acquire knowledge (justified/warranted belief) that p on the basis of their testimony that p. These two cases specifically undermine TEP-N. The third type of case involves a speaker who fails to have knowledge (justified/warranted belief) that p because she has an undefeated defeater for believing that p (i.e., she

---

[22] In the appendix to this book, I shall argue against the view that memory is a merely preservative epistemic source, just as I shall argue in this chapter against the view that testimony is a merely transmissive epistemic source.

[23] For ease of exposition, I shall sometimes focus on only one epistemic property, such as warrant. The arguments in this paper, however, are completely general, and apply just as well to justification and knowledge (and even, at times, to rationality).

fails the justification or warrant condition of knowledge), but a hearer who nonetheless acquires knowledge (justified/warranted belief) that p on the basis of her testimony that p. This case undermines both TEP-N and the much weaker TEP-N* endorsed by Dummett and Fricker.

To begin, consider the following:

CREATIONIST TEACHER: Stella is a devoutly Christian fourth-grade teacher, and her religious beliefs are grounded in a deep faith that she has had since she was a very young child. Part of this faith includes a belief in the truth of creationism and, accordingly, a belief in the falsity of evolutionary theory. Despite this, she fully recognizes that there is an overwhelming amount of scientific evidence against both of these beliefs. Indeed, she readily admits that she is not basing her own commitment to creationism on evidence at all but, rather, on the personal faith that she has in an all-powerful Creator. Because of this, Stella does not think that religion is something that she should impose on those around her, and this is especially true with respect to her fourth-grade students. Instead, she regards her duty as a teacher to involve presenting material that is best supported by the available evidence, which clearly includes the truth of evolutionary theory. As a result, after consulting reliable sources in the library and developing reliable lecture notes, Stella asserts to her students, "Modern-day *Homo sapiens* evolved from *Homo erectus*," while presenting her biology lesson today. Though Stella herself neither believes nor knows this proposition, she never shares her own personal faith-based views with her students, and so they form the corresponding true belief solely on the basis of her reliable testimony.

Now, given Stella's commitment to creationism, she does not know (believe with justification/warrant) that modern-day *Homo sapiens* evolved from *Homo erectus* because she does not believe this proposition, i.e., she fails the belief condition of knowledge. But because she reliably conveys this information to her fourth-grade students, and does not provide them with any relevant undefeated defeaters, they acquire the knowledge (justified/warranted belief) in question on the basis of her testimony. Moreover, we can flesh out CREATIONIST TEACHER in various ways so that the students clearly satisfy the justification or warrant condition of knowledge, no matter what view of these concepts is at issue. For instance, we can suppose that the children have grown up in environments in which they have not acquired any reasons to favor evolutionary theory over creationism or vice versa. We can also assume that the students have excellent positive reasons for accepting the testimony of Stella, e.g., her reports typically covary with their perceptual experiences, the reports of their parents and classmates, and so on. Thus, according to both broadly externalist and internalist accounts of justification or warrant, the children clearly acquire the knowledge (justified/warranted belief) in question on the basis of Stella's testimony.[24]

What CREATIONIST TEACHER reveals is that an *unreliable believer* may nonetheless be a *reliable testifier*, and so may reliably convey knowledge (justified/warranted belief) to a hearer despite the fact that she fails to possess it herself.[25] For, although Stella ignores the relevant evidence with respect to her doxastic states concerning evolutionary theory—thereby leading her to lack the belief that modern-day *Homo sapiens* evolved from *Homo erectus*—she bases her testimony regarding this topic firmly on such evidence. This enables Stella to impart knowledge (justified/warranted belief) to her students that she fails to possess herself, thereby showing that TEP-N is false.

There are three ways in which one can deny that cases like CRE-ATIONIST TEACHER provide a counterexample to TEP-N. The first is to deny that Stella's testimony is the *source* of the children's knowledge in question, the second is to deny that the children actually do come to have the relevant *knowledge* of evolutionary theory, and the third is to deny that the teacher's statement qualifies as an instance of *testimony*.[26] I shall examine these in turn.

To argue that Stella's testimony is not the source of the children's knowledge is tantamount to denying that she is a link in the testimonial chain of evolutionary knowledge. But what, we might ask, could justify

---

[24] A recent article in *The New York Times* (February 12, 2007, "Believing Scripture but Playing by Science's Rules") about Dr Marcus R. Ross, a creationist who also just finished a geosciences PhD in paleontology, makes clear that the situation described in CREATIONIST TEACHER is by no means merely a thought experiment. As the author of the article writes, "For him, Dr. Ross said, the methods and theories of paleontology are one 'paradigm' for studying the past, and Scripture is another. In the paleontological paradigm, he said, the dates in his dissertation are entirely appropriate. The fact that as a young earth creationist he has a different view just means, he said, 'that I am separating the different paradigms.'" (I am grateful to Cristina Lafont for bringing this article to my attention.)

[25] It should be noted that CREATIONIST TEACHER undermines views that are even weaker than TEP-N. For instance, John Hardwig argues in his (1991) that a speaker must *believe* that *p* in order for her testimony to give a hearer a good reason to believe that *p*. But obviously Stella's testimony can give her students a good reason to believe that *Homo sapiens* evolved from *Homo erectus*, despite the fact that she does not believe this proposition herself. Hence, even Hardwig's much weaker thesis is falsified by CREATIONIST TEACHER.

[26] For ease of exposition, I shall, in what follows, focus primarily on knowledge. All of my remarks in this section, however, apply equally to justification and warrant as well.

such a claim? For, *ex hypothesi*, the children are not relying on or consulting any textbooks, but are forming their beliefs solely on the basis of the report made by Stella. Perhaps one way to defend this position is to argue that a person who functions as a mere instrument for transmitting knowledge cannot be considered a testimonial epistemic source. For example, one might claim that it is actually the authors of the books on evolutionary theory from which Stella derived her lecture notes who are the links in the testimonial chain leading to the students in question. Stella is merely an instrument for transmitting the knowledge of evolutionary theory from the authors of the books to the children in the elementary school, and hence such cases do not pose a problem for TEP-N.

Now one obvious way of responding to this objection is simply to modify CREATIONIST TEACHER so that the authors in question are merely interested in the topic of evolutionary theory but are themselves also creationists. This will, I take it, lead the proponent of TEP-N to point to the sources from which the authors in question derived their information on evolutionary theory, so as to avoid the counterexample. And I suppose we can add further modifications and objections until ultimately we trace the chain back to Darwin himself. This, however, is an unwelcome consequence. For not only is it a counterintuitive picture of the way we think of testimony, but it is also question-begging. To see this, let us ask the following question: if the teacher in our envisaged case *had had* the requisite belief, would she have been the source of the children's knowledge, or would it have been Darwin? I take it that the proponent of TEP-N would respond that, in this case, the teacher would be the source of the knowledge in question precisely because such a view is committed to *chains* of testimonial knowledge. That is, hearers need not receive the report that *p* directly from Darwin himself because testimony is a source whereby people can acquire information across times, places, and persons. Given this, it seems natural to assume that the proponent of TEP-N would countenance Stella as the source of the children's knowledge if she had had the requisite belief. But then to deny that she is the source in CREATIONIST TEACHER merely because she lacks the belief at issue is question-begging.

A variant of this first response is to argue that there is a difference between what we might call *direct* and *indirect* testimony and that CREATIONIST TEACHER is an instance of the latter. For example, suppose that I do not believe that Cody ate the last cookie, but I nonetheless report to you that John said that Cody ate the last cookie. Here one might say that what I am testifying to is simply what John said and that it is only in an indirect way that I convey the information about Cody. Similarly, one might argue that even if it is not made explicit in her report, what Stella is testifying to is merely what the authorities on evolutionary theory accept, and hence it is only in an indirect way that she communicates information about evolutionary theory itself. In this way, it may be argued that, as it stands, TEP-N applies only to testimonial knowledge that is acquired in a direct way, and thus CREATIONIST TEACHER does not pose a problem for this view.

However, it is not entirely clear what the criterion could be for distinguishing between direct and indirect testimony such that Stella's report turns out to be an instance of the latter. For, in the above case involving Cody, I report that so and so said that *p* to you, while, *ex hypothesi*, Stella merely reports that *p* to her students. Now the distinguishing mark between direct and indirect testimony cannot be whether the speaker in question believes, or fails to believe that *p*, respectively. For instance, I may believe that Cody ate the last cookie but, because I do not want to be held accountable for divulging this information, I may nonetheless report that John said that Cody ate the last cookie. Here, even though I hold the belief about Cody, one might say that this is still a case of indirect testimony since what I am testifying to is what John said. On the other hand, if the distinguishing mark of direct testimony is that the speaker did not acquire the information in question from another speaker's testimony, this has the unwelcome consequence that most of the reports we make, with the exception of, for example, reports about our first-hand perceptual experiences, are cases of indirect testimony. Given this, the way in which I would distinguish between direct and indirect testimony is by the *content* of the proffered statement: if, on the one hand, I report to you that *p* (whether or not I believe that *p*), then this is a case of direct testimony. On the other hand, if I report to you that so and so said that *p* (whether or not I believe that *p*), then this is a case of indirect testimony. In this way, Stella's assertion that "Modern-day *Homo sapiens* evolved from *Homo erectus*" turns out to be an instance of direct testimony, even though she fails to believe the content of her report.

The second strategy for responding to cases like CREATIONIST TEACHER is to deny that the children in question acquire the relevant knowledge. One way to support this view is to argue that testimony cannot be a source of knowledge if the speaker in question is lying or falsely testifying. For, if one reports that p but does not believe that p, then, it might be argued, it is merely an accident if a hearer comes to believe truly that p on this basis. And since it is widely assumed that there must be some non-accidental connection between a subject's belief that p and the truth in order to rule out Gettier-type cases, one cannot know that p on the basis of a speaker's falsely testifying that p. Given this, one might argue that, broadly speaking, Stella is lying to her students since she is reporting what she herself does not believe, and hence even if her students acquire true beliefs on the basis of her testimony, this is merely an accident.[27]

By way of response here, notice that, *ex hypothesi*, Stella consulted reliable books in the library to develop her reliable lecture notes and, hence, it is unclear how there could be any unacceptable degree of accidentality in CREATIONIST TEACHER. For instance, if there is another elementary school in the area where Stanley teaches evolutionary theory to his students, has the purportedly requisite beliefs, and develops reliable lecture notes that are similar to Stella's in all relevant respects, it seems fairly safe to assume that the children in his school acquire knowledge of evolutionary theory on the basis of Stanley's testimony. But then why wouldn't the children in Stella's school? Why should it matter that Stella is a creationist and does not believe what she is teaching to her students?[28]

The third strategy for defending TEP-N from CREATIONIST TEACHER is to grant that the children acquire the relevant knowledge and that they do so on the basis of Stella's teaching, but to deny that her statement, "Modern-day *Homo sapiens* evolved from *Homo erectus*," qualifies as a genuine instance of testimony. Specifically, one might argue that in order for a speaker to testify, conditions must be satisfied, either about the nature of the proffered statement itself or about the intentions of the speaker, and the satisfaction of such conditions distinguishes testimony from mere statements. In this way, the children may acquire knowledge on the basis of Stella's reports, but this fails to show that they acquire knowledge on the basis of her *testimony*.

[27] See Plantinga (1993b: 82–3) and Chakrabarti (1994: 110) for this type of response.

[28] Indeed, as the second counterexample against TEP-N will show, it seems clear that hearers can acquire knowledge on the basis of the testimony of speakers even when the latter are pathological liars.

Now, as should be clear, Stella's statement, "Modern-day *Homo sapiens* evolved from *Homo erectus*," satisfies the disjunctive conception of testimony that I developed and defended in Chapter 1. Indeed, her statement qualifies as both speaker-testimony and hearer-testimony, for she not only reasonably intends to convey information in virtue of the communicable content of her assertion, but her students also reasonably take her assertion as conveying such information. But even for those who endorse the competing views of the nature of testimony considered in Chapter 1—the narrow view (NVNT), the moderate view (MVNT), and the broad view (BVNT)—Stella's assertion qualifies as testimony *on all three accounts*. For example, according to the NVNT, testifying requires that a competent speaker offer a statement that is both evidence in an objective sense and directed to those who are in need of evidence on the matter, while the MVNT requires that a speaker both intend that her audience believe that she is competent and that she offer a statement that is directed to those whom she believes to be in need of evidence on the matter. But notice: Stella is a competent speaker about evolutionary theory who offers a statement that is not only evidence in an objective sense, it is also directed to those who are, and whom she believes to be, in need of evidence on the matter. Similar considerations apply to the BVNT, where testimony is understood roughly as "people's telling us things" (Audi 1997: 406). Obviously, Stella's saying to her students, "Modern-day *Homo sapiens* evolved from *Homo erectus*," qualifies as a person telling someone something. Thus, according to every view of testimony considered in Chapter 1, Stella satisfies the requisite conditions for testifying. There is, then, no compelling response to CREATIONIST TEACHER, thereby lending further support to the conclusion that TEP-N is false.

A second type of case against TEP-N—one that also involves a speaker failing the belief condition of knowledge but in a substantively different way than Stella in CREATIONIST TEACHER—can be seen by considering the following:

CONSISTENT LIAR: When Bertha was a teenager, she suffered a head injury while ice skating and, shortly afterwards, became quite prone to telling lies, especially about her perceptual experiences involving wild animals. After observing this behavior, her parents became increasingly distressed and, after consulting various psychologists and therapists, finally took her to see a neurosurgeon, Dr Jones. Upon examining her, Dr Jones noticed a lesion in Bertha's brain which appeared to be the cause of her behavior, and so it was decided that surgery would be the best option to pursue. Unfortunately, Dr Jones discovered during the surgery that he couldn't repair the lesion—instead, he decided to modify her current lesion and create another one so that her pattern of lying would be extremely consistent and would combine in a very precise way with a pattern of consistent perceptual unreliability. Not only did Dr Jones keep the procedure that he performed on Bertha completely to himself, he also did this with the best of intentions, wanting his patient to function as a healthy, happy, and well respected citizen.

As a result of this procedure, Bertha is now—as a young adult—a radically unreliable, yet highly consistent, believer with respect to her perceptual experiences about wild animals. For instance, nearly every time she sees a deer, she believes that it is a horse; nearly every time she sees a giraffe, she believes that it is an elephant; nearly every time she sees an owl, she believes that it is a hawk, and so on. At the same time, however, Bertha is also a radically insincere, yet highly consistent, testifier of this information. For instance, nearly every time she sees a deer and believes that it is a horse, she insincerely reports to others that she saw a deer; nearly every time she sees a giraffe and believes that it is an elephant, she insincerely reports to others that she saw a giraffe, and so on.[29] Moreover, because of her consistency as both a believer and a liar, those around her do not have any reason for doubting Bertha's reliability as a source of information. Indeed, in her home community, she is regarded as one of the most trustworthy people to consult on a wide range of topics.[30] Yesterday, Bertha ran into her next door neighbor, Henry, and insincerely though correctly reported to him that she saw a deer on a nearby hiking trail. Since, in addition to his trust in Bertha, it is not at all unlikely for there to be deer on the hiking trail in question, Henry readily accepted her testimony.[31]

---

[29] Notice that because Bertha's ice-skating accident took place when she was a teenager, the content of her wild-animal beliefs was already fixed in a normal way, and hence there is nothing about the example that is incompatible with the truth of a causal theory of content.

[30] In order to avoid the worry that Bertha's false beliefs would eventually be detected, we can also stipulate that, now that she is a young adult, there are very few occasions in which she either interacts with or discusses wild animals. For instance, we can assume that she lives in an urban environment, is allergic to most non-human animal hair and hence rarely has contact with such creatures, and so on.

[31] A similar, though substantially less developed, example can be found in my (1999). There, however, my purpose was simply to argue against a version of TEP framed in terms of knowledge, rather than the general BVT that is my concern here. Moreover, it could plausibly be argued that the example found in my (1999) is a Gettier-type case, whereas I shall later argue that there is simply no compelling sense in which CONSISTENT LIAR is such a case. One further point—compare CONSISTENT LIAR with the following: I know that Margo only reports that it is snowing outside when it is not. Thus, when she reports to me that it is snowing outside, I supplement her testimony with the background information I possess about her testimonial habits and come to know that it is not

The first point to notice about CONSISTENT LIAR is that even though Bertha is a radically *unreliable believer* with respect to her animal sightings, she is nonetheless an extremely *reliable testifier* of this information—indeed, even more reliable than many average testifiers who frequently exaggerate, distort, or are simply wrong in their reports about what is true. For, as a result of the procedure performed by Dr Jones, *nearly every time* Bertha sees a deer, she believes that it is a horse yet reports to others that she saw a deer; *nearly every time* she sees a giraffe, she believes that it is an elephant yet reports to others that she saw a giraffe, and so on. Moreover, this point can be further illustrated by noticing that Bertha's statements satisfy the counterfactuals that are, perhaps, most likely to capture reliability, despite the fact that her beliefs do not. For instance, while Bertha's beliefs are not *sensitive* in Nozick's sense, her statements are, i.e., though Bertha would still believe that p if p were false, she would not state that p if p were false.[32] The same can be said with respect to Sosa's *safety* requirement, i.e., though Bertha would believe that p without it being so that p, she would not state that p without it being so that p. Her statements, then, are safe in Sosa's sense, even though her beliefs are not.[33] Thus, it is clear that Bertha''s *statements*, unlike her *beliefs*, are an excellent epistemic source of information about wild animals.

The second point that should be emphasized about CONSISTENT LIAR is that, though the procedure Dr Jones performed on Bertha renders her a highly reliable testifier with respect to her wild animal sightings, she is nonetheless still an *agent* with intentional states that affect the statements that she offers to others. In this sense, Bertha is importantly different from non-agential mechanisms, such as thermometers and odometers, that may reliably convey information but not through anything reasonably regarded as *testimony*. For instance, Bertha can, if she chooses, refrain from telling Henry anything at all; she can talk about the weather instead; she could tell an unrelated lie (e.g., "I saw an escaped elephant in

snowing outside. As mentioned earlier in this chapter, this kind of knowledge, though in part based on testimony, also relies quite heavily on perception, memory, and inductive inference. Thus, one may plausibly argue that this sort of case does not pose a problem for TEP-N since this thesis applies only to cases of *pure* testimonial belief. But notice that this kind of move cannot be made with respect to CONSISTENT LIAR—the beliefs that Henry forms on the basis of Bertha's testimony are purely testimonial in every relevant sense.

[32] See Nozick (1981).
[33] See Sosa (1996, 1999, 2000, and 2002). See also Williamson (2000) and Pritchard (2005).

the woods"). All of these possibilities are available to Bertha in a way that they are not for thermometers, odometers, and other such non-agential sources of information.[34] For this reason, Henry's learning from Bertha's words falls under the general category picked out by paradigmatic instances of testimony rather than that picked out by such non-testimonial mechanisms.[35]

The third salient feature of CONSISTENT LIAR is that Dr Jones *deliberately* performed procedures on Bertha's brain, not only so that her perceptual errors and lying practices would be highly consistent, but also so that they would combine in such a way so as to render her an extraordinarily reliable testifier. In large part because of the role that Dr Jones plays in Bertha's condition, there is no relevant *accidentality* in the belief that Henry forms on the basis of her testimony and, hence, CONSISTENT LIAR cannot plausibly be regarded as a Gettier-type case.[36] With respect to the truth of the belief in question, it is neither an accident that Bertha reported that there was a deer on the hiking trail nor that Henry came to hold this belief on the basis of her testimony. For, because of her two brain lesions, Bertha is such that *nearly every time* she sees a deer,

---

[34] It is worth emphasizing, then, that Bertha's situation in CONSISTENT LIAR should be read as B, rather than A, below:

A: Bertha is hard-wired such that nearly every time she sees a deer and believes that it is a horse, she thereby reports that she saw a deer.

B: Bertha is hard-wired such that nearly every time she sees a deer and believes that it is a horse, she reports that she saw a deer *when she chooses to report her sighting*.

B, unlike A, makes it clear that Bertha is still very much an agent when it comes to her testimonial practices. (I am grateful to Mark Heller and Ishani Maitra for raising an objection that prompted this note.)

[35] It may be further objected that even if Bertha's statements are an excellent source of information, they do not qualify as *testimony* since our ordinary usage of this term requires that the speaker believe the proposition in question. (I am grateful to Liz Camp, Mark Heller, and Ishani Maitra for pressing an objection that led to the inclusion of this point.) By way of response to this objection, notice first that Bertha's statements clearly satisfy both disjuncts of the account of testimony developed in Chapter 1: Henry not only reasonably takes her assertion as conveying information in virtue of its communicable content, Bertha, unlike non-testimonial sources of information—such as thermometers and odometers—reasonably intends to convey information in virtue of the communicable content of her assertion, even if she does not intend to express the particular content that she does. Moreover, notice that it makes perfect sense to speak of a witness testifying in a courtroom to something that she herself does not believe—it is called perjury.

[36] See Gettier (1963) for the initial formulation of the problem and Shope (1983) for some of the many permutations of Gettier cases. For this response to the sort of testifier found in CONSISTENT LIAR (i.e., that it is a Gettier-type case), see, for instance, Plantinga (1993b: 82–3) and Chakrabarti (1994: 110).

she believes it to be a horse, yet reports that it is a deer. Thus, Bertha's deer-reports nearly always covary with her deer-sightings, despite taking a slight detour through horse-believings. Furthermore, given all of Henry's excellent inductive evidence on behalf of Bertha's testimonial practices, there is also no relevant accidentality in his coming to form the belief in question on the basis of her report. With respect to the justification or warrant of Henry's belief, similar remarks can be adduced: Dr Jones deliberately modified Bertha's first brain lesion and added a second one precisely so that Bertha would turn out to be a reliable testifier.[37] Moreover, there are no close possible worlds in which Dr Jones did not perform the surgery on Bertha, and hence there are no close possible worlds in which Bertha does not have the condition she has. Because of this, there is no sense in which it is an accident that Bertha is a reliable testifier and hence a source of justified or warranted belief.

The fourth feature of CONSISTENT LIAR that is here relevant is that Henry not only fails to possess reasons to doubt Bertha's competence and sincerity, but he is also in possession of excellent positive reasons to accept her testimony. For Henry has no reason to doubt that a deer was in fact on the hiking trail in question, nor does he have counterevidence of any kind for Bertha's testimony. Moreover, because beliefs that are formed on the basis of Bertha's statements nearly always turn out to be true, Henry has acquired excellent inductive evidence for believing her to be one of the most trustworthy people to consult on a wide range of topics. So, when Bertha's extreme reliability as a testifier is combined with his very high degree of justification or warrant for accepting her report, there is simply no reason to deny that Henry's true belief that there was a deer on a nearby hiking trail qualifies as justified, warranted, and known. Thus, in CONSISTENT LIAR, we find a clear case in which a hearer not only acquires justified and warranted belief on the basis of testimony that is insincere, but also comes to have testimonial knowledge of the proposition in question. Furthermore, notice that Bertha fails to possess a belief with the epistemic properties in question, yet Henry forms a belief on the basis of her testimony that does possess these epistemic properties.[38] Here, then,

---

[37] For a compelling discussion of the distinction between accidental truth and accidental justification, see Reed (2000).

[38] In his recent book, Kusch (2002) also argues against TEP-N. In fact, he claims that "almost all testimony is *generative* of knowledge" (Kusch 2002: 68, emphasis added). His argument for this view

we again find a case of testimonial *knowledge (justification, warrant)* without testimonial *transmission,* thereby showing that TEP-N is false.[39]

The upshot of these considerations is that the statements of speakers are *not only the basis, both causally and epistemically, of the beliefs that hearers acquire via testimony, they are also the bearers of epistemic significance.* For as CREATIONIST TEACHER and CONSISTENT LIAR reveal, a speaker doesn't even need to believe the statement she is reporting in order for a hearer to acquire a belief that is justified, warranted, or known on the basis of her testimony. This shows that in order to have a *fully general*

begins by pointing out that *performative testimony* is generative of knowledge. For instance, when a minister says, "I hereby declare you husband and wife," the minister's testimony is, according to Kusch, generating the knowledge that the bride and groom in question were married for all those present at the ceremony. From here, Kusch argues that in addition to individual performatives, there can be *communal performatives,* such as "We hereby declare that it is right to greet people by waving." Such communal performatives are typically made only implicitly, and they are widely distributed across individual instances of testimony. With these two points in place, Kusch goes on to claim that nearly all testimony is partially performative because "[a]lmost all testimony carries parts of widely distributed communal performatives" (Kusch 2002: 67). Hence, Kusch concludes that nearly all testimony is generative of knowledge.

While there are several questions that may be raised with respect to this argument, the central problem is that performative testimony does not generate *testimonial* knowledge because such speech acts are not instances of *testimony.* When a minister says, "I hereby declare you husband and wife," he is not *testifying to* this fact—he is making it the case that this fact obtains. We can, for instance, easily imagine that what renders two people married is not a declaration by a minister but, rather, a waving of a stick. When I see the stick waved, I come to know that the two people in question were married. But surely, this is not *testimonial* knowledge—it is *perceptual* (and partly memorial and inferential) knowledge. I suspect that the fact that performative speech acts involve *words* led Kusch to regard them as instances of testimony. Once we see, however, that the words themselves are not essential to such acts, it becomes clear that Kusch has failed to show that performative speech acts are testimonial and, accordingly, that he has failed to show both that TEP-N is false and that testimony is a generative epistemic source. (For further discussion of Kusch's book, see my (2006e).)

[39] For those who find some of the details of CONSISTENT LIAR a bit too fanciful, the following case can be substituted as a counterexample to TEP-N:

DOUBTING THOMAS: Thomas is a scientist conducting research on the migratory patterns of gray whales and, though he is brilliant, he is crippled by self-doubt. After uncovering evidence that the whales' pattern of migration is actually importantly different from what scientific consensus had thought, his doubts prevent him from coming to believe in the truth of this evidence. Nevertheless, his intellectual integrity leads him to feel an obligation to present his true and reliably acquired research to his colleagues, most of whom readily accept his testimony about the whales' migratory patterns. (Thanks to David Buller for suggesting this type of case.)

Now, even though Thomas's self-doubt prevents him from being a reliable believer regarding the migratory patterns of gray whales, he is nonetheless a highly reliable testifier of this information and so his colleagues can acquire knowledge (justified/warranted belief) on the basis of his testimony. Hence, as with CREATIONIST TEACHER and CONSISTENT LIAR, we have a case in which a hearer acquires knowledge (justified/warranted belief) on the basis of the testimony of a speaker who does not believe and hence does not know (believe with justification/warrant) the proposition to which he is testifying, thereby showing TEP-N to be false.

epistemology of testimony, the epistemic conditions for testimonial beliefs need to be imposed on the statements of speakers, not on their beliefs.[40]

We have seen, then, that TEP-N is falsified by cases involving speakers who fail to believe, and hence know, the proposition to which they are testifying. The final type of case that I shall present involves speakers who fail to believe with justification/warrant, and hence know, the proposition to which they are testifying. Such a case will falsify both TEP-N and the much weaker TEP-N*.

To begin, consider the following:[41]

PERSISTENT BELIEVER: Millicent in fact possesses her normal visual powers, but she has cogent reasons to believe that these powers are temporarily deranged. She is the subject of a neurosurgeon's experiments, and the surgeon falsely tells her that some implants are causing malfunction in her visual cortex. While she is persuaded that her present visual appearances are an entirely unreliable guide to reality, she continues to place credence in her visual appearances. She ignores her well-supported belief in the incapacitation of her visual faculty; she persists in believing, on the basis of her visual experiences, that a chair is before her, that the neurosurgeon is smiling, and so on. These beliefs are all, in fact, true and they are formed by the usual, quite reliable, perceptual processes. As Millicent is walking out of the neurosurgeon's office, she is the only person to see a badger in Big Bear Field. On the basis of this visual experience, she forms the corresponding true belief that there was a badger in this field, and then later reports this fact to her friend Bradley without communicating the neurosurgeon's testimony to him. Bradley, who has ample reason to trust Millicent from their past interaction as friends, forms the corresponding true belief solely on the basis of her testimony.

The first point to notice about PERSISTENT BELIEVER is that *Millicent does not know that there was a badger in Big Bear Field* because *she is not justified or warranted in holding this belief.* In particular, the fact that she believes the

---

[40] It should be emphasized that it is not open to the proponent of the BVT to argue on behalf of a so-called disjunctivist view of the epistemology of testimony in which beliefs are the bearers of epistemic properties in cases where testimonial knowledge is successfully acquired, while statements are the bearers of epistemic properties in those cases where it is not. For notice: testimonial knowledge *is* acquired in CONSISTENT LIAR. Hence, a proponent of a disjunctive view of the epistemology of testimony would have to endorse a completely arbitrary division, according to which beliefs are the bearers of the relevant epistemic properties in all of those cases that do not pose a problem for the BVT while statements are the bearers of these properties in cases that are counterexamples to the BVT. But this view begins to look suspiciously *ad hoc.* It is much like an epistemologist responding to the Gettier problem by insisting that knowledge is justified true belief in non-Gettier cases, while admitting that it is more than this in Gettier cases.

[41] This case is adapted from Goldman (1986: 53–4), though I am using it for a very different purpose.

neurosurgeon that her visual powers are an entirely unreliable guide to reality, without holding any other relevant beliefs, provides her with an undefeated psychological defeater for her visual beliefs. As Goldman says, "are [Millicent's visual beliefs] specimens of knowledge? Intuitively, no. The reason is that Millicent is not justified in holding these beliefs; they contravene her best evidence" (Goldman 1986: 54).

The second point to notice about this case is that *Bradley does know that there was a badger in Big Bear Field on the basis of Millicent's testimony.* For not only does Bradley have excellent positive reasons for accepting Millicent's testimony, but he also possesses no relevant undefeated defeaters. Specifically, since he does not know anything about the neurosurgeon's testimony, he does not believe, nor does he have reason to believe, that Millicent's visual powers are an unreliable guide to reality. Given this, Bradley comes to know (believe with justification/warrant) that there was a badger in Big Bear Field on the basis of Millicent's testimony, even though her believing the neurosurgeon's report undermines her knowing this (believing this with justification/warrant). In this way, Millicent fails the justification or warrant condition of knowledge because she has an undefeated psychological defeater for believing that there was a badger in Big Bear Field, Bradley satisfies the justification or warrant condition of knowledge because he does not have such a psychological defeater, and thus it is possible for a hearer to acquire knowledge (justified/warranted belief) on the basis of a speaker's testimony even when the speaker does not possess the knowledge (justified/warranted belief) in question herself.

But the crucial thing to notice about PERSISTENT BELIEVER is that *Millicent is the first link in the testimonial chain in question.* For even though it is only a two-person chain, it is still a process whereby a hearer acquires knowledge (justified/warranted belief) solely on the basis of a speaker's testimony about a particular first-hand visual experience—indeed one that only the speaker experienced. Moreover, we can certainly imagine a much longer chain in which Bradley reports that there was a badger in Big Bear Field to another hearer, Sanford, who passes it to Marge, and so on, and we can imagine that none of these speakers actually saw the badger in question first-hand. In this way, the chain itself finds its ultimate origin in Millicent, who does not know (believe with justification/warrant) that there was a badger in Big Bear Field. This shows that it is possible for a hearer to come to know (believe with justification/warrant) that *p* on the basis of a speaker's testimony that *p even when the first link in the testimonial chain in question fails to know (believe with justification/warrant) that* p. Thus not only is TEP-N false, but so is the much weaker TEP-N*.[42]

Moreover, once the structure of PERSISTENT BELIEVER is seen, counterexamples of this sort to both TEP-N and TEP-N* quickly proliferate. Here is another such case, though it contains some important differences from PERSISTENT BELIEVER:

SERIOUS STUDENT: While sitting on the lawn reading Descartes' *Meditations* for his History of Modern Philosophy class, Bartholomew finds himself in the grips of skeptical worries that are so strong that he can scarcely be said to know anything at all. That is, his belief that he could now be dreaming is strong enough to defeat the justification (warrant) he has for many of his ordinary beliefs and he is not in possession of any relevant arguments against skepticism. Audrey, a friend and fellow student at the university he attends, approaches Bartholomew, asks him where the nearest Starbucks is, and he reports that it is around the corner—which he believes from having seen it there himself—but does not report his skeptical worries to her. Audrey has never considered any skeptical possibilities at all, and hence does not have any relevant defeaters for her ordinary beliefs. Moreover, she does have positive reasons for accepting Bartholomew's report, e.g., she has perceived a general conformity between his reports and the corresponding facts, she has inductive evidence for believing that speakers are generally reliable when they are giving directions, and so on. Given this, Audrey forms the true belief that there is a Starbucks around the corner solely on the basis of Bartholomew's testimony about his first-hand perceptual experience.

The structure of SERIOUS STUDENT resembles that of PERSISTENT BELIEVER in many crucial respects: the speaker, who is the first link in the relevant testimonial chain, has an undefeated psychological defeater—in this case, it is Bartholomew's belief that he could now be dreaming—that prevents him from having the knowledge (justified/warranted belief) in question, in this case, the knowledge (justified/warranted belief) that Starbucks is around the corner. In spite of this, however, the hearer, who does not possess the undefeated psychological defeater, acquires the relevant knowledge (justified/warranted belief) solely on the basis of the speaker's

---

[42] CONSISTENT LIAR could be read such that Bertha is the first link in the testimonial chain in question, thereby falsifying TEP-N* as well. I focus on PERSISTENT BELIEVER, however, since cases involving defeaters provide interestingly different, though equally compelling, counterexamples to TEP-N* and, *a fortiori*, TEP-N.

testimony. What makes SERIOUS STUDENT interestingly different than PERSISTENT BELIEVER, however, is the nature of the defeater in question and, accordingly, the range of explanations that can be given of the case. For, given that skeptical worries are doing the defeating work in Bartholomew's epistemic system, SERIOUS STUDENT can be given, in addition to the straightforward one involving defeaters, explanations in terms of John Hawthorne's subject-sensitive invariantism and possibly in terms of certain kinds of contextualism.[43] For instance, the differences between Bartholomew and Audrey in the epistemic statuses that they may properly attribute to themselves may be explainable in terms of the fact that different contexts—one skeptical and the other ordinary—are relevant to each of them.[44] More precisely, a testifier in one context may be able to impart knowledge (justified/warranted belief) that she cannot properly attribute to herself to a hearer in another context because, relative to such contexts, they are held to different epistemic standards.

What both PERSISTENT BELIEVER and SERIOUS STUDENT reveal is that *psychological defeaters are not necessarily transmitted via testimony.* For defeaters in this sense are doubts or beliefs *of the speaker in question* that defeat the justification/warrant that *she* has for holding the target belief, thereby rendering the subject who holds it irrational in also holding the defeatee in question. But if a hearer does not hold the psychological defeater in question, then obviously she cannot have the target belief defeated since there is nothing in her doxastic framework to do the defeating work in the first place. Thus, she simply cannot be irrational in holding the relevant target belief. In this way, psychological defeaters do not simply "come along for the ride" when a speaker reports that *p*; instead, the defeater itself must be reported and accepted by the hearer in order for it to be acquired via testimony. This point can be more fully appreciated by noticing that psychological defeaters can clearly prevent the transmission of knowledge via testimony in cases where a speaker knows and reports that *p* but a *hearer* possesses a relevant undefeated defeater. For instance, you might

---

[43] See Hawthorne (2004) and see Cohen (1986, 1988, and 1998), DeRose (1992, 1995, and 1999), and Lewis (1996) for some of the most prominent defenses of contextualism.

[44] To be precise, for Hawthorne's subject-sensitive invariantism, Audrey's self-attribution of knowledge will be evaluated relative to her epistemic and practical context. For the contextualist, on the other hand, Audrey's self-attribution of knowledge will be evaluated relative to her conversational context as a speaker.

truly and with justification or warrant believe that Marcia cheated on the exam because you saw her looking at her notes. But if you report this to me, I may not be justified or warranted in accepting your testimony because I believe that you are an unreliable testifier, thereby providing me with an undefeated psychological defeater for your testimony. Thus, you know that p, report that p to me, and yet I do not know that p because I have an undefeated psychological defeater for your testimony. What proponents of TEP-N and TEP-N* fail to notice is that a *speaker* can have an undefeated defeater that a hearer does not have. I may report that p and even believe that p, but may not know that p because my justification or warrant is defeated by another belief. And unless my hearer also comes to hold this belief, she may know that p on the basis of my testimony while I do not, even when I am the very first link in the testimonial chain in question.[45]

Now, even though I have thus far focused only on the role that psychological defeaters play in individual epistemic frameworks, similar considerations can be adduced involving normative defeaters. For instance, consider the following case involving the failure of the transmissibility of normative defeaters via testimony:

DOGMATIC BELIEVER: Paige is incorrectly told by a neurosurgeon that her vision is extremely unreliable—the doctor is performing the same experiment that Millicent experienced—yet for no rational reason she refuses to accept this diagnosis. So, even though the neurosurgeon's report is false, Paige should accept the diagnosis in question given all of the evidence that she has available to her. Nevertheless, as she is walking out of the doctor's office, Paige sees a car accident on Michigan Avenue, forms the corresponding true belief that there was such an accident, and later reports this fact to her friend, Benny, but does not report the

[45] There are two different ways in which psychological defeaters can fail to be transmitted via testimony. The first is found in PERSISTENT BELIEVER and SERIOUS STUDENT, where a speaker reports that p but fails to report her relevant undefeated defeater. The second way is where a speaker reports that p and reports her relevant undefeated defeater, but the hearer in question is in possession of a defeater-defeater, thereby enabling testimony still to impart knowledge. So, for example, suppose that Bartholomew does report his skeptical worries to Audrey when he tells her that Starbucks is around the corner, but Audrey believes that she has a refutation of skepticism. In such a case, Audrey would still be able to acquire knowledge of the whereabouts of Starbucks on the basis of Bartholomew's testimony, despite the fact that he is the first link in the testimonial chain and fails to have the knowledge in question himself. I focused entirely on the first way in the text, however, since a proponent of TEP-N or TEP-N* may object that this second way in which psychological defeaters can fail to be transmitted via testimony relies too heavily on the hearer's background information and, thus, compromises the purely testimonial nature of the knowledge in question.

neurosurgeon's diagnosis to him. Benny forms the corresponding true belief solely on the basis of Paige's testimony about her first-hand perceptual experience.

While DOGMATIC BELIEVER resembles PERSISTENT BELIEVER in most respects, the central difference is that the defeater in question here is a proposition that the speaker *should believe*, even though she does not as a matter of fact believe it; hence, the speaker has an undefeated normative, rather than psychological, defeater that fails to be transmitted via her testimony to the hearer. For notice: though the neurosurgeon's diagnosis in DOGMATIC BELIEVER is false, Paige has no rational reason for refusing to accept it; otherwise put, she should believe that her vision is highly unreliable, even though she does not. In contrast, Benny has no rational reason for doubting either Paige's perceptual or testimonial practices, and so he should believe solely on the basis of her testimony that there was a car accident on Michigan Avenue. Given this, even though it is irrational for Paige to trust her visual experiences in the face of the neurosurgeon's testimony, such irrationality is not transferred to Benny via her testimony. This enables her to impart knowledge (justified/warranted belief) to Benny that she fails to possess herself—even when she is the first link in the testimonial chain in question—thereby once again showing that both TEP-N and TEP-N* are false.

As we have seen, the failure of the transmissibility of different kinds of defeaters via testimony renders TEP-N and TEP-N* indefensible. For once it is granted, as proponents of these views do, that a hearer can have an undefeated defeater that a speaker does not, then what could justify denying that a speaker can have an undefeated defeater that a hearer does not? That is, what could justify the claim that a speaker's undefeated defeaters are necessarily transmitted to a hearer? Given cases like those above, it seems uncontentious that speakers can have various undefeated defeaters that hearers do not (and, of course, vice versa). This has significant epistemological consequences for the dominant picture of testimonial knowledge (justification/warrant). Since defeaters do not necessarily come along for the ride with reports, testimonial chains can include speakers and hearers with very different epistemic statuses. In particular, a single chain of testimony can include speakers and hearers, some of whom have undefeated defeaters, some defeater-defeaters, some defeater-defeater-defeaters, and so on. Accordingly, such chains can include some speakers who know that *p* and others who fail to know that *p*. Indeed, as I have argued, even the first speaker in a testimonial chain need not know that *p* in order for hearers in the chain to come to know that *p* on the basis of her testimony. Thus, both versions of the necessity thesis—TEP-N and the much weaker TEP-N*—are false.[46]

2.4 The Sufficiency Thesis

In this section, I take up the remaining dimension of TEP—the sufficiency thesis. I shall argue that speaker-knowledge (justification/warrant) is not sufficient for hearer-knowledge (justification/warrant), and hence that the picture dominating the epistemology of testimony, in which epistemic properties are *transmitted* from a speaker's belief to a hearer's, is thoroughly misguided.

Before proceeding, however, one feature of TEP-S that is important to notice is the no-defeater clause (condition (3)). For, on this view, even if there are some cases in which speaker-knowledge (justification/warrant) is sufficient for hearer-knowledge (justification/warrant), the belief that a hearer acquires from a speaker does not *always* possess the relevant epistemic property to the same degree as the speaker's—a hearer may have an *undefeated defeater* for believing the proposition in question that the speaker simply does not possess. But even though the presence of such a defeater may render a hearer's belief less justified or warranted than the speaker's from whom it was acquired, this does not threaten the spirit of TEP-S. For what happens in such a case is that the speaker's belief that *p*, along with its justification or warrant, *is* transmitted to the hearer, but the justification or warrant for the hearer's belief that *p* is then defeated. What

---

[46] It is of interest to note that even in those rare cases where it has been argued that belief is not the central item involved in a testimonial exchange, it is simply replaced with another *mental or cognitive* item rather than with a *linguistic or communicative* item, as I will argue in the next chapter. For instance, in his (1994), Welbourne argues against certain strands of the BVT on the grounds that while beliefs are not appropriate items for transmission, states of knowledge are. Thus, he claims that "our concept of knowledge, unlike our concept of belief, is a concept of something which is essentially transmissible" (Welbourne 1994: 309). Of course, since the arguments offered in this section subsume a knowledge version of TEP-N, moving from belief to knowledge leads us in the wrong direction. But even if we were to bracket this point and accept Welbourne's proposal, we would still be left with the problem of characterizing how beliefs that fall short of knowledge but nevertheless possess justification and warrant are acquired via testimony.

would contradict the spirit of TEP-S would be a case in which a hearer believes that *p* purely on the basis of a speaker's belief that *p*, possesses no relevant defeaters for believing that *p*, and yet still has a significantly different epistemic relation to *p* than the speaker.[47] This is precisely the sort of case I shall provide.

To begin, consider the following:

COMPULSIVELY TRUSTING: Bill is a compulsively trusting person with respect to the testimony of his neighbor, Jill, in whom he has an obsessive romantic interest. Not only does he always trust Jill when he has very good reason to believe her, but he is incapable of distrusting her when he has very good reason to not believe her. For instance, even when he has available to him overwhelming evidence for believing that she is deliberately lying or being deceitful, Bill cannot come to believe this about Jill. Indeed, Bill is such that there is no amount of evidence that would convince him to not trust Jill. Yesterday, while taking his afternoon walk, Bill ran into Jill, and she told him that she had seen an orca whale while boating earlier that day. Bill, of course, readily accepted Jill's testimony. It turns out that Jill did in fact see an orca whale on the boat trip in question, that she is very reliable with respect to her epistemic practices, both in general and in this particular instance, and that Bill has no reason to doubt the proffered testimony. Given his compulsively trusting nature with respect to Jill, however, even if he had had massive amounts of evidence available to him indicating, for instance, that Jill did not see an orca whale, that she is an unreliable epistemic agent, that she is an unreliable testifier, that orca whales do not live in this part of the country, and so on, Bill would have just as readily accepted Jill's testimony.[48]

It is, of course, clear that Jill's belief about the orca whale possesses all of the epistemic properties in question—she is a reliable epistemic agent, both in general and in the particular case at issue, and she did, in fact, see an orca whale while boating yesterday.[49] The crucial question for our purposes is

[47] In his (2000*b*), Peter Graham proposes two different counterexamples to a version of TEP-S, both of which can be interpreted as involving the presence of factual defeaters. In contrast, what I shall provide are counterexamples to TEP-S that do not depend in any way on defeaters, thereby showing that the entire picture of testimony as involving transmission is fundamentally incorrect.

[48] An example that bears some similarities to COMPULSIVELY TRUSTING can be found in Chapter 5. In that chapter, however, I have a different target—there I argue specifically against standard characterizations of non-reductionism in the epistemology of testimony, not the BVT.

[49] Moreover, since there is nothing unusual about Jill's experience of the orca whale, we can assume that she has excellent *reasons* for forming the corresponding belief. This avoids the objection that Jill possesses the relevant knowledge only if an externalist view of epistemic justification or warrant is assumed.

whether Bill knows, or is justified/warranted in believing, that there was an orca whale in the relevant body of water on the basis of Jill's testimony. And here, the answer should clearly be no.

To see this, notice that because of his compulsively good nature with respect to Jill's testimony, Bill is simply *incapable* of being sensitive to the presence of defeaters regarding her reports. In this respect, he is no better epistemically than a subject who has been brainwashed or programmed to accept any report that Jill makes. For were Bill to be inundated with massive amounts of counterevidence, he would have accepted Jill's testimony just as readily as he did in the complete absence of such counterevidence. Indeed, Bill is such that he would have accepted Jill's testimony *under any circumstances*.[50] Because of this, Bill's belief that there was an orca whale in the relevant body of water is *evidentially insensitive* in a way that is clearly incompatible with justification, warrant, and knowledge.[51] Therefore, while Jill's belief possesses all of the epistemic properties in question, the belief that Bill forms on the basis of her testimony possesses none of them. Hence, TEP-S is false.

What COMPULSIVELY TRUSTING reveals is that while a speaker may be both a perfectly reliable believer and testifier, *a hearer may be so constituted as to prevent the epistemic properties of a speaker's belief from being transmitted to her.* This has significant consequences for the BVT. For proponents of the BVT portray the transmission of beliefs as being much like the giving of gifts: if I give you a wrapped box, all you have to do to receive the gift is to receive the wrapped box—the gift, so to speak, comes along for the ride. Similarly, it is thought that if I transmit to you my belief that *p*, all you have to do to receive the epistemic properties it possesses is to receive the belief—the epistemic properties it possesses, so to speak, come

---

[50] In this sense, Bill's epistemic relationship to Jill is importantly different from the epistemic relationship a child bears to her parents or teachers. For while children may be trusting with respect to their caretakers, they certainly are not *compulsively* trusting. For instance, when I responded to a question from my young daughter, Isabella, by saying that houses without chimneys do not pose a problem for Santa Claus because children perhaps do not live in such houses, even at three years old she skeptically remarked, "Surely there are *some* houses without chimneys that have children in them!" In this sense, children, unlike Bill, certainly have the capacity to be sensitive to defeaters with respect to the testimony of their caretakers, even if such a capacity is not frequently exercised. Moreover, if children were like Bill with respect to the testimony of their parents and teachers, then I would have no problem denying testimonial knowledge (justified/warranted belief) to them as well. (I am grateful to comments from Fred Dretske and Ishani Maitra that prompted the inclusion of this point.)

[51] For a more detailed discussion of the nature of this incompatibility, see my (2005) and Chapter 7.

along for the ride. But as we saw in COMPULSIVELY TRUSTING, beliefs are not connected with their epistemic properties the way that gifts are connected with the wrapped boxes that contain them. A hearer may acquire a belief on the basis of a speaker's testimony, and yet not acquire the epistemic properties possessed by the speaker's belief. Moreover, this can happen where it is not explainable by appeal to the defeat of epistemic properties that were in fact transmitted. For Bill's compulsively trusting nature does not make him such that epistemic properties are transmitted to him via Jill's testimony, yet immediately defeated; he is such that epistemic properties *cannot even be transmitted to him in the first place.*[52] Hence, the picture of testimony painted by proponents of the BVT, in which beliefs are passed along with their epistemic properties from a speaker to a hearer, is fundamentally incorrect.[53]

Further support for this conclusion can be provided by examining two other types of cases that undermine TEP-S. Consider the following:

A LUCKY CHOICE: Upon arriving in Chicago for the first time, Pierre asks the closest passerby that he sees, Zoe, for directions to the Sears Tower and she reports that it is six blocks east. While Zoe knows that this is the case, and Pierre has no reason to doubt either her credibility as a speaker or the truth of the proposition to which she is testifying, she is the only reliable speaker in this part of Chicago, completely surrounded by incompetents and liars. Because of this, the fact that Pierre chooses a reliable testifier who correctly points him in the direction of the Sears Tower is entirely a matter of good luck.

Now, even though Zoe knows that the Sears Tower is six blocks east, and Pierre does not possess any relevant defeaters for the report in question, A LUCKY CHOICE represents a testimonial Gettier-type case for the recipient of testimony. In particular, Pierre's luckily choosing the only reliable testifier among the surrounding incompetents and liars is analogous

---

[52] Furthermore, as COMPULSIVELY TRUSTING is described, Bill, as a matter of fact, does *not* have any relevant defeaters for the testimony in question: Jill is very reliable with respect to her epistemic practices, both in general and in this particular instance, and Bill has no reason to doubt the proffered testimony. The epistemic problem with Bill is that, even if there *were* defeaters, he would accept Jill's testimony just as readily as he did in their complete absence.

[53] John MacFarlane (2005) has recently argued that sensitive invariantism of the sort defended by Hawthorne in his (2004) is incompatible with TEP-S because, when combined, these two views allow for "knowledge laundering": "Someone who does not know that p can come to know that p simply by cycling her evidence through someone in less demanding circumstances" (MacFarlane 2005: 134). Given that TEP-S is false, however, sensitive invariantists obviously shouldn't be worried about MacFarlane's conclusion.

to a perceiver luckily seeing the only real barn among surrounding barn facades. Hence, Pierre does not come to know that the Sears Tower is six blocks east on the basis of Zoe's testimony, despite the fact that he satisfies conditions (1)–(3) of TEP-S.[54] Once again, we see that TEP-S is false.

A final case against TEP-S can be seen by considering the following:

ALMOST A LIAR: Phil is compulsively-trusting-Bill's twin brother, though he is not himself compulsively trusting with respect to Jill's testimony. In fact, he is, from an epistemic point of view, quite healthy: he trusts those whom he has good reason to trust—or at least those whom he has no clear reason to distrust—and distrusts those whom he has good reason to distrust. Yesterday, while taking *his* afternoon walk, Phil ran into Jill just after Bill did, and she also told him that she had seen an orca whale while boating earlier that day. Phil, having acquired very good reasons for trusting Jill over the five years he has known her, readily accepted her testimony. It turns out that Jill did in fact see an orca whale on the boat trip in question, that she is very reliable with respect to her epistemic practices, both in general and in this particular instance, that she is generally a very reliable testifier, and that Phil has no reason to doubt the proffered testimony. However, in order to promote a whale watching business she is in the process of starting, she would have reported to Phil—in precisely the same manner—that she had seen an orca whale even if she hadn't. (Of course, she wouldn't have believed that she had seen an orca whale if she hadn't.) Moreover, given the pattern of the whales' travel combined with the particular time of year it is, it is in fact quite surprising that Jill saw an orca whale when and where she did.

There are two central features of ALMOST A LIAR that are important to notice. First, because she wishes to promote her future whale watching business, Jill *would have* reported to Phil that there was an orca whale in the relevant body of water even if there hadn't been one. And, second, given the schedule of the whales' travel coupled with the time of year it is, it was in fact much more likely for Jill *not* to have seen an orca whale when she did than for her to have seen one.

The combination of these two features has the following result: there are nearby possible worlds in which an orca whale was not in the relevant

---

[54] Defeasibility theorists (such as those cited in note 21) may describe this case in terms of Pierre possessing a factual defeater for Zoe's testimony. As I earlier emphasized, however, most proponents of the BVT do not take factual defeaters to be relevant to the satisfaction of condition (3) of TEP-S, and hence will grant that Pierre satisfies all of the conditions of TEP-S. For those who claim that Pierre fails condition (3) because of the presence of a factual defeater, COMPULSIVELY TRUSTING suffices as a relevant counterexample.

body of water, Jill nonetheless reports that there was, and Phil, being in the same evidential situation as he is in the actual world, readily forms the corresponding belief on the basis of Jill's testimony. More generally, Phil's belief about there having been an orca whale in the relevant body of water is *counterfactually insensitive to the truth*. For instance, his belief is neither sensitive (à la Nozick) nor safe (à la Sosa): if p were false, Phil would still believe that p, and Phil would believe that p without it being so that p. Otherwise put, in nearby worlds where it is false that an orca whale was in the relevant body of water, Phil believes that there was one, and there are nearby worlds where Phil believes that an orca whale was in the relevant body of water without this being so. Given this, the true belief that Phil forms on the basis of Jill's testimony not only fails to qualify as knowledge, it also fails to be justified or warranted.[55] Thus, while Jill's belief possesses all of the epistemic properties in question, the belief that Phil forms on the basis of her sincere testimony possesses none of them. Hence, once again, we see that TEP-S is false.[56]

To fully appreciate the consequences of ALMOST A LIAR, it will be helpful to compare it with CONSISTENT LIAR from Section 2.3. Notice first that while CONSISTENT LIAR shows that an *unreliable believer* may nonetheless be a *reliable testifier*, ALMOST A LIAR reveals that a *reliable believer* may nonetheless be an *unreliable testifier*. This is why Henry acquires knowledge (justified/warranted belief) on the basis of Bertha's testimony, despite the fact that she fails to have the knowledge (justified/warranted belief) in question, and why Phil fails to acquire knowledge (justified/warranted belief) on the basis of Jill's testimony, despite the fact that she possesses the knowledge (justified/warranted belief) in question. For, recall that while Bertha's belief is neither sensitive nor safe, the statement that she offers to Henry is both sensitive and safe. In contrast, Jill's orca-whale-belief is both sensitive and safe, but the

---

[55] I should again emphasize, as I did in the Introduction, that I am concerned with the epistemic properties in question only insofar as they bear an intimate connection with knowledge. Thus, there may be some subjective notions of justification that Phil does plausibly possess.

[56] For those who have reservations about either COMPULSIVELY TRUSTING or ALMOST A LIAR in isolation, we can simply combine the features from both so as to have COMPULSIVELY TRUSTING ALMOST A LIAR. This would involve imagining Bill in Phil's scenario, so that we have a hearer who is both evidentially insensitive and counterfactually insensitive to the truth. Given this combination, both reductionists and non-reductionists in particular, and internalists and externalists in general, should agree that the epistemic properties in question fail to be acquired by the hearer.

orca-whale-statement that she offers to Phil is neither. In particular, though Jill would not believe that p if p were false, she would state that p if p were false, and though Jill would not believe that p without it being so that p, she would state that p without it being so that p. So, just as Bertha can give epistemic properties to others that she fails to possess herself, Jill can fail to give epistemic properties to others that she possesses herself (even when testifying truly and sincerely). Both cases, therefore, support the same general conclusion: the *words* of speakers, not their beliefs, are what matter for an epistemology of testimony.

3

A Defense of Learning from Words

3.1 The Statement View of Testimony

In the previous chapter, we saw that both theses of TEP are false and, accordingly, that each component of the BVT is false as well. We are now in a position to see that there is a counterpart version of each component that is true—one involving the *statements* of speakers. Let us call this alternative family of theses the *Statement View of Testimony* (hereafter, the SVT).

According to the SVT, the process of communicating via testimony does not involve a speaker transmitting her belief to a hearer, along with the epistemic properties it possesses. Instead, a speaker offers a statement to a hearer, along with the epistemic properties *it* possesses, and a hearer forms the corresponding belief on the basis of understanding and accepting the statement in question.[1] Statements are not, therefore, merely vehicles for expressing beliefs but, rather, they are the central bearers of epistemic significance themselves.

There are at least three significant consequences of rejecting the BVT in favor of the SVT. First, because proponents of the BVT portray the testimonial exchange as involving merely transmission, testimony is said to be incapable of generating new epistemic features for beliefs—it merely has the capacity to transmit from one person to another beliefs that have already been rendered justified, warranted, or an instance of knowledge via another source. As Alvin Plantinga says, "testimonial warrant, like water, rises no higher than its source...if you tell me something and

---

[1] As I shall argue later in this book, in order for the hearer's testimonial belief in question to be justified, warranted, or an instance of knowledge, further conditions, in addition to those concerning the speaker's statement, need to be satisfied.

I believe it on your say-so, I have warrant for it only if you do"
(Plantinga 1993b: 84, 87). But as we saw in CONSISTENT LIAR and
PERSISTENT BELIEVER, this is not so: a hearer can acquire a belief
that is justified, warranted, and known from a speaker whose own belief
possesses none of the relevant epistemic properties—or, indeed, from a
speaker who does not even have the belief in question. Thus, not only
can testimony function as a *generative* epistemic source, but testimonial
justification (warrant/knowledge)—unlike water—*can* rise higher than
its source.[2]

Second, and closely related, proponents of the BVT maintain that—undefeated defeaters aside—testimonial justification (warrant/knowledge)
cannot fail to rise as high as its source. We have seen, however, that
this is false as well: a hearer's belief may fail to be as justified (warrant-
ed/known) as its source, for reasons having to do with the hearer (as
COMPULSIVELY TRUSTING revealed), the speaker (as ALMOST A
LIAR revealed), or the environment (as A LUCKY CHOICE revealed).

Third, it is nearly received wisdom in the epistemology of testimony
that there are two central criteria that need to be fulfilled in order for a
speaker's testimony to be epistemically acceptable: "the sincerity dimension, concerning the attester's honesty, and the competence dimension,
concerning the attester's having experience or knowledge sufficient to
make it at least likely that if the attester forms a belief that p, then p is true"
(Audi 1997: 409).[3] Otherwise put, in order for a hearer to acquire knowledge (justified/warranted belief) on the basis of a speaker's testimony, the
speaker must be both a *competent believer* and a *sincere testifier*. As we saw in
both CREATIONIST TEACHER and CONSISTENT LIAR, however,
neither a speaker's competent believing nor her sincere testifying is *necessary*
for the acquisition of testimonial knowledge (justified/warranted belief).
And, as we saw in COMPULSIVELY TRUSTING, ALMOST A LIAR,
and A LUCKY CHOICE, a speaker's competent believing combined
with her sincere testifying is not *sufficient* for the acquisition of testimonial
knowledge (justified/warranted belief).

What really matters for the epistemic status of testimony is whether
the speaker is a *competent testifier*, where this is understood in terms of

[2] For arguments leading to a similar conclusion with respect to the epistemic status of memory, see
the appendix.
[3] See also the references in note 5 in Chapter 2.

the reliability—or other form of truth-conduciveness—of the *statement* in question. More precisely, according to the SVT, TEP-N should be replaced with the following *Reliability of the Statement-Necessity* (RS-N) thesis:

> RS-N: For every speaker, A, and hearer, B, B knows (believes with justification/warrant) that p on the basis of A's testimony that p only if A's statement that p is reliable or otherwise truth-conducive.

The reliability of the statement in question can, in turn, be fleshed out in any number of ways.[4] For instance, it may be necessary that the speaker's statement be sensitive, safe, properly or virtuously formed, and so on.[5] Accordingly, it may be necessary that a speaker would not state that p if p were false, or that she would not state that p without it being so that p, or that her statement be offered by testimonial faculties functioning properly or virtuously, and so on.[6] What is of import for our purposes, however, is that being a competent believer and a sincere testifier are epistemically relevant only insofar as they bear on the speaker's capacity to be a competent testifier.[7]

Of course, often times, it is precisely *because* a speaker is insincere or an incompetent believer that she is an incompetent or unreliable testifier. For instance, if I frequently lie or form inaccurate beliefs, more often than not

---

[4] It may be objected that requiring the reliability of the statement in question is too strong a condition for testimonial *justification*. For instance, wouldn't I be justified in believing that the President is currently in Iraq on the basis of reading *The New York Times* even if, for some reason, the reporter's statement fails to be reliable or otherwise truth conducive? Recall, however, what was emphasized in the Introduction: I am concerned with testimonial justification only insofar as it has an intimate connection with testimonial knowledge. There may, then, be some subjective notions of testimonial justification that do not require the reliability of the statement in question.

[5] See Nozick (1981); Sosa (1996, 1999, 2000, and 2002), Williamson (2000), and Pritchard (2005); Plantinga (1993b); and Sosa (1991), respectively.

[6] If one fleshes out RS-N in terms of the requirement that the statement is produced by testimonial faculties functioning properly or virtuously, does this pose a problem for CONSISTENT LIAR in Chapter 2? Not necessarily. For one can view Bertha's testimonial faculties as functioning precisely as they ought to in *light of Dr Jones's surgery*. But even if one were to dispute this response, there are obviously other cases in Chapter 2 where no problem of the sort purportedly afflicting CONSISTENT LIAR even arises, such as CREATIONIST TEACHER.

[7] But what if statements themselves cannot be understood apart from the beliefs of speakers? Will my view still be importantly different than the BVT? (I am grateful to Kent Bach, Michael Glanzberg, and Gurpreet Rattan for pressing this point.) Yes. For even if statements cannot be understood apart from *some* of the beliefs of the relevant speakers, all I need for my purposes is that such speakers do not need to believe the *particular* propositions to which they are testifying. In particular, what I need for my RS-N to be importantly different from the BVT is the falsity of TEP-N. And there is no reason to think that plausible accounts of statements will need to depend on the truth of TEP-N.

this will prevent you from acquiring knowledge (justified/warranted belief) on the basis of my testimony. But the reason why you are so prevented is that my insincerity or incompetence has made my *testimony unreliable*, thereby resulting in the failure of RS-N. Moreover, a *hearer's beliefs* about a speaker's sincerity and competence can have epistemic significance. For instance, if I believe that you are a compulsive liar or an unreliable epistemic source, then even if you are neither of these, the mere fact that I believe you are can provide me with an undefeated psychological defeater for accepting your testimony. Hence, my beliefs about your sincerity and competence can prevent me from acquiring knowledge (justified/warranted belief) on the basis of your testimony.

As with TEP-N, RS-N expresses only a necessary condition for testimonial justification (warrant/knowledge). A complete view of the epistemology of testimony will, then, require further conditions, including (2) and (3) from TEP-S. Thus, at a minimum, the SVT will include the following:

> SVT: For every speaker, A, and hearer, B, B knows[8] (believes with justification/warrant) that p on the basis of A's testimony that p only if (1) A's statement that p is reliable or otherwise truth-conducive, (2) B comes to believe that p on the basis of the content of A's statement that p, and (3) B has no undefeated defeaters for believing that p.

Now, RS-N and the SVT are the statement versions that parallel TEP-N and the BVT. However, for those convinced by the cases discussed in Chapters 1 and 2 that motivate accepting TEP-N′ and (2′) of TEP-S (instead of TEP-N and (2) of TEP-S)—such as Virginia coming to believe that it is cold outside on the basis of my saying that her hat and gloves are in the closet—RS-N may be substituted with the following modified version:

> RS-N′: For every speaker, A, and hearer, B, B knows (believes with justification/warrant) that p on the basis of A's testimony only if (i) A's statement is reliable or otherwise truth-conducive, and

---

[8] Of course, for testimonial *knowledge*, a condition will need to be added to the SVT requiring the truth of B's belief that p.

>   (ii) B's belief that p is appropriately connected with the content of A's statement.[9]

Accordingly, the SVT may be substituted with the weaker:

>   SVT′: For every speaker, A, and hearer, B, B knows (believes with justification/warrant) that p on the basis of A's testimony only if (1) A's statement is reliable or otherwise truth-conducive, (2) B comes to believe that p on the basis of an appropriate connection with the content of A's statement, and (3) B has no undefeated defeaters for believing that p.[10]

For ease of expression, I shall continue to focus on TEP-N and the SVT. But, for the record, since I am convinced that hearers can acquire testimonial knowledge both from nonverbal communication and from pragmatic implicatures, I endorse the slightly weaker RS-N′ and SVT′.

Now, it is not my purpose at this point to provide a fully complete account of testimonial justification (warrant/knowledge), and so I shall not defend the SVT as such.[11] Rather, the SVT provides the *framework for a complete epistemology of testimony*, one that places the statements of speakers at the center of the acquisition of testimonial knowledge. Hence, strictly speaking, we do not learn from one another's *beliefs*—we learn from one another's *words*.[12] A failure to appreciate this has resulted in the widespread acceptance of a picture of testimony that is fundamentally incorrect. Thus, in order to make genuine progress in the epistemology of testimony, we need to stop looking at what speakers *believe* and focus, instead, on what speakers *say*.

My arguments, both against the BVT and in support of the SVT, have drawn some objections. In the remainder of this chapter, I shall take up three different kinds of criticism of my work found in the literature—targeting my counterexamples, my positive view, and my overall approach to theorizing about the epistemology of testimony—and show

---

[9] Of course, if RS-N is replaced with RS-N′, more will need to be said about the "appropriate connection" found in condition (ii).

[10] Again, more will need to be said about the "appropriate connection" in (2) if the SVT is replaced with the SVT′.

[11] In fact, I argue for conditions on testimonial justification (warrant/knowledge) beyond those found in (1)-(3) of the SVT in Chapters 5, 6, and 7.

[12] Even more strictly speaking, we learn from one another's acts of communication (so as to allow for learning from others in the non-linguistic ways discussed in Chapter 1, such as through a nod or pointing).

that each is unsuccessful. In so doing, I shall further strengthen the positive case for the SVT.

3.2 Objection to Counterexamples

In recent work, Robert Audi has attempted to defend the BVT from the arguments I raised in the previous chapter.[13] In particular, he argues that CREATIONIST TEACHER does not in fact undermine TEP-N because it is doubtful that the students in question acquire knowledge on the basis of Stella's testimony. To this end, he raises two central objections.[14] First, he writes:

> One question raised by [CREATIONIST TEACHER] is whether the kind of cognitive malfunction in question makes [Stella] insufficiently reliable for [her] (true) attestation to ground knowledge. For to fail to believe on evidence one takes to be good (to the degree required by the case) is a kind of malfunction ([Stella] does not have to have highly specific beliefs about the evidence but [her] standard must be high enough to make it plausible to say that its role enables the students to know that *p*). (Audi 2006: 30)

According to Audi, then, it is questionable whether the students in CREATIONIST TEACHER in fact know that *Homo sapiens* evolved from *Homo erectus* because Stella's cognitive malfunction may undermine her reliability.

---

[13] Audi (2006 and 2007).

[14] There are two additional objections that Audi raises to CREATIONIST TEACHER in his (2006), but they target the version of this counterexample found in my (1999). In that version, the creationist in question teaches evolutionary theory to her students because it is required by the school at which she is employed. Given this, Audi asks, first, whether the testimonially based beliefs of the children are adequately grounded "if the teacher would have taught a false theory in the same disbelieving way, had this been required by [her] job?" (Audi 2006: 29). Second, Audi considers a modified version of the case where the school in question would not require anyone to teach a theory that is not well-evidenced, and asks: "do the students perhaps believe or presuppose something to this effect? ... [M]ight an essential part of their basis for believing [Stella], or for knowing on the basis of [her] testimony, be that background belief or presupposition?" (Audi 2006: 29). Given that the version of CREATIONIST TEACHER in Chapter 2 has Stella teaching evolutionary theory to her students solely because she recognizes that it is best supported by the available scientific evidence, however, it should be obvious that neither of these questions is relevant. For there is simply no reason to believe either that Stella would teach a false theory to her students in a similarly disbelieving way, or that the students actually base their beliefs about evolutionary theory on the presupposition that their school would not require Stella to teach a theory that is not well-evidenced. But in any case, these features can simply be stipulated in the very construction of the counterexample, thereby altogether avoiding both of Audi's worries.

By way of responding to Audi here, notice that it is not at all clear that a speaker such as Stella in CREATIONIST TEACHER suffers from a cognitive malfunction in the first place. For instance, a person who fails to believe that she is going to die, despite overwhelming evidence showing that her terminal cancer has spread, may have cognitive faculties that are functioning precisely as they ought to in such circumstances. For a subject's cognitive faculties may have evolved or been designed to function in such a way that she ignores evidence—even when it is regarded as good—when other relevant factors are at issue, such as self-preservation or survival. Thus, the mere fact that Stella fails to believe in accordance with evidence that she regards as good does not support the conclusion that she suffers from a cognitive malfunction.

More importantly, however, even if it is granted that Stella in CRE-ATIONIST TEACHER *does* suffer from a cognitive malfunction, it is a malfunction with respect to her *believing*, not with respect to her *tes-tifying*. For recall that while Stella disregards evidence when it comes to her doxastic states concerning evolutionary theory, she firmly grounds her statements concerning evolutionary theory in such evidence. Indeed, it is for precisely this reason that I argued in Chapter 2 that unreliable believers can nonetheless be reliable testifiers. Given this, there is no reason to regard such a cognitive malfunction—if there is one—as being incompatible with the students acquiring knowledge on the basis of Stella's testimony.

The second objection that Audi raises to CREATIONIST TEACHER can be found in the following passage:

Given [Stella's] willingness to deceive the students, why should we view what [s]he says when [s]he has evidence as sufficiently representative of [her] testimonial com-munications to give [her] present testimony the epistemic (knowledge-grounding) status it is supposed to have...? The problem is that, given [her] willingness to deceive the students regarding p, there are relevantly similar cases in which [she] does so without even believing the evidence supports p and where it is false. Why, given that willingness, should we take [her] devotion to the existence of evidence to be adequately stable? (Audi 2006: 30)

According to Audi, then, Stella's behavior in CREATIONIST TEACHER makes it likely that there are nearby possible worlds in which she deceives her students regarding p, where p is not only false, but also where Stella doesn't even believe that the evidence in question supports p.

Now, the most obvious way to respond to this objection is simply to build into the counterexample that Stella's commitment to testifying on the basis of the available evidence is highly stable, particularly when it comes to her students. Indeed, this is the most natural and plausible interpretation of her character: while Stella allows her faith to guide the formation of her own personal beliefs, she recognizes that her testimonial practices—especially when she is teaching biology to her young pupils—must be governed by the available scientific evidence. Given this, her testifying practices where her students are concerned are firmly and consistently grounded in the available evidence.

Moreover, it is a mistake to regard Stella's teaching evolutionary theory to her students as deception in any reasonable sense of the word.[15] For, even though Stella is reporting to her students what she herself does not believe, she is doing so in an attempt to have them believe in accordance with the available scientific evidence. We can even imagine that she regards belief in creationism as something that should be grounded only in a personal relationship with God—thus, reporting what she does in fact believe concerning evolutionary theory (namely, that it is false), and having the students form the corresponding beliefs solely on the basis of her testimony, would be to deceive them in Stella's eyes. Given this, Stella's testifying that *Homo sapiens* evolved from *Homo erectus* can be understood as an attempt to *avoid* deceiving her students.

I conclude, then, that Audi has not provided a compelling reason to question the force of CREATIONIST TEACHER against TEP-N.

3.3 Objection to RS-N

Goldberg's Objection

In a recent paper, Sanford Goldberg argues that testimonial knowledge can be acquired through testimony that is unreliable, insensitive, and unsafe.[16] In so doing, then, he rejects both TEP-N and the logically weaker RS-N that I endorse. In this section, I shall show not only that the particular kinds of cases purporting to establish this conclusion fail, but also that there are good reasons to conclude that all such counterexamples to

---

[15] I say more about this in Section 4.4 of the next chapter.   [16] Goldberg (2005).

RS-N—i.e., those involving testimonially based knowledge from unreliable testimony—are destined to fail.

To begin, Goldberg provides the following example:

MILK: Frank is a writer who religiously wakes up every morning at 7:30 AM and promptly spills out whatever milk is remaining from the pint he purchased the day before, placing the empty carton back in the refrigerator until noon. After remaining in the kitchen from 7:30 until noon writing, he always removes the empty milk carton from the refrigerator at precisely noon and throws it away. Last night, Mary and her son Sonny spent the night at Frank's and, after looking in the refrigerator at 7:40 AM, Mary tells Sonny that there is milk for him to have with his daily breakfast of cereal. As luck would have it, Frank forgot that he had bought milk yesterday, and so there is indeed milk in the carton. Upon hearing Mary's testimony, Sonny forms the belief that there is milk in the refrigerator, and Frank realizes that he forgot to pour out the milk this morning.

According to Goldberg, the following three claims are true of the testimonial exchange in MILK:

1. Mary's testimony that there is milk in the refrigerator is unreliable, insensitive, and unsafe.
2. Sonny comes to know that there is milk in the refrigerator.
3. Sonny's belief that there is milk in the refrigerator has its epistemic properties on the basis of Mary's testimony.

The truth of (1), (2), and (3) would indeed show that a hearer can come to know that p on the basis of a speaker's unreliable, insensitive, and unsafe testimony that p, a conclusion that would fly in the face of not only TEP-N, but also my RS-N.

I shall argue, however, that (1), (2), and (3) cannot all be simultaneously true of the testimonial exchange in MILK. In particular, either (1) and (3) are true, but (2) is false—i.e., Mary's testimony is unreliable, insensitive, and unsafe and Sonny believes that there is milk in the refrigerator on the basis of Mary's testimony, but such a belief does not qualify as knowledge—or (1) and (2) are true, but (3) is false—i.e., Mary's testimony is unreliable, insensitive, and unsafe and Sonny does come to know that there is milk in the refrigerator, but not on the basis of Mary's testimony. Either way, Goldberg has failed to show that testimonial knowledge can be acquired from testimony that is unreliable, insensitive, and unsafe and, therewith, he has failed to provide a counterexample to my RS-N.

Let us take a closer look at (2). According to Goldberg, Sonny knows that there is milk in the refrigerator because his belief satisfies the following reliability, sensitivity, and safety conditions:

(Rel) In situations similar to the present one, Sonny would form the testimonial belief that there is milk in the refrigerator only if there were milk in the refrigerator.

(Sen) If there hadn't been milk in the refrigerator, Sonny wouldn't have formed the testimonial belief that there is milk in the refrigerator.

(Saf) It couldn't have easily been the case that Sonny formed the testimonial belief that there is milk in the refrigerator, and yet there is no milk in the refrigerator.

But why, one might ask, is Sonny's belief reliable, sensitive, and safe in these ways? With respect to (Sen), Goldberg writes:

Had there been no milk in the fridge, this would have been because Frank dumped it (and put the empty milk carton back in the fridge). As noted above, in such a situation Mary would still have testified as she did; but Frank (who is a fixture in the kitchen, and so who is in the kitchen in most or all of the nearest worlds) would have immediately spoken up against that testimony, informing his uninitiated guests of his strange practice. In that case Sonny would not have consumed Mary's testimony, and so would have *refrained* from forming the testimonial belief that there was milk in the fridge. (Goldberg 2005: 303, original emphasis)

Similar considerations, Goldberg claims, apply to (Rel) and (Saf): had Sonny formed the belief that there is milk in the refrigerator, this would have been a case in which Frank did not correct Mary's testimony. But, given Frank's character combined with his constant presence in the kitchen, the only cases in which he would not speak up against Mary's testimony are those, like the actual one, in which he realizes that he failed to pour out the milk from the previous evening. In all such cases, then, there *would* be milk in the refrigerator and hence Sonny's belief would be reliable. Moreover, any nearby world in which the carton in the refrigerator is empty and Mary nonetheless testifies that there is milk in the refrigerator is one in which Frank corrects Mary's testimony, "prompting Sonny to refrain from consuming that testimony" (Goldberg 2005: 304). Thus, Goldberg concludes, Sonny's belief that there is milk in the refrigerator is safe as well.

But notice: when a speaker testifies that *p* at T1 and a hearer has no prior reason for doubting either the speaker in question or the testimony being offered, the natural response for a hearer is to *immediately* form, at T2, the corresponding belief that *p*. Additional information acquired *after* the testimony has been offered, at T3,—whether such information is acquired a couple of seconds or a couple of days later—typically affects whether the speaker *retains* the testimonial belief that has been formed. For instance, suppose that a married couple about whom I know very little, Chloe and Caleb, are hired together by our department, and I meet them at a local restaurant for dinner. During our conversation, Chloe tells me that she has absolutely no fear of heights, after which Caleb immediately responds that she was terrified when they were recently at the top of the Eiffel Tower. Assuming that I have no prior reason to doubt Chloe, the most plausible account of this scenario is as follows: at T1, Chloe testifies that she does not have a fear of heights; I immediately form the corresponding belief at T2; Caleb testifies at T3 that Chloe was recently terrified at the top of the Eiffel Tower, thereby providing me with a defeater for the testimonial belief that I just formed at T2; and, at T4, I abandon my belief that Chloe does not have a fear of heights in light of my newly acquired defeater. Moreover, notice that even if the total amount of time that elapses between T1 and T4 is no more than a few seconds, there is no reason to doubt that T1, T2, T3, and T4 represent events at different moments in time.

Applying these considerations to MILK, we can see that, since Sonny has no prior reason for doubting either Mary or her proffered testimony, the most plausible interpretation of the counterfactual situation in which Mary testifies that there is milk in the refrigerator when, in fact, the milk carton is empty is similarly as follows: at T1, Mary testifies that there is milk in the refrigerator; Sonny immediately forms the corresponding belief at T2; Frank testifies at T3 that the milk carton is empty, thereby providing Sonny with a defeater for the testimonial belief that he just formed at T2; and, at T4, Sonny abandons his belief that there is milk in the refrigerator in light of his newly acquired defeater. Thus, the comparison between the actual sequence of events in MILK and the relevant counterfactual situation is:

Actual:	Counterfactual:
T1: Mary testifies that *p*	T1: Mary testifies that *p*
T2: Sonny forms the belief that *p*	T2: Sonny forms the belief that *p*
T3: Frank silently monitors	T3: Frank corrects Mary's testimony
T4: Sonny retains the belief that *p*	T4: Sonny abandons the belief that *p*

But once this comparison is made clear, it becomes apparent that at the time in the counterfactual situation relevant to determining whether (Rel), (Sen), and (Saf) are true of Sonny's belief—T2—Sonny in fact *forms* the belief that there is milk in the refrigerator. This shows that, contrary to what Goldberg maintains, the testimonial belief that Sonny forms in MILK is in fact unreliable, insensitive, and unsafe. His belief is *unreliable* since Sonny *would* form the belief at T2 that there is milk in the refrigerator on the basis of Mary's testimony even if there weren't milk in the refrigerator. What Frank's monitoring would do in such a counterfactual situation is prevent Sonny from *retaining* such a belief at T4, not prevent him from *forming* it at T2. Similarly, Sonny's belief is both *insensitive*—since, if there hadn't been milk in the refrigerator, Sonny would have nonetheless formed the belief that there is milk in the refrigerator on the basis of Mary's testimony—and *unsafe*—since it could have easily been the case that Sonny formed the testimonial belief that there is milk in the refrigerator despite the fact that there is no milk in the refrigerator. Again, Frank's testimony would simply lead to Sonny's relinquishing his testimonial belief immediately after forming it.[17]

Here, then, is the first horn of the dilemma facing Goldberg: while (1) and (3) are true of the testimonial exchange in MILK, (2) is false. For given that Sonny's belief that there is milk in the refrigerator fails (Rel), (Sen), and (Saf), Goldberg's defense of (2)—that Sonny comes to know that there is milk in the refrigerator—is undermined. Thus, Goldberg has failed to defend his central thesis that testimonial knowledge can be acquired from testimony that is unreliable, insensitive, and unsafe.

There is, however, a way that Goldberg may attempt to resist this conclusion: he may grant that Sonny's belief in MILK fails (Rel), (Sen),

---

[17] Could Goldberg simply modify MILK so that Sonny forms testimonial beliefs rather *slowly*, thereby ensuring that Sonny would not form the belief that there is milk in the refrigerator on the basis of Mary's testimony *prior to* Frank's contribution? Thus, the comparison between the actual sequence of events in MILK and the relevant counterfactual situation would be as follows:

Actual:	Counterfactual:
T1: Mary testifies that p	T1: Mary testifies that p
T2: Frank silently monitors	T2: Frank corrects Mary's testimony
T3: Sonny forms the belief that p	T3: Sonny refrains from forming the belief that p

While this modification to MILK may indeed avoid the problem here discussed, it succumbs to the objection discussed below (which I shall call the second horn of the dilemma for reasons that will become apparent)—i.e., that Goldberg can save the truth of (1) and (2), but only at the cost of losing (3). In particular, since the second horn of the dilemma facing Goldberg arises when Sonny's belief is assessed *after* Frank's contribution, it doesn't matter whether his contribution is made at T3 or at T2.

and (Saf), but argue that such a belief nonetheless satisfies slightly modified versions of these conditions. In particular, he may argue that (Rel), (Sen), and (Saf) should be replaced with the following:

(Rel*) In situations similar to the present one, Sonny would *retain* the testimonial belief that there is milk in the refrigerator only if there were milk in the refrigerator.

(Sen*) If there hadn't been milk in the refrigerator, Sonny wouldn't have *retained* the testimonial belief that there is milk in the refrigerator.

(Saf*) It couldn't have easily been the case that Sonny *retained* the testimonial belief that there is milk in the refrigerator, and yet there is no milk in the refrigerator.

The modified (Rel*), (Sen*), and (Saf*), then, are not relevant to the epistemic properties of Sonny's belief at T2 but, rather, to such properties at T4. In particular, these conditions bear on the properties that his belief possesses *after* Frank's crucial contribution is made to Sonny's epistemic situation—either through his silent monitoring of Mary's testimony or through his active correction of what she reports. Since it is clear that Sonny's belief at T4 satisfies (Rel*), (Sen*), and (Saf*), it may be argued that his belief that there is milk in the refrigerator is thereby relevantly reliable, sensitive, and safe at T4. And this, Goldberg may conclude, is sufficient to support (2) and, therewith, his central thesis that testimonial knowledge can be acquired through testimony that is unreliable, insensitive, and unsafe.

While this response may indeed provide a defense of (2)—the claim that Sonny comes to know that there is milk in the refrigerator—it does so at the cost of losing (3), i.e., the claim that his belief has its epistemic properties on the basis of Mary's testimony. For what it reveals is that, though Mary's testimony is *causally responsible* for Sonny's acquiring the belief that there is milk in the refrigerator, Frank's silent monitoring is what *confers on the belief its positive epistemic status* at T4. This is evident from the fact that Sonny's belief—which is unreliable, insensitive, and unsafe when assessed in relation to only Mary's contribution at T2—*becomes* reliable, sensitive, and safe in light of Frank's contribution at T3. It is, then, simply not the case that Sonny comes to know that there is milk in the refrigerator *on the basis of Mary's testimony*. Given Frank's essential epistemic contribution, the source of Sonny's knowledge at T4 is, at best, Mary's-testimony-plus-Frank's-silent-monitoring. But then the strongest conclusion that can be drawn from MILK is the obvious and uncontentious claim that knowledge can be acquired through unreliable, insensitive, and unsafe testimony that combines with additional support to become a reliable, sensitive, and safe epistemic source. Otherwise put, while this move preserves the truth of (1) and (2) with respect to the testimonial exchange in MILK, (3) is no longer true.

Goldberg himself considers this very objection in his paper, and offers a two-pronged response. On the first prong, suppose that Sonny is aware of Frank's silent monitoring of Mary's testimony, and explicitly relies on this silence in believing that there is milk in the refrigerator. According to Goldberg, Frank's role in such a case is no different from background reasons that hearers invoke in their acceptance of much testimonial knowledge. To illustrate this, he asks us to consider a case involving Ralph, who knows that Nancy has a subconscious fear of dogs that causes her to assert only things of which she is absolutely certain whenever a dog is present. Thus, when Ralph hears Nancy assert that *p* in the presence of a dog, he takes the dog's presence to indicate that Nancy's testimony is worthy of being trusted on this occasion. Assuming Ralph then comes to know that *p* through Nancy's testimony, the presence of dogs is an empirical condition that grounds Ralph's belief in the trustworthiness of Nancy's testimony, no different from other signs of sincerity and/or competence in ordinary testimonial exchanges. Goldberg then writes:

For this reason, it would be wrongheaded to hold that Ralph's knowledge is really knowledge through Nancy's-testimony-as-given-in-the-presence-of-a-dog; at least it would be wrongheaded to say this if it meant that Ralph's knowledge is *not* properly regarded as knowledge through Nancy's testimony. Similarly for the case of Sonny's reliance on Frank's silence: it would be wrongheaded to hold that Sonny's knowledge is really knowledge through Mary's-testimony-as-monitored-by-Frank; at least it would be wrongheaded if this meant that Sonny's knowledge is *not* knowledge through Mary's testimony. (Goldberg 2005: 305)

Thus, Goldberg concludes that the role that Frank plays in Sonny's coming to know that there is milk in the refrigerator does not jeopardize the truth of (3), at least not without also jeopardizing the testimonial nature of much of the ordinary knowledge that we acquire from the assertions of others.

But there are two crucial differences between the knowledge held by Sonny and that held by Ralph. First, while Frank's silent monitoring itself *confers the epistemic status on Sonny's belief,* the presence of dogs merely *causes Nancy's testimony to be reliable which,* in turn, *confers the epistemic status on Ralph's belief.* Unlike Frank's contribution to Sonny's state at T4, then, the presence of dogs does not play any *direct epistemic role* in Ralph's relevant state and, therefore, in no way threatens to compromise Nancy's role as the source of his knowledge. Given this clear asymmetry between Frank's silence and the presence of dogs relative to the beliefs in question—i.e., the former makes a direct epistemic contribution to the belief in question while the latter does not—there is a principled reason to deny that Ralph's knowledge is really knowledge on the basis of Nancy's-testimony-as-given-in-the-presence-of-a-dog while, at the same time, maintaining that Sonny's knowledge is really knowledge on the basis of Mary's-testimony-as-monitored-by-Frank.

Second, and related, Ralph's awareness of the presence of dogs indicates *that Nancy's testimony is reliable,* whereas Sonny's awareness of Frank's silent monitoring indicates *that there is milk in the refrigerator*—that is, it indicates that Mary's testimony is true. Otherwise put, while Ralph's reason for accepting Nancy's testimony is in the form "Feature ϕ indicates that S's testimony that p is reliable," Sonny's reason for accepting Mary's testimony is in the form, "Feature ϕ indicates that p is true."[18] The former supports the *general testimony*; the latter supports the *particular proposition* testified to. Unlike the awareness of the presence of dogs, then, the awareness of Frank's silent monitoring provides *independent* epistemic support for Sonny's believing that p. Once again, this asymmetry reveals an important and principled difference between the knowledge acquired by Sonny and that acquired by Ralph. Hence, the first prong of Goldberg's response fails.

Goldberg's second prong asks us to assume that some version of externalism with respect to knowledge is correct, and then to suppose that

---

[18] Goldberg attempts to gloss over the differences between the reasons possessed by Ralph and Sonny by saying that both subjects have beliefs about the *trustworthiness* of the relevant testifiers, where "trustworthiness" is understood as follows: "testimony is trustworthy when a hearer's belief in it (acceptance of it) would yield a reliable belief" (Goldberg 2005: 306). But even if we grant Goldberg this rather counterintuitive conception of trustworthiness—counterintuitive because testimony can be trustworthy on such a view for reasons that are entirely disconnected from both the speaker and the testimony in question—the point that is being made here still stands: Ralph's reason for accepting Nancy's testimony is in the form "Feature ϕ indicates that S's testimony that p is reliable," while Sonny's reason for accepting Mary's testimony is in the form, "Feature ϕ indicates that p is true." So, even if both of these reasons can be subsumed by Goldberg's conception of trustworthiness, this doesn't affect the fact that they are nonetheless importantly different.

Sonny is not aware of Frank's silent monitoring of Mary's testimony. In such a case, Goldberg argues that Frank's role should be regarded as simply a locally invariant feature of the relevant environment that should be held fixed when evaluating the general reliability of Sonny's belief. For instance, in determining whether your belief that there is a fox currently in your backyard is safe, we might hold fixed the fact that, though your neighbor has a dog that frequents your backyard that is indistinguishable from a fox, she never—absolutely never—lets her dog out when you are home. Your neighbor's dog-letting-out practice, then, is a locally invariant feature of your environment that should be held fixed when the general reliability of your backyard-fox-belief is evaluated, thereby resulting in such a belief being reliable, sensitive, and safe. Moreover, the mere fact that such a feature is relevant to the assessment of the epistemic features of your belief does not render the source of the resulting knowledge perceiving-a-fox-in-light-of-the-neighbor's-dog-letting-out-practice rather than merely perceiving-a-fox. Similarly, according to the second prong of Goldberg's response, Frank's silent monitoring is simply a locally invariant feature of Sonny's environment that results in his acquiring knowledge that there is milk in the refrigerator without compromising Mary's role as its source.

This response, however, is subject to the same problem afflicting Goldberg's first prong: Frank's direct epistemic contribution to Sonny's belief that there is milk in the refrigerator *does* compromise Mary's role as the source of his knowledge, even when he is regarded as simply a locally invariant feature of the relevant environment. To see this, notice that the neighbor's dog-letting-out-practice merely enables your reliable perceptual faculties to function in an environment that is conducive to acquiring true fox-beliefs—your faculty of vision, however, is what is ultimately responsible for the epistemic properties your fox-belief possesses. In contrast, Frank's silent monitoring doesn't merely enable reliable testimony to function in an environment that is conducive to acquiring true milk-beliefs, for Mary's testimony is itself unreliable. Instead, Frank's role is what is ultimately responsible for the epistemic properties that Sonny's milk-belief possesses.

One way of making this point particularly vivid is by noticing that Mary's testimony can be substituted with any other source, no matter how unreliable, insensitive, and unsafe it might be; so long as that source causes Sonny's belief that there is milk in the refrigerator, and so long as Frank's role remains fixed, *Sonny's belief would still possess the same epistemic profile that it possesses in MILK.* For instance, suppose that everything remains the same in MILK except that, rather than Mary testifying that there is milk in the refrigerator, an unreliable, insensitive, and unsafe automatic device flashes a sign that reads "Milk" when Sonny opens the refrigerator. Given Frank's unusual milk-spilling habit, while this device typically flashes such a sign when there is merely an empty carton in the refrigerator, today Frank forgot to pour out the contents of the carton from the night before. So, his silent monitoring of the unreliable, insensitive, and unsafe device results in Sonny acquiring knowledge that there is milk in the refrigerator. Now, while Sonny's belief that there is milk in the refrigerator has a different causal origin in this case, it possesses the *same* epistemic profile that it possesses in the original case of MILK. In contrast, consider substituting your seeing the fox in your backyard with an alternative source, such as your friend telling you that there is a fox in your backyard. In such a case, your belief that there is a fox in your backyard possesses an *entirely different* epistemic profile, grounded in the testimonial practices of your friend rather than in features of your faculty of vision. This reveals that while Goldberg is correct that locally invariant features of the environment can affect the evaluation of a given belief without compromising its original source—as is the case in your backyard-fox-belief—Frank's silent monitoring in MILK is simply not such a feature. Hence, the second prong of Goldberg's response fails as well.

We have seen, then, that either Sonny believes that there is milk in the refrigerator on the basis of Mary's testimony, but such a belief does not qualify as knowledge, or Sonny's belief that there is milk in the refrigerator qualifies as knowledge, but not on the basis of Mary's testimony. Either way, Goldberg has failed to show that testimonial knowledge can be acquired through testimony that is unreliable, insensitive, and unsafe and, thus, he has failed to provide a counterexample to RS-N.

A General Defense of RS-N

One feature of MILK that may be regarded as ultimately responsible for its failure as a counterexample to RS-N is that the epistemic properties of Sonny's belief are provided by another agent—Frank. In particular, it may be thought that the epistemic role of Mary's testimony is usurped by the presence of another testifier, whose agency, one might argue, precludes his being treated merely as a locally invariant feature of the environment.

Thus, even if Frank is simply silently monitoring Mary's testimony, his presence results in Sonny knowing that there is milk in the refrigerator but not on the basis of Mary's testimony. So, perhaps a more compelling case can be made against RS-N by constructing a counterexample that has only two agents involved in the testimonial exchange in question—the speaker and the hearer.

To this end, the counterexample must possess the following features:

(a) S's testimony that p is unreliable, insensitive, and unsafe.
(b) H comes to know that p.
(c) H's belief that p has its epistemic properties on the basis of S's testimony.
(d) S and H are the only two agents epistemically relevant to the case.

Given that Frank's role was of paramount importance to the knowledge acquired in MILK, however, how can (a)–(d) all be true without someone occupying his position in the counterexample in question? Perhaps this can be achieved if the feature enabling H to come to know that p lies, not in the behavior of another agent, but in H herself. Suppose, for instance, that there is a hearer who is so constituted that she is non-inferentially sensitive to features in speakers—even when they are offering testimony that is unreliable, insensitive, and unsafe—that enable her to arrive at beliefs that are reliable, sensitive, and safe.[19] Such sensitivity must be non-inferential so as to ensure that (c) is satisfied, i.e., that H comes to know that p on the basis of S's testimony rather than on the basis of inference from background information. Given this, perhaps H's ability here can be understood as analogous to that of the chicken sexer: much like a chicken sexer is able to just "see" that a chick is either male or female, maybe by picking up on very subtle perceptual cues, H is such that she is able to just "see" that a given statement is to be accepted.

One problem with this comparison between the chicken sexer and the hearer, however, is that there is a dilemma lurking regarding the ability at work in the testimonial case. Consider, on the one hand, understanding H's ability in terms of H being sensitive to subtle perceptual cues about the *sincerity* of speakers. While it may be plausible to regard a hearer as having such an ability—maybe, for instance, H is sensitive to different

[19] This general type of objection to my RS-N was made by John Greco in conversation.

degrees of eye fluttering, facial tics, and other common signs of sincerity and insincerity—the sincerity of an unreliable testifier is not going to do much by way of providing H with a reliable, sensitive, and safe belief. For even the most sincere of speakers can often lead hearers astray, so long as their sincerity combines with the relevant doxastic incompetence. Thus, H having a sensitivity to sincerity is not going to be sufficient to satisfy (b) and (c) in the face of (a).

So, consider, on the other hand, understanding H's ability in terms of H being sensitive to subtle perceptual cues directly about the *truth* of statements offered by speakers. Whether or not S believes that her statement is true, then, H is capable of just "seeing" that the statement is true or false. While such a sensitivity may indeed be sufficient to satisfy (b) and (c) in the face of (a), it is entirely unclear how to understand both such an ability and the relevant cues that would reliably indicate that certain statements are true. For if H is genuinely coming to know something from S that H didn't know already, then what subtle perceptual cues could H be sensitive to that a given statement is *true* rather than merely *believed by S to be true*? Indeed, there just do not seem to be any plausible features that are reliably connected with true statements in general that could play such a role for H. Thus, given that the chicken sexer's ability is presumably the result of some sort of sensitivity to very subtle perceptual cues rather than a magical or supernatural ability, the absence of such cues in the testimonial case renders the analogy with chicken-sexing, at best, strained.

But perhaps we can understand H's sensitivity to the truth of testimony, not in terms of an ordinary ability like the chicken sexer's, but in terms of an *extraordinary ability,* either one that was God-given or otherwise non-accidentally bestowed upon H. For instance, consider the following:

COFFEE: Emma was born with an extraordinary ability to non-inferentially detect the truth of the testimony of those around her: nearly every time a speaker's statement is true, she feels a slight throb in her right temple, and nearly every time a speaker's statement is false, she feels a slight throb in her left temple. Moreover, Emma's ability not only has a great deal of internal support—over the years, she has acquired numerous excellent reasons for trusting her extraordinary ability—it also functions reliably regardless of whether the speaker in question herself believes the statement being offered. Today, Emma met Mandy, her college roommate, who also happens to be a pathological liar. Worried that Emma will discover her condition and leave her without a roommate, Mandy decides to randomly intersperse a couple of truths into the conversation. So, Mandy truly reports that there is coffee in the kitchen, despite the fact that she is generally an unreliable testifier and that her choice to reveal this one truth was arbitrarily selected. Moreover, that there is in fact coffee in the kitchen is quite surprising: just as Mandy's caffeine-addicted mother was about to pour the last cup of coffee out of the pot to drink, a cardinal hit the glass window in the kitchen, causing her to run outside to check on the bird. Nevertheless, given Emma's extraordinary ability, her right temple throbs upon hearing Mandy's statement, resulting in her forming the corresponding belief.

Notice, first, that (d) is obviously true of COFFEE: Mandy and Emma are the only two agents who are epistemically relevant to the case. For, unlike Frank's silent monitoring in MILK, though Mandy's mother affects the counterfactual stability of there being coffee in the kitchen, she does not make any direct epistemic contribution to Emma's belief.

Second, given Mandy's general unreliability as a testifier combined with her random selection of the truth in question, (a) is also clearly true of COFFEE. In particular, it is true both that in situations similar to the present one, Mandy would have reported that there is coffee in the kitchen even if there weren't some and, if there hadn't been coffee in the kitchen, Mandy would have nonetheless reported that there was some. Mandy's testimony is, then, both unreliable and insensitive. Moreover, given how coincidental it is for the bird to hit the window at the precise moment her caffeine-addicted mother was pouring the last cup of coffee out of the pot, it could have easily been the case that Mandy reported that there is coffee in the kitchen without this being so. Thus, her testimony is unsafe as well.

Third, given Emma's extraordinary truth-detecting ability when it comes to the testimony of others combined with her excellent reasons for trusting such an ability, (b) is also clearly true of COFFEE. For, in all of the relevant nearby worlds, if there hadn't in fact been coffee in the kitchen when Mandy reported that there was some, Emma would have felt a slight throb in her left, rather than right, temple, thereby leading to her refraining from forming the corresponding belief. More precisely, Emma's belief that there is coffee in the kitchen is reliable—in situations similar to the present one, Emma would form the testimonial belief that there is coffee in the kitchen only if there were some; sensitive—if there hadn't been coffee in the kitchen, Emma wouldn't have formed the testimonial belief that there is some; safe—it couldn't have easily been the case that Emma formed the testimonial belief that there is coffee in the kitchen, and yet there isn't some; and internally rational—Emma has acquired numerous excellent reasons for trusting her truth-detecting ability.

This leaves us with (c): does Emma's belief that there is coffee in the kitchen have its epistemic properties *on the basis of Mandy's testimony*? Here the answer should clearly be no. For notice: Mandy's acquiring knowledge from the statements of speakers merely has to be *causally triggered* by someone—anyone—saying something true. But surely the mere fact that a speaker's words *cause* a hearer to know a given proposition is inadequate for the resulting knowledge to qualify as relevantly testimonially based. For instance, suppose that your uttering statements about the color of flowers causes my knee to twitch in various ways which, in turn, reliably causes true beliefs in me about the weather in China. Suppose, further, that I have epistemically good reasons for believing not only that I have such a condition, but also that it is a reliable epistemic source for forming beliefs about China's weather. In such a case, even though your words causally trigger events that result in my knowing, e.g., that it is currently 65 degrees in Beijing, surely I do not know this *on the basis of your testimony* that, e.g., roses are red. Indeed, your testimony does not contribute in any way to the epistemic status of my beliefs about China's weather. Because of this, whatever we choose to call the source responsible for my knowing that it is currently 65 degrees in Beijing—whether it is clairvoyance, ESP, or some other extraordinary capacity—it should be clear that it is not testimony.

Similar considerations apply in the case of COFFEE. For, even though the actual content of Mandy's testimony plays a more substantive causal role in Emma's knowing that there is coffee in the kitchen than your statement about the color of flowers plays in my knowing the weather in China, the two cases are on a par from an epistemic point of view. In particular, in neither case does the testimony in question contribute in any way to the epistemic status of the hearer's belief: while my China-weather-belief is justified or warranted on the basis of my extraordinary knee-twitching ability combined with my good reasons for trusting such a source, Emma's coffee belief is justified or warranted on the basis of her extraordinary temple-throbbing ability combined with her good reasons for trusting such a source. In both cases, then, the testimony itself simply drops out of the epistemic picture, a fact that clearly seems sufficient to disqualify the knowledge in question from being testimonially based. Hence, given that (c) is not true of Emma's knowledge, COFFEE fails to provide a counterexample to RS-N.

A Necessary Condition for Testimonially Based Knowledge

One of the central arguments raised against both MILK and COFFEE is that the hearer's knowledge in such cases fails to be acquired on the basis of the speaker's testimony, thereby precluding them from functioning as counterexamples to RS-N. But, one might ask, are there general principles showing that the knowledge acquired in such cases is not testimonially based? Otherwise put, what are the minimal requirements necessary for an instance of knowledge to be properly regarded as testimonial?

Though I shall not attempt a complete answer to this question, at least one condition that is necessary for H to know that p on the basis of S's testimony is this: the content of S's testimony must be epistemically responsible for at least some of the epistemic properties of H's knowing that p. Let us call this condition *Testimonial Epistemic Responsibility*, or TER. Now why should we accept this condition? Well, to reject TER is tantamount to saying that H's knowing that p can be based on S's testimony despite the fact that the content of S's testimony does not contribute in any way to the epistemic status of H's knowing that p. But surely this is wrong. For while such knowledge may be *causally triggered by testimony*, it simply doesn't makes sense to say that it is *testimonially based* when the content of the testimony in question does not itself make any epistemic contribution. And testimonially based knowledge is, after all, what the whole debate surrounding both TEP-N and RS-N is about.

Compare: suppose that my faculty of memory unreliably triggers my believing that you have glasses, but my seeing you wearing glasses is what confers epistemic value on such a belief. Surely, there is no sense in which we would regard the resulting knowledge as memorial or memorially based. If my seeing you wearing glasses is what is doing all of the epistemic work, then the resulting knowledge is perceptual, regardless of memory's role in the causal origin of the belief.

With TER in place, we can now see that the problems afflicting both MILK and COFFEE are general problems that will affect any purported counterexample to RS-N in which a hearer knows that p on the basis of a speaker's unreliable, insensitive, and unsafe testimony that p. Consider the following:

(i) In order to construct a relevant counterexample to RS–N, it needs to be shown that testimonially based knowledge can be acquired from testimony that is unreliable, insensitive, and unsafe.

(ii) If the testimony in question is itself devoid of epistemic value, however, then the epistemic properties possessed by the knowledge the hearer acquires must come entirely from something other than the testimony.

(iii) But then the knowledge in question will fail TER and will, therefore, fail to qualify as testimonially based knowledge.

(iv) Hence, a relevant counterexample to RS–N involving unreliable, insensitive, and unsafe testimony cannot be constructed.

Both MILK and COFFEE provide concrete instances of purported counterexamples to RS–N that are subsumed by this argument, i.e., they fail TER because the epistemic properties in question derive from something other than the testimony in question. In MILK, the unreliability[20] of Mary's testimony is offset by Frank's silent monitoring and, in COFFEE, the unreliability[21] of Mandy's testimony is offset by Emma's extraordinary truth-detecting ability. The result in both cases is that the knowledge in question fails to be testimonially based.

But what if one constructed a counterexample to RS–N in which the testimony itself wasn't unreliable, insensitive, and unsafe but, rather, was simply not reliable, sensitive, and safe *enough* to satisfy RS–N? In such a case, couldn't a hearer's knowledge, though epistemically supplemented with something other than the testimony in question, still satisfy TER because at least some of the epistemic properties would be due to the speaker's testimony?

One way of answering this question is by returning to the original thesis that I opposed in Chapter 2, which holds that speaker-knowledge (justification/warrant) is a necessary condition of testimonial knowledge (justification/warrant). In particular:

TEP–N: For every speaker, A, and hearer, B, B knows (believes with justification/warrant) that p on the basis of A's testimony that p only if A knows (believes with justification/warrant) that p.

---

[20] By "unreliability" here, I mean that Mary's testimony is unreliable, insensitive, *and* unsafe.

[21] Again, I mean here that Mandy's testimony is unreliable, insensitive, *and* unsafe.

Now notice how incredibly simple it would be to construct counterexamples to TEP-N if cases of so-called hybrid knowledge—i.e., cases in which the knowledge in question is based on more than one source—were regarded as relevant to this thesis. We can imagine with great ease cases in which H has acquired background information, about either S or the proposition being testified to, that enables H to derive knowledge from S's testimony that p, despite the fact that S herself does not know that p. Consider, for instance, the following two cases:

OWL: Hank is Clara's ophthalmologist and friend, and he knows from examining her that she has excellent eyesight. He also knows from their friendship that she suffers from debilitating self-doubt that causes her to erroneously believe that her vision is highly unreliable. Earlier today, Clara saw Hank at the store, and she told him that she thought she may have seen an eastern screech-owl in a nearby tree. On the basis of this testimony in conjunction with his knowledge both of Clara's excellent eyesight and of her self-doubt, Hank comes to know that she saw such an owl. Nevertheless, Clara's debilitating self-doubt in her own cognitive faculties prevents her from knowing that she saw an eastern screech-owl in the tree in question.

HAWK: Gordon completely lacks the ability to distinguish among birds of prey: every large bird with talons that he sees he believes is a red-tailed hawk. Felicia, on the other hand, is an ornithologist who specializes in birds of prey, and she knows that the only raptors that perch in a local state park are a pair of red-tailed hawks. (Any other birds of prey that attempted to encroach on the hawks' territory would be quickly chased away, especially now that there are eggs in the nest.) Today, Gordon tells Felicia that he saw a red-tailed hawk in a tree in their local state park, a fact that Felicia comes to know through his testimony in conjunction with her relevant background knowledge of the raptors that live in this park. Nevertheless, Gordon's complete inability to distinguish among birds of prey prevents him from knowing, on the basis of just his sighting, that the bird that he saw was indeed a red-tailed hawk.

In both OWL and HAWK, we have cases in which a hearer acquires knowledge in part from a speaker's testimony and in part from at least one other source—such as perception or inference—despite the fact that the speaker in question does not possess the relevant knowledge. As should be clear, such cases are a dime a dozen. All that one needs to do to construct such a case is provide the hearer with information that enables her to rule out the feature that prevents the speaker from possessing the knowledge in question.

But what should be equally clear is that proponents of the TEP–N will be unimpressed with these sorts of attempts at producing counterexamples to their thesis. For what they will say is that their thesis was never intended to apply to every case in which testimony plays merely *some* role in the resulting knowledge. More precisely, they will deny that TEP–N is true of cases of hybrid knowledge.[22] Indeed, if proponents of TEP–N did maintain that their thesis applied to cases of hybrid knowledge, then TEP–N would be so obviously false—as OWL and HAWK show with ease—that it would be difficult to make sense out of the fact that so many epistemologists continue to regard it as true.

Which brings us back to the initial question: couldn't a hearer's knowledge be epistemically supplemented with something other than the testimony in question and yet still satisfy RS–N because at least some of the epistemic properties would be due to the speaker's testimony? As should be clear at this point, my answer to this question is that RS–N was never expected to apply to cases of hybrid knowledge. For obviously the minimal reliability of a speaker's testimony may combine with some other source to produce knowledge in a hearer. But just as such hybrid knowledge is not the kind relevant to TEP–N, so too it is not the kind relevant to RS–N. Indeed, notice that in the formulations of both TEP–N and RS–N, it is B's knowing that *p on the basis of A's testimony that p* that is taken to be the relevant topic at hand. Compare: when a theory of the epistemology of perception is offered, the theory isn't expected to necessarily subsume

---

[22] Though it may prove difficult to fully distinguish what I am calling "hybrid knowledge" from knowledge that is sufficiently pure, I take it that the distinction is intuitive enough for present purposes. For instance, the knowledge in OWL and HAWK is different in obvious ways from the following:

FALCON: My husband, whom I know is both skilled at distinguishing among raptors and trustworthy when testifying, phoned me at work to say that he saw a peregrine falcon flying near a downtown skyscraper earlier today. Since the corresponding belief I form is true, reliably formed, and rational, I come to know that my husband saw a peregrine falcon today on the basis of his testimony.

Unlike in OWL and HAWK, even though the background information I have of my husband in FALCON plays some epistemic role in my coming to know that he saw a peregrine falcon—thereby preventing the knowledge in question from being *purely testimonial* in the strictest sense of the word—his testimony is clearly what is most responsible for my coming to know that he saw a peregrine falcon, and thus the resulting knowledge is *sufficiently pure* to qualify as testimonially based. Indeed, notice that in both OWL and HAWK, the relevant background information is necessary to *offset epistemic defects* in the testimony in question, whereas in FALCON, the background information merely *adds additional epistemic support* to testimony that is already appropriately truth-conducive. These differences should be adequate—at least for present purposes—for distinguishing "hybrid knowledge" from knowledge that is sufficiently testimonially based.

cases of knowledge that are partially perceptual and partially testimonial. Similarly, a theory of the epistemology of testimony shouldn't be expected to necessarily subsume cases of knowledge that are partially testimonial and partially, say, perceptual, memorial, or inferential. Hence, cases of hybrid knowledge simply go beyond the scope of RS-N and thus fail to serve as counterexamples to the necessity of such a condition for testimonially based knowledge.

We have seen, then, not only that both MILK and COFFEE fail to provide counterexamples to RS-N, but also that testimonially based knowledge *cannot* be acquired from unreliable, insensitive, and unsafe testimony. Thus, there is no reason to doubt, and very good reason to accept, the necessity of RS-N for testimonially based knowledge.

3.4 Objection to Approach

The final objection to my view that I shall consider in this chapter targets my overall approach to theorizing about testimony as an epistemic source. According to Elizabeth Fricker:

Knowledge *gained through trust in testimony* is always and necessarily second-hand knowledge. [A] trusting hearer gains knowledge from what she is told only if the teller speaks from his knowledge. This being so, it seems that telling and testimony more broadly, like memory, is not an original source of knowledge but merely a conduit for it. Memory and testimony do not on their own generate new items of knowledge, but only ... transmit them. The following principle is true:

> T: If H knows that P through being told that P and trusting the teller, there is or was someone who knows that P in some other way—*not* in virtue of having been told that P and trusting the teller.

(Fricker 2006*b*: 603–4, first emphasis added)

So, Fricker is here endorsing TEP-N—or, at the very least TEP-N*—with respect to, not all testimonial knowledge, but only the narrower category of *knowledge gained through trust in testimony*.[23] I say "or, at the very least

---

[23] I am grateful to Mark Heller, Brian McLaughlin, and, especially, David Sosa for also suggesting a response of this sort in conversation. Timothy Williamson makes a similar move when he writes:

TEP-N*'" because the second sentence of the above quotation looks like an endorsement of TEP-N: Fricker says that a trusting hearer acquires testimonial knowledge that p only if the speaker herself knows that p. The formulation of T, however, looks like a commitment to TEP-N*; for Fricker here says that a trusting hearer acquires testimonial knowledge that p only if someone—perhaps the first link in the relevant testimonial chain—knows that p in a non-testimonial way. For our purposes, however, it will not be important to settle which version of the necessity condition Fricker endorses, not only because my arguments in Chapter 2 target both theses, but also because the central objection that she raises against me focuses on my overall method of theorizing. She writes:

> Lackey...argues that one can acquire knowledge that P from testimony that P, even though the testifier does not know that P. I agree with her...Where I disagree with Lackey, is on how testimony as an epistemic source is best theorized. I have described the case where the hearer forms belief in what she is told due to her trust in the teller, taking her speech act at face value, as an expression of knowledge. The result that a recipient of testimony can come to know what she is told only if the teller speaks from knowledge holds only for this relatively narrow category. I believe this is the distinctive core mechanism we need to identify, to understand the nature of testimony as a socio-linguistic means of spreading knowledge. (Fricker 2006b: 603, fn. 27)

There are two main points here: first, Fricker claims that, while the conditions found in TEP-N and TEP-N* may not be true of testimonial knowledge in general (because of the considerations found in Chapter 2), they are nonetheless true of the narrower category of knowledge gained through trust in testimony. Second, she maintains that this narrower category should be the focus of the epistemology of testimony because it is the distinctive core mechanism by which knowledge is spread from speaker to hearer. Both points, I shall argue, are unmotivated.

"Someone who does not know p lacks the authority to assert p, and therefore cannot pass that authority on to me by asserting p, no matter how plausibly he gives me the impression that he has done so. Although there are special cases in which someone comes to know p by hearing someone who does not know p assert p (Lackey 1999), the normal procedure by which the hearer comes to know p requires the speaker to know p too" (Williamson 2000: 257). Thus, just as Fricker responds to my counterexamples to TEP-N in Chapter 2 by simply restricting her thesis to *knowledge gained through trust in testimony*, Williamson here responds to my cases (some versions of which were published in my (1999)) by restricting his endorsement of TEP-N to the *normal procedure by which knowledge is gained through testimony*. Given this similarity, most of my objections to Fricker will apply, *mutatis mutandis*, to Williamson as well.

Notice, first, that it is entirely unclear why this narrower category of knowledge through trust in testimony is of interest *from an epistemological point of view*. For, as we saw in CREATIONIST TEACHER, CONSISTENT LIAR, and PERSISTENT BELIEVER from Chapter 2, testimonial knowledge can be acquired without the satisfaction of either TEP-N or TEP-N*. Moreover, it is not the case that knowledge subsumed by Fricker's narrower category—knowledge gained through trust in testimony—is *better epistemically* than knowledge subsumed only by the broader category. For instance, recall that Stella from CREATIONIST TEACHER consulted reliable sources in the library and developed reliable lecture notes from which to teach evolutionary theory to her students. We can even imagine that Stella became quite an expert on this topic through all of her research, acquiring a rich and detailed understanding of evolutionary theory that has not only breadth but depth as well. Now compare the knowledge that her students acquire to that gained through trust by Blanche's students, where Blanche in fact believes that *Homo sapiens* evolved from *Homo erectus* but does so merely on the basis of scattered fragments of information that she has absorbed through the course of her life. Blanche, then, speaks from knowledge—and so her students thereby acquire knowledge of evolutionary theory through *trust* in her testimony—while Stella does not, and so her students thereby acquire knowledge of evolutionary theory only through her testimony *simpliciter*. But whose students' beliefs are better-grounded from an epistemic point of view? Assuming that the students in the two classes have the same amount of relevant background information about their respective teachers, it seems clear that Stella's students' beliefs are better epistemically than Blanche's students' beliefs. For, even though Stella does not speak from knowledge, as Blanche does, her understanding of evolutionary theory is far superior and her testimony is far more reliable than Blanche's. Thus, knowledge gained through trust in testimony does not carve out a domain that is better epistemically than testimonial knowledge *simpliciter*.

Second, if, in light of my counterexamples in Chapter 2, Fricker simply responds by saying that everything that she once said about testimonial knowledge *simpliciter* is now restricted to the narrower category of knowledge gained through trust in testimony—with nothing about the latter carving out an interesting epistemic domain—then obviously such a response is guilty of being *ad hoc*. (Imagine someone responding to a counterexample purporting to show that justification is not a necessary condition for knowledge by saying that everything that was once said about knowledge is now restricted to a narrower category of knowledge with justification. Obviously, such a response would be unimpressive if this narrower category failed to pick out an interesting epistemic kind.) Fricker, in fact, considers precisely this sort of objection to her response, and writes:

Since there are other ways in which knowledge that P can be gained from observing testimony that P, which do not conform to T, am I protecting my thesis that knowledge through trust in testimony is essentially second-hand knowledge through a definitional stop which renders the result uninteresting? I do not think so. When I take another's word for it that P, I trust her in a way that makes my relation to her different from when I treat the fact of her apparent confident belief that P as one piece of evidence to be weighed with the rest. I take her utterance at face value, as nothing less than what it purports to be, an assurance that P, and an expression of knowledge. I treat my teller with respect, in a way that I do not when I treat her expressed belief merely as defeasible evidence. One might say that I treat her as an end, not merely as a means. (Fricker 2006b: 607)

There are several problems with this response. Why, for instance, does the mere fact that Blanche believes that *Homo sapiens* evolved from *Homo erectus* result in her students treating her differently from the way in which Stella's students treat their teacher? *Ex hypothesi*, the students are *not aware* of the doxastic attitudes of their respective teachers—so the mere presence or absence of the teachers' beliefs, about which the students have no relevant information, does not even seem capable of affecting how the students treat their teachers. Moreover, even if we grant Fricker everything that she says in the above quotation—that Stella's students in CREATIONIST TEACHER are not showing her the proper respect because they are treating her merely as a means, rather than as an end—such a conclusion lacks any *epistemic* import. For, while this kind of treatment may have moral significance, particularly if one is a Kantian, there is no reason to think that treating a person as an end affects any features or properties that are distinctively epistemic, such as reliability, sensitivity, safety, evidential relations, rationality, and so on.[24] Consider: if Stella and Blanche offer statements that are equally reliable (safe, sensitive, and so on) in similar cognitive environments to students who have similar background beliefs

---

[24] I shall say more about this general line of argumentation in Chapter 8.

regarding their respective teachers, what could differ epistemically about the testimonial beliefs that the students thereby acquire? Presumably Fricker would respond that one set is acquired on the basis of trust in testimony, while the other set is not. But this just begs the obvious question: why does trust in this sense carve out a domain that is of any epistemological interest?

Third, it is, in fact, rather perplexing that Fricker calls the knowledge acquired by hearers like Blanche's students, but not that acquired by hearers like Stella's students, knowledge gained through *trust in testimony*. For aren't Stella's students *trusting her testimony* in an intuitive sense? And isn't Stella, by virtue of her commitment to offer to her students only assertions that are supported by the available evidence, providing *testimony that is worthy of being trusted*? Given this, knowledge gained through trust in testimony seems, from an intuitive point of view, a fitting label for the conception of testimonial knowledge found in my SVT. For my view stresses the import of focusing on the *testimony* of speakers rather than on their doxastic states. In contrast, the difference between Stella and Blanche that seems to be motivating Fricker's narrower category of knowledge lies in their respective *belief systems*—Blanche believes what she is testifying to, while Stella does not. Accordingly, it would be more appropriate for Fricker to call her narrower category *knowledge gained through trust in a speaker's beliefs*. But then we are right back to the arguments against the BVT in Chapter 2: unreliable believers can nonetheless be highly reliable testifiers, and the latter is what is necessary for the acquisition of testimonial knowledge.

Finally, my SVT provides a *unified account* of all of the knowledge that is acquired through testimony, one that captures the knowledge acquired from both speakers like Stella and speakers like Blanche. Indeed, my view has the resources to explain the sort of transmission Fricker is interested in, if or when such a process actually occurs: the epistemic properties of a speaker's belief are transmitted *via her statement (or other act of communication)* to the recipient of her testimony. In this way, transmission is epistemically important only insofar as it bears on the satisfaction of RS-N. This point is evidenced by the fact that testimonial knowledge (justification, warrant) can be acquired even after the counterfactual removal of a speaker's belief, so long as the statement in question remains reliable. So, what would a theory of Fricker's narrower category of testimonial knowledge through trust add to my view? She does not say. And why would anything *need* to be added? We already have a theory—the SVT—that explains the epistemic properties of *both* of these categories of testimonial knowledge.

Hence, Fricker has not given a compelling reason to accept either her claim that TEP-N and TEP-N* are true of the narrower category of knowledge gained through trust in testimony or her claim that this narrower category should be the focus of the epistemology of testimony. Given this, combined with the unsuccessful attempts to challenge CREATIONIST TEACHER and RS-N discussed earlier, proponents of the BVT have failed to challenge both my arguments against the Belief View of Testimony and my positive Statement View of Testimony. Thus, contrary to nearly every view in the current epistemological literature, we can conclude that hearers learn from the words of speakers, not from their beliefs.

4

Norms of Assertion
and Testimonial Knowledge

4.1 The Knowledge Norm of Assertion

A view growing in popularity in the recent philosophical literature is
that only knowledge warrants assertion. More precisely, the following
is frequently taken to be the central norm of assertion (hereafter, the
Knowledge Norm of Assertion, or the KNA):

KNA: One should assert that *p* only if one knows that *p*.[1]

So, for instance, Timothy Williamson says that his view can be "sum-
marized in the slogan 'Only knowledge warrants assertion'" (Williamson
2000: 243).[2] Following this view, Jason Stanley maintains that "*assertion
is ... conceptually connected to knowledge ... one ought only to assert what one
knows*" (Stanley 2005: 10–1, original emphasis). Similarly, Keith DeRose
claims that "one is positioned well-enough to assert that P iff one knows
that P" (DeRose 2002: 180). And John Hawthorne concurs: "[t]he practice
of assertion is constituted by the rule/requirement that one assert something
only if one knows it" (Hawthorne 2004: 23).[3]

Now, a norm governing assertion is the rule that needs to be followed in order to offer a proper assertion, much like we have rules that
need to be followed in order to properly perform in certain competitive

---

[1] I am formulating the KNA as specifying only a necessary condition for proper assertion, though
some proponents of this norm, such as DeRose (2002) and perhaps Hawthorne (2004), take knowledge
to be both necessary and sufficient for proper assertion.

[2] See also his (1996).

[3] Other proponents of the KNA include Unger (1975), Brandom (1983 and 1994), Reynolds (2002),
Adler (2002), and Fricker (2006*b* and 2007). Cohen (2004) says that he is "not unsympathetic" to
the view.

sports.[4] Of course, as with many other norms, the KNA can be, and frequently is, violated. I may, for instance, assert that pollution is killing our local wildlife when I only suspect that this is the case. According to proponents of the KNA, in cases such as this—where an assertion is made in the absence of the corresponding knowledge—the asserter in question is properly subject to criticism. Thus, Hawthorne maintains that "if someone asserts *p*, it is proper to criticize that person if she does not know that *p*" (Hawthorne 2004: 23). In a similar spirit, Williamson holds that "asserting that P without knowing that P is doing something without having the authority to do it, like giving someone a command without having the authority to do so" (Williamson 2000: 257).

What these passages suggest is that there is an intimate connection between our assessment of asserters and our assessment of their assertions. In particular, *asserters* are in violation of a norm of assertion and are thereby *subject to criticism* when their *assertions* are *improper*.[5] An analogy with competitive basketball may make this point clear: suppose a player steps over the free throw line when making his foul shot. In such a case, there would be an intimate connection between our assessment of the player and our assessment of the free throw—we would, for instance, say that the player is subject to criticism for making an improper shot. There is, however, an important dissimilarity between the norms of assertion and the rules of games: the rules of most games are stipulated, and thus it is a relatively straightforward matter to tell whether a player is in violation of them—we can simply look it up in the rule book.[6] Because of this, there is no need to consult our intuitions regarding whether we feel that the players of the games in question are subject to criticism. In contrast, when theorizing about norms of assertion, we are often

[4] Those who espouse the KNA are typically silent on the nature of the "ought" or "should" operative in the norm of assertion. For instance, when introducing the KNA, Hawthorne writes, "I shall not try to tackle the thorny question as to the nature of the 'ought' that is in play here" (Hawthorne 2004: 23, fn.56). Even if this is a thorny issue, for present purposes the analogy with competitive sports may be illuminating: following the norm of assertion is necessary for proper assertion, just as following the rules of basketball is necessary for proper basketball playing.

[5] It should be noted, however, that asserters can be subject to criticism without being *blameworthy* in the assertions they offer, as happens when, for instance, an asserter unknowingly violates a norm of assertion. For more on these issues, see Section 4.5.

[6] Of course, there are aspects of determining whether a rule of a game has been violated that are not always a straightforward matter: referees, for instance, may disagree over factual matters of the play—did the player really step over the free throw line?—and over the interpretation of the rules of the game—does this rule apply in this particular context?

trying to figure out what the norms themselves are. Because of this, it is fairly common for those working on this topic to take our intuitions regarding whether we feel that asserters are subject to criticism as *evidence* for concluding that a norm of assertion has been violated. Thus, if an asserter seems appropriately subject to criticism *qua* asserter, then this is taken to be a good reason to conclude that a norm of assertion has been violated.

Considerations regarding the KNA have been quite heavily relied upon to provide support for TEP-N. For instance, Williamson says:

> It is...pointful to ask why we have such a speech act as assertion in our repertoire...No doubt we need a speech act something like assertion, to communicate beliefs, but could we not have done so just as well by using a speech act whose rule demanded less than knowledge?...One obvious answer is that we need assertion to transmit knowledge. In normal circumstances, when the hearer knows that the speaker asserted *p*, the speaker has no reputation for unreliability, and so on, a speaker who asserts *p* thereby puts a hearer in a position to know *p* if (and only if) the speaker knows *p*. (Williamson 2000: 267)[7]

In a similar spirit, Steven Reynolds writes:

> we require someone who testifies that *p* to know that *p*...What purpose does this requirement serve?...One purpose of requiring knowledge might be to encourage testimony that can produce knowledge in the recipients. It seems that if you tell me that *p*, I can thereby come to know that *p* only if you already know it. Requiring knowledge for testimony would thus probably produce more knowledge. (Reynolds 2002: 141–2)

And François Recanati maintains that "[i]t is a part of our prototype of assertion that if someone asserts that *p*, he knows that *p* and wishes the hearer to share his knowledge" (Recanati 1987: 183).

In addition to the support apparently derived for TEP-N from the KNA, such a norm has recently been invoked to directly argue against the cases I put forth in Chapter 2, such as CREATIONIST TEACHER. For instance, Jonathan Adler writes: "Examples like [CREATIONIST TEACHER] are problematic, however, since if the [speaker] lacks knowledge, then, in

---

[7] Immediately following the quoted passage above, Williamson adds, "(see Lackey 1999 for some qualifications)." As I argued in Chapter 3 in my discussion of Fricker, however, I doubt that this type of move will provide an adequate response to the range of counterexamples to TEP-N found in Chapter 2.

asserting, he violates the [KNA]" (Adler 2006). And Elizabeth Fricker argues that "the speech act of assertion is... governed by the norm: one should assert that P only if one knows that P... in asserting that P, the asserter gives her word that P entitles her audience to believe that P on the strength of her say-so, so that her audience may complain if P subsequently turns out to be false, or the asserter not to have known it to be true" (Fricker 2007: 104). Given this, combined with her further argument that the hearer in a testimonial exchange needs to have epistemic warrant for believing that a speaker wouldn't easily assert that *p* unless she knows that *p*, Fricker claims that cases like CREATIONIST TEACHER fail for the following reason: since part of a hearer's basis for a given testimonial belief is the "justified belief that the attester speaks from knowledge, then if that is false her own belief is based on a false premise, and so, even if true, is not itself knowledge" (Fricker 2007: 104).

In this chapter, I shall argue that the KNA is false. In particular, I shall show that there are cases in which a speaker asserts that *p* in the absence of knowing that *p* without being subject to criticism in any relevant sense, thereby showing that knowledge cannot be what is required for proper assertion. I shall then develop and defend an alternative norm of assertion—what I shall call the *Reasonable to Believe Norm of Assertion*, or the RTBNA—that not only avoids the problems afflicting the KNA, but also more fully and coherently accommodates our general intuitions about both asserters and their assertions. Given this, I shall conclude that support for TEP-N cannot be derived from considerations about proper assertion, both because the KNA is false and because the speakers in some of the relevant counterexamples, such as Stella in CREATIONIST TEACHER, in fact satisfy the RTBNA.[8]

---

[8] It should be noted that the speakers in some of my counterexamples to TEP-N, such as Bertha in CONSISTENT LIAR, do not satisfy the RTBNA. However, there are at least two reasons why this is not problematic. First, it is not at all clear why satisfying the norm of assertion is required in the first place for a speaker to impart testimonial knowledge (justification, warrant) to a hearer. For instance, Jonathan Adler in the above quotation presents it as obvious that violating the norm of assertion precludes a speaker from conveying knowledge to a hearer. But why? As I argued in Chapters 2 and 3, unreliable believers can nonetheless be reliable testifiers, and the latter is what is of import for the acquisition of testimonial knowledge. Second, even if, for whatever reason, one holds that the acquisition of testimonial knowledge requires that the speaker in question satisfy the norm of assertion, I provide cases where the RTBNA *is* satisfied, such as CREATIONIST TEACHER.

4.2 Two Initial Objections

Before turning to my own argument against the KNA, let me begin with two initial objections that may be raised to the view that knowledge is the norm of assertion. The first objection involves assertions that are not known by the asserter in question—because they are false, unjustified, or both—but are nevertheless appropriate given the circumstances of the situation. For instance, suppose that I, knowing that it is urgent for you to get to your destination, shout "That is your train" upon seeing a train approach the station. Despite my asserting this, however, I do not know this to be the case: I merely believe that it is very likely that it is your train. According to Williamson:

Such cases do not show that the knowledge rule is not the rule of assertion. They merely show that it can be overridden by other norms not specific to assertion. The other norms do not give me warrant to assert p, for to have such warrant is to satisfy the rule of assertion. (Williamson 2000: 256)

Presumably, proponents of the KNA would offer similar responses to countless other cases of this sort: I assert to my terminally ill friend, "I know that you will survive this," even though I am aware that all of the evidence suggests otherwise; I assert to my relative who is riddled with self-doubt, "I know that you will pass this exam," even though I am aware of her poor performances in the past, and so on.

The second initial objection to the KNA is grounded in cases like the following: "it is winter, and it looks exactly as it would if there were snow outside, but in fact that white stuff is not snow but foam put there by a film crew of whose existence I have no idea" (Williamson 2000: 257). Given that I have every reason to believe that the white stuff I see is snow, I assert that there is snow outside to my neighbor. Of course, since there is not in fact snow outside, my assertion is offered in the absence of the corresponding knowledge required by the KNA, thereby violating such a norm. Similarly, suppose that Wendy correctly sees the only real barn that, unbeknownst to her, is completely surrounded by barn facades and asserts to me, "There was a barn in the field we just passed," on this basis. In such a Gettier-type situation, the accidental truth of Wendy's belief prevents her from having the relevant knowledge, despite the fact that she has excellent evidence for holding the belief in question.

Notice that in both types of cases, the speaker in question *reasonably believes that she knows* the relevant proposition in question. Because of this, it may be argued that it is inappropriate to criticize such a speaker for asserting without knowing, thereby showing that the KNA is too strong a requirement for assertion. If this line of reasoning is correct, then the KNA should be replaced with a weaker norm, such as the following (hereafter, the *Reasonable Belief Norm of Assertion* or the RBNA):

> RBNA: One should assert that *p* only if one reasonably believes that one knows that *p*.

According to the RBNA, then, an asserter is not subject to criticism for asserting that which she reasonably believes she knows, even if infelicitous circumstances lead her to assert a proposition that as a matter of fact falls short of knowledge. Thus, the RBNA, unlike the KNA, is able to accommodate the intuitions above—namely, that I am behaving appropriately when I assert that there is snow outside and that Wendy is undeserving of criticism when she asserts that there was a barn in the field that was just passed. For in both cases, the speaker in question reasonably believes that she has the relevant knowledge even though she in fact fails to possess it.

Despite these intuitions, however, proponents of the KNA do not regard these sorts of cases as counterexamples to their thesis. For instance, regarding the assertion involving snow above, and the weaker RBNA that it supports, Williamson maintains:

On the [RBNA] account...my assertion "There is snow outside" satisfies the rule of assertion. Yet something is wrong with my assertion; neither [the Belief Norm of Assertion[9]] nor the [RBNA] account implies that [there is]. They can allow that something is wrong with my belief that I know that there is snow outside, for it is false, but that is another matter. The [BNA] and [RBNA] accounts lack the resources to explain why we regard the false assertion itself, not just the asserter, as faulty. (Williamson 2000: 262)[10]

---

[9] This is:

(BNA) One must assert that *p* only if one believes that one knows that *p*.

[10] Notice that this passage is not at odds with the connection discussed earlier between asserters being subject to criticism and improper assertions since Williamson is here talking about the faultiness of the asserter *qua* believer rather than *qua* asserter. Hence, there is no reason to doubt that faultiness *qua* asserter can be understood in terms of offering improper assertions.

So the *mere falsity* of the assertion—even if it in no way results from something for which the person in question is responsible—renders both the asserter and the assertion faulty. This faultiness, then, purportedly grounds the sense in which a central norm of assertion has been violated in cases involving highly reasonable but false belief, thereby resulting in the relevant asserter being deserving of criticism. Similar remarks presumably apply to assertions involving Gettierized beliefs: the fact that an assertion involves a belief that is only accidentally true renders the speaker deserving of criticism and her assertion improper relative to the goals of assertion.

But, surely, it may be argued, there is a clear sense in which speakers who assert reasonably believed falsehoods and Gettierized beliefs are *not* subject to criticism. For the faultiness of the assertions in such cases results from infelicitous circumstances, not from any sort of blameworthy behavior on the part of the asserters. Here is where Keith DeRose's distinction between *primary* and *secondary* propriety/impropriety is relevant:

As happens with other rules, a kind of secondary propriety/impropriety will arise with respect to [the KNA]. While those who assert appropriately (with respect to this rule) in a primary sense will be those who actually obey it, a speaker who broke this rule in a blameless fashion (one who asserted something she didn't know, but reasonably thought she did know) would in some secondary sense be asserting properly. (DeRose 2002: 180)

According to DeRose, then, if an act is governed by a given norm, primary propriety/impropriety is determined by whether the act actually conforms to the norm, and secondary propriety/impropriety is determined by whether the agent in question reasonably believes that the act conforms to the norm. This enables proponents of the KNA to explain how subjects who assert, for instance, reasonably believed falsehoods and Gettierized beliefs are behaving, in one sense, appropriately and, in another sense, inappropriately: such assertions are made in a blameless fashion and are thus proper in a secondary sense, despite the fact that they violate the norm of assertion and are thereby improper in a primary sense.

More could certainly be said both about these two initial objections and the responses offered by proponents of the KNA.[11] Nevertheless, I

---

[11] In fact, I will say much more about these objections and responses in Section 4.5, when I argue not only that the distinction between primary and secondary propriety/impropriety is spurious, but also that it is counterintuitive to regard assertions of reasonably believed falsehoods (particularly in evil

bring up these cases only to put them aside for now. The central type of counterexample I raise to the KNA will be unlike any of these cases and, as such, will not be subsumed by any of these responses.

4.3 Selfless Assertion

In this section, I shall present what I take to be the strongest type of counterexample to the KNA. It will involve a phenomenon that I shall call *selfless assertion*.

To begin, consider the following two cases, along with a slightly modified version of CREATIONIST TEACHER from Chapter 2:

RACIST JUROR: Martin was raised by racist parents in a very small-minded community and, for most of his life, he shared the majority of beliefs held by his friends and family members. After graduating from high school, he started taking classes at a local community college and soon began recognizing some of the causes and consequences of racism. During this time, Martin was called to serve on the jury of a case involving a black man on trial for raping a white woman. After hearing the relatively flimsy evidence presented by the prosecution and the strong exculpatory evidence offered by the defense, Martin is able to recognize that the evidence clearly does not support the conclusion that the defendant committed the crime of which he is accused.[12] In spite of this, however, he can't shake the feeling that the man on trial is guilty of raping the woman in question. Upon further reflection, Martin begins to suspect that such a feeling is grounded in the racism that he still harbors, and so he concludes that even if he can't quite come to believe that the defendant is innocent himself, he nonetheless has an obligation to present the case to others this way. Shortly after leaving the courthouse, Martin bumps into a childhood friend who asks him whether the "guy did it." Despite the fact that he does not believe, and hence does not know, that the defendant in question is innocent, Martin asserts, "No, the guy did not rape her."

DISTRAUGHT DOCTOR: Sebastian is an extremely well-respected pediatrician and researcher who has done extensive work studying childhood vaccines. He

demon worlds) and Gettierized beliefs as improper. But my main argument against the KNA shall not depend on cases involving these sorts of assertions, especially since it is clear that at least some proponents of this norm, such as Williamson, do not find either kind of assertion problematic for the KNA. (Whether such proponents are correct in finding such assertions unproblematic for their norm is, of course, another matter.)

[12] I am assuming that the defendant in question did not in fact commit the rape of which he is accused.

recognizes and appreciates that all of the scientific evidence shows that there is absolutely no connection between vaccines and autism.[13] However, shortly after his apparently normal 18-month-old daughter received one of her vaccines, her behavior became increasingly withdrawn and she was soon diagnosed with autism. While Sebastian is aware that signs of autism typically emerge around this age, regardless of whether a child received any vaccines, the grief and exhaustion brought on by his daughter's recent diagnosis cause him to abandon his previously deeply-held beliefs regarding vaccines. Today, while performing a well-baby check-up on one of his patients, the child's parents ask him about the legitimacy of the rumors surrounding vaccines and autism. Recognizing both that the current doubt he has towards vaccines was probably brought about through the emotional trauma of dealing with his daughter's condition and that he has an obligation to his patients to present what is most likely to be true, Sebastian asserts, "There is no connection between vaccines and autism." In spite of this, at the time of this assertion, it would not be correct to say that Sebastian himself believes or knows this proposition.

MODIFIED CREATIONIST TEACHER: Stella is a devoutly Christian fourth-grade teacher, and her religious beliefs are grounded in a deep faith that she has had since she was a very young child. Part of this faith includes a belief in the truth of creationism and, accordingly, a belief in the falsity of evolutionary theory. Despite this, Stella fully recognizes that there is an overwhelming amount of scientific evidence against both of these beliefs. Indeed, she readily admits that she is not basing her own commitment to creationism on evidence at all but, rather, on the personal faith that she has in an all-powerful Creator. Because of this, Stella does not think that religion is something that she should impose on those around her, and this is especially true with respect to her fourth-grade students. Instead, she regards her duty as a teacher to include presenting material that is best supported by the available evidence, which clearly includes the truth of evolutionary theory. As a result, while presenting her biology lesson today, Stella asserts to her students, "Modern-day *Homo sapiens* evolved from *Homo erectus*," though she herself neither believes nor knows this proposition to be true.[14]

Though there are some obvious differences among these cases, they are united in all being instances of what I earlier called selfless assertion. There

---

[13] Again, I am assuming that this is true, i.e., that there is no connection between vaccines and autism.

[14] As mentioned in note 24 from Chapter 2, a recent article in *The New York Times* (February 12, 2007, "Believing Scripture but Playing by Science's Rules") about a creationist who also just finished a geosciences PhD in paleontology makes clear that the sort of situation described in MODIFIED CREATIONIST TEACHER is not merely a thought experiment.

are three central components to this phenomenon: first, a subject, for purely non-epistemic reasons, does not believe (and hence does not know) that p;[15] second, despite this lack of belief, the subject is aware that p is very well-supported by all of the available evidence; and, third, because of this, the subject asserts that p without believing and, hence, without knowing that p.

The combination of these three features has the following result: a subject offers an assertion in the absence of knowledge and is not subject to criticism in any relevant sense. Indeed, in all of the above cases, the subject in question, *qua* asserter, is *appropriately subject to praise*: a racist juror, whose verdict can determine the future of an innocent defendant, is able to transcend his own racism and thereby offers an assertion that is both true and evidentially excellent; a well-respected pediatrician, whose patients depend on him for their health, is able to recognize his own emotional distress and thereby offers an assertion that is both true and clearly supported by all of the available evidence; and a fourth-grade teacher, whose students depend on her for their education, is able to put aside her own purely faith-based religious beliefs and thereby offers an assertion that is both true and evidentially impeccable. Moreover, in all of these cases, the subject offers the assertion in question precisely *because* he/she recognizes that it is supported by an overwhelming amount of excellent evidence, evidence

---

[15] It should be noted that the attribution of no belief that p in the above cases should not be understood as being inferred from the attribution of the belief that not-p. Indeed, in this respect, there seems to be an important difference between RACIST JUROR and DISTRAUGHT DOCTOR, on the one hand, and MODIFIED CREATIONIST TEACHER, on the other hand. For in the first two cases, it would not be accurate to describe the subjects in question as believing that not-p; rather, it would be most accurate to describe them as believing neither that p nor that not-p at the time of the assertion in question. For instance, where p in DISTRAUGHT DOCTOR is the proposition that there is no connection between vaccines and autism, it is not clear that Sebastian believes that not-p at the time of the relevant assertion, i.e., that Sebastian believes that there *is* a connection between vaccines and autism when he asserts that there is not such a connection. Indeed, the most plausible way to understand this case is that his daughter's recent diagnosis of autism leaves him feeling utterly confused, believing neither that p nor that not-p but withholding belief whether p. Given this, Sebastian's lack of belief that p cannot be inferred from the attribution of the belief that not-p since Sebastian does not necessarily believe that not-p. Thus, while it *is* accurate to describe Stella in MODIFIED CREATIONIST TEACHER as believing that not-p—i.e., she believes that Modern day *Homo sapiens* did not evolve from *Homo erectus* when she asserts that they have—this cannot be a *general* explanation of the attribution of no belief that p in the three cases of selfless assertion. (I am grateful to an anonymous referee for a question that led to the inclusion of this note.)

that the subject either cannot or will not allow to govern his/her own doxastic states.[16]

The upshot of these considerations, then, is that *it is a mistake to require proper assertion to pass through the doxastic states of the asserter.*[17] For, in cases of selfless assertion, even though the person in question may be subject to criticism *qua believer*, she is nonetheless subject to praise *qua asserter.*[18] For instance, while Martin is unable to prevent his residual racism from determining his *doxastic states* regarding the defendant's guilt, he does not allow it to govern his relevant *assertions*. Similarly, although Sebastian's grief and exhaustion directly affect his *states of believing* about the connection between vaccines and autism, he is able to overcome these impediments with respect to his *assertions*. Hence, one can properly assert that *p* in the absence of knowing that *p* without being subject to criticism as an

---

[16] Josh Parsons and Roger White both suggested to me that the subjects in cases of selfless assertion may be read as actually weakly believing the propositions that they are asserting. While I agree that there may be cases of this sort—where a subject believes that she doesn't believe that *p* but in fact weakly believes that *p*—it is also surely possible that there are subjects like those found in cases of selfless assertion. And this possibility suffices for my counterexamples to the KNA.

[17] Of course, this is not to say that proper assertion need not pass through *any* doxastic states of the asserter. For instance, in cases of selfless assertion, the asserter in question has beliefs about the evidence supporting the proposition being asserted. The point is, rather, that proper assertion need not pass through doxastic states sharing the same content as the assertion being offered.

[18] It is of interest to note that cases of selfless assertion undermine even substantially weaker conceptions of assertion, such as the belief view endorsed by Kent Bach and Robert Harnish (1979)—one must assert that *p* only if one believes that *p*—and the justification view defended by Jonathan Kvanvig (forthcoming)—one must assert that *p* only if one justifiedly believes that *p*. Such cases may also pose a problem for both Robert Stalnaker's (1978) model in which, generally, what is asserted will be what the asserter in question believes, and will result in the transferring of the speaker's belief to the relevant hearer(s), and for Bernard Williams's conception of insincere assertion, which can be found in the following passage: "sincere assertions do not necessarily have the aim of informing the hearer; but insincere assertions do have the aim of misinforming the hearer. In the primary case, they aim to misinform the hearer about the state of things, the truth of what the speaker asserts. Derivatively, they may aim to misinform the hearer merely about the speaker's beliefs; the speaker may know that the hearer will not believe what he falsely asserts but he wants her to believe that he himself believes it" (Williams 2002: 73–4). Now, while the speakers in cases of selfless assertion assert what they themselves do not believe—and thus qualify as offering insincere assertions on Williams's view—they do not *aim to misinform* their hearers in either the primary or the derivative senses discussed above. For instance, Stella clearly does not aim to misinform her students about the evolution of *Homo sapiens* from *Homo erectus*, nor is it plausible that she aims for her students to believe that she herself believes this. In fact, she may positively aim for her students to believe merely that the evidence overwhelmingly supports the truth of evolutionary theory, regardless of what she herself believes. Thus, Stella may aim for them to form no relevant beliefs about what she herself believes. In such a case, contrary to Williams's view, Stella insincerely asserts that *p* to her students with no relevant aim to misinform her hearers regarding *p*.

asserter in any sense, thereby showing that a norm of assertion has not been violated.[19] The KNA is, therefore, false.[20]

4.4 Objections and Replies

In this section, I shall consider the most compelling objections to my arguments against the KNA, and show each to be unsuccessful in achieving its desired end.

First, it may be argued that the statements in question in the three cases *do not qualify as genuine assertions*. In particular, one may claim that an assertion requires that the asserter in question "speak for herself" and therefore regard the proffered statement as somehow being truly her own

---

[19] It should be noted that Williamson distinguishes between *reasonable assertion*, in which an asserter is blameless in asserting that *p*, and *warranted assertion*, in which an asserter has the epistemic authority to assert that *p*. Given this distinction, could Williamson argue that asserters in cases of selfless assertion offer reasonable and therefore blameless assertions that are nonetheless unwarranted? (I am grateful to Ted Poston for raising this point.) By way of response to this objection, notice that the asserters in all three cases have enough epistemic support for the propositions in question such that they would know them were they to believe them. Indeed, asserters in cases of selfless assertion can even be experts in their fields and so they are often in a better epistemic position relative to the propositions in question than non-experts are who in fact know such propositions. For instance, Sebastian in DISTRAUGHT DOCTOR is an extremely well-respected pediatrician and researcher who has done extensive work studying childhood vaccines, and so he is clearly in a better epistemic position with respect to the evidence supporting the lack of connection between vaccines and autism than a non-expert is. Because of this, it is not at all plausible to claim that a non-expert on vaccines *would have the epistemic authority* to assert that there is not a connection between vaccines and autism *but Sebastian would not*; accordingly, there is no room for plausibly arguing that Sebastian's assertion is reasonable or blameless but unwarranted. Hence, Williamson's distinction between reasonable and warranted assertion cannot be invoked to save the KNA from cases of selfless assertion.

[20] An anonymous referee suggested to me that cases of selfless assertion may instead show that belief is not a necessary condition of knowledge. While it obviously lies outside the scope of this paper to defend the thesis that belief is a necessary condition for knowledge, let me say that such a claim is nearly universally accepted in the epistemological literature. Indeed, even Williamson (2000: 3), who argues that knowledge cannot be analyzed in terms of belief—i.e., belief cannot be a conjunct of a non-circular necessary and sufficient condition for knowledge—nevertheless seems to hold that belief is an insufficient but necessary condition for knowledge. He says that, "If believing *p* is conceptualized as being in a state sufficiently like knowing *p* 'from the inside' in the relevant respects, then belief is necessary for knowledge, since knowing *p* is sufficiently like itself in every respect, even though knowledge is conceptually prior to belief" (Williamson 2000: 3). The account of belief Williamson goes on to develop, according to which "believing *p* is, roughly, treating *p* as if one knew *p*" (Williamson 2000: 47), is precisely of this sort.

In any case, my thesis here can simply be read in the following conditional form: *if* belief is a necessary condition for knowledge, then the KNA is false (as well as the BNA and the RBNA). This conditional form of the argument, however, doesn't weaken my conclusion since all of the proponents of the KNA discussed in this paper accept the antecedent.

rather than, for instance, the general medical profession's or the scientific community's. Since the speakers in instances of selfless assertion do not personally identify with their proffered statements, it may be concluded that they are not therefore offering genuine assertions.[21] Hence, the above cases would not be counterexamples to the KNA.[22]

By way of response to this objection, notice that the only element that distinguishes the statements in cases of selfless assertion from those that would satisfy the KNA is the lack of belief on the part of the speaker. For, in all three cases, the statement in question is an ordinary declarative sentence that is not only non-accidentally true, it is also so well supported epistemically that it would be known if only it were believed. Because of this, the objection that the statements in the above cases are not instances of genuine assertion boils down to the thesis that S must believe that *p* in order to genuinely assert that *p*. But then it follows that it wouldn't be possible to assert a lie, which is clearly the wrong result. For telling a lie is a paradigmatic instance of an assertion that, though genuine, is in violation of the norms governing assertion. Thus, while a person who asserts that *p* with the intention to deceive is undoubtedly subject to criticism, that she didn't really offer an assertion doesn't seem to be among her problems.

A second objection that one may raise to cases of selfless assertion is that, because the relevant asserter in such cases is asserting what he or she does not truly believe, there is a clear sense in which he or she is *lying*. Accordingly, such an asserter is manipulating, cheating, or otherwise deceiving the hearer in question and is thereby subject to criticism *qua asserter*. For instance, in asserting that the defendant did not commit the rape in question, Martin is presenting this to his childhood friend as indeed representing his own view on the issue. Likewise, in asserting that there is no connection between vaccines and autism, Sebastian is presenting this to the parents of his patient as truly being his own considered view of the matter. Because such assertions do not in fact correctly represent the beliefs of the asserters, they are instances of lying and, as such, constitute clear violations of a norm of assertion.

---

[21] It should be noted that this response is not even *prima facie* plausible in RACIST JUROR, since there is no broader community that could plausibly be the bearer of Martin's assertion about the innocence of the defendant.

[22] I am grateful to Matt McGrath for raising this objection.

To see that this objection is unpersuasive, notice first that in cases of selfless assertion, there is absolutely no intention on the part of the asserter to deceive or otherwise mislead. Indeed, quite the contrary is true—the asserter in question *positively intends to not deceive or mislead her hearer* and, as a result, asserts what she herself does not believe. This is relevant to whether it is appropriate to characterize instances of selfless assertion as genuine lies. For instance, according to Augustine's well-known account of lying in *De mendacio*, a lie requires both (a) S asserting that *p* where S does not herself believe that *p*, and (b) S asserting that *p* with the deliberate intention to deceive.[23] Moreover, Augustine claims that, "[t]he objectionable feature of lying is the desire to deliberately mislead in what one says," not the fact that one asserts what one does not truly believe.[24] If Augustine is correct, then, the asserters in all three cases would not be lying since they would fail to satisfy condition (b). Indeed, in cases of selfless assertion, the asserter in question recognizes that she may not be a reliable believer relative to the topic at hand and, because of this, deliberately satisfies (a) in order to fail (b), that is, she asserts what she herself does not believe in order to avoid deceiving her hearers.[25] But even if one does not wish to embrace Augustine's general conception of lying, it should surely be

---

[23] In a similar spirit, James Van Cleve says, "You are not a liar just because you say something false. Lying is saying what you *believe* false in an effort to deceive another" (Van Cleve 2006: 51, original emphasis).

[24] *De mendacio* 3.3.

[25] It may be objected that if a speaker is aware both (I) that all of the available evidence supports that *p* and (II) that she nonetheless fails to believe that *p*, then such a speaker must accept that her attitude of disbelief toward *p* is arational—a conclusion that a subject may not be able to coherently or rationally accept about herself.

By way of response to this objection, notice that it is not necessarily true that a speaker must accept that her attitude of disbelief toward *p* is arational in light of her awareness of (I) and (II). Consider, for instance, Stella's situation in MODIFIED CREATIONIST TEACHER. Stella's belief in evolutionary theory is entirely grounded in her own personal faith-based religious beliefs, which she may regard as being disconnected from evidential constraints. But Stella may nonetheless hold the further belief that it is *sometimes rational to believe propositions for non-evidential reasons*, particularly those that concern religion. In particular, Stella may reject the presumed connection between evidence and rationality, believing instead that rationality requires that we sometimes hold beliefs for non-evidential reasons (e.g., for reasons grounded in faith or spirituality).

Alternatively, Stella may not reject the presumed connection between evidence and rationality and may therefore regard her disbelief toward *p* as both non-evidential and arational, but may nonetheless believe that there are grounds for beliefs deeper than—or at least comparable to—those provided by evidence or reason. In particular, she may regard beliefs grounded in faith or spirituality as arational but not thereby deficient or defective. Either way, then, an awareness that (I) and (II) are true of one's current state does not necessarily lead to a conclusion about oneself that one cannot coherently or rationally accept.

granted that, at the very least, there are two radically different kinds of lying: those involving the satisfaction of both (a) and (b) and those involving the satisfaction of only (a). It should be further granted that only asserters who lie in the first sense are necessarily subject to criticism and thus in violation of a norm of assertion. For there is simply no reasonable sense in which a subject who recognizes that she is an unreliable believer relative to a given proposition and, so as to make it more likely that her hearer will form a belief that is best supported by the available evidence, asserts what she fails to believe herself, is subject to criticism *qua* asserter.

A third and related objection that may be raised to the arguments from the previous section is this: suppose that the hearer in each of the cases above were to ask the asserter in question whether he or she believes or knows the proposition asserted. Wouldn't the hearer *feel* cheated or deceived upon learning that the answer to these questions is no? For instance, wouldn't the parents of Sebastian's patient feel misled or otherwise manipulated when their pediatrician admits that he does not himself believe or know that that there is no connection between vaccines and autism? Similarly, wouldn't the students in Stella's class feel cheated upon learning that their teacher does not herself believe in the truth of evolutionary theory? These plausible reactions to the asserters in question, one may argue, strongly suggest that a norm of assertion has indeed been violated in cases of selfless assertion.[26]

When all of the relevant details of the cases of selfless assertion are considered, however, it becomes clear that these are not the reactions most likely to be had by the hearers in question. For instance, surely the childhood friend of Martin would not prefer that he assert what he truly believes about the defendant's guilt, for this would result in Martin *offering an assertion based purely on racism*. Similarly, the parents of Sebastian's patient would not desire that he assert what he truly believes about vaccines and autism, since this would amount to Sebastian *offering an assertion caused by the emotional grief, distress, and exhaustion of his daughter's newly diagnosed autism*. And the students in Stella's class would not want her to assert what she truly believes about evolutionary theory, as this would lead to Stella *offering an assertion grounded in her own purely faith-based personal relationship with God*. Rather, in each of these cases, the hearers in question would prefer that

---

[26] I am grateful to Timothy Williamson for pressing this objection.

the speakers offer assertions that are best supported by the evidence, which is precisely what they do. Indeed, if the hearers learned the reasons why the asserters do not have the beliefs in question, they would clearly not feel cheated but grateful that the asserters have fitted their assertions to the evidence rather than to their confused doxastic states.

A final point worth emphasizing about the central argument above is that it relies on only three claims regarding knowledge and assertion: first, that knowledge requires belief; second, that one can offer an assertion in the absence of the corresponding belief; and, third, that some assertions offered in the absence of the corresponding belief are proper. The first two claims are accepted by nearly every available theory of knowledge and assertion and thus do not depend on any particular view in epistemology or the philosophy of language. And the third claim, grounded in the above three cases, is intuitively compelling. Hence, it should be widely accepted that such cases of selfless assertion provide convincing counterexamples to the KNA.

4.5 The Spuriousness of Secondary Propriety/Impropriety

If the KNA fails, then what is the central norm of assertion? By way of answering this question, I shall begin by taking seriously the widely accepted thesis that there is a very intimate connection between violating norms and deserving criticism. In particular, when a person is subject to criticism *qua* asserter, I shall regard this as being very good evidence for concluding that a norm of assertion has been violated.

But, one might immediately ask, doesn't DeRose's distinction between primary and secondary propriety/impropriety provide us with a way to reject this thesis? For recall that if an act is governed by a given norm, primary propriety/impropriety is determined by whether the act actually conforms to the norm, while secondary propriety/impropriety is determined by whether the agent in question reasonably believes that the act conforms to the norm. Given this, an asserter may be deserving of (secondary) criticism even if her act conforms to the norm in question, and may be behaving appropriately (in a secondary sense) even if her act violates such a norm.

Indeed, this is precisely how Matthew Weiner recently argues on behalf of the following competitor to the KNA (hereafter, the *Truth Norm of Assertion*, or the TNA):

TNA: One should assert that *p* only if it is true that *p*.

Now, it may be argued that the TNA is obviously far too weak to be the central norm of assertion. For what if one truly asserts that *p* on the basis of extremely poor evidence, e.g., one asserts a lucky guess or a correctly believed product of wishful thinking? Surely, one may claim, the asserter in these instances would be legitimately subject to criticism despite satisfying the TNA. Given the TNA's inability to account for the impropriety of these kinds of correct assertions, it may be concluded that more than mere truth is needed for the central norm of assertion.

Not so fast, says the proponent of secondary propriety and impropriety. Even if, according to the TNA, an asserted lucky guess turns out to be primarily proper, it can nonetheless be secondarily improper and thereby subject to criticism. As Weiner writes, "if assertion is governed by the truth norm, an assertion is secondarily improper if the speaker does not have reason to believe that it is true" (Weiner 2005: 236). Hence, because you do not have reason to believe that your lucky guess is true, it is improper in a secondary sense to offer the corresponding assertion. Similarly, if you have reason to believe that which is in fact false, your assertion of this falsehood is secondarily proper despite being primarily improper.

In what follows, however, I shall argue that the notions of secondary propriety and impropriety are spurious: either a speaker is behaving appropriately and is not subject to criticism *qua* asserter, in which case she has not violated a norm of assertion, or she is behaving inappropriately and is subject to criticism *qua* asserter, in which case she has violated a norm of assertion. There is simply no room for acts being secondarily proper or improper.

Let us begin with the notion of secondary propriety. Notice, first, that norms of assertion are the rules that need to be followed in order to offer a proper assertion, much like we have rules that need to be followed in order to properly perform in certain competitive sports. So, for instance, if Toby crosses over the line of scrimmage when making a forward pass, he may rightly be criticized for failing to play professional football by the rules. In other words, this particular pass is improperly made because it does not follow the rules governing professional football. Suppose further, however, that Toby's contact lens had earlier fallen out during the game, and so his impaired vision causes him to reasonably believe that his forward pass was made without crossing over the line of scrimmage. Would we then say that Toby's pass is secondarily proper, despite the fact that it is primarily improper? No. Given the rules of professional football, there is no sense in which Toby's pass is *proper*. Rather, the impaired vision brought on by the loss of his contact lens provides Toby with an excellent *excuse* for making an *improper* pass. Otherwise put, while his particular circumstances render his violation of the rules of the game *blameless*, Toby's pass is nonetheless one that *shouldn't have been made* in order to successfully play professional football. This is evidenced by the fact that no referee, upon hearing the story about his contact lens, would allow Toby another chance at his pass.

Secondary impropriety is similarly misguided when applied to the rules for performing in competitive sports. Suppose, for instance, that because of Toby's impaired sight, he cannot see precisely where the line of scrimmage is. Despite this, he makes a lucky guess as to its exact whereabouts and, on this basis, successfully makes his forward pass without crossing over the line. Would we regard his pass as secondarily improper because, even though Toby did not in fact cross over the line of scrimmage, he did not have reason to believe this? Once again, the answer is clearly no. Toby, *qua* professional football player, neither behaved in ways that he shouldn't have nor did he violate any of the rules of the game. Moreover, there is no reasonable sense in which he is subject to criticism. For, even if the players on the opposing team later found out that Toby did not know whether he crossed over the line when making his pass, none of them would rightly regard him as somehow cheating. They may, to be sure, regard him as failing to be fully praiseworthy for making the pass in question, but this is a different matter. Again, this is borne out by the fact that his team's field position would still include the relevant yards, even if the referee learned about the circumstances involving Toby's contact lens.

Approaching this issue from a slightly different angle, notice that with respect to a given act, α, the question may be asked: relative to the goal of proper ϕing, should the agent have performed α or not? If the answer here is affirmative, then there is good reason to conclude that α is in accordance with the norms governing proper ϕing. But then what room is there for α being improper in some secondary sense? Perhaps the act fails to be particularly *praiseworthy* or *deserving of full credit*—as when Toby luckily makes his forward pass without crossing over the line of scrimmage—but this does not render it *improper* in any reasonable sense. If, however, the answer to the above question is negative, i.e., the agent should not have performed α, then there is good reason to conclude that α violates the norms for proper ϕing. But then, again, what room is there for the act being proper in some secondary sense? The agent may be *blameless* or have an excellent *excuse* for performing such an improper act—as when Toby crosses over the line of scrimmage because of his missing contact lens—but this does not render the act *proper* in any reasonable sense.

Notice that similar considerations apply in many other domains. For instance, suppose that a moral theorist provides the following account of moral rightness:

MR: Action A is morally right only if A possesses feature x.

Suppose further that cases are presented in which an action fails to possess feature x, but the agent in question reasonably believes that the action possesses this feature. The familiar response in moral theory is not to argue that there are two kinds of moral rightness—primary and secondary—but, rather, to distinguish moral rightness from a different property, such as excusability or blamelessness. Thus, the standard move for a conseqentialist is not to classify actions that an agent reasonably believes will bring about the best consequences but actually fail to do so as secondarily right; instead, such actions are regarded as wrong, but excusable or blameless. Similarly, suppose that an epistemologist provides the following account of knowledge:

K: Belief B is an instance of knowledge only if B possesses feature x.

Again, the familiar response to cases in which a belief fails to possess feature x but the subject in question reasonably believes that the belief possesses this feature is not to argue that there are two kinds of knowledge—primary and secondary—but to distinguish knowledge from excusable or blameless belief. Thus, true beliefs that are believed to be reliably formed but are in fact unreliably formed are not taken by reliabilists as instances of secondary knowledge, but as obvious cases of beliefs that are blamelessly held but not knowledge. To invoke a primary/secondary distinction in these sorts of cases when familiar concepts, like excusability or blamelessness, suffice is to obscure the relevant issues rather than to resolve the disagreements that motivated such a move in the first place.

Applying these considerations to the practice of assertion, it should be clear that the notions of secondary propriety and impropriety are spurious. For if S asserts that *p* in violation of a norm of assertion, then, relative to being a proper asserter, S *should not have made the assertion in question*. If S asserts that *p* because S reasonably believes that asserting that *p* satisfies the norm of assertion even though it in fact does not, then S may be blameless or have a good excuse for offering an improper assertion. But this does not make either the assertion or the asserter proper in any reasonable (or secondary) sense. Accordingly, if S asserts that *p* in accordance with a norm of assertion, then, relative to being a proper asserter, S *should have made, or was permitted to make, such an assertion*. If S does not have reason to believe that her assertion satisfies the norm of assertion, then S may not deserve full praise or credit for offering a proper assertion. But this does not render either the assertion or the asserter improper in any clear (or secondary) sense.

The above considerations show, therefore, that Weiner cannot invoke the notions of secondary propriety and impropriety in an effort to make the TNA more plausible. Given that the TNA requires only truth for assertion, its proponents must accordingly live with the counterintuitive conse-quences that follow from such a norm. There are two dimensions to such consequences that I take to be the most debilitating. On the one hand, truth is not sufficient for proper assertion, and thus the TNA is far too weak a norm to govern assertion. For, on such a view, lucky guesses and correctly believed products of wishful thinking turn out to be proper. If I, for instance, correctly assert that the President is currently in Paris merely because I make a lucky guess, then, according to the TNA, this turns out to be a legitimate assertion that is not subject to criticism. Or if I truly assert that I got the job for which I applied merely because I convinced myself of this through wishful thinking, then such a norm regards my proffered assertion as proper. But surely both kinds of assertions are clearly improper; indeed, it is precisely because of the obvious illegitimacy of such assertions that Weiner invoked the notion of secondary impropriety in the first place.

On the other hand, truth is not necessary for proper assertion, and thus the TNA is far too strong a norm to govern assertion. For, on such a view, assertions offered by our twins in evil demon worlds[27] and imprecise assertions turn out to be improper. For instance, if my twin, who is the unfortunate inhabitant of an evil demon world, acquires on the basis of experiences indistinguishable from my own the same sorts of beliefs as me, then her beliefs should be regarded as reasonable.[28] Given this, my twin also should not be subject to criticism for offering the same assertions as me, even if the truth value of our respective assertions varies significantly. According to the TNA, however, while I may be acting in perfect accordance with the norm of assertion, my twin is consistently violating such a norm and is therefore open to constant criticism. This seems like the wrong result.[29] Similar considerations apply with respect to imprecise assertions. For instance, suppose that you ask me how tall I am and I assert that I am 5 feet, 4 inches. Strictly speaking, however, suppose that I am 5 feet, 3 $7/8$ inches. My assertion about my height, then, violates the TNA since it is false that I am 5 feet, 4 inches tall. Similar cases abound: the weatherman asserts that there is a 40 percent chance of rain tomorrow, when in fact there is only a 39.96 percent chance; a friend asserts that she is 28, when in fact she is 27 years, 364 days old; a contractor asserts that the room is 10 x 11 feet, when in fact it is 9 feet, 11 inches by 10 feet, 11 inches; a scientist asserts that the temperature of the water is 33.65 degrees Celsius when in fact it is 33.65432 degrees Celsius; a friend asserts that it is 6:00 p.m. when in fact it is 6:01 p.m., and so on. In all of these cases, the assertions in question are false because they are not absolutely precise, but they nonetheless seem perfectly proper.[30]

Now, the proponent of the TNA may respond here that imprecise assertions *are* improper, but the norm governing assertion is overridden by other norms in such cases. This would make imprecise assertions

---

[27] For a discussion of the original new evil demon problem, see Cohen and Lehrer (1983).

[28] This assumes, of course, that the way that I form beliefs in the actual world results in them being reasonable.

[29] As mentioned earlier, the KNA has the very same problem with assertions involving reasonably believed falsehoods (and Gettierized beliefs as well). Indeed, DeRose introduces the distinction between primary and secondary propriety/impropriety as a way of accommodating the intuition that there is clearly something proper about assertions of this sort. But given that this distinction is spurious, the intuitive correctness of these assertions cannot be accommodated within the framework of the KNA. Hence, they pose further problems for the KNA, in addition to those deriving from cases of selfless assertion.

[30] For these reasons, then, I disagree with Williamson's suggestion in the following passage that the mere falsity of an assertion renders it improper: "[some rival accounts] lack the resources to explain why we regard the false assertion itself, not just the asserter, as faulty" (2000: 262).

similar to Williamson's case of asserting, "That is your train," when I merely believe that it is very likely that it is your train. But notice: in Williamson's case, urgent practical circumstances explain why one might offer the stronger assertion, rather than the weaker "That might be your train." In the circumstances involving imprecise assertions, however, there need not be other relevant factors that explain why more precise assertions are not offered. When a friend tells me the time while we are taking a stroll, for instance, there need not be any practical circumstances that prevent her from saying 6:01 p.m. or 6:00:30 p.m., rather than 6:00 p.m. Moreover, even if imprecise assertions could be treated as similar to Williamson's train example, it is extremely counterintuitive for a norm of assertion to regard such a vast number of ordinary assertions—ones that cut across many different topics, contexts, and asserters—as improper. Yet this is precisely what the proponent of the TNA is forced to do.

The upshot of these considerations, then, is that those who appeal to the secondary propriety and impropriety distinction cannot have it both ways. If proponents of the KNA and the TNA wish to divorce satisfaction of a given norm from what the subject reasonably believes to be the case about satisfaction of the norm, then they cannot sneak the intuitive mileage of substantively different norms—ones that do not embrace such a divorce—through the back door of secondary propriety and impropriety. According to their views, even if one reasonably believes one's assertion is true or known, the fact that it is not true or known renders one in violation of the norm of assertion and, thereby, leaves one subject to criticism. If proponents of the KNA and TNA find this consequence so counterintuitive that invoking secondary propriety and impropriety seems necessary, this is probably good reason to conclude that the norms themselves are false.

4.6 The Reasonable to Believe Norm of Assertion

We have now seen, first, that cases of selfless assertion show that the KNA is false and, second, that the notions of secondary propriety and impropriety cannot be invoked to vindicate this norm—or the TNA—from the problems facing it. What, then, is the correct norm of assertion?

In response to this question, I propose the following *Reasonable to Believe Norm of Assertion* (hereafter, the RTBNA):

> RTBNA: One should assert that *p* only if (i) it is reasonable for one to believe that *p*, and (ii) if one asserted that *p*, one would assert that *p* at least in part because it is reasonable for one to believe that *p*.[31]

There are several points to notice about the RTBNA. First, the RTBNA does *not* include for proper assertion the condition that one *reasonably believe* that *p*, but only the importantly weaker requirement that it is *reasonable for one to believe* that *p*. This is crucial to the RTBNA's ability to countenance cases of selfless assertion as instances of proper assertion. For in such cases, the asserter in question not only fails to know that *p* when it is being asserted, she also fails to believe—reasonably or otherwise—that *p*; nevertheless, she has substantial evidence indicating that such a proposition should be believed, thereby rendering it reasonable for her to believe that *p*. Hence, cases of selfless assertion clearly satisfy the RTBNA.[32]

The second point to notice about the RTBNA is that, though it does not require that the subject reasonably believe that *p* when it is being asserted, it subsumes cases in which the subject does reasonably believe that *p*. For instance, my twin in an evil demon world who falsely but reasonably asserts everything that I do in the actual world satisfies the RTBNA because her reasonably believing that *p* entails that it is reasonable for her to believe that *p*. So, whereas stronger norms that require belief on the part of the asserter incorrectly exclude some cases of proper assertion that the weaker RTBNA captures—such as those involving selfless assertion—the RTBNA is able to include all of the relevant cases that stronger norms requiring reasonable belief subsume.

The third feature of the RTBNA to notice is the inclusion of (ii), i.e., the requirement that, if one asserted that *p*, one would assert that *p* at least in part because it is reasonable for one to believe that *p*. This is included to prevent cases from qualifying as proper assertions where, though it is

---

[31] Though clause (ii) of the RTBNA subsumes clause (i), I leave them expressed separately so as to make it clear that there are two necessary conditions for proper assertion, one requiring reasonableness and another requiring that the assertion in question be at least partly grounded in this reasonableness.

[32] It is of interest to note that cases of selfless assertion do not satisfy the RBNA (one should assert that *p* only if one reasonably believes that one knows that *p*) discussed in Section 4.2 of this chapter.

reasonable to believe that p, a speaker's asserting that p is, or would be were she to assert that p, entirely disconnected from this reasonableness.[33] For instance, consider the following:

ALARMIST: Gertrude has an overwhelming amount of excellent evidence available to her for believing that Oliver is the person who forgot to turn the alarm on before leaving the bank that employs both of them. She doesn't believe that this is the case, however, because she has romantic feelings for Oliver that cloud her rational judgment about his behavior. Nonetheless, when Gertrude is questioned by her supervisor about the alarm, she asserts "Oliver forgot to turn it on," merely to avoid any suspicion that she was involved in this oversight.

Now, while Gertrude has substantial evidence for believing that Oliver forgot to turn the alarm on before leaving their place of employment, she asserts that this is the case merely to avoid suspicion that she was involved in such an error. The RTBNA provides the correct result here: even though it is reasonable for Gertrude to believe the proposition she asserts, she does not assert it even in part because of this reasonableness and, hence, her assertion is improper.[34]

It is worth noting that competing norms, such as the TNA and the KNA, face similar problems. In particular, though it may be true that p or S might know that p, S's assertion that p may be entirely disconnected from this truth or knowledge. For instance, Hilda may have good reason to truly believe that her brother recently traveled to San Francisco—he told her about his vacation there a few weeks ago—but her daughter's recent trip to the emergency room may have caused her to temporarily forget this fact. Thus, when she asserts to a nurse in the hospital that she knows someone who just came back from California, merely to make small talk and to get her mind off her daughter's illness, her assertion both satisfies the TNA and is secondarily proper in Weiner's sense, i.e., it is true and she has reason to believe that it is true. But, given that the crisis in Hilda's life caused her to forget this reason, the proffering of such an assertion is

---

[33] This additional requirement may be understood as being analogous to the clauses epistemologists add to their analyses of knowledge in an attempt to rule out Gettier cases—i.e., cases of accidentally true, yet justified, belief. In both cases, it is not enough that the belief/assertion is true, justified, or reasonable—there must also be the proper relation between them.

[34] It is worth making explicit that cases of selfless assertion will clearly satisfy both clauses of the RTBNA since a central component of such a phenomenon is that the speaker asserts that p *because* it is very well supported by all of the available evidence.

entirely disconnected from its truth, thereby rendering it no different than a lucky guess. Similar considerations can be adduced regarding cases where a speaker knows a given proposition and has reason to believe that she knows it, but is temporarily distraught and forgetful and asserts this proposition for reasons that are entirely disconnected from this knowledge. Since the obvious illegitimacy of asserting lucky guesses is what motivated the introduction of secondary impropriety in the first place, proponents of the TNA and the KNA should include a clause requiring that, if one asserted that p, one would assert that p at least in part because it is true/known that p.

Fourth, the RTBNA derives support from the way in which criticisms of assertions are commonly offered. For instance, we frequently say, "Why would you believe that?" or "You don't have reason to think that." Of course, a proponent of the KNA may respond that we also criticize assertions by accusing speakers of lacking knowledge. We may say "How do you know that?" or "You couldn't know that" when a speaker offers an assertion that is deemed improper. But implicit in these challenges is the expectation that the asserter will respond with some *reason for believing* that the proposition asserted is true. A natural response to "How do you know that North Korea tested a nuclear bomb?" is "I read it in the *The New York Times*." Here, I am offering my reason for believing that such a nuclear bomb was tested in response to a question challenging my knowledge. Thus, the central way in which assertions are criticized—where the speaker is accused of lacking reasons for believing the proposition in question—is exactly what the RTBNA predicts.

Fifth, the notion of "reasonableness" operative in the RTBNA should not be understood in a purely subjective manner. That is to say, the mere fact that a subject regards it as reasonable to believe that p does not make it reasonable to believe that p. In order for it to be reasonable for a subject to believe that p in the sense required by the RTBNA, there needs to be epistemic support available to the subject that makes it in the actual world, as a matter of objective fact, likely that it is true that p. The clause "in the actual world" not only enables the RTBNA to countenance the assertions of our twins in evil demon worlds as proper, but it also captures the intuition that what is of import is the connection between epistemic support and likely truth when things are working as they should. How much support is required here?

One way of understanding the RTBNA is as follows: it is reasonable for S to believe that *p* only if S has epistemic support that is adequate for S's knowing that *p* were S to truly believe that *p*. Otherwise put, minus belief and truth, the RTBNA would require everything epistemic that the KNA does.[35] While this strategy avoids the counterexamples involving selfless assertion in a way that would probably be most amenable to proponents of the KNA, it is not the one that I favor. For such a view has the consequence that all assertions involving Gettierized beliefs are improper and, accordingly, that such asserters are thereby subject to criticism. So, for example, if I assert "There is a barn" on the basis of my visual experience of seeing a barn, then the fact that unbeknownst to me it is surrounded by barn facades renders my assertion improper on this reading of the RTBNA. If one finds this consequence unattractive—as I do—then the threshold of epistemic support needed for reasonableness operative in the RTBNA should be at least slightly lower than what is required for knowledge.[36] How much lower? Though I shall not here attempt a decisive answer to this question, a plausible answer is that the notion of reasonableness in the RTBNA requires as much epistemic support as is needed for *justified belief*. More precisely: it is reasonable for S to believe that *p* only if S has epistemic support that is adequate for S's justifiedly believing that *p* were S to believe that *p* on that basis.[37]

---

[35] Indeed, if the proponent of the KNA wishes to avoid only my counterexamples involving selfless assertion, the RTBNA could include truth as well. But, of course, our twins deceived by evil demons would then be subject to criticism for offering the same assertions as we do in the actual world, which seems to be the wrong result.

[36] If a proponent of the KNA does not find such a consequence counterintuitive—as Williamson's position seems to be (in conversation)—then the threshold of epistemic support needed for reasonableness operative in the RTBNA can be read as being as high as what is needed for knowledge.

[37] In his (2005), Matthew Weiner proposes counterexamples to the KNA that, if successful, would pose a similar problem for the RTBNA. He writes: "Take the following case of prediction: Captain Jack Aubrey has had long experience of naval combat against the French Navy. He and young Lieutenant Pullings have been watching French ships maneuver off Mauritius all day. At 2 p.m., Aubrey says to Pullings,

(3) The French will wait until nightfall to attack.

Consider also the following case of retrodiction: Sherlock Holmes and Doctor Watson are brought to a crime scene. Holmes scans the scene and says (truthfully, as it turns out),

(4) This is the work of Professor Moriarty! It has the mark of his fiendish genius.

Holmes, at this point, has not found any evidence (in the criminal rather than epistemological sense) incriminating Professor Moriarty, but he is sticking his neck out based on his sense of what Moriarty's crimes are like ....These cases pose a problem for the knowledge account. They seem to be proper assertions in the absence of knowledge; the speakers' grounds for belief fall short of those necessary for knowledge, yet the assertions do not seem wrong or odd" (Weiner 2005: 230–1).

But regardless of the exact details of the RTBNA, it is clear that such a norm of assertion not only countenances cases of selfless assertion as proper, it also sanctions both assertions of Gettierized beliefs and those made by our twins in evil demon worlds. Since such asserters do not seem subject to criticism in any reasonable sense, these are clear and compelling advantages that the RTBNA has over rival norms of assertions. The case for replacing the KNA with this norm of assertion is not yet complete, however, since there are two central and formidable objections to the RTBNA that still need to be discussed.

4.7 Counterexamples to the RTBNA

Support for preferring the KNA to rival views that require anything less than knowledge for assertion—such as the RTBNA—comes from considering two central phenomena: Moorean paradoxes and lottery propositions.[38] Let us begin with the former.

Consider the following two assertions:

1. Albatrosses are birds, but I don't believe that they are.
2. Albatrosses are birds, but I don't know that they are.

Fortunately, neither case provides a compelling counterexample to the KNA or the RTBNA. On the one hand, if the prediction or retrodiction in question is genuinely based merely on a "hunch" (Weiner 2005: 231)—or otherwise fails to have epistemic support adequate for reasonable belief—then the relevant asserter should offer a *qualified* rather than a *flat-out* assertion. For instance, rather than (3), Aubrey should instead offer a suitably qualified assertion, such as:

(3*) I suspect that the French will wait until nightfall to attack.

Unlike (3), (3*) does not have the potential to mislead Pullings into believing that Aubrey is privy to additional information regarding the French attacking. For notice: if Aubrey is truly working *merely on the basis of a hunch*, then it is unclear what would justify offering the flat-out assertion found in (3) rather than the qualified version in (3*).

What is often the case with both predictions and retrodictions, however, is that one does in fact possess epistemic support sufficient for reasonably believing a proposition, but one is unable to fully conceptualize or articulate one's support, perhaps because of cognitive or pragmatic limitations. Thus, on the other hand, Aubrey might in fact be working with more than a hunch—in particular, he may have epistemic grounds adequate for reasonably believing (3)—but not be in a position to articulate his support. In such a case, Aubrey would be entitled to flat-out assert (3), but then such an assertion would also be reasonable to believe, thereby satisfying the RTBNA. (Indeed, I suspect that the fact that Aubrey and Holmes are known as experts in their respective fields might be the source of whatever intuitive pull Weiner attempts to generate from these cases.) Either way, then, Weiner's cases fail to provide compelling counterexamples to the RTBNA.

[38] My presentation of these issues relies heavily on Williamson's discussion in his (2000).

Moore famously noted that assertions of these general forms—that is, of either the form "p, but I don't believe that p" or of the form "p, but I don't know that p"—seem quite paradoxical.[39] For instance, upon hearing you offer (1) and (2), one may rightly ask, "Well, if you take yourself to neither know nor believe that albatrosses are birds, then why are you asserting that they are?" At least *prima facie*, one may think it is unclear what you could reasonably offer by way of response to such a question.

Advocates of the KNA are in an excellent position to account for the paradoxical nature of asserting Moorean sentences: if only knowledge warrants assertion, then, in order to legitimately assert the conjunctions found in (1) and (2), both conjuncts of each sentence must be known by the asserter. Thus, regarding (1), in order to appropriately assert that albatrosses are birds, you need to know that they are. Given that knowledge entails belief, this conjunct is true only if you believe that albatrosses are indeed birds. Hence, you know the first conjunct of (1) only if the second conjunct is false, i.e., you know that albatrosses are birds only if it is false that you don't believe that they are. Similar considerations apply to (2): in order to legitimately assert that albatrosses are birds, the KNA requires that you know that they are. But then it turns out, again, that you know the first conjunct of (2) only if the second conjunct is false, i.e., you know that albatrosses are birds only if it is false that you don't know that they are.

Let us now turn to lottery propositions. Suppose that Sabrina bought a ticket in a very large lottery. While the drawing has already taken place and only one ticket has won, the result has not yet been made public. As a matter of fact, Sabrina's ticket has not won. Nevertheless, her friend, Mervin, who has no inside information regarding the outcome of the lottery, flat-out asserts to Sabrina merely on the basis of the relevant probabilities:

3.   Your ticket did not win.

Given that Mervin's grounds for asserting (3) are merely probabilistic, they seem intuitively inadequate for making such an unqualified assertion. Because of this, Williamson maintains that Sabrina will be "entitled to feel some resentment" when she later discovers the nature of these grounds (Williamson 2000: 246). For Mervin was representing himself to Sabrina as having a kind of authority to make the outright assertion which he

---

[39] See Moore (1962).

in fact lacked. Hence, there is a clear sense in which he "was cheating" (Williamson 2000: 246).

Again, proponents of the KNA have the resources to explain the data involving (3) with ease: intuitively, such lottery propositions, even when believed on very good probabilistic grounds, do not qualify as instances of knowledge. In offering (3), therefore, Mervin is asserting that which he does not know. If the KNA is correct, then, Sabrina's resentment is perfectly justified: Mervin, in offering an assertion that fails to be known, is violating a central norm of assertion. Substituting the KNA with a norm that requires anything less than knowledge, however, will leave us hard-pressed to explain what is wrong with these sorts of assertions. For, even if (3) is true, believed, and based on excellent probabilistic grounds, it is still improper for Mervin to flat-out assert, in the absence of inside information, that Sabrina did not win the lottery in question.

We have seen, then, that proponents of the KNA have the resources to clearly explain the impermissibility of flat-out asserting both instances of Moore's paradox and lottery propositions. The RTBNA, however, is taken to be at a significant disadvantage here. For since such a norm requires reasonableness rather than knowledge, it is said that assertions involving both of these kinds of propositions will at times satisfy the RTBNA. Regarding Moorean paradoxes, instances of selfless assertion, among possible others, provide clear examples in which the RTBNA countenances such assertions as appropriate. For example, it is reasonable for Sebastian in DISTRAUGHT DOCTOR to believe both *that there is no connection between vaccines and autism* and *that he neither believes nor knows that this is the case*. Accordingly, his asserting "There is no connection between vaccines and autism, but I don't believe that this is the case" and "There is no connection between vaccines and autism, but I don't know that this is the case" both satisfy the RTBNA and are thus permissible assertions according to this norm. Similarly, the very good probabilistic grounds for lottery propositions presumably render it reasonable to believe in their truth. Hence, so long as a speaker asserts a lottery proposition, such as that found in (3) above, *because* of this reasonableness, these assertions are taken to satisfy the RTBNA.

Let me begin my response to these two central problems for the RTBNA by focusing on assertions involving Moorean paradoxes. The first point to notice here is that there are very few sentences of the form found in either

(1) or (2) that will actually satisfy the RTBNA. For, in order to conform to such a norm, it needs to be reasonable for S to believe that *p and* it needs to be reasonable for S to believe that she either fails to believe or know that *p*. Certainly, both of these conjuncts will be true of very few of our ordinary beliefs. For instance, consider the sentences found in (1) and (2). If it is reasonable for me to believe that albatrosses are birds—which I assume it is—then it is unclear what circumstances could make it such that it is also reasonable for me to believe that I either fail to believe or know that albatrosses are birds, especially when reasonableness is understood in terms of the amount of epistemic support needed for justified belief. This is not to say that there aren't such circumstances—perhaps it is possible for an ornithologist to have very good evidence for believing that albatrosses are birds, but also be aware of enough conflicting evidence that makes it reasonable for her to doubt whether she in fact *knows* that albatrosses are birds. But, regardless of whether such conjunctions are possible, the point that is of import here is that it will be quite rare for Moorean paradoxes to satisfy the RTBNA.

Of course, even if it is rare, there are some Moorean paradoxes that clearly *do* satisfy the RTBNA on my view: namely, cases involving selfless assertion. In order to account for such assertions, let us begin by considering the following two cases:

LOSING DRINKER: Nadia and Hank know both that their friend Nina tends to go to the bar only when she loses a tennis match and that this is a fact that is generally known by all of her friends. However, Nadia knows further that Nina went to the bar today to have a drink with her opponent despite having won her tennis match. Nevertheless, while discussing Nina's recent tennis matches, Nadia asserts to Hank, "Nina went to the bar earlier today after her tennis match."

CHURCH THIEF: Quinn, Manfred, Rosalind, and Dolores are all currently at Starbucks drinking coffee and Quinn knows both that Dolores stole the money that was discovered to be missing earlier today from a local church's collection basket and that Manfred strongly suspects that Rosalind is the one who committed this crime. Nevertheless, Quinn asserts to Manfred, "Someone in this coffee shop stole the money from the church's collection basket earlier today."

Both the assertion made by Nadia in LOSING DRINKER and that made by Quinn in CHURCH THIEF satisfy all of the norms of assertion that have been thus far considered: the propositions in question are reasonable, true, and known by their respective asserters, and hence the corresponding assertions satisfy the RTBNA, the TNA, and the KNA. Yet, despite this, the assertions being offered are obviously problematic and the asserters in question are clearly subject to criticism.

What is the precise problem with the asserters and their assertions in these cases? In both cases, the speaker is offering an assertion that she or he knows will be *misleading* in the context at hand. For instance, even though Nadia's assertion that "Nina went to the bar earlier today after her tennis match" is reasonable, true, and known, she knows that Hank will form the further *false* belief that Nina lost her tennis match. By omitting the information that this is one of the rare times that Nina went to the bar after winning her tennis match, then, Nadia is offering an assertion that she knows will be misleading to Hank. Similarly, despite the fact that Quinn's assertion that "Someone in this coffee shop stole the money from the church's collection basket earlier today" is reasonable, true, and known, he knows that Manfred will form the additional *false* belief that Rosalind is the thief in question. His failing to add that Dolores stole the money is, then, tantamount to indirectly lying to Manfred.

Moreover, it is not only asserters who *know* that their assertions will be misleading who are subject to criticism or otherwise problematic. For instance, suppose that because of laziness, carelessness, or some other epistemic vice, both Nadia and Quinn in the above cases fail to realize that their assertions will be misleading to their respective interlocutors. Despite this, the circumstances are such that it is *reasonable for them to believe that their assertions will be misleading.* Such asserters are also clearly subject to criticism for asserting what they *should* believe is misleading, in much the same way that one who fails to know that she is speeding, but should know it, is nonetheless deserving of a speeding ticket. Yet, none of the three norms thus far considered—the RTBNA, TNA, or the KNA—have the resources to regard any of these assertions as improper.

What LOSING DRINKER and CHURCH THIEF, combined with their slightly modified versions, show is that there is an additional norm governing assertion, one that rules out as proper assertions that it is reasonable to believe are misleading in the contexts in which they are offered. More precisely, proponents of the RTBNA, TNA, and the KNA should all embrace something like the following *Not Misleading Norm of Assertion* (hereafter, the NMNA):

NMNA: S should assert that p in context C only if it is not reasonable
for S to believe that the assertion that p will be misleading
in C.

According to the NMNA, then, the assertions made by Nadia and Quinn
both turn out to be improper because the asserters in question know that
their assertions will be misleading (*a fortiori*, it is also reasonable for them
to believe this). Moreover, notice that the NMNA is different from the
following stronger norm:

NMNA*: S should assert that p in context C only if it is reasonable for
S to believe that the assertion that p will not be misleading
in C.

While the stronger NMNA* requires that S have positive epistemic support
for believing that her assertion will not be misleading in C, the weaker
NMNA requires only that S not have reason for believing that her assertion
will be misleading in C. Unlike the NMNA*, then, the weaker NMNA
allows assertions to be permissible when asserters do not have any relevant
information about whether they will be misleading or not.

Applying these considerations to Moorean paradoxes, we are now in
a position to see that the NMNA rules out the permissibility of asserting
such paradoxes in most circumstances, even when they involve selfless
assertions. For, again, consider Sebastian in DISTRAUGHT DOCTOR:
it is reasonable for him to believe both *that there is no connection between
vaccines and autism* and *that he neither believes nor knows that this is the case*. But
now imagine that he asserts to the parents of his patients either, "There is
no connection between vaccines and autism, but I don't believe that this is
the case," or "There is no connection between vaccines and autism, but I
don't know that this is the case." Surely, it is extremely unlikely that such
an assertion will prompt in his interlocutors the belief that though there
is very good evidence for believing that there is no connection between
vaccines and autism, Sebastian fails to believe or know this because of
the grief and exhaustion brought on by his daughter's recent diagnosis
of autism. Rather, such an assertion is most likely to lead to Sebastian's
hearers either forming *no* relevant beliefs at all, because they are confused
by its oddity, or to forming *false* beliefs, because they are trying to plausibly
explain its oddity away. It would, for instance, be natural for them to falsely

believe that the medical profession requires that Sebastian say that there is not such a connection, despite the fact that he believes that there are *good* reasons to suspect that vaccines do cause autism. Moreover, assuming that his hearers do not have any privileged information about their doctor's personal life, it is clearly reasonable for Sebastian to believe that such odd assertions—as those found in Moorean paradoxes—will be misleading to his interlocutors.

Similar considerations apply to other cases of selfless assertion. Suppose, for instance, that Martin in RACIST JUROR asserts to his childhood friend either, "No, the guy didn't rape her, but I don't believe that this is the case," or "No, the guy didn't rape her, but I don't know that this is the case." Again, it is highly unlikely that Martin's friend will come to believe that though there is excellent evidence for believing in the defendant's innocence, Martin fails to believe this because of his residual racism. Instead, this odd assertion is most likely to lead to his friend forming either *no* relevant beliefs or *false* beliefs, e.g., that though the prosecution didn't adequately prove that he committed the rape, there are *good* reasons to believe in the defendant's guilt. Furthermore, if we assume that the hearer in question does not have any privileged information, either about the case or about Martin's psychology relative to the race of the defendant, then it is reasonable for Martin to believe that assertions of these Moorean paradoxes will lead to the formation of either no relevant beliefs or to such false beliefs on the part of his hearer, thereby making them misleading.

Now, is the NMNA a constitutive norm of assertion, such as the RTBNA, TNA, and KNA purport to be, or is it a pragmatic norm of conversation, on a par with a Gricean maxim? One plausible answer here is that the NMNA either can be subsumed by or is at least akin to Grice's Maxim of Quantity: "Make your contribution as informative as is required for the current purposes of the exchange" (Grice 1989: 30–1). In all of the above cases, the speakers in question offer assertions that can be seen as failing the NMNA because they offer either *too little* or *too much* information. For instance, both Nadia and Hank omit crucial information that lead to their assertions being misleading: if Nadia had added that Nina won her tennis match today and if Hank had added that the thief in question is not Rosalind, both assertions would have satisfied the NMNA by being as informative as is required for the current purposes of the respective exchanges. Similarly, speakers who assert Moorean versions of selfless assertions offer either too little or too much information: too little, if they fail to explain away the oddity of their assertions—e.g., Sebastian can satisfy the NMNA by explaining to his hearers the whole story involving his daughter's recent diagnosis of autism and the grief and exhaustion he has been experiencing; too much, if they add to their assertion that *p* the conjuncts "I do not believe that *p*" or "I do not know that *p*"—e.g., Sebastian can satisfy the NMNA by merely asserting, as he does in DISTRAUGHT DOCTOR, "There is no connection between vaccines and autism."

But, one might ask, if Sebastian asserts only that there is not a connection between vaccines and autism, won't he be guilty of offering an assertion that it is reasonable to believe will lead to his hearers forming false beliefs? For isn't it likely that the parents of his patient will form the false beliefs that Sebastian both believes and knows that there is no connection between vaccines and autism? While there may be times when this is true, this is where Grice's requirement that the contribution be "as informative as is required for the current purposes of the exchange" is relevant. For when the parents in DISTRAUGHT DOCTOR ask Sebastian about the purported connection between vaccines and autism, they are interested in *the fact of the matter* on this issue, not the personal beliefs he has about such a topic in the midst of grief and exhaustion. Given the current purposes of the exchange—namely, to provide the parents of his patient with the best medical advice about vaccines—it would not only be irrelevant for him to express his personal beliefs, but it would also be misleading in achieving the desired end. Similar considerations apply in RACIST JUROR and MODIFIED CREATIONIST TEACHER: the current purposes of these exchanges do not require that Martin offer an assertion grounded in his residual racism or that Stella assert to her students what is the result of her own personal relationship with God. Rather, both contexts require that the speakers in question offer what is best supported by the evidence, which is precisely what they do. This is importantly different both from LOSING DRINKER and CHURCH THIEF above, and from Moorean versions of selfless assertions, all of which are misleading relative to the purposes of the exchanges in question. For instance, in CHURCH THIEF, Quinn's assertion to Manfred is misleading with respect to the question of who stole the money missing from the local church's collection basket, which is precisely the topic at hand. So, in order to make this point explicit, we can modify the NMNA as follows:

> NMNA**: S should assert that p in context C only if it is not reasonable
> for S to believe that the assertion that p will be misleading in
> C relative to the purposes of the exchange in question.

According to the NMNA**, then, assertions of Moorean paradoxes, even those involving selfless assertions, are usually impermissible.

Let us now turn to assertions involving lottery propositions. The first point to notice is that it is not universally accepted that subjects *do* in fact lack knowledge of lottery propositions.[40] For given a commitment to fallibilism, it is not obvious why excellent probabilistic grounds for believing a true lottery proposition would fail to be adequate for knowledge. Hence, it is at least not clear that proponents of the KNA have the advantage that they are said to have here over advocates of the RTBNA.

Second, even if we suppose that knowledge is *not* had of lottery propositions, assertions of such propositions are surely not always improper. For instance, if my friend Hannah, who is 3 months pregnant and will not receive another paycheck for at least a week, is considering spending her last 4 dollars on lottery tickets rather than on prenatal vitamins, surely it is permissible and indeed proper for me to flat-out assert, "You are *not* going to win the lottery." Similarly, if my cousin, Sean, is considering buying a car that far exceeds his financial capabilities on the grounds that he might have won a lottery in which the drawing has already taken place but the results have not yet been made public, it is clearly proper for me to flat-out assert, "You did *not* win the lottery." In cases such as this, flat-out assertions involving lottery propositions, even if they are not known, invite neither resentment nor criticism from the relevant hearers, thereby showing that they are not in violation of a norm of assertion.

Third, even if we suppose that knowledge is *not* had of lottery propositions and that there are clear instances in which asserting these propositions is *improper*, such assertions, like those involving Moorean paradoxes, will generally fail the NMNA**. In particular, in cases where it is truly improper to assert lottery propositions, such assertions will frequently be impermissible precisely *because they are misleading,* where this misleading nature is both

---

[40] See, for instance, Reed (forthcoming).

directly relevant to the purposes of the exchange in question and reasonably anticipated by the asserter.[41] For instance, if I flat-out assert to a woman I just met on a train, "You did not win the lottery," it would be natural for her to form the *false* belief that I have some sort of inside information about the results of the drawing when in fact I do not. Furthermore, such a false belief is both relevant to the purposes of our exchange and one that I could reasonably expect her to form. Similar considerations apply to most other assertions of lottery propositions that are genuinely improper. In contexts where it is clear that an asserter is appropriately subject to criticism—unlike those above involving my assertions to Hannah and Sean—the central problem in offering lottery propositions is that they are apt to mislead hearers into believing that inside information about the lottery is possessed by the speaker.[42] Given this likelihood to mislead, then,

---

[41] It is of interest to note that this way of explaining the impermissibility of some assertions involving lottery propositions is importantly different than the Gricean strategy considered by Williamson (2000) and defended by Weiner (2005). For instance, regarding Sarah's asserting to Alice, "Your ticket didn't win," Weiner responds: "Briefly, the idea is that there is a norm, akin to Grice's Cooperative Principle (1989, 26), that one's utterances have some point. It would be pointless for Sarah to tell Alice that her ticket hadn't won unless Sarah had some inside information not obviously available to Alice. Accordingly, when Sarah asserts that Alice's ticket did not win, she implicates that she has inside information. Because Sarah lacks inside information, Alice has the right to feel resentful. This resentment is grounded in the falsehood of Sarah's implicature rather than in the mere fact of Sarah's having asserted what she does not know" (Weiner 2005: 232). There are three points I should like to make about this response. First, there are some assertions of lottery propositions that *clearly do have a point*. For instance, in the example in the text, the point of the assertion I offer to my friend Hannah is that she should spend her remaining money on prenatal vitamins rather than on lottery tickets with wildly improbable odds. So, if Weiner regards all assertions of lottery propositions as impermissible, his Gricean explanation is, at best, only partial. Second, even with respect to assertions of lottery propositions that fail to have as obvious a point as the one I offer to Hannah, it is *highly doubtful that such assertions are even frequently pointless*. For instance, I may assert that you are going to lose the lottery to prevent you from having unrealistic expectations about your odds, or to remind you of your present modest financial situation, or to encourage you to begin looking for reliable employment, and so on, all of which clearly give a point to my assertions. Indeed, it is only in the most unusual and unlikely cases that assertions of lottery propositions would accurately be regarded as pointless. Third, given that Weiner regards assertions involving predictions and retrodictions that are based purely on hunches as proper, *it is not at all clear why he regards lottery propositions as problematic in the first place*. For instance, consider my assertion to Hannah, "You are *not* going to win the lottery." Such an assertion is rightly regarded as a prediction. But surely my basis for believing this proposition is significantly better than the hunches grounding the predictions that Weiner considers proper. Given this, it is curious that Weiner regards assertions of lottery propositions as being importantly different from predictions and retrodictions, so much so that he goes to great lengths to rule out the permissibility of asserting the former yet relies on the latter as his sole counterexamples to the KNA.

[42] There is an alternate way for proponents of the RTBNA to handle lottery propositions, one that would be most attractive to those who are inclined to accept the KNA but nonetheless find cases of selfless assertion compelling counterexamples. First, one could characterize the notion of reasonableness operative in the RTBNA in terms of *justified belief, where justification is taken to be necessary and, when*

though assertions of lottery propositions satisfy the RTBNA, those that are truly improper will nonetheless generally fail the NMNA**.[43]

Hence, neither lottery propositions nor Moorean paradoxes—the two central objections to norms requiring anything less than the KNA—pose a problem for the RTBNA.

4.8 Concluding Remarks

We have seen that cases of selfless assertion show that the KNA is false, and that the distinction between primary and secondary propriety cannot be invoked either to defend the KNA or to support replacing this norm with the TNA. We have also seen that the RTBNA provides a plausible middle ground between these two rival views. For, unlike the KNA, the RTBNA rightly recognizes that assertions need not pass through the doxastic states of asserters in order to be proper, particularly when such states are riddled with prejudice or confusion. At the same time, however, the RTBNA, unlike the TNA, appreciates that assertions that float entirely free from adequate epistemic support—such as lucky guesses—are not proper in any significant sense. Finally, we have seen that the RTBNA not only

---

combined with truth, belief, and a Gettier-condition, sufficient for knowledge. Otherwise put, one could argue that minus belief, truth, and a Gettier-condition, the RTBNA requires everything epistemic that the KNA does. Second, one could argue along the following lines: if lottery propositions are indeed not known, what prevents them from being known? The answer here has to be something involving the *level of epistemic support* possessed for believing such propositions. As the proponent of this strategy is using the term, then, the answer involves the *justification* condition for knowledge. For standard lottery propositions are believed to be true, often are true, and are typically not believed in Gettier-type situations. This leaves only the distinctively epistemic condition of justification as the culprit purportedly preventing knowledge of lottery propositions. But if there is not enough epistemic support for knowledge of lottery propositions, then there is not enough epistemic support for satisfying the RTBNA understood in this way. In particular, where p is a lottery proposition, S's epistemic support will be inadequate for S's justifiedly believing that p, whether or not S as a matter of fact believes that p. According to this reading of the RTBNA, then, it may not be reasonable for subjects to believe lottery propositions, thereby rendering it improper for such propositions to be asserted. Hence, lottery propositions would not pose a problem for those who accept this reading of the RTBNA.

[43] I say "generally" because there may be some assertions involving lottery propositions that are impermissible yet not misleading. For instance, I may say to my friend, "You did not win the lottery," and we may both know that I am not privy to any inside information regarding the results. Here, Weiner may be correct that the problem with my assertion in such a case is that it is *pointless*, and hence that a conversational norm akin to Grice's Cooperative Principle renders it impermissible. The mistake Weiner makes, however, is to suppose that all—or even most—lottery propositions are impermissible because they are pointless.

avoids all of the problems facing its rivals, but it also accommodates the two central advantages of the KNA—the impermissibility of asserting both lottery propositions and Moorean paradoxes.

Thus, the KNA cannot be relied upon to defend TEP-N from the counterexamples raised in Chapter 2 since such a norm does not govern the practice of assertion in the first place. Moreover, the speakers in some of these counterexamples, such as Stella in CREATIONIST TEACHER, clearly satisfy the RTBNA, which is the norm that I have argued *does* govern assertion. Hence, even if one claims that the acquisition of testimonial knowledge requires the satisfaction of the norm of assertion on the part of the speaker, the arguments in Chapter 2 nonetheless succeed in undermining TEP-N. Either way, then, considerations about assertion support not only the rejection of the Belief View of Testimony, but also the acceptance of the Statement View of Testimony.

A final note, on the consequences of accepting the RTBNA over the KNA: some of the most important epistemological views in recent years—e.g., contextualism and speaker sensitive invariantism—have been grounded in large part in a close consideration of the semantics of knowledge ascriptions. The KNA has been one of the central supports for these linguistically motivated views.[44] If, however, the KNA is false, and ought to be replaced by the RTBNA, the proper focus in epistemology should begin to shift back to traditional considerations involving justification, warrant, evidence, and so on—which is where it should have been all along.

---

[44] See, for instance, DeRose (2002) and Hawthorne (2004).

5

A Critique of Reductionism and Non-Reductionism

5.1 Preliminary Remarks

In previous chapters, I argued that the proper focus in the epistemology of testimony should be on what speakers say, not on what they believe. In this chapter, I turn to the question: what, if anything, needs to be added to the SVT for a complete epistemology of testimony? Otherwise put, what precisely is needed in order for a speaker to successfully acquire justified or warranted belief, and ultimately knowledge, through either the spoken or written word of others? This question is at the center of the epistemology of testimony, and the current philosophical literature contains two main options for answering it: *reductionism* and *non-reductionism*. While reductionists argue that the epistemic status of testimony is ultimately reducible to sense perception, memory, and inductive inference, non-reductionists maintain that testimony is just as basic epistemically as these other sources. The aim of this chapter is to challenge the current terms of the debate by showing that there are serious problems afflicting both non-reductionism and reductionism.

Before proceeding, however, I should make a point of clarification. There will be two central questions at issue in this chapter: first, are positive reasons necessary for acquiring testimonially based knowledge and, second, are the epistemic properties of such knowledge—such as justification and warrant—ultimately reducible to the epistemic properties of purportedly more basic sources, such as sense perception, memory, and inductive inference? Reductionists answer affirmatively, while non-reductionists respond negatively, to both of these questions. For ease of discussion, I shall sometimes in this chapter focus specifically on testimonial justification and warrant—for instance, since the truth, belief, and anti-Gettier components of testimonial knowledge are obviously not reducible to other sources in the way that the distinctively epistemic condition may be, it is far simpler to focus on testimonial justification or warrant when talking about reductionism. At other times, I shall focus on testimonial knowledge—for instance, since non-reductionists deny that the epistemic properties of testimony are reducible to other sources in the first place, their view can be discussed in terms of testimonial knowledge with considerable ease. These differences, however, should not cloud the fact that, ultimately, the central questions at issue concern the conditions for, and nature of, *testimonially based knowledge*.

5.2 Reductionism

Characterizing Reductionism

Reductionism, though not nearly as popular in the contemporary literature as its non-reductionist rival, has a rich history.[1] The most well-known proponent of this view is David Hume, and the following passages from his essay on miracles are often taken to be the most explicit and earliest characterization of reductionism in the epistemology of testimony:

There is no species of reasoning more common, more useful, and even necessary to human life, than that which is derived from the testimony of men and the reports of eye-witnesses and spectators. This species of reasoning, perhaps, one may deny to be founded on the relation of cause and effect. I shall not dispute about a word. It will be sufficient to observe, that our assurance in any argument of this kind is derived from no other principle than our observation of the veracity of human testimony, and of the usual conformity of facts to the reports of witnesses. It being a general maxim, that no objects have any discoverable connexion together, and that

---

[1] Proponents of different versions of reductionism include Mackie (1970), Hume (1977), Fricker (1987, 1994, 1995, and 2006a), Adler (1994 and 2002), Lyons (1997), Lipton (1998), Shogenji (2006), and Van Cleve (2006). For nice discussions of Hume's version of reductionism, see Faulkner (1998) and Root (2001). Lehrer (2006) develops a view that is neither reductionist nor non-reductionist, but instead focuses on the trustworthiness that he claims is required on the part of both the speaker and the hearer in the acquisition of testimonial knowledge. Faulkner (2000) develops a hybrid reductionist/non-reductionist view of testimonial justification and knowledge. While Faulkner endorses a view that is in some ways similar to the dualist view I will defend in the next chapter, he espouses TEP-N*, which I rejected in Chapter 2.

all the inferences, which we can draw from one to another, are founded merely on our experience of their constant and regular conjunction; it is evident, that we ought not to make an exception to this maxim in favour of human testimony, whose connexion with any event seems, in itself, as little necessary as any other. (Hume 1977: 74)

The reason why we place any credit in witnesses and historians, is not derived from any *connexion*, which we perceive *a priori*, between testimony and reality, but because we are accustomed to find a conformity between them. (Hume 1977: 75)

According to a Humean view, then, hearers must observe a constant and regular conjunction between the reports of speakers and the corresponding facts in order to accept testimony with justification or warrant. For instance, I may perceive a constant conformity between the instances of your testimony and reality and, on this basis, inductively conclude that you are a generally reliable epistemic source. If these inductively-based reasons are not themselves derived from further testimony, then my testimonial justification or warrant can be reduced to perceptual, memorial, and inferential justification or warrant.

Recent reductionists sometimes impose slightly laxer requirements than those found in Hume. For instance, Paul Faulkner writes:

Given that a speaker's intentions in communicating need not be informative and given the relevance of these intentions to the acquisition of testimonial knowledge ... [i]t is doxastically irresponsible to accept testimony without *some background belief in the testimony's credibility or truth*. In the case of perception and memory, rational acceptance requires only the absence of defeating background beliefs. In the case of testimony, rational acceptance requires the presence of supporting background beliefs.

This demand of responsibility may be expressed as a criterion of justification. *An audience is justified in forming a testimonial belief if and only if he is justified in accepting the speaker's testimony.* (Faulkner 2000: 587–8, first emphasis added)

In requiring that the hearer merely have *some* background information about the credibility or truth of the testimony in question—which perhaps can be satisfied without having specific information about the speaker herself—Faulkner's condition here may be read as being weaker than Hume's. Similarly, Elizabeth Fricker maintains:

In claiming that a hearer is required to assess a speaker for trustworthiness, I do not mean to insist, absurdly, that she is required to conduct an extensive piece of MI5-type "vetting" of any speaker before she may accept anything he says as true.... My insistence is much weaker: that the hearer should be discriminating in her attitude to the speaker, in that she should be continually evaluating him for trustworthiness throughout their exchange, in the light of the evidence, or cues, available to her. This will be partly a matter of her being disposed to deploy background knowledge which is relevant, partly a matter of her monitoring the speaker for any tell-tale signs revealing likely untrustworthiness. (Fricker 1994: 149–50)

Once again, since Fricker requires that a hearer *deploy relevant background information* and *monitor* the speaker for trustworthiness, her version of reductionism may be read as being weaker than Hume's, who is often understood as demanding that reliance on testimony occur "only when [the hearer] has checked for himself the credibility of the witnesses he trusts" (Coady 1992: 80).[2]

Yet, despite these differences, contemporary reductionists share with Hume a commitment to two theses central to reductionism. The first is what we may call the *Positive Reasons Thesis*: justification or warrant is conferred on testimonial beliefs by the presence of appropriate *positive reasons* on the part of hearers. Since these reasons cannot themselves be ultimately testimonially grounded—otherwise there would be circularity, i.e., testimonial beliefs ultimately justifying other testimonial beliefs—they must depend on resources provided by other epistemic sources, which typically include sense perception, memory, and inductive inference. This gives rise to the second thesis—what we may call the *Reduction Thesis*. Because the justification or warrant of testimonial beliefs is provided by non-testimonially grounded positive reasons, testimonial justification or warrant is said to *reduce* to the justification of sense perception, memory, and inductive inference.[3] As James Van Cleve says: "My view...is that testimony gives us justified belief and reflective knowledge not because it shines by its own light, but because it has often enough been revealed true

---

[2] In this passage from Coady (1992), he is directly talking about J. L. Mackie's view, but seems to attribute this same version of reductionism to Hume. It should be noted, however, that there is disagreement on how best to interpret Hume's view of testimony. See, for instance, Traiger (1993), Faulkner (1998), and Root (2001).

[3] As Fricker says, "Reductionists about testimony hold that, if testimony is to be vindicated as a source not merely of belief, but of knowledge, our epistemic right to believe what others tell us must be exhibitable as grounded in other epistemic resources and principles—perception, memory, and inference—which are regarded by them as both more fundamental, and less problematic" (Fricker 1995: 394).

by our other lights. On this point, I find myself uncharacteristically on the side of Hume rather than Reid" (Van Cleve 2006: 69).

Thus, let us formulate reductionism with respect to testimonial justification and warrant in the following way:

R: For every speaker, A, and hearer, B, B believes that *p* with justification/warrant on the basis of A's testimony if and only if:

(R1) B believes that *p* on the basis of the content of A's testimony, and

(R2) B has sufficiently good non-testimonial positive reasons to accept A's testimony.

Now, though most reductionists do not explicitly include a condition like (R1) when presenting their view, I have done so to prevent some of the cases discussed in Chapter 2—such as your saying, in a soprano voice, that you have a soprano voice, and my coming to believe that you do entirely on the basis of hearing your soprano voice—from qualifying as *testimonially* justified or warranted. I have also formulated R in terms of "A's testimony" rather than in terms of "A's testimony that *p*," so as to allow some of the other cases discussed in Chapter 2—such as Virginia coming to believe that it is cold outside on the basis of my testimony that her hat and gloves are in the closet—to qualify as *testimonially* justified. Finally, notice that condition (R2) requires that the positive reasons be *non-testimonial*—this is to allow testimonial justification or warrant to reduce to perceptual, memorial, and inferential justification or warrant.

But, one might ask, what exactly is being reduced to what on the reductionist's view? Otherwise put, what are the relata of testimonial reduction? Two different answers are given to this question. The first answer—a view often called *global reductionism*—is that the justification/warrant of testimony as a source of belief reduces to the justification/warrant of sense perception, memory, and inductive inference. In particular, global reductionists maintain that in order to justifiedly accept a speaker's report, a hearer must have non-testimonially based positive reasons for believing that testimony is generally reliable.[4]

---

[4] More precisely, this is one version of global reductionism. The other version requires that "a hearer have evidence that *most of what she has ever learned through testimony is true*, where this evidence does not in any way rest on knowledge acquired by her through testimony" (Fricker 1994: 134). Though this weaker version of global reductionism avoids some of the objections raised to the stronger one, it faces

There are, however, at least three problems with global reductionism that render it ultimately an untenable view of testimonial justification or warrant. The first is that, before accepting any testimony at all, including that of their parents and teachers, very young children would have to wait until they had checked the accuracy of enough different kinds of reports from enough different speakers to conclude that testimony is generally reliable. Not only is it wildly implausible to suppose that most young children—or even adults—are capable of engaging in such a process, it also becomes mysterious how they would be able to acquire the conceptual and linguistic tools needed for an induction to the general reliability of testimony without accepting some testimony in the first place.[5] Thus, if global reductionism is true, the very cognitive tools needed to acquire testimonial justification or warrant would be inaccessible to epistemic agents, thereby leading ultimately to skepticism about testimonial knowledge.

The second problem is that in order to have non-testimonially based positive reasons that testimony is generally reliable, one would have to be exposed not only to an appropriately random, wide-ranging sample of reports, but also to an appropriately random, wide-ranging sample of the corresponding facts. Both are problematic. With respect to the reports, most of us have been exposed only to a very limited range of reports from speakers in our native language in a handful of communities in our native country. This limited sample of reports provides only a fraction of what would be required to legitimately conclude that testimony is *generally* reliable. With respect to the corresponding facts, a similar problem arises: the observational base of ordinary epistemic agents is simply far too small to allow the requisite induction about the reliability of testimony. As C. A. J. Coady says:

it seems absurd to suggest that, individually, we have done anything like the amount of field-work that [reductionism] requires ... many of us have never seen a baby born, nor have most of us examined the circulation of the blood nor the actual geography of the world nor any fair sample of the laws of the land, nor have we made the observations that lie behind our knowledge that the lights in the sky

---

problems of its own. Most notably, in the absence of a good reason to believe that *most of what one has ever learned through testimony* adequately and non-randomly represents either *testimony in general* or *testimony that one will encounter in the future*, it is unclear why this would justify the inference that future acceptances of testimony will be justified.

[5] For a detailed discussion of some of the specific epistemic issues that arise regarding young children's acceptance of testimony, see Chapter 7.

are heavenly bodies immensely distant nor a vast number of other observations that [reductionism] would seem to require. (Coady 1992: 82)

Moreover, with many reports, such as those involving complex scientific, economic, or mathematical theories, most of us simply lack the conceptual machinery and background information needed to properly check the reports against the facts. Once again, then, global reductionism leads to skepticism about testimonial knowledge, at least for most epistemic agents.

The previous two points focused on our ability to *know* or *determine* whether testimony is a generally reliable epistemic source. A third problem with global reductionism—one that has not been properly appreciated but is, to my mind, the most debilitating objection—is that it is questionable whether there even is an epistemically significant *fact of the matter* here.[6] To see this, consider, for instance, the following epistemically heterogeneous list of types of reports, all of which are subsumed under "testimony in general": reports about the time of day, what one had for breakfast, the achievements of one's children, whether one's loved one looks attractive in a certain outfit, the character of one's political opponents, one's age and weight, one's criminal record, and so on. Some of these types of reports may be generally highly reliable (e.g., about the time of day and what one had for breakfast), generally highly unreliable (e.g., about the achievements of one's children, the looks of one's loved ones, and the character of one's political opponents), and generally very epistemically mixed, depending on the speaker (e.g., about one's age, weight, and criminal record). Because of this epistemic heterogeneity, it is doubtful, not only whether "testimony" picks out an epistemically interesting or unified kind, but also whether it even makes sense to talk about testimony being a generally reliable source.

Otherwise put, even if it turned out that the majority of testimonial reports are, as a matter of fact, both true and properly formed, this information would not have much epistemic significance. For concealed in this percentage are all sorts of epistemically salient facts: some people

---

[6] A notable exception is Fricker (1994). As she says, "looking for generalisations about the reliability or otherwise of testimony ... as a homogenous whole, will not be an enlightening project. Illuminating generalisations, if there are any, will be about particular types of testimony, differentiated according to subject matter, or type of speaker, or both ... [W]hen it comes to the probability of accuracy of speakers' assertions, and what sorts of factors warrant a hearer in trusting a speaker, *testimony is not a unitary category*" (Fricker 1994: 139, emphasis added).

offer mostly false reports, some kinds of reports are mostly false, many true reports are about very mundane facts, and so on. Because of this, the mere fact that testimony is *generally* reliable—if indeed it is—would have very little epistemic bearing on any *particular* instance of testimony. For instance, suppose that I came to learn that 70 percent of all reports are both true and properly formed. What relevance would this information have to whether a particular instance of testimony is epistemically acceptable? Very little. For this information is so broad and conceals so many epistemically important differences that it would have virtually no straightforward epistemic application. Thus, even if global reductionism were entirely successful and it could be shown that testimony is generally reliable, this conclusion would have very little epistemic significance in itself.

The second version of reductionism—often called *local reductionism*—is that the justification/warrant of each particular report or instance of testimony reduces to the justification/warrant of instances of sense perception, memory, and inductive inference. Specifically, local reductionists claim that in order to justifiedly accept a speaker's testimony, a hearer must have non-testimonially based positive reasons for accepting the particular report in question. As Elizabeth Fricker says, "My reliance on a particular piece of testimony *reduces locally* just if I have adequate grounds to take my informant to be trustworthy on this occasion independently of accepting as true her very utterance" (Fricker 1995: 404).

There are, however, two importantly different ways of understanding the local reductionist's Positive Reasons Thesis. The first is:

PR-N: Appropriate positive reasons are *necessary* for testimonial justification/warrant.

The second, stronger, interpretation is:

PR-N&S: Appropriate positive reasons are *necessary and sufficient* for testimonialjustification/warrant.

But notice: in order for testimonial justification or warrant to be *reducible* to sense perception, memory, and inductive inference, the positive reasons in question must be fully sufficient for justifying, or conferring warrant on, the relevant testimonial belief. Otherwise, there would be an asymmetry between the epistemic status of the *testimonial belief being reduced* and the *positive reasons doing the reducing,* thereby preventing the possibility of just such a reduction. Because of this, *the Reduction Thesis of the local reductionist's view depends on reading the Positive Reasons Thesis as the stronger PR-N&S.* In what follows, however, I shall argue that PR-N&S is false.[7]

Rejecting Reductionism

To begin, consider the following:

NESTED SPEAKER: Fred has known Helen for five years and, during this time, he has acquired excellent epistemic reasons for believing her to be a highly reliable source of information on a wide range of topics. For instance, each time she has made a personal or professional recommendation to Fred, her assessment has proven to be accurate; each time she has reported an incident to Fred, her version of the story has been independently confirmed; each time she has recounted historical information, all of the major historical texts and figures have fully supported her account, and so on. Yesterday, Helen told Fred that Pauline, a close friend of hers, is a highly trustworthy person, especially when it comes to information regarding wild birds. Because of this, Fred unhesitatingly believed Pauline earlier today when she told him that albatrosses, not condors (as is widely believed), have the largest wingspan among wild birds. It turns out that while Helen is an epistemically excellent source of information, she was incorrect on this particular occasion: Pauline is, in fact, a highly incompetent and insincere speaker, especially on the topic of wild birds. Moreover, though Pauline is correct in her report about albatrosses, she came to hold this belief merely on the basis of wishful thinking (in order to make her reading of *The Rime of the Ancient Mariner* more compelling).[8]

Now, does Fred believe with justification or warrant that albatrosses have the largest wingspan among wild birds on the basis of Pauline's report? Intuitively, no. For, even though Helen's testimony provides Fred with excellent positive reasons for accepting the report in question, Pauline is not only a generally unreliable speaker, but she is also reporting a belief which, though true, fails to be reliably produced or appropriately truth-conducive.

---

[7] Strictly speaking, I shall argue that the weakest version of only the *Reduction Thesis* of reductionism is false, leaving the general Positive Reasons Thesis of reductionism untouched. (Indeed, I shall argue later in this chapter that PR-N is correct.) However, since I am taking the Reduction Thesis to be an essential part of reductionism (what, after all, is reductionism with no reduction?), a view that merely includes the Positive Reasons Thesis does not qualify as reductionist.

[8] A point of clarification: I refer to this case as NESTED SPEAKER because the justification/warrant for accepting one speaker's report is *nested within* the positive reasons for accepting another speaker's report. More precisely, the justification/warrant for accepting Pauline's testimony is nested within the positive reasons for accepting Helen's testimony.

Because of this, the testimony that Pauline offers to Fred also fails to be reliably produced or appropriately truth-conducive, thereby preventing it from leading to justified or warranted belief for Fred.[9]

What NESTED SPEAKER reveals is that the possession of good positive reasons by a hearer is not sufficient for accepting a speaker's testimony with justification or warrant. Why? Because the possession of positive reasons on behalf of a speaker's report, even objectively excellent ones, *does not necessarily put one in contact with testimony that is reliable*. There is, then, a further necessary condition for testimonial justification or warrant, one that requires that a speaker's testimony be reliable or otherwise truth-conducive. This additional "speaker-condition" can be fleshed out in different ways. For instance, as we saw in Chapter 2, many would require that a speaker herself *competently believe* the proposition to which she is *sincerely testifying* in order for it to qualify as justified or warranted belief for her hearers.[10] Of course, I argued in this same chapter that neither competence nor sincerity is necessary for testimonial justification or warrant, and instead defended the view that the speaker's *statement* needs to be reliable or otherwise truth-conducive. But the point that is of import here is that it is a condition that cannot be subsumed merely by requiring the possession of appropriate positive reasons on the part of the hearer. The presence of such reasons is, therefore, not sufficient for testimonial justification or warrant. Accordingly, the stronger reading of the Positive Reasons Thesis—i.e., PR-N&S—is false.[11]

---

[9] This is not to say that a belief that fails to be reliably produced or appropriately connected with the truth will *necessarily* render a report based on such a belief unreliable. Indeed, as we saw in Chapter 2, the epistemic status of beliefs and reports can come apart so that an unreliable believer can nonetheless be a reliable testifier. Rather, the problem with Pauline's testimony in NESTED SPEAKER is that her unreliability as a believer leads her to also be an *unreliable testifier*.

[10] For discussions specifically about the role of competence and sincerity in testimony, see, for instance, Welbourne (1979, 1981, 1986, and 1994), Hardwig (1985 and 1991), Ross (1986), Fricker (1987, 1994, 1995, 2006a, and 2006b), Plantinga (1993b), McDowell (1994), Audi (1997, 1998, and 2006), Owens (2000 and 2006), Root (2001), Adler (2002 and 2006), Moran (2005), Faulkner (2006), and Sosa (2006).

[11] A proponent of reductionism may object to the conclusion of NESTED SPEAKER by arguing that justification—unlike, for instance, warrant and knowledge—is primarily an *internalist* notion. For instance, if I were a brain-in-a-vat and had no idea that I was, one might argue that I would still be *justified* in believing that I am here typing at this computer, even if I do not *know* that I am. Similarly, one might claim that in NESTED SPEAKER, the belief that Fred forms on the basis of Pauline's radically unreliable testimony is *justified*, even if it does not qualify as *knowledge*. (I am grateful to Peter Graham for pressing this point.)

By way of response to this objection, recall my emphasis in the Introduction that I am not only using "justification" and "warrant" interchangeably, but also that I am understanding these concepts as

This, in turn, means that the Reduction Thesis of reductionism is false. For, if the Reduction Thesis were correct, there wouldn't be any difference between the epistemic status of the *testimonial belief being reduced* and the *positive reasons doing the reducing*. That is, to the extent that the positive reasons were justified or warranted, so, too, should the testimony in question be justified or warranted. This is just what it would mean for testimonial justification/warrant to be *reduced* to the justification/warrant of sense perception, memory, and inductive inference. But notice: in NESTED SPEAKER, we have an example in which there is precisely such an epistemic difference. In particular, Fred's positive reasons are fully epistemically justified/warranted and yet the testimonially based belief in question is not.

There are, however, at least three central objections that a reductionist may raise to this conclusion. First, it may be argued that the conclusion drawn from NESTED SPEAKER follows only if an externalist view of epistemic justification or warrant is assumed. In particular, it may be claimed that, if reliability is not a necessary condition of justification or warrant, then the unreliability of Pauline's testimony does not prevent Fred's testimonial beliefs from being justified or warranted. And since internalists do in fact deny the necessity of reliability for justification or warrant, NESTED SPEAKER succeeds as a counterexample to reductionism only if a substantive assumption is made, one that reductionists are likely to reject from the start.

Notice, however, that any plausible view of epistemic justification or warrant must preserve the connection between a belief's being justified or warranted and its being likely that such a belief is true. For instance, Laurence BonJour claims, "any degree of epistemic justification, however small, must increase to a commensurate degree the chances that the belief in question is true ... for otherwise it cannot qualify as epistemic justification at all" (BonJour 1985: 8). Similarly, Scott Hendricks maintains that "[a] theory of justification must preserve the connection between a belief's

bearing a necessary connection with knowledge. Moreover, it is not at all uncommon in the literature to find justification being discussed, either entirely or partially, in externalist terms. To name just a few, see Alston (1989), Goldman (1992), and BonJour and Sosa (2003). Still further, many reductionists are equally reductionistic about warrant and knowledge (though, of course, a truth-condition is added when testimonial knowledge is at issue). Hence, for those who hold that justification is a purely internalist notion, my arguments in this section can simply be recast as arguments against reductionism about testimonial *warrant* or *knowledge*.

being justified and a belief's being likely to be true" (Hendricks 2005: 405). Now, internalists will attempt to secure the connection between epistemic justification (warrant) and truth one way—say, through the presence of certain kinds of mental states—while externalists will attempt to do so another way—say, through truth-tracking. But both internalists and externalists are committed to justification or warrant *having* an appropriate connection with the truth. This connection, however, is precisely what is missing in NESTED SPEAKER. For while Helen's testimony makes probable that Pauline's testimony is likely to be true, Pauline's testimony that albatrosses have the largest wingspan does not make probable the truth of this proposition. The fact that Pauline's testimony does not make probable the proposition about albatrosses is thus enough to render Fred's belief unjustified, regardless of whether internalism or externalism is assumed.

Second, it may be argued that NESTED SPEAKER simply describes a testimonial Gettier-type case, one in which a hearer's belief is justified or warranted but true merely by accident. In particular, one may claim that, because of the excellent reasons he has for trusting Pauline, the true belief that Fred acquires from her testimony is *justified or warranted*. Our intuition that something is epistemically defective in such a case can be explained by the fact that Fred's belief nevertheless falls short of *knowledge*.

By way of response to this objection, it will be helpful to compare NESTED SPEAKER with the following:

UNNESTED SPEAKER: Max has known Ethel for ten years and, over the course of these years, he has acquired excellent epistemic reasons for believing her to be a highly reliable source of information on a wide range of topics. Indeed, during this time, she has never offered, to Max or anyone else, a report that has been either insincere or improperly formed. Currently, however, Ethel is in the midst of a personal crisis, which she effectively conceals from those around her, and her emotional state of mind leads her to report to Max that her purse has been stolen, despite having absolutely no evidence for thinking this to be the case. Max, detecting nothing amiss, readily accepts Ethel's testimony. Now, it turns out that Ethel's purse was in fact stolen: while she was at a coffee shop earlier today, a young man slipped it off her chair and into his backpack.

Notice first that in UNNESTED SPEAKER, Max not only has excellent epistemic reasons for accepting Ethel's testimony, but *Ethel is also a generally reliable testifier.* The problem is simply that, on this particular occasion, Ethel acts completely out of epistemic character and offers a report for which she lacks adequate evidence. What's more, she gets veridically (though not financially!) lucky: her report turns out to be true. Because of this, one may plausibly regard UNNESTED SPEAKER as a Gettier-type case, i.e., a case of justified or warranted true belief that falls short of knowledge. In particular, one may argue that Max's excellent positive reasons for Ethel's testimony combined with her general reliability as a testifier render his true belief about the stolen purse justified or warranted, though not an instance of knowledge.[12] Accordingly, UNNESTED SPEAKER would fail to show that there can be a difference between the epistemic status of the testimonial belief being reduced and the positive reasons doing the reducing.

In NESTED SPEAKER, however, while Fred has excellent positive reasons to accept Pauline's testimony, *she is not a reliable testifier in any sense of the word.* For not only does Pauline hold her belief about the wingspan of albatrosses on the basis of wishful thinking, but she is also in general a highly incompetent and insincere testifier. In other words, with respect to most topics most of the time, Pauline believes to be true what is in fact false, reports what she herself does not believe, or both. Thus, positive reasons can come apart from even *general* reliability. Moreover, given the degree and depth of Pauline's unreliability, there is simply no plausible sense in which the belief that Fred forms on the basis of her testimony could be justified or warranted. Unlike UNNESTED SPEAKER, then, NESTED SPEAKER simply cannot be plausibly regarded as a Gettier-type case.[13]

One may pursue a third line of resistance to NESTED SPEAKER, however, by arguing that Fred's "excellent epistemic reasons" on behalf of Pauline's testimony are not "appropriate" in the relevant sense. For, one may say that the only positive reasons that are appropriate are ones that render it likely in an objective sense that the testimony in question is true. Since Helen is incorrect in her assessment of Pauline, it may be

---

[12] Let me emphasize that this is how *one* might plausibly construe the case; it is not, however, how *I* would characterize it. Despite the fact that Ethel is a generally reliable testifier, I would hold that Max's belief on the basis of her testimony fails to be justified or warranted because the report itself is not reliably produced. On my view, the virtue of NESTED SPEAKER, in comparison with UNNESTED SPEAKER, is that it entirely precludes this sort of plausible reading.

[13] I am grateful for an exchange with Sandy Goldberg that prompted the addition of both UNNESTED SPEAKER and the discussion contrasting it with NESTED SPEAKER.

thought that such an assessment fails to provide Fred with positive reasons that satisfy this criterion.

But, as NESTED SPEAKER is described, Fred *does* have reasons that, by one measure, render it objectively likely that Pauline's testimony is true. In particular, Fred's positive reasons place those beliefs from Pauline's testimony in a category that contains beliefs that are or would be mostly true; namely, *those beliefs that are supported by Helen's testimony*. For instance, were Fred to decide between accepting the reports of two different speakers, one of whom has the support of Helen's testimony and another who lacks this support, most of the time Fred would do well to accept the reports of the former. That is, most of the time, forming beliefs from sources supported by Helen's testimony would lead to the truth. In this sense, then, the positive reasons that Fred possesses for Pauline's testimony *do* render it likely in an objective sense that her testimony is true. The problem is that, by other measures of objective likelihood, Fred's positive reasons *do not* render it likely that Pauline's testimony is true. Fred's belief about the wingspan of albatrosses also belongs to a category that contains beliefs that are or would be mostly false; namely, *those beliefs that are supported by Pauline's testimony*. Moreover, because Pauline is the direct source of the belief, it is clear that her unreliability is not offset by the excellence of Fred's reasons for believing her. So, although Fred does have excellent positive reasons for believing Pauline's testimony, the belief in question is not justified or warranted.[14]

It is, therefore, not enough for testimonial justification or warrant that a hearer have even epistemically excellent positive reasons for accepting a speaker's testimony—the speaker must also do her part in the testimonial exchange by offering testimony that is reliable or otherwise truth-conducive. Thus, PR-N&S is false and, accordingly, reductionism in the epistemology of testimony is false.

---

[14] A further reductionist strategy for resisting the conclusion of NESTED SPEAKER is to make it part of the definition of "appropriate" that the reasons in question lead hearers to reports that bear a reliable connection with the truth. This would make it impossible for a subject to have appropriate positive reasons for believing a report that wasn't reliably connected with the truth. This strategy, however, has at least one of two unattractive consequences. It either (i) makes the requirement for positive reasons so externalistic that it undermines the central motivation for endorsing the Positive Reasons Thesis in the first place; namely, to preserve a link between epistemic justification/warrant and subjective rationality. Or (ii), it makes the requirements for testimonial justification/warrant so stringent that there would be far less testimonial justification/warrant than is intuitively acceptable.

5.3 Non-Reductionism

Characterizing Non-Reductionism

Given the problems facing reductionism, let us now turn to non-reductionism to see if this view of testimony fares any better. Non-reductionism is the most widely accepted view of testimonial knowledge (justification/warrant) in the current literature.[15] Such a view is standardly traced back to the work of Thomas Reid and the following passage is frequently cited, not only in its support, but also as arguably the earliest explicit endorsement of non-reductionism:

The wise author of nature hath planted in the human mind a propensity to rely upon human testimony before we can give a reason for doing so. This, indeed, puts our judgments almost entirely in the power of those who are about us in the first period of life; but this is necessary both to our preservation and to our improvement. If children were so framed as to pay no regard to testimony or authority, they must, in the literal sense, perish for lack of knowledge.

I believed by instinct whatever they [my parents and tutors] told me, long before I had the idea of a lie, or a thought of the possibility of their deceiving me. Afterwards, upon reflection, I found they had acted like fair and honest people, who wished me well. I found that, if I had not believed what they told me, before I could give a reason for my belief, I had to this day been little better than a changeling. And although this natural credulity hath sometimes occasioned my being imposed upon by deceivers, yet it hath been of infinite advantage to me upon the whole; therefore, I consider it as another good gift of Nature. (Reid 1983: 281–2)

According to Reid, then, accepting the testimony of others couldn't require having non-testimonially grounded positive reasons—as reductionists require—since we must all rely on the reports of our parents and

---

[15] Proponents of various versions of non-reductionism include Austin (1979), Welbourne (1979, 1981, 1986, and 1994), Evans (1982), Reid (1983), Ross (1986), Hardwig (1985 and 1991), Coady (1992 and 1994), Burge (1993 and 1997), Plantinga (1993b), Webb (1993), Dummett (1994), Foley (1994), McDowell (1994), Strawson (1994), Williamson (1996 and 2000), Goldman (1999), Schmitt (1999), Insole (2000), Owens (2000 and 2006), Rysiew (2002), Weiner (2003), Sosa (2006), Goldberg (2006), and Goldberg and Henderson (2006). Some phrase their view in terms of knowledge, others in terms of justification or entitlement, still others in terms of warrant. Audi (1997, 1998, and 2006) embraces a non-reductionist view of testimonial knowledge, but not of testimonial justification. Stevenson (1993), Millgram (1997), and Graham (2006) defend restricted versions of non-reductionism. As mentioned earlier, I shall, for ease of exposition, focus almost entirely on non-reductionism with respect to knowledge in this chapter. However, much of what is said applies, *mutatis mutandis*, to non-reductionism with respect to justification and warrant.

caretakers long before we possess any evidence regarding their reliability or trustworthiness.[16] Thus, testimony is an irreducible source of knowledge (justification/warrant), on an epistemic par with sources that are often taken to be more basic, such as sense perception, memory, and inductive inference.

More recent endorsements of non-reductionism add to Reid's characterization that, though the presence of positive reasons is not necessary to acquire testimonially based knowledge, the absence of negative reasons is. This requirement, though considerably weaker than either version of the reductionist's Positive Reasons Thesis, is included to prevent the compatibility of testimonial knowledge and doxastic irrationality or irresponsibility. So, for instance, John McDowell maintains that "knowledge is available to be picked up ... by someone whose taking the speaker's word for it is *not doxastically irresponsible* ... it is obviously doxastically irresponsible to believe someone about whom one *has positive reason to believe he is not trustworthy, or not likely to be informed about the subject matter of the conversation*" (McDowell 1994: 210–11, emphasis added). Similarly, Tyler Burge writes that "[a] person is entitled to accept as true something that is presented as true and that is intelligible to him, *unless there are stronger reasons not to do so*" (Burge 1993: 467, emphasis added). Following this view, Matthew Weiner accepts the principle: "We are justified in accepting anything that we are told unless there is positive evidence against doing so" (Weiner 2003: 257). And Robert Audi claims that "gaining testimonially grounded knowledge normally requires *only having no reason for doubt about the credibility of the attester*" (Audi 1998: 142, emphasis added). The underlying thought here is that so long as there is no available evidence *against* accepting a speaker's report, the hearer has no positive epistemic work to do in order to accept the testimony in question.[17] Otherwise put, non-reductionists maintain that, so as long as there are no relevant undefeated defeaters,

---

[16] I discuss this particular point in much more detail in Chapter 7.

[17] This is a broad characterization, with subtler or more robust versions of non-reductionism not always clearly subsumed by it. For instance, Goldberg (2006) requires also that the hearer have "the epistemic right to rely on" the testimony of the speaker in question (2006: 128); Goldberg and Henderson (2006) require that the hearer "monitor" the speaker for signs of incompetence and insincerity; and Graham (2006) claims that the justification provided by the "event or state of comprehending the attester's presentation-as-true that P ... may fall short of on balance justification (even if undefeated)" (2006: 94). In my direct arguments against non-reductionism later in this chapter, however, even these subtler versions, particularly Goldberg (2006) and Goldberg and Henderson (2006), will be subsumed.

hearers can acquire testimonally based knowledge *merely* on the basis of a speaker's testimony.

There are two different kinds of undefeated defeaters that are typically taken by non-reductionists to be relevant here—what we called in Chapter 2 *psychological defeaters* and *normative defeaters*. Psychological defeaters, it may be recalled, are doubts or beliefs that are had by S, yet indicate that S's belief that p is either false or unreliably formed or sustained, while normative defeaters are doubts or beliefs that S ought to have, yet indicate that S's belief that p is either false or unreliably formed or sustained. According to non-reductionism, then, acquiring testimonially based knowledge is an extremely simple epistemic process that functions well between speakers and hearers unless it is interrupted by the presence of an undefeated defeater.

In this section, my purpose shall be, first, to provide a precise and plausible formulation of non-reductionism in the epistemology of testimony. In so doing, I shall show that non-reductionism, as it is currently characterized in the literature, is a wholly inadequate view of testimonial knowledge. Specifically, I shall argue that, in addition to the absence of undefeated defeaters, there are at least three further conditions that need to be added to this view to render it plausible. Thus, I intend to show that acquiring knowledge through the word of others is a process that is far more complicated and easily interrupted than proponents of non-reductionism maintain. I shall then argue that, even with such a precise and plausible formulation of their view, non-reductionists face a serious problem. I shall conclude, then, that neither reductionism nor non-reductionism provides an adequate theory of the epistemic status of our testimonial beliefs.

A Necessary Condition on the Testimony

An initial formulation of non-reductionism with respect to testimonial knowledge can be expressed in the following way:[18]

---

[18] Since my ultimate goal is to characterize the minimal requirements needed to render any version of non-reductionism with respect to testimonial knowledge plausible, I shall speak simply of "non-reductionism," where this is not meant to refer to any particular non-reductionist's position. It should also be clear that, in what follows, NR is the *weakest* formulation of the non-reductionist's position, which I begin with for dialectical purposes. As I shall soon show, many non-reductionists replace condition (NR3) with a stronger one, such as TEP-N from Chapter 2.

> NR: For every speaker, A, and hearer, B, B knows that p on the basis
> of A's testimony if and only if:
>
> (NR1) B believes that p on the basis of the content of A's testi-
> mony,
>
> (NR2) B has no undefeated (psychological or normative) defeaters
> for A's testimony, and
>
> (NR3) it is true that p.

Now, as was the case with our formulation of R in the previous section, I have not only included condition (NR1), despite the fact that most non-reductionists do not explicitly include a condition like this when presenting their view, I have also formulated NR in terms of "A's testimony" rather than in terms of "A's testimony that p." Both of these additions are based on the relevant considerations from Chapter 2, but can easily be substituted with their stronger counterparts. Condition (NR2) replaces the reductionist's requirement for positive reasons with a weaker one requiring merely the absence of undefeated defeaters, and condition (NR3) is included simply to distinguish testimonially based knowledge from testimonially justified or warranted belief. Thus, according to NR, *any true report* from *any kind of speaker* can lead to testimonial knowledge for *any sort of hearer;* the only epistemic obstacle to such a process is the presence of an undefeated defeater.

But now consider the following sort of case:

INCOMPETENT AGENT: Margaret is an extremely incompetent epistemic agent, continually forming perceptual beliefs without wearing her required pre-scription eyeglasses, testimonial beliefs on the basis of reading *The National Enquirer*, introspective beliefs when she is intoxicated, and so on. One day, Margaret again fails to wear her corrective lenses and forms the belief that there is a great horned owl in a tree 50 feet away. Her belief happens to be true. Later that day, Margaret meets someone on the street named Eleanor, reports her owl sighting to her, and Eleanor comes to believe that there was a great horned owl in a neighborhood tree on the basis of Margaret's testimony. Moreover, since it is possible for great horned owls to be in this neighborhood and Eleanor knows nothing about Margaret's epistemic habits, there are no undefeated defeaters for the report in question, that is, Eleanor neither believes nor has evidence available to her such that she should believe that Margaret's report is false or unreliable.

Does Eleanor know that there was a great horned owl in a neighborhood tree? Intuitively, no, despite the satisfaction of conditions (NR1)–(NR3). For even though Eleanor's *response* to the proffered testimony is not epistemically defective, Margaret's *testimony* is. In particular, Margaret's report of her perceptual belief, though true, fails to be reliably produced or appropriately connected with the truth, thereby preventing it from leading to knowledge for her hearers. What this type of case shows, therefore, is that there is a further condition necessary for testimonial knowledge, one that requires that *the proffered testimony be reliable, truth-conducive, or otherwise epistemically acceptable*.

Now, as we saw in Chapter 2, many non-reductionists have recognized the need to strengthen condition (NR3) and have, therefore, replaced it with TEP-N. So, for instance, Michael Welbourne maintains that "[a]*ll* that is required of a listener who understands a knowledgeable teller if the knowledge is to be successfully transmitted to him is that he *believe* the teller" (Welbourne 1986: 5–6, original emphasis). Welbourne is, therefore, requiring TEP-N here since the speaker in question must be "knowledgeable," that is, she must have the knowledge in question herself in order to pass it to a hearer. But even though substituting (NR3) with TEP-N adequately addresses the problem found in INCOMPETENT AGENT—Eleanor does not know that there was a great horned owl in a neighborhood tree because Margaret does not speak from knowledge—we also saw in Chapter 2 that such a condition is in fact too strong a requirement for testimonial knowledge. So, let us reformulate the non-reductionist's view of testimonial knowledge, not by replacing (NR3) with TEP-N, but by adding RS-N to NR*, which was defended in Chapter 3:

NR*: For every speaker, A, and hearer, B, B knows that *p* on the basis of A's testimony if and only if:
(NR1) B believes that *p* on the basis of the content of A's testimony,
(NR2) B has no undefeated (psychological or normative) defeaters for A's testimony,
(NR3) it is true that *p*, and
(NR4) A's testimony is reliable or otherwise truth-conducive.

Hence, in addition to the presence of undefeated defeaters, there is a further epistemic obstacle to the acquisition of testimonial knowledge—namely, the unreliability of the testimony in question. Accordingly, only true reports made by *reliable testifiers* can become testimonial knowledge for hearers.[19]

A Necessary Condition on the Hearer

Even the revised NR* is not an adequate account of testimonial knowledge, however, because there is a second problem for non-reductionism. Consider, for instance, the following case, which bears many similarities to COMPULSIVELY TRUSTING from Chapter 2:

COMPULSIVELY GOOD-NATURED: Stuart is a compulsively good-natured epistemic agent. Not only does he always think highly of other people, he is incapable of thinking poorly of them even when the circumstances clearly call for doing so. That is, even when Stuart has good evidence available to him for thinking, e.g., that someone is lying to him, deceiving him, betraying him, and so on, he can't come to believe this. One day, Gilbert, a friendly neighbor down the street, tells Stuart that he saw a cougar in a nearby hiking trail and Stuart, of course, readily accepts his testimony. Now, it turns out that Gilbert did in fact see a cougar in the aforementioned hiking trail, that he is very reliable with respect to both his epistemic and testimonial practices in this case, and that Stuart has no reason to doubt the proffered testimony. But, given Stuart's compulsively good nature, even if he had massive amounts of evidence available to him indicating, e.g., that Gilbert did not see a cougar, that he is an unreliable epistemic agent, that he is an unreliable testifier, that cougars do not live in this part of the country, and so on, he would have nonetheless accepted Gilbert's testimony.

Does Stuart know that there was a cougar in a nearby hiking trail on the basis of Gilbert's testimony? To my mind, the answer is no. For the only epistemic requirement placed on the hearer in NR* is condition (NR2). And although Stuart does, as a matter of fact, satisfy this condition by virtue of not having any undefeated defeaters for Gilbert's report, the way in which he satisfies it is inadequate for testimonial knowledge.

To see this, notice that because of Stuart's compulsively good nature, he simply *lacks the capacity* to be sensitive to the presence of defeaters. In this respect, Stuart is—as was true of Bill in COMPULSIVELY TRUST-ING—no better epistemically than a subject who has been brainwashed

---

[19] This problem resembles the one that NESTED SPEAKER poses to reductionism: namely, that the possession of good positive reasons by a hearer is not sufficient for accepting a speaker's testimony with justification or warrant since the possession of such reasons, even objectively excellent ones, does not necessarily put one in contact with testimony that is reliable.

or programmed to accept any report that is made by any speaker. For Stuart is such that he would have accepted Gilbert's testimony *under any circumstances*.[20] Because of this, the mere fact that Stuart does not have any undefeated defeaters for Gilbert's testimony is clearly not enough to satisfy condition (NR2) of NR* in a way that has epistemic value. Clocks, telephone poles, and coffee cups also do not have any defeaters in this trivial way.[21] In order for satisfaction of the no-defeater condition to properly reflect on the epistemic agent, the agent in question must have the *general capacity* to recognize and process counterevidence; otherwise put, the agent must *substantively* satisfy the no-defeater condition.

So, could the non-reductionist simply add a condition requiring the substantive satisfaction of (NR2)? Although the addition of this requirement would successfully prevent epistemic agents like Stuart from acquiring testimonial knowledge, there is a deeper problem with NR*. Consider, for instance, the following case:

COMPULSIVELY PARANOID: While in her home community, Beatrice is a compulsively paranoid epistemic agent. Though she has a bit of evidence suggesting that a few of her neighbors have lied to her in the past, she has come to be utterly convinced that everyone in her neighborhood is constantly trying to deceive her, undermine her successes, and destroy her reputation. At the same time, however, she is equally certain that those around her know that she is suspicious of them. Because of this, Beatrice is confident that she is actually surrounded by very reliable testifiers. For given their intent to deceive her coupled with their suspicion that she knows about their intent, Beatrice concludes that everyone will in fact report what they believe under the assumption that she will believe the opposite. One day, Beatrice runs into her neighbor Beverly, whom she has no good epistemic reason to distrust, and Beverly tells her that there is a golden eagle's nest in a local tree. Upon receiving this report, Beatrice reasons thusly: "Beverly wants to deceive me but she also knows that I am suspicious of her. So, she has reported to me that there is a golden eagle's nest in a local tree, believing that I will disbelieve her. But I know her strategy and will thwart her plan to deceive me by

---

[20] Let me emphasize that the problem with Stuart is not that he is simply a *gullible* epistemic agent with respect to incoming testimony. For I take it that even very gullible people have the *general capacity* to appreciate counterevidence, even if they are very bad at doing so. Thus, very gullible people, though capable of substantively satisfying the no-defeater condition, simply fail to do so very often. By contrast, because Stuart is compulsively good-natured, he is psychologically incapable of appreciating counterevidence and thus he is epistemically defective in a much deeper way than the merely gullible. For that reason, Stuart cannot satisfy the no-defeater condition in anything but a trivial way.

[21] I shall develop this point in much more detail in Chapter 7.

accepting her testimony. Therefore, I will believe that there is a golden eagle's nest in a local tree." Now, the report in question is in fact true, Beverly is a reliable testifier, and Beatrice does not believe, or have evidence available to her such that she should believe, that Beverly's report is either false or unreliable. Moreover, Beatrice is capable of being sensitive to defeaters and, when she is outside of her home community, she is even appropriately sensitive to them.

Does Beatrice know that there is a golden eagle's nest in a local tree on the basis of Beverly's testimony?[22] Even though she substantively satisfied condition (NR2), in addition to fulfilling conditions (NR1), (NR3), and (NR4), the answer is clearly no. For while Stuart's problem *was the complete absence of the capacity to be sensitive to defeaters*, Beatrice's problem is that she is *inappropriately sensitive to defeaters*. Otherwise put, even though she has the general capacity to be sensitive to defeaters, her sensitivity mechanism is defective or malfunctioning in an important sense. And while this defect or malfunction is *truth-preserving* with respect to incoming testimony in Beatrice's home community, it is not *knowledge-preserving*.

Notice, first, that because of Beatrice's compulsively paranoid nature, she is overly sensitive to the presence of counterevidence. On the basis of scanty evidence that a few of her neighbors have lied to her in the past, she has come to believe that everyone in her neighborhood is intent on deceiving her. So, while Stuart is such that he can't believe that there is counterevidence present when there is, Beatrice is such that she believes that there is counterevidence present even when there is not. In both of these cases, however, there is a clear sense in which the hearer in question is an unreliable or improperly functioning recipient of testimony. For even though Beatrice, unlike Stuart, substantively satisfies condition

---

[22] It should be emphasized that Beatrice's inference does not interfere with the belief in question being testimonial in origin. For it does not differ in any epistemically significant way from a rational inference. For instance, suppose Beatrice were to reason thusly: "Whenever Beverly has told me something in the past, it has turned out to be true. So, I have reason to believe that Beverly is a reliable testifier. I will, therefore, accept her testimony in this particular case." Now, it is plausible to suppose that this sort of rational inference is tacitly operative in much of the testimony that is accepted, and yet we rightly regard the resulting knowledge as testimonial in origin. Hence, similar considerations should apply with respect to Beatrice's acceptance of Beverly's testimony in COMPULSIVELY PARANOID.

However, if one is still troubled by the role of inference in the formation of Beatrice's belief, the case can simply be modified so that she does not engage in any particular inference about Beverly's current piece of testimony. Rather, Beatrice forms the belief in question by following a general strategy of accepting the testimony of her neighbors, where this strategy is underwritten by her inference that her neighbors are trying to deceive her but know that she is suspicious of them, thereby rendering them generally reliable testifiers.

(NR2), she does so irrationally and fortuitously. In particular, she has two irrational beliefs which, when combined, quite luckily lead to the absence of relevant counterbeliefs and counterevidence. And even though this lucky coincidence preserves the truth of the belief in question, neither explicit irrationality nor luck of this sort is compatible with testimonial knowledge.

But, even more importantly, let us briefly consider the non–reductionist's rationale for including condition (NR2) in the first place. If this weren't a necessary condition on such a view, hearers could acquire testimonial knowledge from any reliable speaker, no matter how irrational or epistemically irresponsible such acceptance was. It is precisely to avoid this radically counterintuitive picture that non–reductionists include the no-defeater condition. Testimonial knowledge is defeasible, through the presence of either an undefeated psychological or normative defeater. We can, therefore, accept much of what we are told on simple trust according to non–reductionism, but not where this acceptance is epistemically irrational or irresponsible. However, if this is the rationale for the inclusion of condition (NR2), then it should be all the more clear that a subject like Beatrice does not acquire knowledge under the circumstances described above. For, as previously mentioned, it is clear that the process by which she comes to accept the testimony in question is highly irrational. Thus, by the non–reductionist's own admission that explicit irrationality is incompatible with knowledge, Beatrice turns out to not have the testimonial knowledge in question.

What the two cases above show, therefore, is that in order to acquire knowledge from the testimony of a speaker, *the hearer in question has to be a properly functioning or reliable recipient of testimony,* where having the capacity for and being appropriately sensitive to defeaters are at least two central components of this broader requirement.[23] Let us, then, reformulate the non–reductionists's view in the following way:

NR**: For every speaker, A, and hearer, B, B knows that p on the basis of A's testimony if and only if:
> (NR1) B believes that p on the basis of the content of A's testimony,

---

[23] For further discussion of "proper function" and "reliability," see Plantinga (1993b) and Goldman (1986), respectively.

(NR2) B has no undefeated (psychological or normative) defeaters for A's testimony,

(NR3) it is true that p,

(NR4) A's testimony is reliable or otherwise truth-conducive, and

(NR5) B is a reliable or properly functioning recipient of testimony.[24]

So, in addition to both the reliability of the testifier in question and the absence of undefeated defeaters, there is a further condition needed to render non-reductionism acceptable. Even those proponents of non-reductionism who saw the need for a condition on the speaker's testimony, however, have missed this crucial aspect of testimonial knowledge. But the need for it should be clear: even if speakers are perfectly reliable testifiers, hearers need to be reliable recipients of their testimony. And, despite the fact that most non-reductionists think the inclusion of (NR2) sufficiently ensures this, we have seen that such a condition can be satisfied trivially, irrationally, and luckily, none of which is adequate for testimonial knowledge.

A Necessary Condition on the Environment

Even the twice revised NR** is not an adequate account of testimonial knowledge, however, because there is a third problem for non-reductionism. Consider, for example, the following case:

INSULAR COMMUNITY: Marvin is an epistemically impeccable recipient of testimony. Not only does he have the capacity for being sensitive to defeaters, but he is also appropriately and reliably sensitive to them when accepting the reports of others. One evening, while on a road trip, Marvin stops in a small town to find a hotel for the night and he encounters a large group of people

---

[24] In a complete account of testimonial knowledge, more will need to be said about the level of generality appropriate for this condition. It may, for instance, be too weak epistemically to require merely that the hearer be a properly functioning or reliable recipient of testimony with respect to the acceptance of A's testimony that p. For, what if this is the only statement for which a hearer would satisfy condition (NR5)? Some may here doubt whether this is enough to enable the acquisition of testimonial knowledge. On the other hand, it may be too strong epistemically to require that the hearer be an overall properly functioning or reliable recipient of testimony. A hearer may, for instance, be inappropriately sensitive to defeaters about her political beliefs. But surely, one might claim, this should not prevent her from satisfying condition (NR5) when acquiring scientific beliefs, for which she is impeccably sensitive to defeaters.

gathered for an annual neighborhood parade. Out of this large crowd, Marvin quite fortuitously focuses on Alfred, the only member of this epistemic community who reliably shares information with "outsiders," and asks him where they are. Alfred tells Marvin that they are in Smithville. Now, it is true that they are in Smithville, Alfred is a reliable testifier with respect to this information, and Marvin, not knowing that the testimonial habits of the members of this community are extremely unreliable when "outsiders" are involved, readily accepts the proffered testimony. Moreover, because he has no reason for thinking that Smithville differs from his own community in any epistemically relevant way, Marvin does not believe, or have evidence available to him such that he should believe, that Alfred's report is either false or unreliable.

Does Marvin know that he is in Smithville on the basis of Alfred's testimony? To my mind, the answer to this question is clearly negative, despite the satisfaction of conditions $(NR1)-(NR5)$ of NR^{**}.[25] For, even though both the speaker and the hearer in our envisaged case are reliable participants in the testimonial exchange in question, the epistemic circumstances are not suitable to the reception of reliable testimony.[26]

To see this, notice that the fact that Marvin acquires a justified or warranted true belief about his whereabouts is, in large part, due to good fortune. For not only is Alfred surrounded by a crowd of testifiers who are extremely unreliable sources of information for "outsiders," but Marvin is also completely unaware of the epistemic habits of both the inhabitants of Smithville in general and of Alfred in particular. Because of this, that he approaches Alfred rather than any of the other members of Smithville, encounters a reliable testifier rather than an unreliable one, and acquires a true belief rather than a false one, are all strokes of good luck.

Now, the precise nature of the problem with this sort of luck can be diagnosed in two different ways. First, one may argue that the problem with Marvin's belief is that it is merely an *accident that it is true rather than false* and

---

[25] I should note that it is not open to the non-reductionist to argue that the fact that Marvin is unaware of the epistemic habits of this new community provides him with an undefeated defeater for accepting the testimony in question (and, accordingly, that he fails condition (NR2) of NR**). For to require that Marvin have some basis for thinking that the inhabitants of Smithville are reliable testifiers is to require that he have *positive reasons* for accepting Alfred's report with justification or warrant, a requirement that non-reductionists explicitly reject. And, since Marvin has no reason to believe that Smithville differs epistemically from his own community, there is no other sense in which he could be said to have a defeater for Alfred's testimony.

[26] Since Plantinga (1993*b*) includes a condition on the environment in his general account of warrant, his view of testimonial knowledge will most likely avoid this sort of problem.

is thereby a Gettier-type case.[27] For instance, consider one of the famous examples illustrating this sort of accidentality: Albert is driving down the street, sees a barn in a field, and forms the true belief that there is a barn in the field on the basis of this perceptual experience. However, unbeknownst to Albert, the barn that he saw is the only real one, completely surrounded by barn facades.[28] In this way, just as Albert's belief that there is a barn in the field could equally have been false, so too Marvin's belief about his whereabouts could equally have been false. Hence, in both cases, the belief in question is true, but only by accident. Second, one may claim that the problem with Marvin's belief is that it is merely an *accident that it is justified rather than unjustified*.[29] Specifically, it may be argued that INSULAR COMMUNITY differs from standard Gettier-type cases by virtue of the accidentality being located at the justificatory level rather than at the level of truth. For, one may contend, the fact that Marvin acquired the true belief that he is in Smithville is not, in one sense, an accident: Alfred is a perfectly reliable testifier, both in general and with respect to this information. Instead, that Marvin used a reliable source of information rather than an unreliable one and, accordingly, acquired a justified belief rather than an unjustified one is where the accidentality comes in.

It is not necessary that we here choose between these competing diagnoses. For the general problem that INSULAR COMMUNITY points to is that *the environment in question needs to be suitable for receiving reliable testimony*.[30] Because the epistemic community that Marvin

---

[27] See Gettier (1963) for the initial formulation of the problem and Shope (1983) for some of the many permutations of Gettier cases.

[28] This case is originally due to Carl Ginet, but first appeared in print in Goldman (1976).

[29] See Reed (2000) for the distinction between accidental truth and accidental justification.

[30] It has been suggested to me by Frederick Schmitt that the problem of INSULAR COMMUNITY might be better resolved by including a "metareliability" condition. (See, for instance, Schmitt (1987 and 1999).) In particular, rather than locating the problem with Marvin's testimonial belief in his epistemic environment, the deeper problem, it is argued, is that Marvin is unable to distinguish reliable sources of testimony from unreliable ones. In this way, if we include a metareliability constraint that requires that the recipient of testimony select a reliable source via the capacity to distinguish the reliable sources from the unreliable, then the problem of INSULAR COMMUNITY would be avoided. I suspect, however, that even if such a metareliability constraint would adequately address the problem of INSULAR COMMUNITY, most non-reductionists would regard such a condition as being far too strong. For, in most cases, the natural way in which a recipient of testimony could satisfy such a metareliablity constraint would be via the acquisition of positive reasons on behalf of those sources that are reliable. And since the requirement for positive reasons is precisely what divides non-reductionism from reductionism, a condition of this sort threatens one of the central tenets of non-reductionism: namely, that testimonial knowledge can be acquired in the complete absence of any reason to believe

encounters is filled with massively unreliable testifiers, the only way that Marvin could acquire true beliefs that are justified or warranted in this environment (without access to further information) is through good fortune. Moreover, this sort of problem can arise in a multitude of ways: one may fortuitously pick up the only reliable book or magazine on a shelf, or turn on the only reliable radio or television station, and so on. Thus, even if both the speaker and hearer in question are epistemically impeccable, being situated in a massively unreliable epistemic environment can nonetheless prevent the acquisition of testimonial knowledge. So, let us reformulate the non-reductionist's view in the following way:

NR***: For every speaker, A, and hearer, B, B knows that p on the basis of A's testimony if and only if:

(NR1) B believes that p on the basis of the content of A's testimony,

(NR2) B has no undefeated (psychological or normative) defeaters for A's testimony,

(NR3) it is true that p,

(NR4) A's testimony is reliable or otherwise truth-conducive,

(NR5) B is a reliable or properly functioning recipient of testimony,

and

(NR6) the environment in which B receives A's testimony is suitable for the reception of reliable testimony.

There may, of course, be further conditions that need to be added to yield a fully satisfactory epistemology of testimony—for instance, though we have seen that the Reduction Thesis of reductionism is false, we have yet to evaluate the Positive Reasons Thesis of this view. My purpose here, however, is simply to show that NR*** expresses the minimal requirements for a non-reductionist account of testimonial knowledge. Thus, unlike the versions found in the current literature in the epistemology of testimony, a precise description of non-reductionism is that *properly functioning recipients*

that the testifier in question is reliable. Therefore, since my purpose at this point is to formulate the *minimal* requirements for a non-reductionist view of testimonial knowledge, and since a metareliability condition is considerably stronger than one on the epistemic environment, I shall include the latter condition rather than the former in my final version of non-reductionism.

of testimony may defeasibly acquire knowledge from the true reports of *reliable speakers* in an *epistemically suitable environment*.

Rejecting Non-Reductionism

Now that we have a precise characterization of non-reductionism with respect to testimonial knowledge, we can turn to assessing whether it is an epistemologically adequate view. To this end, notice that even with the addition of the conditions found in NR***, it is central to the non-reductionist's view to altogether reject both versions of the reductionist's Positive Reasons Thesis, that is, to maintain that positive reasons are neither necessary nor sufficient for testimonial knowledge (justification/warrant) (and, accordingly, that testimonial knowledge (justification, warrant) is an irreducible epistemic source). Thus, the non-reductionist holds that, so long as the hearer is properly functioning and there is no evidence *against* accepting a speaker's report, the hearer has no positive epistemic work to do in order to acquire knowledge (justified/warranted belief) on the basis of the testimony in question. In what follows, however, I argue that this is false—hearers *do* have some positive work to do for testimonial knowledge (justification/warrant). Specifically, I show that although PR-N&S is false, PR-N is nevertheless true—that is, despite the fact that NESTED SPEAKER revealed that positive reasons cannot be *both* necessary *and* sufficient for testimonial justification/warrant, the possession of such reasons is nonetheless a necessary condition. Thus, I show that non-reductionism in the epistemology of testimony is false.

To begin, notice that in denying even the weaker reading of the Positive Reasons Thesis of reductionism—i.e., PR-N—non-reductionists commit themselves to saying that testimonial knowledge can be acquired in the complete absence of *any* relevant positive reasons on the part of the hearer. Let us, therefore, consider such a case.

ALIEN: Sam, an average human being, is taking a walk through the forest one sunny morning and, in the distance, he sees someone drop a book. Although the individual's physical appearance enables Sam to identify her as an alien from another planet, he does not know anything about either this kind of alien or the planet from which she comes. Now, Sam eventually loses sight of the alien, but he is able to recover the book that she dropped. Upon opening it, he immediately notices that it appears to be written in English and looks like what we on Earth would call a diary. Moreover, after reading the first sentence of the book, Sam forms the corresponding belief that tigers have eaten some of the inhabitants of the author's planet during their exploration of Earth. It turns out that the book is a diary, the alien does communicate in English, and it is both true and reliably written in the diary that tigers have eaten some of the inhabitants of the planet in question. Moreover, Sam is not only a properly functioning recipient of testimony, he is also situated in an environment that is suitable for the reception of reliable reports.[31]

Now, since the book in question is written by an alien, Sam truly has no epistemically relevant positive reasons: he has no common-sense alien-psychological theory, he has no beliefs about the general reliability of aliens as testifiers, he has no beliefs about the reliability of the author of this book, he has no beliefs about how "diaries" function in this alien society, and so on. Moreover, if Sam attends to the narrative voice of the author in the hope of trying to assess her competence and sincerity, he would be engaged in a fruitless activity since there is no reason to believe that signs of competence and sincerity on the planet in question correspond to these signs on Earth. Sam cannot even compare the content of the reports in this diary to his background beliefs since he does not know that the words in this book are used in the same way that we on Earth use them. So, here is a case in which a hearer truly fails to have any positive reasons on behalf of a speaker's testimony. Let us suppose, further, that there is nothing about the diary that provides Sam with relevant psychological or normative defeaters, and thus he clearly satisfies conditions (NR1)–(NR6) with respect to accepting the alien's testimony. The crucial question we now need to ask, then, is whether Sam knows that tigers have eaten some of the inhabitants of the planet in question on the basis of the alien's diary.

Here the answer should clearly be no. Despite the fact that Sam's belief satisfies all of the conditions in NR***, it seems plainly irrational epistemically for him to form the belief in question on the basis of the alien's testimony. For, it may very well be accepted practice in alien society to be insincere and deceptive when testifying to others. Or, normal alien psychology may be what we Earthlings would consider psychosis. Or, the language that the aliens use, though superficially indistinguishable from English, may really be Twenglish, where Twenglish uses the

---

[31] Obviously, the mere fact that there is at present one alien in Sam's environment—who happens to be an extremely reliable testifier—does not at all call into question whether condition (NR6) is satisfied.

"negation" sign for affirming a proposition. Or, "diaries" in the alien society may be what we on Earth regard as science fiction, and so on. For all Sam knows when he reads the book, each of these scenarios is just as likely as the possibility that these aliens are reliable testifiers who speak English. But, in the absence of any way to discriminate among these possibilities, it seems clear that the appropriate epistemic response is to withhold belief.[32]

It is of further interest to note that the general diagnosis offered of ALIEN appeals only to features to which non-reductionists are already committed. To see this, recall that a central condition of non-reductionism (expressed as NR2 above) requires that the hearer in question not possess any relevant undefeated defeaters for accepting a speaker's report. For instance, if I believe that you frequently lie but nevertheless come to believe that owls are raptors on the basis of your testimony, then, according to non-reductionism, my testimonial belief fails to qualify as justified, warranted, or known, even if it is in fact true and reliably formed in an appropriate environment. Why? Because even non-reductionists agree that testimonial knowledge (justification/warrant) is incompatible with at least certain kinds of epistemic *irrationality*.[33] What ALIEN reveals, however, is that accepting a speaker's report in the complete absence of positive reasons can be just as epistemically irrational as accepting such a report in the presence of an undefeated defeater—indeed, perhaps even more so. If I, for example, have an undefeated psychological defeater by virtue of believing that you *occasionally* lie, would it be more epistemically irrational for me to trust your testimony than it would be for Sam to trust the alien's in the absence of positive reasons? Not at all. For while Sam knows *absolutely nothing* about the alien in question, I have all sorts of beliefs, both about humans in general and about you in particular, that are relevant to my acceptance of your testimony—for instance, I believe that humans often speak sincerely, that reports on Earth are usually offered to communicate information, that

---

[32] It was suggested to me by Lizzie Fricker that another type of example that may make the same general point would be a person receiving testimony over the internet, with absolutely no epistemically relevant information about the source of the testimony. (Fricker also mentions this sort of case in her (2002).)

[33] Even outside the epistemology of testimony, this is a very widely accepted view. For instance, adding a no-defeater condition to theories of epistemic justification/warrant that are otherwise externalist has become the standard response given to the counterexamples found in BonJour's (1980 and 1985). See, for instance, Nozick (1981), Goldman (1986), and Plantinga (1993b).

you do not exhibit any clear signs of being deceptive, and so on. Against the background of all of this incredibly rich positive information, my belief that you merely occasionally lie seems rather epistemically insignificant when compared with the fact that Sam doesn't even know whether aliens actually speak English. Accepting testimony in the absence of positive reasons can, then, be even more irrational than accepting testimony in the presence of undefeated defeaters. Thus, by showing that epistemic irrationality is involved in accepting a speaker's report in the complete absence of positive reasons—even more so than in some cases in which undefeated defeaters are present—ALIEN poses a challenge to non-reductionists on their own terms.[34]

Now, one way the non-reductionist may respond to ALIEN is to deny that Sam satisfies the relevant conditions in his acceptance of the contents of the "diary." Specifically, it may be argued that Sam fails the no-defeater condition because a context like that envisaged above, in which there is absolutely no epistemically relevant information about the speaker, report, or context, provides the hearer in question with evidence against the testimony in question. For instance, consider the following passage from Plantinga:

[Y]ou embark on a voyage of space exploration and land on a planet revolving about a distant sun. This planet has a favorable atmosphere, but you know little more about it. You crack the hatch, step out, and immediately find something that looks a lot like a radio; it periodically emits strings of sounds that, oddly enough, form sentences in English. The sentences emitted by this instrument express propositions only about topics of which you have no knowledge: what the weather is like in Beijing at the moment, whether Caesar had eggs on toast on the morning he crossed the Rubicon ... and the like. A bit unduly impressed with your find, you initially form the opinion that this quasi radio speaks the truth: that is, the propositions expressed (in English) by those sentences are true. But then you recall that you have no idea at all as to what the purpose of this apparent instrument is, whether it *has* a purpose, or how it came to be. You see that the probability of its being reliable, given what you know about it, is for you inscrutable. Then (in the absence of investigation) you have a defeater for your initial belief that the thing does, in fact, speak the truth ... If you don't have or get further information about its reliability, the reasonable course is agnosticism about that proposition. (Plantinga 2000: 224–5)

---

[34] I am grateful to comments from Joe Shieber that prompted the addition of this point.

The scenario described by Plantinga in this passage bears some striking similarities to that envisaged in ALIEN: in both cases, there is a testimonial source about which a hearer knows nothing at all, and the intuition we are invited to share is that it would be epistemically irrational for the hearer in question to form beliefs on the basis of this source. But, it may be asked, if the hearer possesses a defeater for trusting the radio in Plantinga's scenario, then why doesn't Sam possess a defeater for trusting the diary in ALIEN?

Rather than supporting non-reductionism, however, this response essentially concedes the necessity of positive reasons for testimonial justification or warrant. For, as both ALIEN and Plantinga's scenario are described, there is nothing about the source in question that suggests that its reports are either false or unreliable. If, for instance, the "diary" found in the forest had written in it that bison laid eggs, or the "radio" found on the new planet reported that Abraham Lincoln and Sigmund Freud were currently at lunch together, then the hearers may rightly be described as possessing undefeated defeaters for the corresponding beliefs. But the only negative reason it is appropriate to say that Sam has with respect to the alien's diary or that you have regarding the radio is *the absence of positive reasons*. Since the fundamental difference between reductionism and non-reductionism is precisely over the need for positive reasons, it is simply not available to the non-reductionist to claim that defeaters are present in such cases. Otherwise put, if the complete absence of positive reasons amounts to the presence of a defeater, then non-reductionism essentially collapses into reductionism on this issue.

A second response the non-reductionist may offer to ALIEN can be extracted from the view found in Goldberg and Henderson (2006).[35] According to Goldberg and Henderson, the non-reductionist need not sanction gullibility or irrationality on the part of a hearer in a testimonial exchange since such a view can incorporate a "monitoring requirement" into her epistemology of testimony. In particular, it is not enough on such a view that a hearer merely does not possess undefeated defeaters for a given testimonial belief; the hearer must also be actively monitoring for their presence.[36] Now, applying this response to the context at hand, the non-reductionist may argue that, while reading the alien's diary,

---

[35] A similar view with respect to mundane testimony can be found in Fricker (1994 and 1995).

[36] According to Goldberg and Henderson, actively monitoring requires "*being on the lookout*" for defeaters rather than the stronger "*going out and looking*" for them (Goldberg and Henderson 2006: 610).

Sam must be monitoring for the presence of any signs of the author's being either incompetent or insincere. And being on the lookout for defeaters in this way, it may be urged, renders Sam's acceptance of the contents of the diary not irrational, as is suggested in the original ALIEN case.

By way of response to this move, there are two points I should like to make. First, with respect to ALIEN, both non–reductionists who require monitoring and those who do not arrive at the same verdict: Sam comes to know that tigers have eaten some of the inhabitants of the planet in question on the basis of the alien's diary.[37] For, as was emphasized above, there is nothing about the situation described in ALIEN that suggests that the reports found in the diary are either false or unreliable. So, even if it is required that the recipient of testimony be on the lookout for counterevidence, there are not any relevant defeaters present for her to pick up on in ALIEN, thereby delivering precisely the counterintuitive consequence at issue. Moreover, if the non–reductionist then argues that the mere absence of positive reasons provides the monitoring hearer with a defeater, then this amounts to the first response above which, as I argued, essentially collapses into reductionism. Second, notice that it is entirely unclear, and indeed doubtful, that monitoring in a situation such as that found in ALIEN even makes sense as a meaningful requirement. For, as I emphasized above, Sam has no common-sense alien-psychological theory, he has no information about the general reliability of aliens as testifiers, he has no beliefs about how diaries function in this alien society, he has no reason to think that signs of competence and sincerity on the planet in question correspond to these signs on Earth, and so on. Given this, what exactly would Sam's monitoring while reading the alien's diary accomplish? Sure, he may be monitoring the alien's diary in the same way he would monitor a fellow human's, but why think that this would be an effective strategy for detecting defeaters in this alien society? The upshot of these considerations is that the addition of a monitoring requirement does nothing

---

[37] This should come as no surprise given that standard versions of non–reductionism will regard the so-called monitoring requirement proposed by Goldberg and Henderson as simply being subsumed by the no–normative–defeater requirement. For instance, if Greta should be, but is not, suspicious of Raul's honesty regarding his whereabouts last night, the standard non–reductionist will say that she has a normative defeater for his testimony that he was at Starbuck's, while Goldberg and Henderson will say that she was not properly monitoring Raul's testimony for signs of incompetence and insincerity. But the verdict that these two views arrive at is the same.

to help the non-reductionist avoid the counterintuitive consequences found in ALIEN.

A third strategy for denying the force of ALIEN is to argue that the non-reductionist's principle applies only to testimony offered by humans because only those who are members of *our* institution of testimony fall under it. The aliens may very well have their own institution of testimony on their planet, and their practices and epistemic principles may be quite similar to ours. But we cannot assume this similarity. Non-reductionism would thus be limited in its applicability to only members of our species and, accordingly, Sam would fail to acquire knowledge (justified/warranted belief) on the basis of the alien's testimony.

An obvious response to this objection is simply to modify the counterexample so that the testifier in question is in fact a member of our institution of testimony. For instance, suppose that Sally has been in a coma for the past two months and, upon waking, discovers that she has lost all of her previous knowledge except for her competence with the English language. Upon leaving the hospital, she stumbles upon a diary of an unknown author and begins reading it. Now, *ex hypothesi*, Sally no longer has common-sense beliefs about human psychology, she no longer has beliefs about the general reliability of humans as testifiers, she no longer has beliefs about how diaries function in our society, and so on. Is Sally justified in accepting the contents of the diary? Since this case is similar to the alien example in all *epistemically relevant* respects, the answer must be no. So, restricting the scope of non-reductionism to humans will not avoid this objection.

Furthermore, it seems that the primary explanation for why different epistemic standards would be invoked, depending on whether the speaker in question is a human or an alien, is precisely that we have all sorts *of epistemically relevant beliefs about our institution of testimony, and fail to have them in the case of the aliens.* For consider: why aren't we entitled to assume that the aliens are like us in all relevant respects? The natural answer seems to be that we do not have any *reason* to believe that this is the case. Thus, the very criterion for saying who is or is not a member of our institution of testimony is simply whether we have positive reasons for their testimony—which begs the question.

We have seen, then, that the hearer must also do her part in a testimonial exchange by having at least some epistemically relevant positive reasons for accepting the report in question. Thus, PR-N is true and, accordingly, even the version of non-reductionism found in NR*** fails to provide an adequate epistemology of testimony. The two dominant views of the epistemic status of testimonial beliefs, then—reductionism and non-reductionism—are both false.

6

Dualism in the Epistemology of Testimony

6.1 Dualism

In a testimonial exchange, information is typically conveyed between two central participants: the speaker and the hearer. My diagnosis of what has gone wrong in the epistemology of testimony is this: reductionists and non-reductionists alike have attempted to place nearly all of the epistemic work on only one or the other of these participants and, in so doing, have ignored the positive epistemic contribution that needs to be made by the other.

Reductionists, on the one hand, focus entirely on the *hearer* in a testimonial exchange. For, in order for testimonial justification or warrant to be reduced to the justification or warrant of perception, memory, and inference, all of the epistemic work needs to be shouldered by the hearer since it is precisely *her* positive reasons that are supposed to provide the reductive base. Reductionists, then, are committed to saying, first, that the reasons possessed by a hearer wholly determine the epistemic status of a given testimonial belief, and, second, that nothing about the speaker (apart from what may already be captured by the hearer's positive reasons) has epistemic relevance to the justification or warrant of a hearer's testimonial belief. But, as we have seen, both of these theses are false. For, as NESTED SPEAKER showed, no matter how excellent a hearer's positive reasons are on behalf of an instance of testimony, a speaker may still be offering a report that is thoroughly unreliable. Because of this, an adequate account of testimonial justification/warrant must include a condition requiring that the testimony in question is reliable or otherwise properly truth-conducive.

Non-reductionists, on the other hand, capture the work that needs to be done by the *speaker* in a testimonial exchange, but neglect the positive contribution that a hearer needs to make. Specifically, they correctly require the reliability of the speaker's testimony, but then mistakenly assume that the hearer merely has to satisfy the no-defeater condition. However, as ALIEN showed, no matter how reliable a speaker's testimony is, this cannot by itself make it rational for a hearer to accept her report. For this, the hearer needs to have some epistemically relevant positive reasons on behalf of the testimony in question.[1]

The upshot of these considerations is that it takes two to tango: the positive epistemic work of testimonial beliefs can be shouldered neither exclusively by the hearer nor by the speaker. To put this point somewhat crudely, the speaker-condition ensures reliability while the hearer-condition ensures rationality for testimonial knowledge (justification/warrant).[2] Thus, we need to look toward a view of testimonial knowledge (justification/warrant) that gives proper credence to its *dual nature*, one that includes the need for the reliability of the speaker (from non-reductionism) and the necessity of positive reasons (from reductionism). Accordingly, an adequate view of testimonial justification or warrant needs to recognize that the justification or warrant of a hearer's belief has *dual sources*, being grounded in both the reliability of the speaker and the rationality of the hearer's reasons for belief. More precisely, in light of these considerations, combined with those motivating the inclusion of conditions (NR4) and (NR5) of NR***, we should accept what I shall call *dualism*[3] in the epistemology of testimony, which includes at least the following:

D: For every speaker, A, and hearer, B, B knows (believes with justification/warrant) that *p* on the basis of A's testimony only if:

(D1) B believes that *p* on the basis of the content of A's testimony,

(D2) A's testimony is reliable or otherwise truth-conducive,

(D3) B is a reliable or properly functioning recipient of testimony,

(D4) the environment in which B receives A's testimony is suitable for the reception of reliable testimony,

---

[1] As I argued in the previous chapter, this conclusion is true even for more robust versions of non-reductionism, such as that found in Goldberg and Henderson (2006).

[2] I say "crudely" because I do not want to suggest either that the speaker-condition is entirely divorced from questions of rationality or that the hearer-condition is entirely divorced from questions of reliability.

[3] Of course, my use of this term has no direct bearing on its use in other contexts, such as in the philosophy of mind.

(D5) B has no undefeated (psychological or normative) defeaters for A's testimony, and

(D6) B has appropriate positive reasons for accepting A's testimony.[4]

Because dualism specifies only necessary conditions, there may be other conditions that need to be added for a complete epistemology of testimony.[5] What is of import, here, however, is that testimonial knowledge (justification/warrant) requires positive epistemic contributions from *both* the speaker *and* the hearer. Though this point is not acknowledged by the standard views in the current literature, it should be obvious: acquiring testimonial knowledge (justification/warrant) involves an exchange between *two* parties. And, in order for such an exchange to properly result in knowledge (justification/warrant), both parties need to do their epistemic work.[6]

6.2 The Scarcity of Information Objection

Let us now take a closer look at the specific conditions expressed in dualism. Conditions (D1)–(D5) should be rather familiar at this point: (D1) ensures that the resulting knowledge (justification/warrant) is *testimonial* in nature, (D2) was defended against TEP-N in Chapters 2 and 3, (D3) and (D4) were argued for in Chapter 5, and (D5) has been discussed and developed throughout most of this book. This leaves (D6), and serious doubts over the plausibility of such a condition have been expressed repeatedly in the literature. Indeed, all of the standard arguments against reductionism focus specifically on the Positive Reasons Thesis. For instance, Mark Owen Webb claims that:

---

[4] (D5) and (D6) could have been combined into a single, simpler formulation; but, since the discussion that follows will focus exclusively on (D6), it seems best to characterize them as separate requirements.

[5] For instance, a condition requiring the truth of B's belief that *p* is needed to distinguish testimonial knowledge from testimonial justification or warrant.

[6] A rough taxonomy of the three competing positions, then, is as follows:

Reductionism: Reduction Thesis and Positive Reasons Thesis (PR-N&S)
Non-Reductionism: No-Reduction Thesis and No-Positive Reasons Thesis
Dualism: No-Reduction Thesis and Positive Reasons Thesis (PR-N)

[t]he cause of the trouble [with reductionism] seems to be the requirement that our beliefs based on the testimony of others be based on beliefs in us about the reliability of testimony. This higher-level requirement...places too great a burden on the believing subject, since it requires of him all kinds of knowledge about people, their areas of expertise, and their psychological propensities, which knowledge most subjects simply lack. (Webb 1993: 263)

Similarly, Laurence BonJour writes:

the potential scope of this sort of [reductionist] justification is severely limited in ways that make it clear that it cannot even begin to provide a general justification for testimonial beliefs. There are far too many people (and other sources) whose testimony I rely on in various ways for all or even very many of them to be certified as reliable via this sort of argument. Moreover, I receive information via testimony on a very wide range of subjects: it would be practically impossible for me to check firsthand concerning very many of these, and quite a few involve matters that I am unable to check even in principle. (BonJour 2002: 172)

And Richard Foley maintains that the problem with reductionism "is that it threatens to cut us off from expertise and information that others have and we lack. ... After all, many people with expertise and information that we lack are people about whom we know little. Hence, there may be little or no basis for us to grant them derivative authority" (Foley 1994: 57–8).[7]

Moreover, even when we do have adequate positive reasons for accepting a speaker's testimony, it is often argued, as P. F. Strawson does, that "the checking process ... consists in nothing other than seeking confirmation from other sources of testimony" (Strawson 1994: 25). Similarly, Frederick Schmitt argues that "[m]y belief in the reliability of... testimony sometimes has what passes for a first-hand inductive base, but this passing first-hand basis is itself indebted to testimony for its justification" (Schmitt 1999: 360).

These quotations express two slightly different concerns about (D6), which can be expressed as follows:

---

[7] In a similar spirit, Frederick Schmitt says that "[t]he objection [to reductionism]...I regard as most persuasive [is] that we have too little first-hand experience to provide a nontestimonial basis for induction to the reliability of testimony in all instances in which testimonial belief is intuitively justified" (Schmitt 1999: 359).

Scarcity of Information Objection (SIO):	Ordinary epistemic agents simply do not have enough information to acquire positive reasons strong enough to justify accepting most of the testimony that is intuitively justified or warranted.
Circularity Objection (CO):	Even when agents do have enough information to justify accepting particular instances of testimony, the positive reasons themselves are often indebted to testimony.

Now, since the Reduction Thesis was the focus of my arguments in Chapter 5, my reasons for rejecting reductionism obviously differ in significant ways from those expressed in the SIO and the CO. But, more importantly, by arguing on behalf of the Positive Reasons Thesis (i.e., PR–N), my view is also targeted by these very objections. My purpose in what follows, then, is to defend condition (D6) of dualism from the SIO and the CO. In this section, I shall focus on the SIO, leaving the CO for the next section.

The first point to notice about the SIO is that one of the primary reasons this objection is raised against reductionists is that proponents of such a view are committed to PR–N&S rather than to PR–N. In particular, in order to preserve the Reduction Thesis of their view, reductionists must claim that positive reasons are both necessary and sufficient for testimonial justification and, therefore, that such reasons carry *all* of the justificatory burden for testimonial beliefs. This, in turn, lends itself to the concern expressed in the SIO: how can we possess enough information to adequately justify all of our testimonial beliefs? For instance, when I ask a stranger on the street for directions to the Empire State Building, do I have enough information about her to justify my accepting her testimony that it is six blocks north? Or, while traveling to London for the first time, do I have enough evidence about a random local British newspaper to adequately justify the beliefs that I acquire while reading it?

This, to my mind, is a very compelling objection to reductionism. But notice: in contrast to reductionism, dualism has the epistemic work being *shared* between the speaker and the hearer, leaving the work for the positive reasons condition far less burdensome. Specifically, since condition (D2) of dualism requires that the testimony in question is reliable and (D3) requires that the hearer is a reliable or properly functioning recipient of the testimony, (D6), along with (D5), merely has to ensure that the hearer's acceptance of the testimony is *rationally acceptable*. On my dualist view, the positive reasons possessed by a hearer need to be such that they render it, at the very least, *not irrational for her to accept the testimony in question*. This is a substantially weaker condition than that required by reductionists, which requires that such reasons not only be sufficient for testimonial justification/warrant, but also that they render it positively rational for a hearer to accept a given instance of testimony. To see this, consider again my accepting the reports of a random British newspaper. Even if I do not have specific beliefs about British newspapers, I have all sorts of beliefs about England, the people who live there, their government, their social and political values, and so on. Surely, this information is enough to make it *not irrational* to form beliefs on the basis of British newspapers, even if it is not itself fully sufficient for *justifying* such beliefs or for rendering the formation of such beliefs positively *rational*.

Second, and also in response to the SIO, it is important to notice that there are all sorts of positive reasons that can have epistemic significance and, therefore, be relevant to the satisfaction of condition (D6) of dualism.[8] For instance, suppose that I know nothing personal about Harold or his testifying habits—I met him for the first time on the subway today. I ask him for directions and, while making direct eye contact with me, he responds in an able and confident manner that my destination is four blocks to the south. Now, despite the fact that I have no background with Harold, I may have a substantial amount of inductive evidence for believing that people are generally both sincere and competent when providing directions in normal contexts, that reports made with sustained eye contact are typically sincere ones, or that reports made ably and confidently are typically competent ones.

More precisely, even if a hearer, B, has not observed the general conformity of prior reports of a speaker, A, and the corresponding facts, B may *have observed a general conformity of other relevant reports and facts*. In particular, there seem to be at least three classes of inductively based positive reasons that are available to epistemic agents for distinguishing between reliable and unreliable testimony.

---

[8] This point has been suggested by other proponents of a positive reasons requirement—most notably, by Fricker (1987, 1994, 1995, and 2002) and Faulkner (2002).

The first class includes criteria for individuating epistemically reliable *contexts* and *contextual features*. Specifically, even if B has not observed a general conformity between A's reports and the truth, B may have observed the general conformity of reports delivered in contexts of kind C and the truth. So, if B believes that A's report is delivered in a C-context, then this, combined with B's inductive evidence regarding contexts of kind C, may give B an epistemically relevant positive reason for A's testimony. For instance, one may take a less critical attitude in the context of an astronomy lecture or a *National Geographic* report than one does in the context of an astrology lecture or a *National Enquirer* report. The explanation for this disparity may appeal not only to the *negative* evidence that has been inductively acquired for reports received in the latter contexts, but also to the *positive* evidence that has been accumulated for believing that reports received in the former contexts tend to be reliable. Or consider the different attitudes that may be taken toward a calm and coherent stranger reporting a robbery a few blocks away versus an apparently confused person who is smelling of alcohol reporting the same information. Again, the difference in responses may be explained by both positive reasons and undefeated defeaters: previous inductive evidence indicates that the contextual features in the first scenario suggest a reliable testifier, while the contextual features in the second scenario suggest an unreliable testifier. Similar remarks can be made about countless other contextual factors, such as facial expressions, eye contact, mannerisms, narrative voice, and so on.

The second broad class of positive reasons includes criteria for distinguishing between different kinds of *reports*. In particular, even if B has not observed a general conformity between A's reports and the truth, B may have observed the general conformity of reports of kind R and the truth. Thus, if B believes that A's report is an instance of kind R, this, combined with B's inductive evidence regarding R-reports, may give B an epistemically relevant positive reason for A's testimony. So, for example, a hearer may quite reasonably take an uncritical stance when a speaker is reporting the time of day, her name, what she had for dinner, and so on—Matthew Weiner (2003) aptly terms the reports found in this class *mundane testimony*. On the other hand, one may take a more critical stance when receiving a speaker's testimony about political matters, the achievements of her children, alien encounters, UFO sightings, and the like. Here, prior evidence acquired about subject matters or types of reports provides recipients of testimony with epistemically relevant positive reasons.

The third class includes criteria for identifying epistemically reliable *speakers*. Specifically, even if B has not observed the general conformity between A's reports and the truth, B may have observed the general conformity of speakers of kind S and the truth. Thus, if B believes that A is an S-speaker, then this, combined with B's inductive evidence regarding S-speakers, may give B an epistemically relevant positive reason for A's testimony. For instance, one may have accumulated inductive evidence for believing that accountants tend to be reliable sources of information about taxes, while politicians in the middle of their campaigns tend to be unreliable sources of information about the characters of their political opponents. In such cases, a pattern of interaction with speakers who fall under various relevant types enables hearers to acquire positive reasons for accepting some of the reports that they are offered.[9]

The upshot of these considerations, then, is that ordinary hearers are confronted with a plethora of epistemically relevant positive reasons that come in a variety of forms. Such reasons are often not explicitly brought to mind but they nonetheless play a crucial role in our epistemic lives, as we tacitly discriminate among and evaluate pieces of incoming information, and compare such input with our background beliefs.[10] This point is borne out by noticing just how difficult it is to construct a case in which a speaker truly fails to have *any* relevant positive reasons for accepting a given report. Indeed, even in ALIEN from Chapter 5, the fact that the book in question is written in what looks like English and appears to be what we would call a diary may provide Sam with positive reasons for thinking the alien's society is similar in some crucial respects to Earth.

It is important to notice, however, that though these reasons guiding our acceptance of testimony are far more abundant and easier to acquire than proponents of the SIO suggest, they are positive reasons nonetheless.

---

[9] The reasons from each of the three classes discussed may be at the level of either tokens or types.

[10] This point is frequently noticed in the case of negative evidence, that is, it is readily acknowledged that average epistemic agents have acquired ample inductive evidence for believing that certain conversational features, such as nervousness, lack of eye contact, and confused behavior, suggest *incompetence, insincerity, and unreliability*. But positive reasons are just the flip side of defeaters. For just as we have accumulated this type of negative inductive evidence, we have also accumulated positive inductive evidence for believing that certain contextual features are indicators of competence, sincerity, and reliability.

This point can be more fully appreciated by contrasting my view with the following passage from Elizabeth Fricker, who is a self-avowed reductionist: "competence may be assumed as default setting... with respect to a subclass of tellings only, viz. those with subject matters for which common sense psychological knowledge licenses one to expect the speaker to be competent about them: such as her name, where she lives, what she had for breakfast, what is in clear view in front of her, and so forth" (Fricker 1995: 405). According to Fricker, then, the default setting for mundane testimony—e.g., reports about what one had for dinner, the time of day, and so on—is assumed competence. Otherwise put, Fricker accepts the non-reductionist's requirements for testimonial justification when it comes to mundane testimony, which can be expressed as follows (hereafter *Non-Reductionism for Mundane Testimony* or NRMT):

> NRMT: For every speaker, A, and hearer, B, B is justified (warranted) in accepting A's mundane testimony unless B has an undefeated defeater for doing so.[11]

Now, while Fricker and I may often agree on the frequency with which testimonial justification/warrant is acquired, we ultimately disagree on *how* it is acquired. On my view, most mundane testimony can be accepted with justification or warrant *because most cognitive agents have acquired ample evidence for believing that speakers tend to be highly reliable when it comes to such reports.* On Fricker's view, most mundane testimony can be accepted with justification or warrant *because, in the absence of undefeated defeaters, competence can be assumed with respect to such reports.*

To see this, consider the following case, which bears some obvious similarities to ALIEN in Chapter 5:

ALIEN-2: George, an average human being, is taking a walk through the forest one brisk afternoon and he sees someone in the distance. Although the individual's physical appearance enables George to identify her as an alien from another planet, he does not know anything about either this kind of alien or the planet from which she comes. When George catches up to the alien, she turns to him and immediately says in what sounds like English that she had oranges for breakfast. Without hesitation, George forms the corresponding belief. It turns out that the

---

[11] Fricker also accepts the non-reductionist's requirements for testimonial justification/warrant with respect to what she calls the developmental phase of cognitive agents' lives. I shall discuss this in Chapter 7.

alien does, in fact, communicate in English, she did have oranges for breakfast, and she is a reliable testifier, both in general and in this particular instance. Moreover, George is not only a properly functioning recipient of testimony, but he is also situated in an environment that is suitable for the reception of reliable reports.

Given Fricker's endorsement of NRMT, she would apparently grant that George acquires justified or warranted belief and knowledge that the alien had oranges for breakfast on the basis of her testimony. For reporting what one had for breakfast qualifies as mundane testimony if anything does. But for the same reasons given in connection with ALIEN in Chapter 5, this seems to be the wrong verdict in ALIEN-2. Moreover, one of Fricker's central motivations for endorsing reductionism in the first place is her view that anyone who accepts testimony in the complete absence of positive reasons is thereby irrational and gullible.[12] However, if one does not have any relevant positive reasons about mundane testimony—and instead merely assumes competence for the sake of convenience, as NRMT permits—why isn't such behavior also marked by irrationality and gullibility? My view, in contrast, not only denies that George acquires the relevant justified or warranted belief and knowledge in ALIEN-2, but also provides an explanation of mundane testimony that is consistent with the requirement of positive reasons found in (D6): we typically accept speakers' reports about such topics because we have a multitude of reasons for believing that reports about the mundane are appropriately truth-conducive.

Thus, once it is clear, first, that the positive reasons required in (D6) only need to render it *not irrational* for the hearer to accept the testimony in question and, second, that there are a *multitude of kinds of reasons* that have epistemic significance, it becomes equally clear that the SIO simply does not pose a problem for dualism.

6.3 The Circularity Objection

Let us now turn to the CO, which is the objection that even when ordinary epistemic agents have enough information to justify particular reports, the positive reasons themselves are often indebted to testimony. The first point that is crucial to notice is that the positive reasons for accepting a speaker's

---

[12] See, for instance, her (1994 and 1995).

testimony required by (D6) can themselves depend on testimony, so long as they are not *ultimately and entirely* testimonially grounded. In particular, in order to avoid circular appeals to testimony, one can reject

(i) For each report, R, the positive reasons justifying R cannot themselves be acquired from the testimony of others.

and still accept

(ii) For each report, R, the positive reasons justifying R cannot ultimately be testimonially grounded, where this means that the justificatory or epistemic chain leading up to R cannot "bottom out" in testimony.

To see this, recall the case of NESTED SPEAKER: through the course of their friendship, Fred acquired excellent inductively-based positive reasons for believing that Helen is a highly reliable source of information on a wide range of topics. Because of this, he readily accepts Helen's testimony that Pauline, a close friend of hers, is a highly trustworthy person, especially when it comes to information regarding wild birds. This, in turn, leads him to accept Pauline's testimony that albatrosses have the largest wingspan among wild birds. To link this up with the above distinction, Fred's positive reasons for Helen's testimony satisfy both (i) and (ii), whereas Fred's positive reasons for Pauline's testimony satisfy only (ii). In particular, Fred's positive reasons for accepting Helen's reports have been acquired via sense perception, memory, and inductive inference, and so they are not based on further testimony in the most direct sort of way. Regarding Pauline's testimony, however, Fred's positive reasons for accepting her report are based on further testimony in this direct sense; but the epistemic chain ultimately "bottoms out" in a non-testimonial source, namely, Fred's inductive evidence for Helen's reliability. It is this weaker sense of being non-testimonially grounded—expressed in (ii)—that is crucial for avoiding circularity. According to dualism, the reasons invoked for accepting a speaker's testimony can, and often are, themselves acquired from the testimony of others. Indeed, there can be epistemic chains involving many more speakers than two. For instance, A's reason for accepting B's testimony may be the testimony of C which, in turn, may be based on the testimony of D, and so on. What is crucial for the satisfaction of (D6) is *that the final link in the epistemic chain in question is non-testimonially justified.*

Perhaps an analogy will help here: in order to avoid both a vicious regress and the problem of circularity, traditional foundationalism requires that a justificatory chain ultimately bottom out in foundational, or basic, beliefs. But it does not require that each justified belief be, in turn, directly justified by a basic belief. Similarly, in order to avoid both a vicious regress and circular appeals to testimony, the positive reasons condition requires that the justificatory chain ultimately bottom out in a non-testimonial source. But, it does not require direct non-testimonial grounding for each testimonial belief.

Moreover, even the final link in the chain can be partially indebted to testimony, so long as there is enough non-testimonial support to render it *not irrational* to accept the report in question. For instance, suppose I form beliefs on the basis of reading an internet site about Howard Dean because Jack, an acquaintance of mine from the Political Science Department, told me that it is a reliable source of information. Why do I trust Jack? In part, because my colleague, Jill, told me that he is an honest, competent, Democrat. However, I have also had enough personal interaction with Jack to acquire a partial non-testimonial basis for relying on his testimony. So long as this partial non-testimonial basis is sufficient to render it not irrational to trust the Howard Dean website, Jack can be the non-testimonial source in which this chain bottoms out.

Thus, *the positive reasons required by (D6) can themselves rely on testimony*, so long as they do not do so entirely and ultimately. Given this, the CO fails to pose a problem for the dualist view of testimonial knowledge found in D.

One more point that is worth mentioning is that doubts may be raised about the very plausibility of the CO itself. James Van Cleve makes this point very nicely in the following passage:

In my opinion, this argument [found in CO] is far from decisive. To begin with, there is no plausibility at all in the ... contention that *any* corroboration of testimony *must* rely on further testimony. For many years of my life, I believed there were such wonders as the Grand Canyon and the Taj Mahal solely on the basis of books and postcards. Now I have verified the existence of those things with my own eyes. (More accurately: I have verified with my own eyes the existence of *such* things, that is, structures matching a certain general description, for I admittedly relied on the testimony of the locals to know *that building is the Taj Mahal*.) To these dramatic episodes of confirmation may be added thousands of more quotidian occurrences of finding beer in the fridge or a restroom down the hall on the right after being told where to look. To be sure, these myriad instances in which I have been able to check on the veracity of testimony firsthand are … only a miniscule fraction of all the instances in which I have believed things on the basis of testimony. But does it follow that any inductive justification I have for believing testimony must be "extremely weak"? Not at all, for what matters is not the proportion of testimonial beliefs I have checked, but the proportion of checks undertaken that have had positive results. I have seen only a tiny fraction of the world's crows, but the ones I have seen have been overwhelmingly black, and that is enough to support my belief that nearly all crows are black. (Of course, the ratio of testimonies checked to testimonies that have proved true varies with different classes of testimony; I have found geography textbooks to be more reliable than presidential press conferences.) (Van Cleve 2006: 67–8)

According to Van Cleve, then, so long as the proportion of positive results of those testimonial beliefs that have been checked is high, one has good reason to accept the testimony in question. Given this, the force of the CO may have been overstated from the very beginning.

6.4 The Generalization Problem

There is a further concern that may be expressed about condition (D6) of dualism. To see this, recall that the argument motivating the inclusion of this condition was ALIEN in Chapter 5. But now, one might ask, couldn't a parallel argument be constructed regarding other, purportedly more basic, epistemic sources, such as sense perception, memory, and inference? For instance, suppose that after her involvement in a car accident, Dolores has complete amnesia with respect to her perceptual faculties, that is, she remembers nothing about either the workings or the deliverances of such faculties. Upon waking from the car accident and seeing the face of her sister, Dolores forms the corresponding perceptual belief. Intuitively, is such a belief justified or warranted? Since this case is similar in all of the relevant respects to ALIEN, shouldn't we conclude here, as we did there, that it would be irrational for Dolores to hold such a belief in the absence of epistemically relevant positive reasons on behalf of her perceptual faculties? If so, there seems to be a problem of overgeneralization here. For now it looks as though positive reasons are needed to justifiedly hold, not just testimonial beliefs, but *any* beliefs. And this, in turn, leads us into all of the problems facing traditional internalist theories of epistemic justification or warrant, such as infinite regresses, circularity, foundations, and so on.

Although a complete response to this concern lies outside the scope of this chapter, I shall here highlight three salient ways in which testimony differs epistemically from other sources of belief. These differences allow us to conclude that, although ALIEN shows that positive reasons are needed for testimony, no similar case can be constructed for our other cognitive faculties; the need for positive reasons thus does not generalize.

First, testimonial beliefs are acquired from *persons*.[13] Persons, unlike other sources of belief, have all sorts of different intentions, desires, goals, motives, and so on. Some of these desires and goals make it very advantageous to lie, to exaggerate, to mislead, and to otherwise deceive. Indeed, recall that in the discussion following ALIEN, some of the considerations motivating the need for a condition like (D6) of dualism were that "it may very well be accepted practice in alien society to be insincere and deceptive when testifying to others. Or, normal alien psychology may be what we Earthlings would consider psychosis." Since both of these possibilities appeal to features distinctive of persons, they are relevant only in the case of testimony.

Of course, it may be argued that other sources of belief can lead us just as far astray epistemically as testimony. For instance, aren't the paradoxes just as misleading as incompetent testifiers, and aren't perceptual hallucinations and illusions just as deceptive as compulsive liars? Given these parallels, it looks like the mere fact that testimonial beliefs are acquired from persons fails to distinguish it epistemically from other sources of belief.

By way of response to this point, notice that there are two aspects that are often involved in rendering a speaker a reliable testifier: her competence as a believer and her sincerity as a testifier.[14] Accordingly, when a hearer acquires a false belief from a speaker, one (or both) of these aspects is

---

[13] I am using the term "person" broadly so that non-human animals from whom we are able to acquire testimonial beliefs qualify as persons in this sense.

[14] Of course, as argued in Chapter 2, neither of these aspects is *necessary* for a speaker to be a reliable testifier, though they are often *constitutive* of being such a testifier. I should also mention that a third aspect involved in rendering a speaker reliable is her *competence as a testifier*. For instance, one who is only beginning to learn English will be an incompetent testifier, not because she is an incompetent believer or an insincere testifier, but because of her relative lack of competence with the English language. (I thank an anonymous referee for this point.) I leave this aspect aside, however, because it does not directly bear on the present point.

frequently responsible: either A reports that p when p is false because A herself erroneously believes that p (i.e., A is an incompetent believer), or A reports that p when p is false because A intends to deceive her hearer (i.e., A is an insincere testifier). But now notice: the paradoxes, perceptual illusions, hallucinations, and so on all parallel only the testimonial case of incompetent believing—there simply is no analogue of insincere testifying with non-testimonial sources of belief.[15] For insincerity involves the *intention* to deceive or mislead, and intentions of this sort are distinctive of persons. When my rational and perceptual faculties lead me astray epistemically, they do not *intend* to do so.[16] Because of this, failures in the case of testimony are much more *unpredictable* than failures in non-testimonial cases.

A second and somewhat related difference between testimony and other epistemic sources concerns the varying degrees of likelihood that such sources are unreliable. For instance, the possible worlds in which most of my perceptual beliefs are indistinguishably false—for instance, worlds in which I am unknowingly a brain-in-a-vat or the victim of an evil demon—are quite distant from the actual world. Indeed, even possible worlds in which *many* of my perceptual beliefs are indistinguishably false are rather far away—worlds, for instance, where my perceptual faculties frequently malfunction and yet I do not suspect that they do. In contrast, the possible worlds in which most of my testimonial beliefs are indistinguishably false—for instance, worlds in which I was raised by parents who belong to a cult, or worlds in which my government is highly corrupt, or worlds in which my society is highly superstitious—are much closer. Indeed, for many people, this is true in the *actual* world. Given this much greater chance for error in the case of testimony, the rational acceptance of the reports of others requires positive reasons in a way that is not paralleled with other cognitive faculties.

This brings us to the third and, to my mind, most important epistemic difference between testimony and other sources of belief. To fully appreciate

---

[15] For a very nice discussion of this point, see Faulkner (2000).

[16] A possible non-testimonial exception to this claim is the relationship between self-deception and certain memories. A subject may, for instance, deceive herself by calling into question memories that are too painful to remember. While this is true, it is quite doubtful whether self-deception can be overtly conscious and therefore intentional in the way that insincere testimony is. What is more plausible is that self-deception takes place at the unconscious level, and indirectly induces false belief. Thus, failures in memory deriving from self-deception are more analogous to failures in perception regarding some sub-personal glitch in how the faculty works.

this point, let us return to our perceptual amnesiac, Dolores, and imagine an average day for her after leaving the hospital: she stops at the store to buy some groceries, bumps into some acquaintances on her way home, watches an episode of *Seinfeld* on TV while eating dinner, and spends some time on the internet before going to bed. Along the way, Dolores forms perceptual beliefs about all sorts of things, including beliefs about the vegetarian items that Trader Joe's carries, the kinds of trees losing their leaves, the number of children her acquaintance now has, which *Seinfeld* episode is on, and the color of the background of the MSN website. Now, because of her perceptual amnesia, Dolores's acquisition of these perceptual beliefs is not governed by any acquired principles of perceptual belief formation. But even in the absence of such principles, it seems reasonable to conclude that the overall status of Dolores's daily perceptual beliefs would be very high epistemically. For Dolores's beliefs are most likely quite similar to those that would have been acquired by a subject in the same circumstances who does have acquired principles of perceptual belief formation governing her acceptance. Why? Because sense perception, like other non-testimonial sources, is fairly *homogenous*—there is, for instance, simply not much of a difference epistemically between Dolores seeing groceries at Trader Joe's and Dolores seeing trees without their leaves. Accordingly, when forming non-testimonial beliefs, subjects do not need to be very discriminating in order to be reliably in touch with the truth.[17]

Now compare Dolores's day with Edna's. Edna, Dolores's best friend, was in the same car accident that caused Dolores's perceptual amnesia. In Edna, however, the accident caused *testimonial* amnesia: she remembers nothing about either the workings or the deliverances of testimony. After leaving the hospital, Edna's day was nearly identical to Dolores's. For instance, she stopped at the same grocery store, bumped into the same acquaintances on the way home, watched the same episode of *Seinfeld*, and

---

[17] My point here is not that all non-testimonial sources are homogenous *to the same extent*—there may, for instance, be more variation between memories from different stages in one's life than there is among different kinds of perceptual experiences. My point is, rather, that there is a striking difference between the amount of variation found within non-testimonial sources as compared with testimony as an epistemic source. Moreover, if there are some non-testimonial sources—perhaps, for instance, inductive inference—that are as epistemically heterogeneous as testimony, then a positive reasons condition may be needed to justifiedly accept the deliverances of these sources as well. What I wish to establish here, however, is that the conclusion of ALIEN does not generalize to *all* epistemic sources.

visited the same internet sites before going to bed. Now, because of her testimonial amnesia, Edna's acquisition of testimonial beliefs along the way was not governed by any principles of testimonial belief formation. As a result, Edna trusted to the same extent all of the testimonial sources she encountered throughout the day—which included a copy of *The National Enquirer* that she read at the grocery store, her acquaintance's three-year-old daughter, the characters of Jerry and George on *Seinfeld*, and an extremist, evangelical Christian internet site she stumbled upon while surfing the web—and she believed everything that she was either told or read along the way—which included testimony that a woman from Georgia was abducted by aliens, that there are *real* princes and princesses at Disneyland, that licking the envelopes of cheap wedding invitations can lead to one's death, and that those who are gay will be sent to eternal damnation.

Did Edna fare as well epistemically as Dolores? Not at all. In the absence of acquired principles governing the acceptance of testimony, Edna was led very far astray epistemically. She trusted *The National Enquirer* as much as she would have trusted *The New York Times*, she trusted a three-year-old's depiction of Disneyland as much as she would have trusted an adult's, she trusted the characters on a sitcom as much as she would have trusted those interviewed in a *National Geographic* documentary, and she trusted the rantings of an extremist, evangelical Christian internet site as much as she would have trusted news found on the MSN website. Because of this, Edna's beliefs are very different from those that would have been acquired by a subject in the same circumstances who does have her testimonial practices governed by such epistemic principles.

Thus, testimony is quite unlike other sources of belief precisely because it is so wildly *heterogeneous* epistemically—there is, for instance, all the difference in the world between reading *The National Enquirer* and reading *The New York Times*. Moreover, this heterogeneity requires subjects to be much more discriminating when accepting testimony than when trusting, say, sense perception.[18] Non-testimonial analogues of ALIEN, therefore,

---

[18] This point can be looked at as two sides of the same coin: on the one side, the radical unreliability of certain testimonial sources is emphasized; on the other side, sense perception's extraordinary reliability is emphasized. (In discussion, I recently heard Keith DeRose highlight this latter side in defense of a reductionist view of testimonial justification or warrant that does not generalize to sense perception.) But both sides amount to the same conclusion: there are important epistemic differences between testimony and sense perception.

simply fail to motivate a positive reasons condition similar to (D6) of dualism.

6.5 Beyond Reductionism and Non-Reductionism

As should now be clear, dualism provides easy resolutions to many of the central and most divisive disagreements between reductionists and non-reductionists.

First, as we have seen, a central component of reductionism—indeed, the one for which the view derived its name—is that the justification or warrant of testimony *reduces* to the justification or warrant of sense perception, memory, and inductive inference. Testimony does not, therefore, make any justificatory contributions of its own—whatever appearances there are to the contrary can ultimately be reduced to the epistemic contributions of these other sources. Otherwise put, if reductionism is true, there is *no* specifically testimonial justification/warrant and, thus, no distinctly testimonial knowledge. There is only justification/warrant or knowledge for beliefs acquired *through* testimony. But this view gives testimony far too little epistemic credit. For, as we saw in NESTED SPEAKER in Chapter 5, the reliability of the report in question is not something that can be reduced to perceptual, memorial, and inferential justification/warrant. Since the reliability of the report in a testimonial exchange is a necessary condition of the justification/warrant of beliefs acquired via testimony, testimonial justification/warrant itself is not reducible. Thus, contrary to reductionism, there *is* justification/warrant, and hence knowledge, that is distinctly testimonial in nature.

Second, non-reductionists claim that since testimony is just as basic a source of justification/warrant as sense perception, memory and inductive inference, hearers may be justified/warranted in accepting the reports of speakers, albeit defeasibly, *merely* on the basis of a speaker's testimony. In this way, testimony is construed as an independent and autonomous source of justification/warrant, needing neither the direct input nor the assistance of any other sources.[19] But this view gives testimony far too

---

[19] There are two qualifications to this thesis: first, though other epistemic sources are not necessary for justification/warrant and knowledge, according to standard characterizations of non-reductionism,

much credit. As we saw in ALIEN, to accept a speaker's testimony *in the complete absence* of positive reasons on behalf of the testimony in question is to exhibit an epistemically unacceptable kind of irrationality, one that is incompatible with testimonial justification/warrant. Moreover, since there would be vicious circularity if the positive reasons were themselves entirely and ultimately acquired via testimony, direct input and assistance are needed from sense perception, memory, and inductive inference. Thus, contrary to non-reductionism, testimonial justification/warrant *depends on* the justificatory resources of other epistemic sources.

In showing the need for positive epistemic work from both the speaker and hearer, then, we have seen that testimonial justification or warrant is neither reducible to nor completely independent from sense perception, memory, and inductive inference. Thus, insofar as we wish to make genuine progress in the epistemology of testimony, we need to move beyond the debate between reductionism and non-reductionism.

they are of course needed for accessing the testimony of others, e.g., sense perception is required to hear the spoken testimony of others. Second, even if these other epistemic sources do not provide justification for accepting the testimony of speakers, they can inhibit justification and knowledge by generating undefeated defeaters.

7

Positive Reasons, Defeaters, and the Infant/Child Objection

7.1 The Infant/Child Objection

In the previous two chapters, I argued that while the Reduction Thesis of reductionism is false, the weaker Positive Reasons Thesis—PR-N—which holds that appropriate positive reasons are necessary, though not sufficient, for testimonial justification or warrant, is nonetheless true. Such a requirement figures into my dualist view of testimonial knowledge as condition (D6). In this chapter, I shall discuss a central objection—which I shall call the *Infant/Child Objection* (henceforth, the ICO)—that is frequently raised by non-reductionists as a nearly decisive reason to favor their view over reductionism. Since the ICO depends on only the reductionist's acceptance of the weaker PR-N, however, it targets a thesis that I am committed to as well. Thus, to the extent that the ICO succeeds, it undermines *both* reductionism and dualism.[1]

The ICO begins by pointing to the apparent fact that infants and young children lack the cognitive capacity to acquire the non-testimonial positive reasons required by PR-N. Because of this, they are said to be incapable of satisfying the reductionist's—and, therewith, the dualist's—requirements for testimonial justification or warrant. Thus, on such views, infants and young children are devoid of testimonial knowledge. Yet, surely, it is urged, a two-year-old can know that there is apple juice in the refrigerator when her mother says that there is. Let us outline the ICO in the following way:

---

[1] I shall actually later argue that this is not entirely accurate since the dualist's version of PR-N is weaker than the reductionist's. At this point, however, this rough characterization of the problem will suffice.

1. According to PR-N—which is endorsed by both reductionists and dualists—for every speaker, A, and hearer, B, B's belief that p is justified or warranted on the basis of A's testimony only if B has appropriate positive reasons for accepting A's testimony.
2. However, infants and young children lack the cognitive capacity for acquiring and possessing appropriate positive reasons.
3. Therefore, infants and young children are incapable of satisfying PR-N.
4. Infants and young children do have at least some testimonial knowledge.
5. Therefore, reductionism and dualism are false.

Because non-reductionists require the satisfaction of the no-defeater condition (henceforth, the NDC)[2] instead of PR-N, however, their view is said to be immune to such an argument. For, while non-reductionism requires only the *absence* of negative reasons (i.e., of psychological and normative defeaters), reductionism and dualism also require the *presence* of positive reasons. So, even if infants and young children are incapable of having reasons, they can nonetheless satisfy the non-reductionist's requirements merely by accepting testimony in the absence of negative reasons.[3] As Robert Audi says, "[i]f, as seems a reasonable assumption, gaining testimonially based knowledge normally requires only having no reason to doubt the attester's credibility, then [a non-reductionist view of testimonial knowledge] encounters no difficulty. If a tiny child perhaps *can* have no reason for doubt, at least the child has none" (Audi 1997: 415).

In this chapter, I shall challenge this presumed asymmetry between reductionism and dualism, on the one hand, and non-reductionism, on the other hand. Specifically, I shall argue, first, that if the ICO indeed undermines reductionism and dualism, then a variant of it similarly undermines non-reductionism. Thus, considerations about the cognitive capacities of infants and small children do not effectively discriminate between these

---

[2] Though I shall, for the sake of ease of exposition, often speak simply of the "no-defeater condition," this should be read throughout this chapter as the "no-undefeated-defeater condition." Similar considerations apply, *mutatis mutandis*, to "no-normative-defeater condition" and to "no-psychological-defeater condition."

[3] I do not mean to suggest here that the no-defeater condition is the *only* requirement imposed by non-reductionist views of testimonial justification or warrant; rather, I mean that, *relative to requirements involving reasons*, the non-reductionist requires only the absence of negative reasons, while the reductionist also requires the presence of positive ones.

three theories of testimonial justification or warrant. I shall then argue that to the extent that there is any asymmetry of this sort between those who endorse PR-N and those who do not, it is one that is advantageous to those who require positive reasons. Finally, I shall show that there are good reasons to doubt premise (2) of the ICO at the outset, thereby rendering this purportedly devastating objection to the proponent of PR-N benign.

7.2 Trivial and Substantive Satisfaction

To begin, consider the import of the no-defeater condition for the non-reductionist's view of testimonial justification or warrant. If this weren't a necessary condition on such a view, hearers could be justified in accepting *any reliable report*, no matter how much available evidence there was to the contrary. It is precisely to avoid this radically counterintuitive picture of testimony that non-reductionists include the NDC. Testimonial justification or warrant is defeasible, through the presence of either an available psychological or normative defeater. According to non-reductionism, then, we can accept much of what we are told on simple trust, but not where this acceptance is epistemically irrational or irresponsible, i.e., not in the presence of undefeated defeaters.

There are, however, importantly different ways of satisfying a condition. For instance, one of the reasons it doesn't make sense to impose a "no-lying condition" on a chair is because chairs cannot lie. To say that a chair has satisfied such a condition merely because it hasn't lied, without taking into account whether the chair has the capacity to lie, trivializes what satisfaction of such a condition means. Of course, considerations of this sort apply to persons as well. For example, suppose that in order to live a truly moral life, an agent has to satisfy the "no-betrayal condition," that is, an agent has to live her life without committing any acts of betrayal. Suppose further that Vivienne has never committed an act of betrayal because she has been in a persistent vegetative state since the age of two. Once again, the only sense in which this condition is satisfied is trivial—specifically, given her circumstances, Vivienne *wasn't capable of failing to satisfy it*. While in a persistent vegetative state, a person simply lacks qualities that are essential to committing acts of betrayal, e.g., consciousness, ongoing relationships, commitments, and so on. Thus, though Vivienne hasn't committed any acts of betrayal, she has satisfied the no-betrayal condition in only a trivial sense.

What these considerations suggest is that if we impose a no-ϕing condition on X, then there is a crucial difference between what we might call *trivial satisfaction* and *substantive satisfaction* of such a condition, a difference that depends on X's capacity to ϕ. In particular, let us put forth the following:

Trivial Satisfaction:	If X does not ϕ merely because X does not have the capacity to ϕ, then X has *trivially* satisfied the no-ϕing condition.
Substantive Satisfaction:	If X has the capacity to ϕ and does not ϕ, then X has *substantively* satisfied the no-ϕing condition.

But what, one might ask, is the significance of this distinction? What, that is, does substantive satisfaction give us that trivial satisfaction does not?

The answer to this question will depend on the nature of the condition at issue. If, for instance, the condition is a moral one, then trivial satisfaction does not add to the moral worth of the agent herself. Not lying because one does not have the capacity to lie does not make one a morally better person. Of course, there is a sense in which the world is a better place than it would have been had there been more lies in it. But this is not something that is attributable to the agent in any significant sense.[4]

With these points in mind, let us turn to the relationship that infants and young children bear to defeaters. Consider, first, normative defeaters— doubts or beliefs that a subject ought to have, which indicate that her belief that *p* is either false or unreliably formed or sustained. Otherwise put, normative defeaters are *negative reasons* or reasons *against* holding a given belief. For instance, recall Tyler Burge's claim that "[a] person is entitled to accept as true something that is presented as true and that is intelligible to him, unless *there are stronger reasons not to do so*" (Burge 1993: 467, emphasis added). Similarly, recall John McDowell's statement that "knowledge is available to be picked up only by someone whose taking the speaker's word for it is not doxastically irresponsible ... it is obviously doxastically irresponsible to believe someone about whom one *has positive reason to*

---

[4] See Reed (2007) for more on the relevant notion of "attributability" here.

believe he is not trustworthy, or not likely to be informed about the subject matter of the conversation" (McDowell 1994: 210–11, emphasis added).[5] In both of the passages, the NDC precludes being justified or warranted in accepting a speaker's testimony in the presence of negative reasons.

But if, as proponents of the ICO contend, infants and young children are cognitively incapable of having positive reasons, *then so, too, are they incapable of having negative reasons.* Reasons are reasons, whether they are for or against holding a given belief. In this way, positive reasons and normative defeaters go hand in hand: if a subject is unable to have the former, then she is also unable to have the latter. Accordingly, *the only sense in which infants and young children can satisfy the no-normative-defeater condition* (henceforth, the NNDC) *is trivial.*

Why, one might ask, is this important? The epistemic import of this fact depends on the particular circumstances in which the belief is held. In those cases where there is no counterevidence for the belief in question, trivial satisfaction of the NNDC adds nothing to the epistemic worth of the subject. For, if a subject is simply incapable of having negative reasons for her beliefs, then even if there *had* been counterevidence present, the condition would have been trivially satisfied nonetheless. Indeed, this sort of satisfaction would have obtained *under any circumstances.* Hence, trivial satisfaction of the NNDC does not indicate any sort of sensitivity on the part of the subject to evidence either for or against her own beliefs. But without a proper sensitivity to one's epistemic surroundings, it is merely a lucky coincidence that one ends up satisfying the NNDC. This, of course, is why even many of the staunchest externalists maintain that epistemic justification or warrant and knowledge depend on a subject forming beliefs out of a sensitivity to the way that things are in the world. *At best*, then, trivial satisfaction of the NNDC is epistemically worthless: clocks, telephone poles, and coffee cups satisfy such a requirement in this trivial way.

At worst, however, this sort of trivial satisfaction is more problematic than mere epistemic worthlessness. For, unlike clocks, telephone poles, and coffee cups, infants and young children can have beliefs and also be

---

[5] I should mention that negative reasons are just positive reasons *against* believing a proposition, i.e., positive reasons to *not* believe a proposition. I have chosen to use the term "negative reason," however, in order to keep clearly distinct the requirement for positive reasons and the requirement for the absence of normative defeaters. Thus, although McDowell speaks of positive reasons against believing a speaker's testimony, he is here (in my terms) simply requiring the absence of normative defeaters.

presented with evidence against those beliefs. That is, there can be cases in which there is counterevidence present for the belief in question and yet the NNDC is trivially satisfied in spite of this. Indeed, if infants and young children are incapable of having negative reasons, then even if they are inundated with *massive* amounts of counterevidence for one of their beliefs, this cannot provide them with a reason to alter their doxastic systems. In other words, such counterevidence cannot function as a normative defeater on this view.[6] Because of this, infants and young children can satisfy the no-normative-defeater condition and justifiedly hold a belief even when, from an epistemic point of view, they *clearly should not*. This result not only flies in the face of the underlying rationale for including the no-defeater condition in the first place, but it is epistemically absurd as well.

Thus, if infants and young children lack the capacity to appreciate reasons, then reductionism and dualism, on the one hand, and non-reductionism, on the other hand, all have a problem: reductionism and dualism are too strong because such views prevent infants and young children from being justified or warranted when intuitively they are, and non-reductionism is too weak because such a view allows infants and young children to be justified or warranted when intuitively they are not.

7.3 Negative Reasons and Counterevidence

But why, one might ask, must normative defeat be understood in terms of negative reasons in the first place? Granted, this is how most non-reductionists *do* characterize normative defeaters. But couldn't normative defeat instead be fleshed out simply in terms of *the presence of counterevidence*?

In particular, consider the following line of argument: there seems to be an important asymmetry between positive and negative evidence. While a subject cannot be justified or warranted in believing that p on the basis of evidence that she does not appreciate, a subject's justification or warrant for believing that p can be defeated by evidence that she does

---

[6] Strictly speaking, then, there is a difference between the presence of *counterevidence* and having a *normative defeater*. While the former is merely evidence against one's belief, the latter is counterevidence that gives one a *reason* to make changes in one's epistemic system. In the next section, however, I shall argue that if infants and young children cannot have reasons, then it is doubtful whether counterevidence can even be present to them in any reasonable sense.

not—perhaps even cannot—appreciate. For instance, I cannot be justified or warranted in believing that the President is currently in China on the basis of newspaper articles that I do not read, but the reports in these newspaper articles can nonetheless defeat my justified or warranted belief that the President is currently in Iraq, even if I do not read them.[7] Because of this, the non-reductionist can propose the following alternative account of normative defeat:

> ND: The presence of negative evidence, E, for a subject, S, defeats the positive epistemic status of S's belief that p just in case E sufficiently supports a proposition indicating that p is either false or unreliably formed or sustained, regardless of whether S has the capacity to appreciate E.

Now, if ND is substituted for the characterization of normative defeaters in terms of negative reasons, then the asymmetry between non-reductionism, on the one hand, and reductionism and dualism, on the other hand, can be preserved relative to the ICO. For, even if infants and young children lack the capacity to appreciate evidence, the presence of negative evidence can still function as a normative defeater in their belief systems. According to ND, therefore, infants and young children would be able to substantively satisfy the NNDC even if they are cognitively incapable of possessing positive reasons for their beliefs.

Despite the virtues of this approach for the non-reductionist's view, there are compelling reasons to reject it. The first point to notice is that ND fails to support the standard view regarding the epistemic problem posed by normative defeaters; namely, that a subject who holds a belief in the face of an undefeated normative defeater is being *epistemically irrational and/or irresponsible*. For instance, in discussing a classic example of normative defeat, Laurence BonJour says that such a subject is "being thoroughly irrational and irresponsible" in disregarding the evidence in question. (BonJour 1985: 39) Similarly, in the earlier quotation, John McDowell claims that knowledge is incompatible with doxastic irresponsibility, where this is understood, in part, in terms of holding a belief in the face of undefeated normative defeaters. But if a subject completely lacks the capacity to appreciate

---

[7] This asymmetry between positive and negative evidence can be seen in some of the well-known examples found in Harman (1968, 1973, and 1980).

counterevidence, then it simply doesn't make sense to say that such a subject is being "thoroughly irrational" or "doxastically irresponsible" in holding a belief in the presence of an undefeated normative defeater. This would be like saying that I am being morally irresponsible in failing to grow wings and fly to help a child falling from a tree. Surely, there is no coherent sense of being irresponsible, either epistemically or morally, in failing to do something that one simply cannot do.

Second, and more importantly, if the subject in question completely lacks the capacity to appreciate counterevidence, then it is unclear how to understand the clause in ND that reads, "The presence of negative evidence, D, for a subject, S." Typically, this would be understood, roughly, in terms of the evidence that S can reasonably be expected to be aware of which, in turn, would be understood, at least in part, in terms of the cognitive capacities of the subject in question. This is, of course, why it is thought that the presence of an undefeated normative defeater renders it epistemically irrational and/or irresponsible to hold the defeatee in question. But if a subject simply cannot appreciate evidence, then there is *no* evidence that S can reasonably be expected to be aware of.

So, the non-reductionist may try to cash out "The presence of negative evidence, E, for a subject, S" in terms of the evidence that is somehow *physically available to S*. Perhaps, for instance, the evidence that is in S's *immediate or nearby physical environment* is present to S in this sense. This, however, will not do. Surely, the reports of an open newspaper on a blind person's desk are not necessarily relevant negative evidence for her belief that *p*, despite the fact that they are to be found in her immediate physical environment.

Perhaps, then, this clause in ND should be understood in terms of the evidence that is *present to S's senses*. For the problem in the above case seems to be that while the contents of the open newspaper are in the blind person's immediate physical environment, they are not present to her senses. But now consider the following: I am standing in a room with Olga, who speaks both English and Polish. I justifiedly believe and report to Olga that the bakery down the street is open and she says in Polish that she saw a sign on their door this morning saying that it is closed for the next month for remodeling. Now, Olga's statement is "present to my senses" and it is evidence against my belief that the bakery is open. Nevertheless, because

I lack the capacity to appreciate it, the intuitive response is to say that the justification or warrant for my belief about the bakery is *not* defeated.

What these cases suggest is not only that the physical availability and sensual presence of negative evidence, by themselves, do not have much epistemic significance, but also that the concept of normative defeat is intimately connected with cognitive capacities. Because of this, the non-reductionist may attempt to flesh out "The presence of negative evidence, E, for a subject, S" in terms of *the cognitive abilities of a person who could appreciate the presence of counterevidence.*[8] But, surely, if it requires the cognitive abilities of a *genius* to appreciate the presence of a certain piece of negative evidence, the evidence in question should not necessarily defeat the justified or warranted beliefs of average adults and children. So, this clause in ND cannot be understood in terms of the capacities of *anyone* who could appreciate the presence of counterevidence.

A more promising strategy is to characterize "The presence of negative evidence, E, for a subject, S" in terms of *the cognitive abilities of a normal or average adult.* Thus, if the evidence in S's "cognitive" environment is such that a *normally functioning adult* could appreciate it, then the evidence in question would be present to S, regardless of S's own capacities. There are, however, two problems with this approach. First, there is what we may call the *high end problem*: suppose that Polly is a superb mathematician who correctly and justifiedly believes that her checkbook is not balanced. Polly, however, fails to notice both that her checkbook is lying open on the desk and that the bottom line says that the account is balanced. Now, while a normal adult could appreciate this information, Polly would see a subtle mathematical error that a normal adult would miss. Nevertheless, on this view, Polly would no longer be justified or warranted in believing that her checkbook is not balanced simply because those with mathematical capacities inferior to her own could appreciate the presence of relevant misleading information. Intuitively, this seems like the wrong result.[9]

Second, there is the *low end problem*: suppose that Noah is watching the evening news and both his one-year-old daughter and his three-year-old daughter are in the living room with him. While the news is on, there is a report that M&M's pose a choking hazard for young children.

---

[8] This characterization is very similar to what Stewart Cohen (1986) calls an *intersubjectively evident* defeater.

[9] For other cases of this sort, see Reed (2001).

Now, assuming there is no reason to doubt this report, does it defeat the justification or warrant of their respective beliefs that M&M's are safe for young children? The answer to this question seems different for all three of them: clearly, Noah's justification or warrant is defeated, perhaps his three-year-old's is, and it is extremely doubtful that his one-year-old's is. Why? Because Noah clearly has the capacity to grasp the relationship between his belief that M&M's are safe for young children and the report that M&M's pose a choking hazard for young children, his three-year-old most likely has a grasp of this relationship relative to her beliefs, though probably not as clear as her father's, and it is extremely doubtful that his one-year-old has any such grasp at all. According to the above characterization, however, not only would Noah and his daughters all have defeated beliefs, but the negative evidence in question would also be equally present to them. Once again, this seems like the wrong result. Thus, fleshing out the presence of negative evidence in terms of the cognitive capacities of normal adults delivers the wrong results at both the high end (with above average adults) and the low end (with infants and young children).

The upshot of these considerations is that the very concept of evidence being present to a subject *is intimately connected with the cognitive capacities of the subject in question.* Thus, even if the non-reductionist discards talk of negative reasons in favor of counterevidence, the same question arises: if infants and young children do not have the capacity for reasons, then how can anything count against their beliefs epistemically?

7.4 Non-Reductionism and Psychological Defeaters

Even if infants and young children are incapable of substantively satisfying the no-undefeated-defeater requirement when it comes to normative defeaters, however, the non-reductionist may nonetheless argue that they are at least capable of doing so with respect to psychological defeaters. In particular, since psychological defeaters are doubts or beliefs rather than reasons, and since infants and young children *can* have doubts or beliefs, such defeaters do not suffer the same fate as their normative counterparts. Thus, so long as the NDC is understood as precluding *only* undefeated psychological defeaters, it may be thought that the non-reductionist's view avoids the above objection.

The first point to notice is that without the inclusion of the no-normative-defeater condition, non-reductionism will simply not be a plausible view of testimonial justification or warrant. For instance, consider Owen, a highly dogmatic and close-minded epistemic agent who has massive amounts of epistemically good evidence available to him for believing that the President has engaged in illicit business transactions. Nevertheless, because of his dogmatism and close-mindedness, he refuses to accept this information and persists in believing with the same degree of conviction that the President has conducted his professional life impeccably. Owen, therefore, has an undefeated normative, but not psychological, defeater for his belief about the President.[10] But surely he should not be justified or warranted in believing that the President has a flawless professional record merely because his dogmatism and close-mindedness prevent him from acquiring a psychological defeater. It is for precisely this reason that normative defeaters are so central to the tenability of the non-reductionist's position.

Second, if infants and young children lack the capacity for reasons, then it is questionable whether they can indeed satisfy the no-psychological-defeater condition (henceforth, the NPDC) in a substantive way. For recall that the problem with subjects who continue to hold a belief for which they have an undefeated psychological defeater is that they would be epistemically irrational in doing so. Such a diagnosis is highly normative—in these cases, such subjects are receiving a negative epistemic evaluation because they are ignoring the dictates of rationality. However, if, as non-reductionists maintain, infants and young children are *incapable* of having positive reasons, then there is a clear and important sense in which such subjects are not bound by the constraints of rationality and hence cannot receive such a negative evaluation. In particular, creatures who are incapable of having positive reasons can be neither rational nor irrational; instead, they are *arational*.

To see this, notice that if a 15-month-old baby cannot have a reason for her belief that there is milk in her bottle, then it does not make sense to say that she is epistemically irrational for also believing that Mommy just said that we ran out of milk. For, if such an infant is too cognitively underdeveloped to have reasons for her beliefs, then she also seems to

---

[10] For various examples of this sort, see BonJour (1980 and 1985).

be too cognitively immature to receive such a negative evaluation. In this way, there is, strictly speaking, a difference between *counterbeliefs* and *doxastic defeaters*.[11] While the former are merely beliefs, the content of which conflicts with an already held belief, the latter are counterbeliefs that contribute epistemic irrationality to an agent's doxastic corpus. Otherwise put, to say that an agent has a counterbelief is a *descriptive* statement, while saying that an agent has a psychological defeater is a *normatively* loaded evaluation. Given this distinction, if infants and young children cannot have reasons for their beliefs, then, even if they can have counterbeliefs, they are incapable of having psychological defeaters. Thus, they are capable of satisfying the NPDC in only a trivial way.

The import of this parallels the earlier considerations regarding normative defeaters. In those cases where there is not a counterbelief for the belief in question, trivial satisfaction of the NPDC does not positively contribute to the epistemic assessment of the subject in question. For, if a subject lies outside the domain of rationality altogether, then even if there *had* been a counterbelief present, its existence could not have rendered such a subject epistemically irrational. Because of this, the way in which infants and young children satisfy the NPDC is on an epistemic par with the way my pencil holder satisfies such a requirement: it is simply not possible for either to fail to satisfy it. At best, then, trivial satisfaction of the NPDC fails to reflect any sort of epistemic sensitivity on the part of the subject in question and is, therefore, epistemically worthless.

At worst, however, there can be cases in which the NPDC is trivially satisfied in spite of the presence of a counterbelief. For, if counterbeliefs simply cannot function as psychological defeaters in the epistemic systems of infants and young children, then such cognitive agents will trivially satisfy the NPDC even when, epistemically, they clearly should fail it. Indeed, no matter what occurs in the epistemic lives of such subjects—whether they hold massive amounts of counterbeliefs or none at all—the NPDC will nonetheless be trivially satisfied.

Given this, it seems rather odd to call trivial satisfaction of the no-defeater condition with respect to either normative or psychological defeaters "satisfaction" at all. But whatever word we choose to use, the following

---

[11] I shall here focus only on the difference between counterbeliefs and psychological defeaters, but similar considerations apply to the difference between doubts and psychological defeaters.

point should be made clear: with respect to those subjects who lack the capacity for reasons, there is simply no epistemic difference between allowing trivial satisfaction of the no-defeater condition and not requiring satisfaction of this condition at all. Hence, if the non-reductionist wants the no-defeater-condition to matter epistemically, it had better be understood as requiring substantive satisfaction.

7.5 A Version of the ICO for Non-Reductionism

The considerations from the previous sections show that the plausibility of the non-reductionist's view depends on reading the no-defeater condition—condition (NR2) of NR*** in Chapter 5—as requiring substantive satisfaction. This can be done by building substantive satisfaction into what it means to be a properly functioning recipient of testimony, i.e., into condition (NR4) of NR***, which is what I suggested in Chapter 5. Alternatively, condition (NR2) can be revised in the following way:

(NR2*): B has no undefeated (psychological or normative) defeaters for A's testimony, and B has the cognitive capacity to be sensitive to such defeaters.

Either way, once it is clear that the no-defeater condition requires substantive satisfaction, it becomes equally clear that non-reductionism is subject to a variant of the very argument that its proponents commonly use against reductionism and dualism. In particular, if it is indeed the case that infants and young children lack the cognitive capacity for acquiring and possessing appropriate positive reasons, then the following version of the ICO—which we can call the ICO*—can be put forth:

(1*) According to (NR2*), for every speaker, A, and hearer, B, B's belief that p is justified or warranted on the basis of A's testimony only if B has no undefeated psychological or normative defeaters for A's testimony, and B has the cognitive capacity to be sensitive to such defeaters.

(2*) However, infants and young children lack the cognitive capacity to be sensitive to undefeated psychological and normative defeaters.

(3*) Therefore, infants and young children are incapable of satisfying (NR2*).[12]

(4*) Infants and young children do have at least some testimonial knowledge.

(5*) Therefore, non-reductionism is false.

Thus, considerations about the cognitive capacities of infants and young children do not provide a reason to endorse non-reductionism over either reductionism or dualism.

This conclusion has important implications, not only for proponents of non-reductionism, but also for a well-known reductionist response to the ICO put forth by Elizabeth Fricker. According to Fricker, while appropriate non-testimonial positive reasons are necessary during what she calls the *mature phase* of an epistemic agent's life, they are not necessary during the *developmental phase*.[13] The latter phase is when a subject is acquiring concepts and learning the language, relying in large part on her parents and teachers to guide the formation of her belief system, while the former phase is when such a subject has become a competent speaker of the language. So, on Fricker's view, older children and adults must satisfy the reductionist's requirements for testimonial knowledge, while infants and young children merely have to satisfy the non-reductionists's requirements. Of course, this strategy works as a *response* to the ICO only under the assumption that the non-reductionist does not encounter difficulty in explaining the testimonial knowledge that infants and young children presumably possess. As the arguments in this chapter have shown, however, to the extent that the reductionist faces the ICO, so, too, does the non-reductionist. Thus, Fricker's move here on behalf of the reductionist fails to provide a compelling response to the ICO.

We have seen, then, that if premise (2) of the ICO is correct, then the considerations underlying this premise can be used to support (2*) of the ICO*, thereby showing that non-reductionism is false as well. Thus, at this point, it looks as though non-reductionism, reductionism, and dualism stand or fall together in the face of the Infant/Child Objection.

---

[12] If one chooses to build substantive satisfaction of the NDC into condition (NR4)—which requires that the hearer is a properly functioning recipient of testimony—instead of revising (NR2), then this premise of the ICO*, along with (1*), can simply be appropriately adapted.

[13] See Fricker (1994 and 1995). For a critical discussion of Fricker's view, see Weiner (2003).

7.6 Why the Situation is Even Worse for Non-Reductionism

In fact, however, non-reductionists are in an even worse position than either reductionists or dualists are with respect to the Infant/Child Objection. To see this, consider the following response that the non-reductionist may offer to the above argument: if proponents of non-reductionism indeed have a problem explaining how infants and young children can lose their justification or warrant, *then reductionists and dualists have the very same problem.* For *all three* views of testimonial justification or warrant include the no-defeater condition. Hence, if infants and young children cannot appreciate reasons or evidence, then non-reductionists, reductionists, and dualists alike cannot account for how the justification or warrant of the beliefs of such agents is lost or defeated.

The central reason why this extension of the problem to reductionism and dualism is mistaken is this: if it is indeed correct that infants and young children lack the capacity to appreciate reasons or evidence, then reductionists and dualists can simply say that such subjects *never had testimonial justification/warrant or knowledge in the first place*; they are, rationally, too much like coffee cups or paper clips to have justification/warrant or knowledge. Hence, there was never anything epistemically positive present to be lost or defeated. Once it seems reasonable to say that infants and young children *do* have justification/warrant or knowledge to be lost, then reductionists and dualists can also say that they have at least a minimal capacity to appreciate reasons or evidence. The problem for non-reductionists is that, unlike reductionists and dualists, they are *committed* to granting justification/warrant and knowledge to creatures who lie completely outside the domain of reasons, that is, to creatures who are rationally like coffee cups or paper clips. It is only when one grants justification/warrant and knowledge to these types of creatures that one is left with the problem of explaining how they can lose their justification/warrant and knowledge.

But perhaps one could attempt to extend the problem to reductionism and dualism by arguing in the following way. Both the reductionist and the dualist grant that sometimes infants and young children can appreciate at least *some* evidence and reasons and, accordingly, that they can have justified or warranted beliefs. So, let's imagine a young child at such a point: Harry is justified or warranted in believing that *p* based on evidence he can appreciate. Suppose then that Harry is inundated with counterevidence against his belief that *p*, which he is incapable of appreciating. Since, *ex hypothesi*, Harry was justified or warranted in believing that *p* prior to getting the counterevidence, the only question is whether Harry now *loses* his justification or warrant. And here reductionism and dualism face a dilemma. If, on the one hand, the reductionist and dualist say that Harry *does not* lose his justification or warrant because he cannot appreciate the evidence, then the non-reductionist can say the same thing in response to the argument of Section 7.5 above. The fact that infants and young children satisfy the NNDC in only a trivial sense would then be irrelevant. If, on the other hand, the reductionist and dualist say that Harry *does* lose his justification or warrant, then reductionism and dualism will have to explain, just as non-reductionism does, why this happens despite the fact that Harry cannot appreciate the counterevidence. And non-reductionists could then claim that this problem is really a problem for *every* view, including both reductionism and dualism.

The proponent of PR-N can respond to this argument by making the following two points. First, she can embrace the first horn of the dilemma and say that Harry does *not* lose his justification or warrant. The reasoning is the same as in the case of Olga, the Polish speaker, from Section 7.3 above. Given that Harry cannot appreciate the counterevidence, it does not defeat his justification or warrant. However, the *fact* that there is this counterevidence may nevertheless provide him with what we called in Chapter 2 a factual defeater that prevents his justified or warranted belief from counting as knowledge.

Second, the non-reductionist cannot similarly embrace the first horn of the dilemma and argue that a young child incapable of appreciating *any* counterevidence (let us call her "Mary") does not lose her justification or warrant even though she is apparently inundated with it. As I have argued, the problem with non-reductionism is that nothing—absolutely nothing—can count against the belief of someone like Mary. This is not true in Harry's case, presumably, for if he can appreciate evidence well enough to have a justified or warranted belief, he can also appreciate coun-terevidence. Granted, he cannot appreciate *every* piece of counterevidence (not even adults can do that), but he could appreciate at least *some* pieces of counterevidence. So, there *will* be some things that can count against Harry's justification or warrant. This is the crucial difference between Harry and Mary: Harry is in the logical space of reasons and evidence, but Mary is not.

To this the non-reductionist might object that it is implausible to suppose that infants and young children make a dramatic leap from outside the logical space of reasons and evidence to within it. Surely, the process of cognitive development is a gradual one. The reductionist and the dualist, however, can accept this. It may well be difficult or even impossible to distinguish between an infant that cannot at all appreciate evidence and reasons and an infant that is just beginning to do so. Nevertheless, in order to have a justified or warranted belief, a subject must do better than have just a rudimentary appreciation of some tiny bit of evidence. Rather, she must appreciate evidence sufficiently well to count as having a justified or warranted belief. That is, there is a minimal threshold, whatever it may turn out to be, for the appreciation of evidence that will provide a clear dividing line between Harry and Mary. This minimal threshold is what allows for Harry and Mary to differ in kind and not merely in degree.

It should be clear, then, that for reductionism and dualism, there is no special problem of explaining how infants and young children can lose (or have defeated) justification or warrant. Rather, the same principles governing evidence, justification, warrant, and knowledge in the case of adults govern the beliefs of infants and young children as well. In this sense, then, reductionists and dualists alike reject what we might call "quantum epistemology"—there aren't different rules governing the behavior of the very small.[14] Non-reductionists, however, cannot offer this sort of response, so long as they take infants and young children to be incapable of appreciating evidence and reasons. Thus, the problem of explaining how young children can nevertheless lose justification is a problem *only* for non-reductionism.

---

[14] I owe this point to Baron Reed.

7.7 Infants, Children, and Their Cognitive Environment

In a recent paper, Sanford Goldberg offers a non-reductionist response to an argument such as that found in the ICO*. In particular, he grants that non-reductionists are committed to requiring substantive satisfaction of the NDC for testimonial knowledge, that infants and young children cannot substantively satisfy the NDC, and that infants and young children possess testimonial knowledge, yet he still denies that non-reductionism is false.

Now how does Goldberg accomplish this feat? He writes: "On such a view, although cognitively immature children (taken in isolation from their surrounding social environment) fail to satisfy the No-Defeater requirement, nevertheless such children (taken in the context of their surrounding social environment) can be said to acquire beliefs in such a way as to satisfy this requirement" (Goldberg 2008: 28). According to Goldberg, then, while infants and young children cannot substantively satisfy the NDC *by themselves*, they can nonetheless substantively satisfy such a condition when viewed *in relation to their broader social environment*. In particular, he argues that:

we should consider the role that the child's adult guardians play in the process that eventuates in the young child's consumption of testimony. I submit that adult guardians play three epistemically-relevant roles in this process. First, adult guardians make social arrangements in such a way that children are typically shielded early in life from those who might abuse their trust; second, adult guardians serve as an explicit check on the trustworthiness of interlocutors whom children encounter in the presence of their parents or adult guardians (as in: "Tommy, do you really believe Uncle Myron's story about being the richest man in the world?"; or "Sally, don't believe your brother, he's just saying silly things again"); and third, adult guardians continue to vet the child's subsequent assertions for signs of his having consumed unreliable testimony. I will describe these three roles as the roles of (i) *access-restriction*, (ii) *pro-active monitoring* for credibility, and (iii) *reactive monitoring* for credibility. (Goldberg 2008: 18)

So while infants and young children lack the capacity to be properly sensitive to defeaters, their adult guardians, in performing the three roles found in (i)–(iii), nonetheless enable them to not only satisfy (NR2*), but also to thereby acquire testimonially based knowledge. Goldberg, then, accepts the following restricted version of (3*):

(3**) Therefore, infants and young children are incapable of satisfying (NR2*) *by themselves.*

He also grants that:

(4*) Infants and young children do have at least some testimonial knowledge.

But instead of then granting the falsity of non-reductionism, as found in (5*) of the ICO*, he proposes that:

(5**) Infants and young children are capable of satisfying (NR2*) *when viewed in relation to their adult guardians.*

Given this, Goldberg concludes that the non-reductionist is able to have it all: she can retain the no-defeater condition, require that it be substantively satisfied, concede that infants and young children lack the capacity to substantively satisfy such a condition, but nevertheless grant that such cognitive agents acquire testimonially based knowledge because of the roles played by their adult guardians.

There are, however, at least three central problems with Goldberg's response here. First, such a move fails to preserve the original asymmetry that proponents of the ICO claim exists between non-reductionists, on the one hand, and reductionists and dualists, on the other hand.[15] For once adult guardians are allowed to do the epistemic work for infants and children in satisfying (NR2*), what is to prevent such guardians from also doing their epistemic work in satisfying PR-N? Otherwise put, if caretakers are included in our epistemic evaluation of infants and young children with respect to *negative* reasons, then they should also be included in our epistemic evaluation of such cognitive agents when it comes to *positive* reasons. So, just as Goldberg altered the ICO* by replacing (3*) with (3**) and (5*) with (5**), the reductionist and dualist can replace (3) and (5) of the ICO with the following:

(3′) Therefore, infants and young children are incapable of satisfying PR-N *by themselves.*

---

[15] It is not clear that Goldberg himself is aiming to preserve the original asymmetry between non-reductionists, on the one hand, and reductionists and dualists, on the other hand, but this is certainly an aim of those who endorse the ICO.

(5′) Infants and young children are capable of satisfying PR-N *when viewed in relation to their adult guardians.*

Of course, this is not to say that the reductionist and the dualist *should* accept (3′) and (5′); in fact, I shall argue below that there are independent reasons to reject Goldberg's argumentative strategy here. The point is, rather, that to the extent that such a move succeeds as a defense of non-reductionism, it also succeeds as a defense of reductionism and dualism.

Second, it is an empirical question whether caretakers indeed perform the three roles that Goldberg claims, and there are at least some reasons to doubt that they in fact do, particularly to the extent that Goldberg suggests. For instance, consider his discussion of the access–restriction role that adult guardians presumably perform in the cognitive lives of infants and young children:

During her waking hours, a young child is typically either at home, or else (if outside the home) in the company of an adult guardian. Access to the child is restricted while she is at home, since the walls of the house enable the adults to monitor (literally) who is permitted to enter the home. When not at home the child will encounter strangers, but will do so only in the presence of her adult caretaker, where the caretaker's interest in protecting the child will render her (the caretaker) more attentive to the child's environment. Part of this attentiveness, I submit, is a greater attentiveness on the adult's part to the testimony [proffered] in their mutual presence. The result is that, given the role adults play in achieving (i), the child is typically either in a pre-screened environment, or if she is not, her guardians are more vigilant; but either way, the risk of the child's accepting false testimony is significantly decreased, whether because the risk of *encountering* it is decreased, or because (though the child encounters it) the risk of *consuming* it is decreased. (Goldberg forthcoming; 20–1 of ms., original emphasis)

Now, while Goldberg is certainly correct that caretakers monitor young children's encounters with and consumption of testimony, there is reason to think that he overstates the extent to which this is the case. For instance, the US Census Bureau reported that, in 2002, there were more than 687,000 daycare centers across the country, with about 2 million pre-schoolers being cared for in such centers during the bulk of their parents' working hours.[16] The child/caretaker ratio can vary dramatically in such centers; a

---

[16] See <http://www.cnn.com/2006/US/04/21/modern.mothers/>. This information is taken from a CNN report, dated April 24, 2006, titled: "Deciphering the 'mommy wars'."

group childcare center with one provider, for instance, can be licensed to care for up to 10 children between the ages of three and four, and up to 20 children age five and older.[17] Thus, a 10/1 or 20/1 ratio of children to adults clearly limits the extent to which young children can be individually monitored by their caretakers, leaving a substantial amount of time for interaction with peers. Moreover, 70 percent of daycare centers in the USA rely on television to entertain the children during a typical day, and the average American child spends 1,023 hours a year watching television, compared with the 900 hours a year she spends in school.[18] The majority of this television-watching is done without an adult caretaker sitting next to each child, monitoring his or her encounters with, and consumption of, the incoming information. Indeed, children between the ages of two and seven spend 81 percent of their television-watching time alone and unsupervised.[19] These statistics suggest that at least many young children experience significant amounts of unmonitored exposure to both peers and television, with the extent to which adult caretakers engage in access-restriction, proactive monitoring for credibility, and reactive monitoring for credibility being far more limited than Goldberg assumes. Hence, there are good reasons to doubt the truth of Goldberg's modified (5**) and, therewith, his conclusion that non-reductionism has the resources to explain the testimonially based knowledge possessed by infants and young children.

Third, even if we grant that adult caretakers in fact perform the roles that Goldberg claims, it is not at all clear why this should result in the possession of testimonial *knowledge* by the infants and young children in question. For it is undeniable that guardians typically do much to increase the number of true beliefs, and to decrease the number of false beliefs, that infants and young children acquire on the basis of testimony. But Plato taught us long ago in the *Meno* that while mere true beliefs can often function just as well as knowledge, they nonetheless fall short by lacking the appropriate "tether." Compare: adult caretakers typically engage in various kinds of

[17] See <http://www.illinoisearlylearning.org/faqs/cc-options.htm>. This information is provided by the Illinois Department of Children and Family Services, accessed through the Illinois Early Learning Project.

[18] See <http://www.tvturnoff.org/images/facts&figs/factsheets/FactsFigs.pdf>. This information is provided by the TV-Turnoff Network, which is a non-profit organization that encourages children and adults to watch less television in order to promote healthier lives.

[19] See, again, <http://www.tvturnoff.org/images/facts&figs/factsheets/FactsFigs.pdf>.

behavior to prevent infants and young children from performing actions that are morally objectionable. For instance, a mother may take a toy out of her young son's hand and put it back on the shelf of the store, saying "No, no, Caleb, this belongs to the store, not to us." Or a father may pick up his young daughter and walk away from a social gathering, just as she begins sharing an embarrassing story about her sister. In both cases, the young children end up doing the morally right thing because of the intervention of their parents; but surely we would not characterize the *children* as *morally good agents*. In fact, depending on their age and level of cognitive sophistication, they may not even be properly regarded as moral agents at all, let alone morally good ones. Similar considerations apply in the epistemic realm: a mother may interrupt her son as he is about to tell his sister, incorrectly, that the snake in the window is a real one. In such a case, the young girl ends up with the right beliefs: she acquires a true belief, and avoids a false one, because of the intervention of her mother. But surely we would not characterize the child, who presumably lies completely outside the realm of evidence and reasons, as a *knower* merely because her mother ensures that the correct epistemic results obtain.

Given these three central problems with Goldberg's argument, then, I conclude that he has failed to provide a compelling non-reductionist response to the ICO*.

7.8 Why the Situation is Even Better for Reductionism and Dualism

At this point, we have seen, first, that different versions of the Infant/Child Objection cut across non-reductionism, reductionism, and dualism and, second, that if there is any asymmetry found between those who reject PR-N and those who accept it, it is one that works to the disadvantage of those who reject the requirement for positive reasons. In this final section, I shall argue that the situation regarding the cognitive capacities of infants and young children may be even better for the proponent of PR-N since there are good reasons to reject premise (2) of the ICO at the outset, thereby enabling the reductionist and, especially, the dualist, to altogether avoid this purported problem.

To begin, recall that (2) claims that infants and young children lack the cognitive capacity for acquiring and possessing the positive reasons required by the proponent of PR-N, a premise that is often simply taken for granted by the proponent of the ICO. But recent psychological work examining the processes by which infants and young children accept testimony suggests that such cognitive agents are far more critical and discriminating in believing what they are told than is often thought. For instance, a recent study by Koenig and Echols (2003) reported that 16-month-old infants directed more attention toward human speakers who labeled objects falsely—e.g., "That's a dog" when referring to a cup—than toward those who labeled objects truthfully. Indeed, many infants even corrected, through their own pointing and labeling, the speakers who named objects incorrectly in this way. Similar results were found by Pea (1982), who reported that 18-month-old infants explicitly rejected testimony involving false, but not true, labels of visible objects by saying "no."[20] As Koenig, Clément, and Harris (2004) conclude about these findings, "when human speakers provide information that conflicts with infants' knowledge and experience, infants demonstrate an ability to recognize, correct, and deny assertions that they know to be false" (Koenig, Clément, and Harris 2004: 694).

In addition, there is substantial evidence that young children are quite sensitive to group-based epistemic differences among speakers. For instance, according to Koenig and Harris,

young children appreciate that adults know more than themselves, and that younger children know less (Taylor, Cartwright, & Bowden, 1991). They appreciate that different individuals have different kinds of expert knowledge (Lutz & Keil, 2002; Taylor, Esbensen, & Bennett, 1994). As communicators, young children also show marked sensitivity to the age of a listener by producing simpler, shorter speech to children younger than themselves (Dunn & Kendrick, 1982; Shatz & Gelman, 1973). (2005: 1261)

In all of these cases, young children base their acceptance and offering of testimony on a person's membership in various epistemically relevant groups, such as those grounded in age, degree of expertise, and so on.

Perhaps even more telling for our purposes, however, are several recent studies that show that young children are critical and discriminating in their

---

[20] This was discussed in Koenig, Clément, and Harris (2004).

testimonial practices, not only when it comes to assertions involving what they know to be false or when speakers belong to various epistemically salient groups, but also with respect to the track records of reliability exhibited by individual speakers. In three different studies—Koenig, Clément, and Harris (2004), Clément, Koenig, and Harris (2004), and Koenig and Harris (2005)—3- and 4-year-old children were presented with two testifiers, one who labeled familiar objects correctly and one who labeled them incorrectly. The children were then presented with questions to determine whether they could use information about each speaker's past to gauge the reliability of subsequent testimony received from such speakers. All three studies showed that three- and four-year olds demonstrate *selective trust* in their acceptance of testimony. In Koenig and Harris (2005), for instance, three- and four-year olds were found to: (i) distinguish between knowledgeable and ignorant speakers; (ii) predict the future assertions of such speakers; (iii) seek information from knowledgeable speakers; and (iv) accept new information from knowledgeable speakers.[21] Moreover, when the children were asked to explain the behavior of the unreliable testifier, they gave "predominantly epistemic explanations" (Koenig and Harris 2005: 1273). In particular, when asked why the unreliable testifier "was not good at answering questions," 25 out of the 38 children provided spontaneous answers that referred to the speaker's ignorance—"e.g., 'She didn't know what they were,' 'She wasn't too smart,' 'She never saw them before,' 'She didn't know anything'" (Koenig and Harris 2005: 1272). According to Koenig and Harris, then, the results of their study "suggest that preschool children may be able to attribute knowledge and ignorance to speakers as epistemic traits" (Koenig and Harris 2005: 1273).

These studies show that infants and young children are hardly the uncritical, indiscriminate recipients of testimony that they are often portrayed to be by proponents of the ICO. For not only are such cognitive agents sensitive to the *contents* of the particular assertions being offered (e.g., they reject assertions involving what they know to be false), they are also sensitive to the identity of the *speakers* in question, at the level of both type (e.g., they distinguish adult testifiers from children, and those who have expertise in a given area from those who do not) and token (e.g., they distinguish particular reliable from unreliable testifiers in the light of their

---

[21] See Koenig and Harris (2005: 1269–73).

past track records). Given this, it seems undeniable that infants and young children acquire and possess epistemically relevant positive reasons about the assertions that they are being offered, and that they often rely upon these reasons in their acceptance and rejection of such reports. Thus, there is good reason to reject (2) of the ICO and, therewith, (2*) of the ICO*, from the very beginning.

But what if the non-reductionist were to argue that while these psychological studies may very well establish that infants and young children can possess and rely upon epistemically relevant reasons, they may still be too cognitively underdeveloped to have positive reasons *adequate* for satisfying PR-N. Indeed, this may be precisely what the non-reductionist needs to preserve the original asymmetry of the ICO: such cognitive agents are clearly sensitive to negative evidence and can thereby substantively satisfy the NDC. But it does not follow from this that they can possess positive reasons that are sufficient to *justify* their acceptance of testimony.

Here is where my response will abandon reductionism and apply only to my own dualist view of testimonial knowledge. For the non-reductionist may very well be correct that infants and young children are incapable of acquiring positive reasons that *fully justify* their testimonial beliefs, as is required by reductionism. According to dualism, however, the reasons required by condition (D6) need only render the acceptance of a given instance of testimony *not irrational*. Surely, the abilities that infants and young children demonstrated by discriminating between not only true and false assertions, but also reliable and unreliable testifiers, suffice to satisfy *this* condition. Moreover, it is of interest to note that of the three epistemically relevant classes of reasons discussed in Chapter 6—reasons about contexts, reports, and speakers—the psychological literature cited above shows that infants and young children rely upon at least the last two of these in their acceptance of testimony. This provides even further reason to conclude that such cognitive agents have the capacity to satisfy condition (D6) of dualism.

Thus, we have seen that, first, whatever considerations the non-reductionist invokes on behalf of the ICO can be similarly used by the reductionist and the dualist on behalf of the ICO*; second, to the extent that there is any asymmetry between proponents and opponents of PR-N regarding the cognitive capacities of infants and young children, it is one that favors those who require positive reasons; and, third, there are very good reasons stemming from recent psychological studies to reject premise (2) of the ICO at the outset. Thus, considerations about the cognitive capacities of infants and young children pose no obstacle to fully embracing a dualist view of testimonial knowledge.

8

Trust and Assurance: The Interpersonal View of Testimony

8.1 The IVT

Very recent work in the epistemology of testimony has seen the emergence of a new family of views, one that provides a radically different answer to the question of how testimonial beliefs are justified or warranted than any of the other theories discussed thus far, such as reductionism, non-reductionism, and dualism. Though there are some points of disagreement among some of the members of this family, they are united in their commitment to at least three central theses. First, and perhaps most important, the *interpersonal relationship* between the two parties in a testimonial exchange should be the central focus of the epistemology of testimony. Second, and closely related, certain features of this interpersonal relationship—such as the speaker *offering her assurance* to the hearer that her testimony is true, or the speaker *inviting the hearer to trust* her—are (at least sometimes) actually *responsible for conferring epistemic value* on the testimonial beliefs acquired. Third, the epistemic justification or warrant provided by these features of a testimonial exchange is *non-evidential* in nature. For ease of discussion, let us call the general conception of testimony characterized by these theses the *Interpersonal View of Testimony* (hereafter, the IVT).[1]

In addition to these three central claims, proponents of the IVT further agree that something critical is missing from views of testimony—such as the one defended in this book—that fail to place the interpersonal relationship between speaker and hearer at the center of the epistemology of testimony. For instance, in discussing evidential views of testimonial

[1] Proponents of various versions of the IVT include Ross (1986), Hinchman (2005), Moran (2005 and 2006), Faulkner (2007 and forthcoming), and Wanderer (unpublished).

justification or warrant, Edward Hinchman says, "[w]hen you have evidence of a speaker's reliability you don't *need* to trust her: you can treat her speech act as a mere assertion and believe what she says on the basis of the evidence you have of its truth. You can ignore the fact that she's addressing you, inviting you. You can *treat her as a truth-gauge*" (Hinchman 2005: 580, second emphasis added). In a similar spirit, Angus Ross claims that "[i]f, as hearers, we do see the words a speaker utters as evidence of something... we are not accepting them in the spirit in which they are offered ... *Something important to true communication is missing* when the hearer sees the speaker's words simply as evidence of the existence of a certain state of affairs" (Ross 1986: 73, emphasis added). And Richard Moran maintains that "if we are inclined to believe what the speaker says, but then learn that he is *not*, in fact, presenting his utterance as an assertion whose truth he stands behind, then what remains is *just words*, not a reason to believe anything... [T]he utterance as [a] phenomenon loses the epistemic import we thought it had" (Moran 2006: 283; second emphasis added). According to proponents of the IVT, then, a significant aspect of true communication is missing when a speaker is treated as a mere truth gauge, offering nothing more than words. Given this, the view of testimony that I have developed in this book—in which hearers learn from the *words* of speakers—is a paradigm of the kind of view targeted by these criticisms.

So, in this chapter, I shall critically examine the conception of testimony found in the IVT. In particular, I shall argue that the proponent of the IVT faces a dilemma: either the view of testimony in question is genuinely interpersonal but epistemologically impotent, or it is not epistemologically impotent but neither is it genuinely interpersonal. Either way, the IVT fails to provide a compelling alternative to existing theories in the epistemology of testimony. I shall then show that the criticisms raised by proponents of the IVT to competing views of testimony, such as mine, are fundamentally misguided and hence give us no reason to abandon standard, purely epistemic, conceptions of testimony.

8.2 The First Horn of the Dilemma

Let us begin with the version of the IVT that has come to be known as the *Assurance View*, developed and defended by Angus Ross and, more recently, by Richard Moran.[2] Since Moran provides a thorough and detailed account of this conception of testimony, I shall focus primarily on his view in my discussion. But before proceeding, let me say at the outset that several versions of the IVT contain competing strands of thought, each of which is coherent in isolation but, when combined, result in an incoherent picture of testimony. In what follows, I shall argue that each of these strands will be impaled on one or the other horn of the dilemma I will develop. For ease of exposition, I shall emphasize one of these strands while focusing on the Assurance View and the other strand when discussing what I shall call the Trust View. But, as will become clear, each of these versions of the IVT ultimately contains both strands.

In a recent paper,[3] Richard Moran poses the question: why does a speaker's testimony that p provide a *reason* for a hearer to believe that p? He argues that the standard *Evidential View*—in which a speaker's testimony that p is regarded as merely evidence for believing that p—simply cannot provide an adequate answer to this question. For, since people are known to lie, exaggerate, and otherwise mislead, the Evidential View will be hard pressed to explain how, in light of its intentional character, testimony could count as anything more than a "doctored" form of evidence, and hence a generally less reliable way of learning the beliefs of speakers than more direct routes, such as mind-reading, brain-scans, or private observation of their behavior.

In contrast, Moran argues on behalf of the *Assurance View* of testimony, in which a speaker's testimony that p is understood as the speaker giving his *assurance* that p is true. Since assurance can be given only when it is freely presented as such, Moran claims that a speaker freely assumes responsibility for the truth of p when he asserts that p, thereby providing the hearer with an *additional* reason to believe that p, different in kind from anything given by evidence alone.[4] In particular, the speaker's assertion that p counts as a reason to believe that p in virtue of his *presenting* it as a reason to believe that p, that is, in virtue of his presenting it as having the force of "giving his word," and it is only through this presentation that the assertion in question acquires epistemic value. As Moran says,

---

[2] See Ross (1986) and Moran (2005 and 2006).   [3] Moran (2006).

[4] As Moran says, "it is the special relations of telling someone, being told, and accepting or refusing another's word that are the home of the network of beliefs we acquire through human testimony. And these relations...provide a reason for belief that is categorically different from that provided by evidence" (Moran 2006: 275).

If, unlike a piece of evidence, the speaker's words have no independent epistemic value as a phenomenon, then how do they *acquire* the status of a reason to believe something? It seems that this can only be by virtue of the speaker's there and then explicitly *presenting* his utterance as a reason to believe, with this presentation being accomplished in the act of assertion itself. The epistemic value of his words is something publicly conferred on them by the speaker, by presenting his utterance as an assertion. (Moran 2006: 288)

This, according to Moran, is the only way to adequately account for how the recognition of testimony's intentional character *enhances* rather than *detracts from* the epistemic status of the assertion in question.[5]

At this point, then, the Assurance View appears to clearly be an IVT: the speaker's offering her assurance to the hearer that her testimony is true, which is a non-evidential feature of their interpersonal relationship, is responsible for conferring epistemic value on the testimonial beliefs acquired. Before showing how this reading of the Assurance View succumbs to the first horn of the dilemma (i.e., it is genuinely interpersonal but epistemologically impotent), however, let me raise two initial problems with this view. First, recall Moran's claim that a speaker's testimony acquires epistemic value *only* by virtue of her presenting her utterance as a reason for her hearer to believe the proposition in question. But now suppose that Celeste comes to believe that Chester committed the murder for which he is suspected on the basis of overhearing his soliloquy. It seems quite reasonable to think that Celeste's belief could qualify as knowledge, for we can suppose that Chester's utterance is reliable and that Celeste is a properly functioning recipient of testimony situated in an epistemically appropriate environment who possesses positive reasons for Chester's testimony. But, given that Celeste's knowledge is acquired on the basis of a soliloquy, Chester is not *presenting* his utterance as a reason for her to believe him, nor is he *offering* his assurance to Celeste that his utterance is true. For Chester does not even think that there *is* a relevant hearer, let alone one to whom

---

[5] Of course, there is an enormous difference between *detracting from* and *destroying* the epistemic status of the assertion in question. A proponent of the Evidential View could obviously grant that the intentional nature of testimony *detracts* from the epistemic value of testimony (compared, say, to straight perception), while also holding (i) that testimony is still an adequate source of knowledge and (ii) that testimony provides knowledge that we couldn't get any other way. But notice: though Moran argues for the weaker claim, that the intentional nature of testimony *detracts from* its epistemic value, he needs to argue for the stronger claim—that the intentional nature of testimony *destroys* its epistemic value—in order for there to even be a problem that the Assurance View purportedly solves.

he is presenting or offering anything. Proponents of the Assurance View will, then, be hard pressed to explain the epistemic value that Celeste's belief intuitively possesses despite the absence of the interpersonal features that purportedly confer such value on beliefs.[6]

Second, recall Moran's claim that interpersonal features of a speaker's testimony, particularly the speaker's offering her assurance that p is true, provide the hearer in question with a *reason* to believe that p. Now notice: even views that hold that testimony is not evidence, nor necessarily grounded in evidence, nearly universally maintain that testimonially justified or warranted belief must be appropriately resistant to *counterevidence*. Because of this, both evidential and non-evidential views of testimony typically include a no-undefeated defeater condition, one that rules out the compatibility of testimonial justification or warrant and the presence of available counterevidence. Suppose, for instance, that I have counterevidence for Hubert's testimony that albatrosses have the largest wingspan among wild birds—say, a respectable colleague called into question his credentials as an ornithologist. (This counterevidence serves as an undefeated normative defeater—i.e., it is counterevidence for one's belief, where the counterevidence is such that it *should* be believed, even if one does not actually believe it.) Suppose, also, that you tell me Hubert is one of the best in his field. According to the Assurance View—and indeed all versions of the IVT—certain non-evidential features of our interpersonal relationship provide me with a *reason* for believing that Hubert is one of the best ornithologists in the field, one that is entirely different in kind than a reason provided by evidence. Now, if this is a reason *in an epistemic sense*, it should clearly be capable of functioning as a defeater-defeater for the original counterevidence I had against Hubert's competence as an ornithologist. But here is the problem: if, on the one hand, the epistemic value of your testimony is conceived in wholly non-evidential and interpersonal terms, as all proponents of the IVT maintain, then it is entirely unclear how a purely non-evidential reason could defeat counterevidence. Thus, it is a mystery how your testimony could function as a defeater-defeater for the original undefeated normative defeater I possess regarding Hubert's competence.

---

[6] I shall develop a similar point in even greater detail in the next section of this chapter. I should also note that I recently discovered that a similar objection is raised to the Assurance View by David Owens in his (2006). However, Owens then goes on to argue on behalf of the Belief View of Testimony, which I refuted in Chapter 2.

After all, a defeater–defeater ought to be counterevidence for the original counterevidence. On the other hand, if the proponent of the IVT bites the bullet and claims that the non-evidential reason provided by your testimony simply cannot function as a defeater–defeater, then this amounts to a concession to the epistemological irrelevance of the reasons provided by testimony.

Moreover, it should be clear that this objection can be carried even further. For notice: the original counterevidence calling into question Hubert's credentials as an ornithologist was, *ex hypothesi*, provided by the testimony of a colleague. According to the IVT, then, the interpersonal relationship that I have with this colleague provides me with a reason to doubt Hubert's testimony regarding birds. But now it is utterly mysterious how something purely non-evidential and interpersonal could function as an undefeated normative defeater in the first place. Even further, it is equally mysterious how testimony could ever be defeated on the IVT. For, if the reasons provided by testimony are purely non-evidential, then how could such reasons be defeated by *counterevidence,* such as that found in a paradigmatic normative defeater? The upshot of these considerations is that if the reasons provided by testimony lie entirely outside the realm of evidence, as all proponents of the IVT maintain, then such a view faces the difficult challenge of explaining the relationship between such non-evidential reasons and counterevidence that is capable of defeating such reasons.

Let us now turn to developing the first horn of the dilemma facing proponents of the IVT. To begin, notice that "epistemic" applies to a concept to indicate its being truth-conducive or otherwise intimately related to knowledge; thus, if, for instance, a practice has epistemic value, it would be one that somehow furthers the goal of acquiring true beliefs and avoiding false ones. Because of this, a natural question to ask at this point is what the precise connection is between *a speaker's giving a hearer assurance of the truth of her utterance* and *the truth itself.* Otherwise put, what is the *epistemic* value of a speaker's assurance?

By way of answering this question, Moran says, "the speaker, in present- ing his utterance as an *assertion*, one with the force of *telling* the audience something, presents himself as *accountable* for the truth of what he says, and in doing so he offers a kind of guarantee for this truth" (Moran 2006: 283, original emphasis). In a similar spirit, Ross claims that "[t]he speaker, in taking responsibility for the truth of what he is saying, is offering his hearer not evidence but a *guarantee* that it is true, and in believing what he is told the hearer accepts this guarantee" (Ross 1986: 79–80). In both of these passages, it is suggested that the epistemic significance of assurance lies in the *guarantee of truth* that the speaker offers to her hearer.

But this response is quite puzzling. For, even if a speaker explicitly offers her hearer a guarantee of the truth of her assertion, what does this actually have to do with the *truth itself*?[7] For instance, consider Vera, a radically unreliable believer who consistently offers assertions to her hearers that she sincerely believes to be true but which are wholly disconnected from the truth. Now, since Vera presents herself as accountable for the truth of what she says, Moran and Ross claim that the hearer in question is thereby provided with a guarantee of the truth of what Vera says. But what does this so-called guarantee amount to? Nearly every time Vera offers an assertion to a hearer, it turns out to be false. In this way, she is what we might call a reliably unreliable testifier. Moreover, notice that the point brought out by this case is not merely that a speaker can give her assurance that *p* is true but be wrong on a particular occasion; rather, the point is that a speaker can repeatedly give her assurance that various propositions are true and yet consistently offer utterances that fail to be reliably connected with the truth in any way. A "guarantee" of truth that nearly always turns out to be false, however, is a far cry from anything resembling a genuine guarantee.[8]

There is, however, a slightly different answer to our question regarding the epistemic value of assurance that can be found in the above quotations; namely, that this value derives, not necessarily from the guarantee of truth offered by the speaker, but from the fact that the speaker *assumes responsibility* for the truth of her assertion. To see that this response is distinct from the one just considered, notice that the objection raised to the view that assurance involves a speaker guaranteeing the truth of her assertion clearly does not arise here: a speaker can still assume responsibility for the truth of *p* even if she is not in a position to legitimately provide a guarantee of

---

[7] A further problem with the response offered by Moran and Ross here is that it is not at all clear that either speakers or hearers regard testimonial exchanges as always, or even mostly, involving anything as strong as *guarantees* of truth.

[8] As shall be seen in the next section, there is a passage in Moran's paper where he appears to add a condition to his Assurance View to deal with this sort of problem. I shall later argue, however, that to the extent that he does add such a condition, his view succumbs to the second horn of the dilemma under consideration.

the truth of p. For instance, I can assume responsibility for the truth of my Volvo being in the lot near the football stadium, even if I am aware of the possibility that it could have been stolen since I parked it there this morning. Compare: I can assume responsibility for my daughter's behavior at your house even if I cannot make many guarantees about what her behavior will amount to.

Despite the fact that this answer is clearly different from the previous one, it nevertheless succumbs to a variant of the objection raised above. To see this, let us return to the case of Vera, the radically unreliable believer who is a consistently sincere testifier, and suppose that she tells me that she received a Dalmatian puppy when she was seven years old. As is typical with Vera's tellings, she believes this to be true, though it is in fact false. But let us suppose further that in addition to being false, Vera's assertion doesn't have a shred of epistemic value, e.g., it is unreliably produced, it is produced by a faculty functioning improperly, it fails to track to the truth, it lacks appropriate evidential support, and so on. Now, according to the interpretation of the Assurance View of testimony under consideration, through the very act of telling me and thereby taking responsibility for the truth of the assertion that she received a Dalmatian puppy when she was seven years old, Vera's testimony provides me with a belief that has epistemic value. But why would a speaker's taking responsibility for the truth of a false assertion that has absolutely no independent epistemic value confer epistemic value on it? Recall that the value in question is epistemic—rather than, say, moral or pragmatic—and so it must have some connection with truth-conduciveness or knowledge. Taking responsibility for the truth of p, however, doesn't affect reliability, proper functioning, truth-tracking, evidential relations, or any other feature relevant to the truth of p. Hence, it is unclear what value that is distinctively epistemic can be derived from the act of taking such responsibility.

But, one might ask, couldn't a speaker's taking responsibility for the truth of p affect the hearer's so-called *subjective* epistemic status? For instance, if you take responsibility for the truth of p, couldn't this, at the very least, render me not irrational, not epistemically blameworthy, or not epistemically irresponsible in believing that p and, at most, render me rational, epistemically blameless, and epistemically responsible in believing that p?

While there may be some truth in this response, it fails as a *general* explanation of the epistemic value of assurance for at least two reasons. First, even if a speaker assumes responsibility for the truth of *p*, this does not necessarily render the hearer in question not irrational, not epistemically blameworthy, or not epistemically irresponsible in believing that *p*. Consider: I may take responsibility for my daughter's behavior while she is playing at your house, but this renders her neither not blameworthy nor not irresponsible for carelessly breaking your vase. Similarly, the mere fact that an acquaintance takes responsibility for the truth of her claim that two of my friends are having an affair renders me neither not epistemically blameworthy nor not irresponsible in believing such gossip. This point is even clearer in cases where the hearer in question has either an undefeated psychological or normative defeater for accepting a speaker's testimony that *p*. Surely the mere fact that the speaker takes responsibility for the truth of *p* fails to render the hearer not epistemically blameworthy or not irresponsible in believing that *p* in the face of such a defeater. If, for instance, I have good reason to believe that you are a compulsive liar, it would still be epistemically irresponsible for me to accept your testimony that Conrad stole the missing money, even if you give me your assurance that this is true.

Second, and more importantly, even if we grant that a speaker's taking responsibility for the truth of *p* can confer epistemic value on a hearer's testimonial belief that *p*, surely this should be the case *only under appropriate epistemic circumstances*. For instance, suppose that I walk up to an airplane mechanic and say, "I will take responsibility for the proper functioning of this aircraft." Given that I know nothing about the mechanics of aircrafts, my words would rightly be regarded as hollow even if said with the utmost sincerity and goodwill. Similarly, when Vera, our radically unreliable speaker, takes responsibility for the truth of her assertion that she received a Dalmatian puppy when she was seven, her words should also be rightly regarded as hollow since her faculty of memory is an extremely poor epistemic source for acquiring beliefs. Otherwise put, just as I am in no mechanical position to be taking responsibility for the functioning of aircrafts, so too Vera is in no epistemic position to be taking responsibility for the truth of her memorial beliefs. Hence, it is *only when a speaker's taking responsibility for the truth of her assertion is properly grounded epistemically that it has the capacity to confer epistemic value on testimonial beliefs.*

Otherwise put, in order for assurance to be of interest to the epistemology of testimony, it must be capable of conferring epistemic value on those beliefs acquired on the basis of testimony. But this can only be accomplished when assurance and its relatives—such as taking responsibility for the truth—are themselves properly grounded epistemically. This can be done in any number of ways: a speaker's assurance that p is true may need to track the truth—either à la Nozick's sensitivity requirement[9] or à la Sosa's safety requirement[10]—or be reliably grounded,[11] or be adequately supported by the available evidence,[12] and so on. The point that is crucial here is not the details of how assurance is connected with the truth, but only that it *have* a proper connection with the truth.[13]

The upshot of these considerations, then, is that, as it stands, the Assurance View, though genuinely interpersonal, is epistemologically impotent. For, in the absence of epistemic conditions placed on either the speaker or the hearer in a testimonial exchange, a speaker, A, can give assurance and thereby a justified or warranted belief to a hearer, B, even when A shouldn't be able to (e.g., because A is a radically unreliable testifier), and B can acquire a belief with epistemic justification or warrant from A's assurance, even when B shouldn't be able to (e.g., because B possesses a relevant undefeated defeater). If the Assurance View is going to be a genuine contender in the epistemology of testimony, however, it simply cannot float free from all that is epistemic.

8.3 The Second Horn of the Dilemma

In the previous section, we saw the first horn of the dilemma afflicting versions of the IVT: views of testimony that are genuinely interpersonal turn out to be epistemologically impotent. But, one might ask, why couldn't a proponent of the IVT build into her view a connection between the interpersonal features of testimonial exchanges and properties that are properly truth-conducive or epistemic?

---

[9] See Nozick (1981).
[10] See Sosa (1996, 1999, 2000, and 2002). See also Williamson (2000) and Pritchard (2005).
[11] See, for instance, Goldman (1986).
[12] See, for instance, Conee and Feldman (1985 and 2004).
[13] In the next section, I shall consider a version of the IVT that attempts to provide an appropriate epistemic grounding for the interpersonal properties in question.

In a recent paper, Edward Hinchman defends a version of the IVT that appears to do just this. According to Hinchman, there is an important difference between the act of *telling* someone that *p* and the act of merely *asserting* that *p* in someone's presence. Here is his characterization of this distinction:

How can I entitle you to believe what I tell you? One way is by influencing the evidence available to you, perhaps by making an assertion or otherwise manifesting a belief, which still makes you epistemically responsible for the belief I want you to form. Another is by inviting you to trust me, thereby taking part of that responsibility onto my own shoulders. These two ways of giving an epistemic entitlement work very differently. When a speaker tells her hearer that *p* ... she acts on an intention to give him an entitlement to believe that *p* that derives not from evidence of the truth of "*p*" but from his mere understanding of the act she thereby performs ... [U]nlike acts of mere assertion, acts of telling give epistemic warrant directly. (Hinchman 2005: 563–4)

Now, notice that, like other proponents of the IVT, Hinchman claims that certain non-evidential features of the interpersonal relationship between the speaker and the hearer confer epistemic value on testimonial beliefs. Whereas Moran and Ross claim that this feature is the assurance of truth that the speaker gives to the hearer, Hinchman maintains that this feature is *the speaker's invitation to the hearer to trust her*. Let us call Hinchman's version of the IVT the *Trust View* of testimony.

According to the Trust View, by virtue of A telling B that *p*, A invites B to trust her and thereby assumes some of the responsibility for B's newly acquired testimonial belief that *p*. That is, through inviting B to trust her with respect to *p*, A has the intention to give B an epistemic entitlement to believe that *p*. If B recognizes A's intention to provide such an entitlement, B acquires a testimonial belief that is directly epistemically justified or warranted merely on the basis of accepting A's invitation to trust her.

So far, however, the Trust View faces the same central problem raised in the previous section: since there are no epistemic conditions placed on either the speaker who is inviting the trust or the hearer who is accepting the invitation, justification or warrant can be conferred on testimonial beliefs even when, from an epistemic point of view, it clearly should not be. Aware of this sort of problem, Hinchman adds the following crucial amendment to the Trust View:

Trust is a source of epistemic warrant just when it is epistemically reasonable. Trust is epistemically reasonable when the thing trusted is worthy of the trust—*as long as there is no evidence available that it is untrustworthy*. Assuming satisfaction of this negative evidential condition... when an epistemic faculty is trustworthy *by serving as a reliable guide to the truth*, it makes available an entitlement to believe what it tells you whose basis lies simply in the fact that you trust it. (Hinchman 2005: 578–9, emphasis added)

In order for the acceptance of an invitation to trust to confer epistemic justification or warrant directly on a testimonial belief acquired, then, the following two conditions must be satisfied:

(T1) the speaker's testimony must serve as a reliable guide to the truth, and

(T2) the hearer cannot have any relevant undefeated defeaters (i.e., "evidence available" that the speaker trusted "is untrustworthy") for accepting the invitation to trust the speaker.

Now, as should be clear, the addition of these two conditions puts the Trust View of testimony on the epistemological map. In particular, by virtue of placing epistemic conditions on both the speaker and the hearer in a testimonial exchange, the Trust View avoids the debilitating objection that it is simply impotent for the epistemology of testimony.

Somewhat surprisingly, and in spite of what is suggested by most of his paper, Moran, like Hinchman, seems to be aware of some of the problems underlying the first horn of the dilemma, and so he also appears to amend his Assurance View in the following passage:

Of course, as with any public assumption of responsibility, the appropriate abilities and other background conditions must be assumed to be in place for it to amount to anything. For the speaker to be able to do this it must be assumed by both parties that the speaker does indeed satisfy the right conditions for such an act (e.g., that he possesses the relevant knowledge, trustworthiness, and reliability). These background conditions can themselves be construed as evidential, or at any rate not at the behest of the speaker to determine, but they are not themselves sufficient for giving any epistemic significance to the speaker's words, for the relevance of these conditions only comes into play once it is understood that a particular speech-act is being performed with those words (i.e., an assertion or promise rather than something else). (Moran 2006: 289)[14]

---

[14] It is not entirely clear from Moran's article whether the background conditions in question are *facts of the matter* regarding the speaker (e.g., the speaker needs to in fact possess the relevant knowledge,

So, Moran here seems to be requiring that the speaker's offering of assurance have an appropriate epistemological grounding. Thus, offerings of assurance that float free from speakers' possessing knowledge, or being reliable, or being trustworthy presumably are incapable of conferring epistemic value on hearers' beliefs.[15]

The Trust View, and this modified version of the Assurance View, then, do not succumb to the objection of epistemological impotency, as they both appear to require that the relevant interpersonal features have an appropriate grounding in reliability or some other form of truth-conduciveness. Yet, despite this advantage, such views face problems of their own. For ease of exposition, let us focus on the Trust View, though similar objections can be raised to the modified Assurance View as well.

To begin, while it is true that the addition of conditions (T1) and (T2) above renders the Trust View a genuine contender in the epistemology of testimony, it does so at the cost of making trust itself *epistemically superfluous*. To see this, consider the following:

EAVESDROPPER: Ben and Kate, thinking they are alone in their office building, are having a discussion about the private lives of their co-workers. During the course of their conversation, Ben tells Kate that their boss is having an affair with the latest intern who has been hired by the company, Irene. Unbeknownst to them, however, Earl has been eavesdropping on their conversation and so he, like Kate, comes to believe solely on the basis of Ben's testimony—which is in fact both true and epistemically impeccable—that his boss is having an affair with Irene. Moreover, Kate and Earl not only have the same relevant background information about both Ben's reliability as a testifier and the proffered testimony, they also are properly functioning recipients of testimony who possess no relevant undefeated defeaters.

According to all versions of the IVT, Kate's testimonial belief in EAVES-DROPPER possesses epistemic value that Earl's does not. For, while Ben offered Kate his assurance that his testimony is true and invited Kate to trust him, neither is true of the relationship between Ben and eavesdropping

---

trustworthiness, and reliability) or *assumptions* about the speaker (e.g., it needs to be assumed that the speaker possesses the relevant knowledge, trustworthiness, and reliability). Since mere assumptions would do little, at best, to place the Assurance View on the epistemological map, I will read Moran's background condition as requiring facts of the matter regarding the speaker's epistemic situation.

[15] In this way, both Moran's and Hinchman's views differ in important respects from Faulkner's (2007 and forthcoming).

Earl. Because of this, the epistemic value of Earl's belief about the affair between the boss and intern Irene is inferior to, or at least different from, that of Kate's belief with the same content.

But if Kate and Earl are equally properly functioning as recipients of testimony, have the same relevant background information, both about Ben as a testifier and about the proposition to which he is testifying, and form their beliefs about the boss and Irene solely on the basis of Ben's testimony, then what could distinguish their beliefs epistemically? According to Hinchman's view, the central difference between these two cases is that Kate's, but not Earl's, warrant for believing the boss and Irene are having an affair is acquired simply by recognizing Ben's intention to give her an entitlement to hold this belief. That these two warrants are epistemologically different is apparently evidenced by the purported fact that, were Kate and Earl both to refuse to treat Ben's telling as a source of epistemic warrant, Ben "is entitled to feel slighted" by Kate's refusal but not by Earl's. For Ben has "tendered an invitation to [Kate] to trust [him] and explicitly been rebuffed," whereas Earl was tendered no such invitation and thus cannot slight Ben in this way (Hinchman 2005: 565–6).[16] Other proponents of the IVT hold that Kate, but not Earl, is entitled to "resent" Ben for not being trustworthy or that it is " 'difficult' for [Kate but not Earl] to dissent, even inwardly [from Ben's telling], for to do so will be to challenge [Ben's] authority as a judge of the matter in question" (Ross 1986: 79). The thought underlying these remarks is that there are certain expectations that come along with invitations and offerings and, accordingly, certain attitudes that follow from their being rejected or accepted.

There are, however, at least two central problems with this response. First, it is not at all clear that the differences cited by proponents of the IVT between situations involving the invited and the non-invited in fact hold. For instance, suppose that after the scenario envisaged in EAVESDROPPER, Ben and Earl are later talking at a dinner party and Earl confesses both that he eavesdropped on Ben's conversation with Kate and that he has no relevant information about the boss and Irene other than what Ben reported to Kate. Suppose further that Ben then asks, "So

---

[16] It should be noted that Hinchman restricts this claim to cases in which the hearer refuses to accept the speaker's telling in ways that manifest mistrust in the speaker herself. For instance, a speaker may not be entitled to feel slighted if a hearer refuses to accept her telling about the time of day merely because he doubts the accuracy of her watch (rather than the trustworthiness of her word).

what do you think about the boss and Irene?" and Earl responds, "Oh, I don't believe that the boss and Irene are having an affair." Wouldn't Ben be entitled to feel slighted by Earl's refusal to believe what he reported, even if he did not issue a specific invitation to trust him?[17] Indeed, it is not at all clear that Ben would, or should, feel more slighted by Kate's refusal to believe him than by Earl's, for both are revealing in their refusals their belief that Ben is somehow untrustworthy, either in general or with respect to the topic at hand. It may even be the case that Ben is entitled to feel *more* slighted by Earl's refusal to believe him than by Kate's if we suppose, for instance, that Ben regards Earl, but not Kate, as a friend. Similar considerations apply with respect to the claim that only the invited are entitled to feel resentment for the speaker proving untrustworthy. For suppose that Earl did come to believe Ben's report about the boss and Irene and made practical decisions on this basis—such as choosing not to ask Irene out on a date—only to later discover that Ben was untrustworthy on this topic. Wouldn't Earl be entitled to resent Ben for asserting an unjustified falsehood about the boss and Irene, even if such an assertion was not offered specifically to him?

The second, and more important, problem with the above response is that, even if proponents of the IVT are correct about the purported differences between the situations involving the invited and the non-invited, being entitled to the reactions in question lacks any *epistemological* significance and hence fails to establish that there is an *epistemologically relevant difference* between justification or warrant from telling and justification or warrant from mere asserting. In particular, Ben's being entitled to feel slighted should Kate, but not Earl, refuse his invitation to trust, and Kate's, but not Earl's, being entitled to feel resentment should Ben prove untrustworthy, do not bear in any way on the truth-conduciveness or epistemic rationality of the testimonial beliefs in question. For notice: Ben's inviting Kate but not Earl to trust him does not make it more likely that the testimonial belief in question is true for Kate but not for Earl—they are both receiving testimony with the same degree of reliability, the same kind of truth-tracking, the same amount of proper functioning, and so on.

---

[17] If one wishes to argue that Ben's asking Earl what he thinks about the affair between the boss and Irene amounts to his telling him about the affair, and thereby tendering an invitation to Earl to trust him, then the scenario can be tweaked so that there is no direct contact between Ben and Earl. Perhaps Ben finds out that Earl eavesdropped on his conversation with Kate and yet did not form the belief about the boss and Irene from a mutual friend or from a letter.

Moreover, Kate and Earl have the same relevant background information about both Ben's reliability as a testifier and the proffered testimony, so it is not more rational for Kate to form the relevant belief than it is for Earl. Of course, a situation may be envisaged in which Kate but not Earl has had a deep friendship with Ben since childhood and, because of this, has more reasons to trust Ben's testimony. But this doesn't show that interpersonal features of a relationship can affect the epistemic value of testimonial beliefs; all it shows is that a hearer who possesses *more information* on behalf of the trustworthiness of a given speaker can acquire a testimonial belief that is more justified or warranted than a hearer who does not—an obvious point, but one that fails to support the IVT.

A further difference Hinchman cites between tellings and mere assertions is that, unlike in the case of the former, "one who merely hears, or overhears, a speaker assert that p is not thereby entitled to hold the speaker accountable for providing a reason to believe that p" (Hinchman 2005: 569). Thus, if you tell me that p, I can challenge you to offer a reason to believe that p, but similar considerations fail to apply if you merely assert that p in my presence. Once again, however, this purported difference faces the two objections raised above: first, it is doubtful that there is such a difference and, second, even if there were, it fails to have the needed epistemological significance. Let us begin with the first objection. Suppose that Malcolm tells me that your wife is abusing drugs and you overhear this conversation from the hallway. According to Hinchman, in such a case, only I am entitled to challenge Malcolm to provide reasons for believing that this is true. But why? If Malcolm offers an assertion in a context where he is overheard by you, then why should the mere fact that he is addressing me prevent you from being justified in challenging him? Indeed, given that the information concerns *your* wife, there is an obvious sense in which you are even *more* entitled than I am to hold Malcolm accountable for supporting such a claim, despite the fact that you merely overheard him offer me this telling.

Of course, Hinchman may respond that the relevant difference between you and me here is that if Malcolm cannot produce a reason for believing that your wife is abusing drugs, then he "counts as misleading" me but not you. He writes:

If S tells A that p but cannot when challenged produce a reason to believe that p, she counts as misleading A .... If, on the other hand, S merely asserts that p, then if she cannot produce a reason to believe that *p* she is not culpable for misleading anyone. (Hinchman 2005: 569, fn. 19)

This distinction, however, seems entirely arbitrary. If Malcolm offers information about your wife that I overhear, then he counts as misleading both you and me. Compare: if Malcolm makes an anti-Semitic slur against Olivia Rosenberg that Otis Goldstein overhears, then it would surely be arbitrary to say that he was insulting only Olivia. For instance, if Otis were to challenge Malcolm to defend his comment, we would hardly be impressed by Malcolm responding, "Look, I didn't tell *you* anything, so you cannot regard me as culpable for insulting you."

The second problem with this purported difference between tellings and assertions is that, even if it were genuine, it lacks any epistemological significance. For instance, consider, again, the scenario in which you and I both come to believe that your wife is abusing drugs on the basis of Malcolm's telling me that this is the case. The mere fact that Malcolm addressed only me does not affect any of the epistemic properties of either his testimony or the basis that you and I have for accepting what he says. Indeed, there are countless scenarios that can be envisaged where one who merely overhears a speaker's testimony that *p* acquires a belief with better epistemic support than one who is told that *p*. For instance, suppose that Oscar tells you that the great gray owl is the largest North American owl and I overhear his testimony. Suppose further that while I know that Oscar is an ornithologist, you know only that he is a man whom you frequently bump into at Starbuck's. Surely my belief about the great gray owl has more epistemic value than yours, despite the fact that Oscar *told* this fact to you. Moreover, given that Oscar is an ornithologist, he may be in a better position to challenge someone else's testimony about birds, even if he merely overhears it being offered. Suppose, for example, that he overhears a Starbuck's barista telling her co-worker that the great horned owl is the largest North American owl. Given his expertise on the topic, Oscar may very well be in a better position to challenge the barista to offer reasons for her belief about North American owls than her co-worker is.

What these considerations show is that interpersonal features are not capable of adding epistemic value to testimonial beliefs. This is made clear in EAVESDROPPER: there does not seem to be anything epistemically significant about the fact that, though Kate and Earl both learned about the boss's affair from Ben's testimony, only the former was *told* this. Indeed, the counterintuitive consequences of the IVT quickly proliferate: if you are addressing a particular room of people at a conference, surely the epistemic value of the belief that I acquire on the basis of your testimony does not differ from those acquired by the audience members merely because I overhear your talk from the hallway. Or if you write a book with the intended audience being Democrats, the fact that a Republican reads it should not, by itself, affect the epistemic status of the testimonial beliefs that are thereby acquired. Interpersonal features, then, do not add any epistemic value to testimonial beliefs that is not already contributed by the truth-conducive grounding in question, thereby rendering such features epistemologically impotent.

Thus, while the addition of conditions (T1) and (T2) places the Trust View on the epistemological map, trust itself turns out to be epistemically superfluous. For the reason why it is no longer an utter mystery how justification or warrant could be conferred through the acceptance of an invitation to trust is because conditions (T1) and (T2) do all of the epistemic work. When B acquires a justified or warranted belief that p from A's telling her that p, this is explained through both A's reliability as a testifier with respect to p and B's rationality as a recipient of A's telling her that p (i.e., B does not have any undefeated defeaters for accepting the testimony in question). In providing the *epistemic* explanation of B's newly acquired justified or warranted belief, then, trust in A simply drops out of the picture.

Once trust becomes epistemically superfluous, however, the Trust View ceases to even represent a version of the IVT. For the interpersonal relationship between the two parties in a testimonial exchange is not the central focus of the epistemology of testimony on such a view; nor are features of this interpersonal relationship responsible for conferring epistemic value on the testimonial beliefs acquired—the reliability of the speaker's testimony and the rationality of the hearer's acceptance of the testimony are doing all of the epistemic work. Moreover, it is simply not the case that the epistemic justification or warrant provided by testimony is non-evidential in nature. For, as we saw in Chapters 5 and 7, the substantive satisfaction of the no-defeater condition necessarily requires a sensitivity on the part of the hearer to evidential features of the epistemic situation. Given this, the addition of (T2) adds a distinctively evidential condition to the

Trust View and, accordingly, its satisfaction adds a distinctively evidential feature to the testimonial justification or warrant at issue. Hence, the Trust View ceases to include any of the central theses characterizing the IVT.

Moreover, once conditions (T1) and (T2) are added, it becomes clear that the Trust View is not in any way interestingly different from the views it purportedly replaces. Indeed, all of the talk about invitations to trust and acceptances of trust turns out to be bells and whistles, masking the fact that the Trust View is simply a run-of-the-mill version of non-reductionism[18]—a conception of testimony which, as we saw in Chapter 5, is currently the most widely accepted in the literature. For though there are differences in how the details are spelled out, the heart of non-reductionism is that, in the absence of relevant undefeated defeaters, hearers can acquire justified or warranted beliefs on the basis of a speaker's reliable testimony. And since one of the primary factors motivating the Trust View—and indeed the IVT in general—is its purportedly novel and unique approach to thinking about testimony, the fact that it instead turns out to be simply another characterization of non-reductionism seriously undermines any value it might have contributed to the epistemology of testimony.

The upshot of these considerations is that in an attempt to avoid the first horn of the dilemma by providing an epistemological grounding for the interpersonal features of their views, the proponents of the IVT become impaled on the second horn. In particular, though introducing conditions such as (T1) and (T2) enables these views to avoid the charge of epistemological impotency, it does so at the cost of their interpersonal nature.

Thus, we have seen that there is a general dilemma confronting the proponent of the IVT: either the view of testimony in question is genuinely interpersonal but not epistemological, or it is genuinely epistemological but not interpersonal. In the former case, the IVT will be novel but useless for an epistemology of testimony; in the latter case, the IVT will be epistemologically useful, but not interestingly different from its so-called competitors. The bottom line is this: interpersonal features cannot create

---

[18] Hinchman himself admits that his view is a version of non-reductionism, but maintains that it is a "novel form" that provides "a detailed explanation of how the status of testimony as an irreducible source of warrant is entailed by the nature of the illocutionary act of telling" (Hinchman 2005: 562 and 576). What I am arguing here, however, is that if Hinchman's view is interpreted in a way that has epistemological relevance, then it turns out to not be novel at all. Otherwise put, his view is either novel but not epistemologically relevant, or epistemologically relevant but not novel.

justification or warrant epistemologically *ex nihilo* and hence there is no room for a *genuinely interpersonal* view in the epistemology of testimony.

8.4 The Reasons Generated by Trust Argument

In this section, I shall consider one further attempt to defend the IVT as a contender in the epistemology of testimony. To begin, it is often noted that trusting someone can at times be precisely the factor that motivates that person to behave in a trustworthy fashion. For instance, consider the following scenario:

TRUSTED FELON: Gladys owns a small boutique in the downtown area of her city and, after looking over applicants for an open position as salesperson, she decides to give the job to a convicted felon, Frank. When her exasperated friends question Gladys's judgment, she explains that the very act of placing trust in someone whom one not only has no reason to trust, but also has reason to distrust, may in fact prompt the trusted individual to behave in the way desired. In this particular case, Gladys's reasoning proves correct: Frank is so inspired by her trust that he succeeds in performing his duties at the shop in an honest, fair, and reliable manner.

In TRUSTED FELON, Gladys's trust in Frank is what motivates him to reform his character and carry out his responsibilities with integrity and competence. Indeed, we can even imagine that were it not for her trust, he would have continued down the same path of criminal behavior that he traveled prior to being employed at her boutique. Thus, Gladys's trust is actually responsible for Frank's being trustworthy. What TRUSTED FELON reveals, then, is that, as Diego Gambetta puts it, trust "can generate the very behaviour which might logically seem to be its precondition" (Gambetta 1988: 234).

There are two central explanations that are typically offered of how trust functions in this generative way. First, trust can provide a trustee with an *intrinsic* reason to be trustworthy. In particular, by virtue of manifesting trust, the trustor expects the trustee to be moved to trustworthiness, and thereby takes an evaluative stance toward the trustee. This evaluative stance presumes that the relationship between the trustor and the trustee is one of "shared values, whether of friendship, morality or some other nexus" and thus, if the trustee agrees with this presumption, then she will "have reasons

of friendship, moral reasons or reasons based on whatever other values"
that she shares with the trustor to be trustworthy (Faulkner 2007: 552–3.).
Second, trust can provide the trustee with an *instrumental* reason to be
trustworthy. For if the trustee violates or exploits the trust that is afforded
to her, then the trustor is likely to feel betrayed or resentful, and the trustee
is likely to lose the good opinion of others. As Philip Pettit says:

Like any investment [trust] may have a risky side, for the trustee may not be bound
to act as required. But it is not by any means as risky as it may at first seem. For in
the very act whereby the trustor is put at risk, the trustee is given a motive not to
let that risk materialize. The trustor can bank on the fact that if the trustee does let
the risk materialize then they will suffer the loss of the trustor's good opinion and,
in all likelihood, the cost of gaining a bad reputation among those who learn what
has happened. (Pettit 1995: 216)

Thus, a desire to avoid the negative consequences that typically follow
untrustworthy behavior—such as resentment and a tarnished reputation—can provide the trustee with an instrumental reason to be trustworthy.

Now, suppose that you are deciding whether to trust someone whom
you have just met. While you have no relevant background information
about this person's specific trustworthiness, you are aware of the generative
feature of trust described in TRUSTED FELON, that is, you know that
trust can sometimes motivate a trustee to be trustworthy, either through
intrinsic or instrumental reasons. According to some proponents of the
IVT, an awareness of this generative feature can provide a trustor with a
reason to trust even in the absence of any relevant background information
about the trustee in question. This argument—which we may call the
Reasons Generated by Trust Argument (hereafter, the RGTA)—is nicely
presented by Pettit in the following passage:

1. There are situations where an act of trust will signal to a trustee, and to
   witnesses, that the trustor believes in or presumes on the trustworthiness of the
   trustee—believes in or presumes on his loyalty or virtue or prudence—and
   so thinks well of him to that extent.
2. The trustee is likely to have a desire, intrinsic or instrumental, for the good
   opinion of the trustor and of witnesses to the act of trust.
3. The desire for that good opinion will tend to give the trustee reason to act
   in the way in which the trustor relies on him to act.

Conclusion. And so the trustor, recognizing these facts, may have a reason to trust someone, even when he actually has no reason to believe in the other's pre-existing trustworthiness. (Pettit 1995: 216)

So, if I know absolutely nothing about a given person, my awareness that trust can sometimes generate trustworthy behavior nonetheless provides me with a reason to extend my trust to her. Indeed, even if I have evidence that speaks *against* the trustworthiness of a person, some proponents of the RGTA maintain that trust is still appropriate. For instance, regarding the kind of trust that we find Gladys extending to Frank, Paul Faulkner writes:

A's being justified in affectively trusting S to ϕ depends on A's being justified in believing that S can recognize [her] dependence on S ϕ-ing, and A's being justified in presuming that this will move S to ϕ ... [T]his presumption is only clearly unjustified when the evidence *obliges* A to believe that S will not ϕ. Thus, and supposing the prior facts about [Frank] do not oblige [Gladys] to believe that he will steal once trusted ... ,[Gladys's] trust is not obviously unjustified. (Faulkner 2007: 549)

Now, the final step of this argument is to apply these considerations to the epistemology of testimony; in particular, even if a hearer has absolutely no evidence in favor of a speaker's reliability, sincerity, or general trustworthiness, proponents of the RGTA argue that this awareness is capable of *providing the hearer with a justifying reason for accepting the speaker's testimony.* Unlike motivating reasons, which simply psychologically explain why a subject holds a given belief, "[j]ustifying reasons epistemically support a subject's belief; they ... establish the subject's belief as likely to be true" (Faulkner 2007: 549–50.). So, the thesis put forth here is this: a hearer's awareness of the generative feature of trust—as it is characterized in the RGTA—can render the belief that she forms on the basis of a speaker's testimony epistemically justified even when she has no information on behalf of, and some information against, the trustworthiness of the speaker in question.

In what follows, I shall argue that while this may be the best argument on behalf of the IVT, it nonetheless fails. In particular, I shall show that the proponent of the RGTA faces a dilemma: either the relevant hearer has independent reasons for believing the speaker in question to be trust-responsive, in which case beliefs acquired on the basis of her testimony may be epistemically justified, but not via an awareness of trust's generative nature, or the hearer does not possess independent reasons for believing the speaker to be trust-responsive, in which case beliefs acquired on the basis of her testimony may be grounded in an awareness of trust's generative nature, but they are not epistemically justified. Either way, epistemically justified testimonial beliefs cannot be grounded purely in an awareness of the generative nature of trust.[19]

Before proceeding to the dilemma facing the proponent of the RGTA, let me begin with a general concern about extending considerations arising from the phenomenon of trust to the epistemology of testimony. When focusing on paradigmatic instances of trust, premise (1) is fairly straightforward: there are some situations where an act of trust will indicate to others—e.g., the trustee and relevant witnesses—that the trustor relies on the trustworthiness of the trustee. My leaving my children under your supervision, for instance, clearly reveals that I trust you in countless ways to be sensitive to their needs, to care for them, and to protect them from harm. But trust as it applies to the epistemology of testimony involves a hearer forming a given belief solely on the basis of a speaker's report. Here is the problem: what in the act of believing an instance of testimony can be said to plausibly *signal* that the speaker is regarded by the hearer as trustworthy?[20] Sure, when I trust you with respect to your testimony that *p*, I can loudly announce, "I believe you," or I can very publicly report to someone else that *p* to reveal my belief in your statement. Such signals, however, are clearly quite unusual when it comes to paradigmatic instances of forming testimonial beliefs. Given this, premise (1) will be true of testimonial exchanges in only very rare cases—i.e., it will very infrequently be the case that a hearer signals to others that a speaker's testimony has been trusted—and thus the conclusion of the RGTA, even if otherwise successful, will have extremely limited application in the epistemology of testimony.

There are, however, independent reasons to challenge the success of the RGTA. To see this, let us turn to premise (2), which says that the trustee in question is likely to have a desire, whether intrinsic or instrumental,

---

[19] I shall focus here only on cases where a trustor *fails to have reasons* for believing that a given trustee will be trustworthy. Given that I will argue that epistemic justification cannot be acquired in these cases, similar considerations will obviously apply, though perhaps even more so, to cases where a trustor has *reasons against* believing that a given trustee will be trustworthy.

[20] I am grateful to Jim Van Cleve for raising this point.

for the good opinion of the trustor and relevant witnesses. Now, as stated, (2) clearly glosses over at least three important points. First, this premise is surely true of only *some* trustees. For we all know of plenty of people who care very little about either being trustworthy or having the good opinion of others. Ruthless CEOs of the corporate world, devoted members of the Aryan Brotherhood, and proud and flagrant workers in the adult entertainment industry may care very little about what most people think of them. Second, and more importantly, even among those who generally desire the good opinion of others, (2) will be true relative to only *some* trustors and witnesses. One may, for instance, care very much about people's perceptions, but not when the trustors and witnesses in question are reviled enemies, immature teenagers, racists, pedophiles, and so on. Thus, relative to members of these classes of people, one may be very unlikely to possess the desire for their good opinion. Third, even among those who generally desire the good opinion of the particular trustors and witnesses in question, (2) will be true in only *some* situations or contexts. If one is depressed, intoxicated, deeply distracted, consumed with rage or fear, or otherwise unable to respond appropriately to one's environment, then one may very well be unlikely to form the relevant desire. What these considerations show, then, is that (2) should be clarified in the following way:

2*. *Some* trustees are likely in *some* contexts to have a desire, intrinsic or instrumental, for the good opinion of *some* trustors and of *some* witnesses to the act of trust.

Unlike (2), which would simply be false relative to various trustees, trustors, contexts, and combinations thereof, (2*) makes it clear that the likelihood of a trustee having the desire for the good opinion of a trustor and witnesses depends on the obtaining of a number of relevant factors, and is thus true of a much smaller class of individuals than is suggested by the RGTA.

Similar considerations apply to premise (3) since the truth of this claim also depends on various factors. First, the desire for the good opinion of others will surely tend to give only *some* trustees a reason to act in the way in question. For such a desire may typically fail to be appropriately strong in some trustees, or may simply tend to be defeated or overridden by their other desires and beliefs. Indeed, some people may be such that they are more likely to be moved to trustworthy behavior by *not* being trusted. A frustrated teenager, for example, may be motivated to excel academically to prove to her parents that they are wrong in their belief that she can no longer be trusted to be a responsible student. Second, even among those trustees who are generally inclined to be responsive to trust, the truth of (3) will obviously depend a great deal on the nature of the expected act in question and will thus be true of only *some* such acts. If one is trusted to act in a way that is at odds with one's values or is extremely time-consuming and arduous, for example, then one may be very unlikely to have a reason to act in the way in which the trustor relies on one to act. Third, for reasons that echo those discussed in connection with (2), (3) will be true in only *some* situations and contexts. If, for instance, one is under the influence of drugs or in the midst of a manic episode, then one may be unlikely to have a reason to act in the relevant way. Let us then similarly clarify (3) as follows:

3*. The desire for that good opinion will tend to give *some* trustees in *some* contexts reason to act in *some* of the ways in which the trustor relies on him to act.

The question to which we now need to turn is whether substituting (2) and (3) with the clarified (2*) and (3*) calls into question the conclusion of the RGTA and, ultimately, the thesis that epistemically justified testimonial beliefs can be grounded purely in an awareness of trust's generative nature.

And here the answer is clearly an affirmative one for at least three reasons. To see this, notice, first, that once all of the variables involved in trustees being responsive to trust are emphasized, i.e., once all of the "somes" are inserted into the RGTA, it becomes clear that the phenomenon of trust generating trustworthy behavior is a highly contingent affair that depends on the obtaining of multiple factors. In particular, when I decide to trust S with respect to x, my trust moving S with respect to x depends, at the very least, on S's character, S's regard for others, S's regard for me, S's attitude toward x, and S's current situation or context. When I know absolutely nothing about S, then, my succeeding in choosing a trustee who satisfies all of these relevant factors—i.e., my success in choosing a trustee who is moved by my trust to trustworthy behavior in the context at hand—is *simply a matter of good luck*. For instance, among convicted thieves who are being considered for a position handling funds for a charity, it is plausible to think that there will be a significant number of applicants who will be completely unmoved to honesty by the trust that their employers place in them. When I know nothing relevant about the characters or situations of these applicants, then, my choosing one of the few who will be motivated to reform themselves because of my trust is entirely fortuitous or accidental. Now, applying this to the epistemology of testimony, when a hearer trusts a speaker's testimony merely because she is aware of the generative capacity that trust sometimes has with respect to some individuals in some contexts—without possessing any reason to believe that the particular speaker in question will be trust-responsive in this way—it will be simply a matter of luck if the hearer happens upon someone who is appropriately trust-responsive. But surely luck in this sense is incompatible with the hearer forming epistemically justified beliefs solely on the basis of the speaker's testimony. For recall that the notion of epistemic justification at issue is that which is grounded in reasons that establish a "subject's belief as likely to be true." If a hearer must depend entirely on good fortune in choosing a trust-responsive speaker rather than a non-trust-responsive one, however, then the beliefs formed on the basis of this speaker's testimony clearly fail to be supported by reasons that establish that they are likely to be true. Thus, a hearer's awareness that trust sometimes generates trust—without any reason to suppose that trust-responsiveness will obtain in the specific case at hand—simply fails to render beliefs formed on the basis of the trustee's testimony epistemically justified.

Second, even if a given trustor just so happens to be situated in an environment in which, as a matter of fact, all of the relevant trustees will be moved in those contexts to the trustworthy behavior in question, if the trustor herself lacks reasons for believing that the trustees will be so trust-responsive, it is surely wrong to say that she possesses *justifying reasons* on behalf of the testimony in question. For all the trustor knows, the trustee in question could care not at all about the opinion of others or about the trustor's opinion in particular; or she may in principle be opposed to the behavior or act in question; or she may be so consumed with grief over a recent loss that no amount of trust would motivate her to behave in a trustworthy fashion; and so on. If, from the trustor's point of view, these are all equally open possibilities, then it would be clearly irrational to simply have blind faith that none of them obtain in the situation at hand. And it is widely agreed, even by theorists from radically different epistemological traditions, that explicit irrationality on the part of a subject is incompatible with epistemic justification.

Third, and related, for the trustworthiness of testimony to bear the appropriate connection with the truth, it will often be the case that both a speaker's sincerity and her competence are relevant factors.[21] For instance, in order for my being moved to trustworthiness to render my reports about Word War II likely to be true, I have to be both honest *and* knowledgeable about this historical event. But here is the problem for the proponent of the RGTA: even if a speaker is inspired to be trustworthy because a hearer trusts her, the control that she has over the *competence* dimension of trustworthiness will often be severely limited. Sure, your trusting me may motivate me to check twice before testifying to the sighting of a bald eagle, or to confirm the date of a political event with another source before reporting it. But many testimonial contexts simply preclude this sort of thoroughness and care. Moreover, some people, no matter how hard they try, are simply not competent with respect to certain statements or subject matters. So, for instance, regardless of how committed a scientologist is to the truth, she may nonetheless be wildly unreliable in her reports about mental health. Thus, she can be impeccably thorough and commendably careful but this won't help at all in rendering her reports about mental health likely to be true. Given this, even for those speakers who *are* motivated by a hearer's trust to be trustworthy testifiers, this may fail to have any bearing on their competence, and thus trustworthiness may ultimately fail to have any relevant connection with the truth of their proffered testimony.

Of course, many of the above concerns will not arise, or at least will not be as obviously problematic, if the trustor has some independent reasons for believing that the speaker in question will be relevantly trust-responsive and competent. If, for instance, we all know about our friend Marcia that the opinion of others is exceedingly important to her, that she is extraordinarily reluctant to let people down, and that she is financially savvy, then, so as to motivate her to be trustworthy, we may overtly announce that we are trusting her to advise us on our investments. Clearly, however, what justifies the beliefs that we thereby form on the basis of Marcia's testimony is not any awareness of trust's generative nature but, rather, the background

---

[21] As mentioned earlier, while neither sincerity nor competence is *necessary* for a speaker to be a reliable testifier, the satisfaction of such conditions can nonetheless often be crucial features in rendering a speaker a reliable testifier.

information that we have about her trust-responsiveness and her financial expertise.

The upshot of these considerations, then, is that the proponent of the IVT who defends her view via the RGTA faces a dilemma: either a hearer truly fails to possess independent reasons for believing a given speaker to be trust-responsive, in which case beliefs acquired on the basis of her testimony may be grounded in an awareness of trust's generative nature, but they are clearly not epistemically justified. Or a hearer indeed possesses independent reasons for believing a speaker to be trust-responsive, in which case beliefs acquired on the basis of her testimony may be epistemically justified, but not on the basis of an awareness of trust's generative nature. Either way, we have seen that epistemically justified testimonial beliefs cannot be grounded purely in an awareness of the generative capacity of trust.

8.5 Concluding Remarks

In closing, I shall offer a brief diagnosis of the problems afflicting the IVT. I shall then address the basic criticisms that proponents of the IVT launch at views of testimony that fail to place the interpersonal relationship between speaker and hearer at the center of the epistemology of testimony.

Proponents of the IVT are concerned with the interpersonal relationship that exists between the speaker and the hearer in a testimonial exchange and, even more specifically, with the differences that follow for those who are invited into such a relationship and those who are not. I agree that there may be some rough differences between these two parties. The central place where I part company with proponents of the IVT is with their claim that such differences are *epistemic* in nature.[22] For instance, it is frequently noted that an important difference between *trusting* another and merely *relying* on another is that, if one is let down, one feels betrayed or resentful only in the former case.[23] If I merely *rely* on my car to get me from Chicago to Boston, I may be disappointed or frustrated if it breaks down, but feelings of betrayal or resentment would surely be out of place. In contrast, if I *trust*

---

[22] As should be clear from my arguments in the previous section and from my agreement that there are "rough" differences of the sort described by proponents of the IVT between the invited and the non-invited, I do not think that such differences are without exception.

[23] See, for instance, Baier (1986) and Holton (1994).

my best friend to help me during my illness, I may very well feel betrayed or resentful if she fails to do so. Now this difference, regardless of whether it holds without exception, may very well be psychologically, morally, or even pragmatically relevant. Trusting relationships may generally make us more psychologically vulnerable, e.g., a trusted person may be able to psychologically harm me far more than one who is merely relied upon, may force us to incur various moral obligations, e.g., I may owe a trusted friend far more loyalty than one who merely relies upon me, and may be effective in motivating people to act, e.g., your trusting me may motivate me to keep my promises in ways that mere reliance do not. But where proponents of the IVT go wrong is in the move from these differences to the conclusion that they have *epistemic* significance. The mere fact that I rely on rather than trust you does not necessarily affect the reliability, truth-tracking, proper functioning, evidential grounding, coherence, or any other distinctively epistemic features of either your testimony or my acceptance of it. The upshot, then, is that proponents of the IVT have conflated psychological, moral, or pragmatic significance with epistemic significance.

This conflation is made even clearer when we examine the objections that proponents of the IVT raise to non-interpersonal views of testimony. In the process of motivating the IVT, it is often argued that the current non-interpersonal views of testimony in the literature miss a significant part of true communication. Specifically, the picture painted by such views depicts speakers as being treated by hearers as mere truth gauges, offering words that cannot provide reasons for testimonial beliefs. But what is the *epistemic* problem with treating speakers as mere truth gauges? To be sure, there may be psychological problems with a mother treating her children merely as truth gauges, moral problems with a husband treating his wife merely as a truth gauge, and pragmatic problems with a quarterback treating his teammates merely this way. Given that the central epistemological goal is the acquisition of true beliefs and the avoidance of false ones, however, the epistemic objection here—if indeed there is one—appears to be entirely misguided. Similar considerations can be adduced regarding the other criticisms: even if there is something missing from "true communication" when speakers are treated as mere truth gauges, there is no reason to suppose that true communication is needed for the acquisition of testimonially justified or warranted beliefs. Moreover, as we saw in Chapters 2 and 3, there are very good reasons to think that hearers can acquire not only testimonially justified or warranted beliefs from mere words, but also testimonial knowledge. Hence, even if there are other worries with this sort of treatment, there fails to be a distinctively epistemological problem here.

I conclude, then, that the IVT not only fails to provide a genuine alternative to existing theories in the epistemology of testimony, but the considerations that its proponents invoke to motivate such a view are entirely misguided.

Appendix: Memory as a Generative Epistemic Source

A.1 The Preservation View of Memory

Memory, we are told, is strikingly similar to testimony in several crucial respects. First, and perhaps most significant, neither source is regarded as *generative* with respect to knowledge. In particular, memory *preserves* knowledge from one time to another while testimony *transmits* knowledge from one person to another. In this way, it is said to be true for both memorial knowledge, on the one hand, and testimonial knowledge, on the other hand, that the proposition in question must be *known* when it was originally acquired and, accordingly, that *a source other than memory and testimony, respectively,* must be responsible for its original acquisition. So, for instance, Robert Audi says that:

[j]ust as we cannot know that *p* from memory unless we have *come* to know it in another way, say through perception, we cannot know that *p* on the basis of testimony unless the attester...has come to know it (at least in part) in another way...Memory and testimony...are not generative with respect to knowledge: characteristically, the former is preservative, the latter transmissive. (Audi 1997: 410)

In a similar spirit, Michael Dummett says, "Memory is not a *source*, still less a *ground*, of knowledge: it is the maintenance of knowledge formerly acquired by whatever means" (Dummett 1994: 262, original emphasis).

In addition to the thesis that neither memory nor testimony can generate new knowledge, it is often further noted that neither is a generative epistemic source more broadly. Specifically, both sources are said to be incapable of generating epistemic justification,[1] warrant, rationality, and the like. For example, if I justifiedly believe that *p* on the basis of memory, then I must have acquired this justification in a non-memorial way at an earlier time. Similarly, if my belief that *p* is irrational when it was originally acquired, then it will continue to be just as

---

[1] As has been the case throughout this book, I am here assuming that justification is necessary and, when added to true belief, close to being sufficient for knowledge.

irrational when it is remembered at a later time. Alvin Plantinga makes this point when he writes: "memory beliefs depend, for their warrant, upon the warrant of *earlier* beliefs. I have an orange for breakfast; if this belief has no warrant, then my later belief that I *had* an orange for breakfast will also have no warrant. Memory beliefs are like testimonial beliefs ... the warrant they have is dependent upon the warrant enjoyed by an earlier belief" (Plantinga 1993*b*: 61, fn. 22).[2] In a similar spirit, David Owens claims, "If a belief is irrational when adopted, it remains just as irrational while laid up in memory" (Owens 2000: 156).

We have seen, therefore, that with respect to memorial beliefs in particular, the standard view is that memory cannot make a proposition acquire an epistemic status different than the one it had at the time it was originally acquired. Thus, for example, memory cannot make an unknown proposition known, an unjustified belief justified, or an irrational belief rational—it can only preserve what is already known, justified, or rational.[3] Let us call this the *Preservation View of Memory* (hereafter, the PVM) and formulate it in the following way:

> PVM: S knows (justifiedly believes/rationally believes) that *p* on the basis of memory at T2 only if: (1) S knows (justifiedly believes/rationally believes) that *p* at an earlier time T1, and (2) S acquired the knowledge that *p* (justification with respect to *p*/rationality with respect to *p*) at T1 via a source other than memory.[4]

So, according to the PVM, memory has the capacity only to preserve epistemic features that have already been generated by other sources.

In this appendix, I shall argue that considerations similar to those motivating the rejection of TEP-N in Chapter 2 can be applied to show that the Preservation View of Memory is false. Specifically, I shall claim that it is not necessary for memorial knowledge (justification/rationality) that the belief in question be known

---

[2] This point is attributed to Tom Senor, though Plantinga appears to endorse the thesis as well. For related discussion, see Senor (1993).

[3] Since some proponents of the PVM explicitly discuss rationality, I will add this to my discussion in this appendix. Given this, I will often speak only of "justification" (rather than of "justification or warrant") to avoid cumbersome constructions. But "warrant" should be read into all of the relevant arguments.

[4] As I have formulated it, the PVM has several strands. Not all of the above cited philosophers would endorse every strand. For instance, Audi endorses the PVM with respect to memorial knowledge but not memorial justification. (However, it should be noted that, on Audi's view, justification is not necessary for knowledge. Hence, his claim that memory can generate justification is significantly different from mine in this book since I am assuming that justification is a necessary condition for knowledge. See Audi (1995, 1997, and 1998).) Owens endorses the PVM with respect to rationality and justification for *beliefs*, but not necessarily with respect to rationality and justification for *agents*. See Owens (2000: 157). See also Owens (2006). Nevertheless, the different strands of the PVM have enough in common to warrant discussion together.

(justifiedly believed/rationally believed) when it was originally acquired and, accordingly, that it need not be known (justifiedly believed/rationally believed) in a non-memorial way at this time. In this way, I shall show that condition (1) of the PVM is false and, *a fortiori*, that condition (2) is false as well.[5] Hence, just as I argued in Chapter 2 that testimony is not merely transmissive but can instead generate epistemic features in its own right, I shall here show that memory is not merely preservative but, rather, can function as a generative epistemic source.

A.2 Normative Defeaters

Knowledge, almost everyone agrees, is more than just true belief. But there is far less agreement about what precisely needs to be added to true belief to render it knowledge. Despite this disagreement, however, one point that all parties tend to accept is that knowledge is incompatible with the presence of undefeated psychological and normative defeaters. Recall that a psychological defeater is a doubt or belief that is had by S, and indicates that S's belief that *p* is either false or unreliably formed or sustained, while a normative defeater is a doubt or belief that S ought to have, and indicates that S's belief that *p* is either false or unreliably formed or sustained. The underlying thought here is that certain kinds of counterbeliefs and counterevidence—either that a subject has or should have—contribute epistemically unacceptable *irrationality* to doxastic systems and, accordingly, that justification and knowledge can be defeated or undermined by their presence.

Now, with these points in mind, consider the following:

CORRUPT MAYOR: Two days ago, Arthur was visiting his Aunt Lola and, while they were eating lunch, she mentioned to him without disclosing the source of her information that the mayor of their city had been caught accepting bribes in exchange for political favors. Arthur unhesitatingly formed the corresponding belief. At the same time, however, there was a vast conspiracy on the part of the mayor's allies to protect his political reputation, and so they exploited their high-powered connections in the media to cover up this indiscretion. To this end, they convinced all of the major newspapers and television stations to report that the mayor's political opponents had orchestrated a plan to win the upcoming election by falsely presenting him as having been the recipient of bribes. However,

---

[5] Condition (1) requires that the proposition in question be known (justifiedly believed/rationally believed), while condition (2) specifies the way in which the proposition needs to be known (justifiedly believed/rationally believed). If, however, the proposition doesn't need to be known (justifiedly believed/rationally believed), as I shall show, then it doesn't need to be known (justifiedly believed/rationally believed) in a particular sort of way.

because both Arthur and Aunt Lola rarely pay attention to the news, they were entirely unaware of all of the stories surrounding the mayor. Thus, unbeknownst to both Arthur and Aunt Lola, every major newspaper and television network was reporting that the mayor had not accepted bribes and was instead the victim of a devious scheme at the very time that Arthur was forming the belief that the mayor had been the recipient of bribes on the basis of Aunt Lola's testimony. Now, as it turns out, the mayor had in fact accepted bribes in exchange for political favors, all of the reports to the contrary were false, Aunt Lola was not only a highly reliable source of information in general, but had also heard this news directly from the mayor's epistemically reliable secretary, and Arthur's true belief about the mayor was reliably formed.

Since then and, once again, unbeknownst to Arthur and Aunt Lola, the scheme to cover up the mayor's indiscretion has been exposed, and all of the major newspapers and television stations are now reporting that the mayor did accept political bribes. At the present time, then, there no longer are vast amounts of available evidence indicating that the mayor had been framed. Throughout all of this, Arthur has remained blissfully ignorant of all of the relevant reports, and he currently continues to believe that the mayor was the recipient of bribes solely on the basis of remembering Aunt Lola's original testimony.[6]

Now, when Arthur first acquired his belief that the mayor had accepted bribes in exchange for political favors (at T1), he had an undefeated normative defeater for this belief and, accordingly, failed to have the knowledge in question at this time. Specifically, because every major newspaper and television station was reporting that the mayor had instead been framed by his political opponents, Arthur should have believed that the mayor had *not* actually been the recipient of such bribes.[7]

---

[6] This case is inspired by examples found in Harman (1968, 1973, and 1980). The diagnosis that Harman and others have offered as to why a subject such as Arthur lacks knowledge is that neglecting various social expectations can prevent one from having knowledge of certain relevant propositions. While this description of CORRUPT MAYOR is plausible, I am not here committing myself to this particular diagnosis of the situation. Instead, I am appealing to the *intuitive plausibility* of the claim that Arthur ought to hold the belief in question, however the nature of this ought is cashed out. For any who remain unconvinced that the belief in question is one that Arthur ought to have, see the next two counterexamples.

[7] It was suggested to me by an anonymous referee that this case could be described, not in terms of a normative defeater, but rather as involving what I called a factual defeater in note 21 of Chapter 2. In order to avoid this alternative analysis, however, we could simply modify the case so that there is a factual defeater-defeater at T1 for the defeater in question. For instance, we could stipulate that there is at least one fairly unknown newspaper that is reporting that the mayor had accepted bribes and that the reports to the contrary were merely part of a scheme to cover up this indiscretion. This true proposition would, then, defeat the original factual defeater at T1. But since this newspaper is relatively unknown and all of the major newspapers are making reports to the contrary, this proposition is not something that the subject ought to believe in any reasonable sense. There would, then, not be

At the present time (at T2), however, it is no longer the case that Arthur should hold this belief because all of the major newspapers and television stations have ceased reporting this false information. Arthur, then, does not have an undefeated normative defeater at T2 for his belief about the mayor. Given that the presence of this defeater was the only factor preventing Arthur's true belief from being an instance of knowledge at T1, its absence enables him to have the knowledge in question at T2. So, Arthur knows at T2 that the mayor had accepted bribes in exchange for political favors without knowing this proposition when it was originally acquired at T1. Thus, with respect to knowledge in particular, CORRUPT MAYOR shows that both conditions (1) and (2) of the PVM are false.[8]

What the above case reveals is that *a subject's relation to normative defeaters can change over time as a result of changes in the external environment,* thereby enabling memory to generate knowledge. In particular, if the presence of an undefeated normative defeater is the only factor preventing a belief from being an instance of knowledge, then such a belief can become memorial knowledge at a later time when changes in the external environment result in the absence of such a defeater.[9]

There are, however, two central ways in which one may attempt to deny that CORRUPT MAYOR provides a counterexample to the Preservation View of Memory. First, one may deny that Arthur *does not* have the knowledge in question at T1. Second, one may deny that he *does* have the knowledge at T2. Let us examine these in turn.

In order to deny that Arthur does not know at T1 — that is, to affirm that he *does* know at this time — that the mayor had accepted political bribes, one may simply point to all of the epistemically positive features of his belief. For, Arthur's belief at T1 was true, reliably produced via the testimony of Aunt Lola, and formed through Arthur's reliable cognitive faculties. Moreover, the evidence against Arthur's belief

---

a normative defeater-defeater for the belief in question at T1. Hence, with this modification, the only available analysis would be that Arthur has a normative defeater at T1 for his belief that the mayor was the recipient of bribes.

[8] Though I think that there is a clear sense of both rationality and epistemic justification that memory generates in CORRUPT MAYOR, I shall restrict my conclusion here to knowledge since there are many competing and divergent views regarding the former concepts. Nevertheless, the conclusion that is drawn in the next two sections will show that memory can generate rationality and epistemic justification in addition to knowledge.

[9] Why, one might ask, are we not attributing the generation of the epistemic status of knowledge in CORRUPT MAYOR to the environment in question rather than to memory? (I owe this objection to an anonymous referee.) The reason is this: a change in an environment has epistemic significance only relative to some particular faculty of a given subject. The only plausible candidate for a faculty operative in this case is memory insofar as the subject in question is not perceiving or inferring anything. Hence proper credit for the generation of the epistemic properties at T2 should be understood to accrue to memory as it functions in the environment in question.

about the mayor was produced by sources that were unreliable with respect to the information in question. So why, one might ask, is such unreliable counterevidence capable of preventing an otherwise epistemically impeccable belief from being an instance of knowledge?[10]

One diagnosis of CORRUPT MAYOR is that even though Arthur is not actually aware of the evidence against his belief about the mayor, there are certain pieces of information that one is expected to be aware of by virtue of being a member of society, and the mere fact that one happens to be ignorant of such information does not enable one to have knowledge that everyone else lacks.[11] As Ernest Sosa notes, "[i]t seems plausible...that knowledge has a further 'social aspect,' that it cannot depend on one's missing or blinking what is generally known" (Sosa 1991: 27). Were Arthur to turn on any channel of the evening news, pick up any local newspaper, or chat with almost anyone on the street, he would have believed that the mayor had *not* accepted political bribes. So, Arthur's having a true belief rather than a false one at T_1 depends on his being ignorant of information that is, so to speak, "common knowledge."[12] And unless this sort of ignorance is appropriately grounded (e.g., on some occasions, one may have good reason for deliberately remaining ignorant of certain pieces of "common knowledge"), it is incompatible with having the knowledge in question.

The second strategy for defending the PVM from CORRUPT MAYOR is to grant that Arthur does not have the knowledge in question at T_1, but to argue that he doesn't have this knowledge at T_2 either. In particular, one might claim that because of the massive amount of evidence against Arthur's belief about the mayor, such a belief was not formed in a reliable way when it was originally acquired. After all, the epistemic negligence Arthur exhibits in CORRUPT MAYOR is a type of cognitive defect, and it is plausible to think that a cognitive defect of

---

[10] It was suggested to me by Robert Almeder that false propositions cannot, strictly speaking, be either evidence or counterevidence and hence cannot function as normative defeaters in the relevant sense. Even if this is correct, however, the proposition in question that is actually doing the defeating work is true; namely, *that every major newspaper and television network is reporting that the mayor had not accepted bribes and was instead the victim of a devious scheme.*

[11] For instance, John Pollock says, "[w]e are 'socially expected' to be aware of various things. We are expected to know what is announced on television, and we are expected to know what is in our mail. If we fail to know all these things and that makes a difference to whether we are justified in believing some true proposition P, then our objectively justified belief in P does not constitute knowledge" (Pollock 1986: 192).

[12] Pollock calls these "common knowledge" defeaters. One may find the term "common knowledge" misleading here since the content of the reports in question is false. However, as mentioned in note 10 above, the proposition that is doing the defeating work, i.e., *that every major newspaper and television network is reporting that the mayor had not accepted bribes and was instead the victim of a devious scheme,* is appropriately described as common knowledge.

this sort undermines the agent's ability to reliably form true beliefs regarding the subject matter in question.[13]

By way of response to this point, notice that, as CORRUPT MAYOR is described, both of the processes responsible for the production and formation of Arthur's belief about the mayor are, in fact, reliable: Aunt Lola is a highly reliable testifier in general and with respect to the particular information in question, and Arthur is a reliable recipient of her testimony. For, though epistemic negligence of the sort Arthur exhibits in the above case may be a cognitive defect, it does not necessarily affect a subject's ability to reliably form true beliefs. This is just the converse of the familiar point that even the most responsible epistemic agent may still fail to be reliable. In this way, just as epistemic responsibility and reliability can come apart, so too can epistemic negligence and unreliability. Indeed, it is for precisely this reason that the inclusion of the no-defeater condition is taken to be an *additional* constraint on knowledge, one that cannot simply be subsumed by the reliability condition. There is, then, no reason to doubt that Arthur has the knowledge in question at T2. Thus, CORRUPT MAYOR shows that, contrary to the PVM, memory can function as a generative source with respect to knowledge.

A.3 Psychological Defeaters

In this section, I shall present a further case against the PVM. This example differs from the previous one in two central ways: first, the following case exploits certain features about psychological, rather than normative, defeaters. Second, unlike CORRUPT MAYOR which showed only that memory can generate knowledge, the conclusion to be drawn from this example is that memory can function as a generative epistemic source more broadly—that is, that in addition to knowledge, justification and rationality can be generated by memory as well.

With these points in mind, consider the following case:

CULT FRIENDS: While an undergraduate in college, Nora was a very careful and epistemically reliable recipient of testimony, with one notable exception: she

---

[13] In a similar spirit, one may argue that it is merely an accident that Arthur has a true belief rather than a false one at T1 because he *could have just as easily* turned on the evening news or read the newspaper and formed the belief that the mayor had *not* been the recipient of bribes. And because this sort of accidentality is relevant to the very formation of the belief in question, one might claim that it still prevents Arthur from knowing at T2 that the mayor had accepted bribes, despite the changes in the external environment at this time. However, as CORRUPT MAYOR is described, both Arthur and Aunt Lola rarely pay attention to the news, and so it is simply not the case that he could have just as easily formed the false belief that the mayor had not accepted political bribes. Therefore, it is not an accident that Arthur has a true belief rather than a false one at T1 and, accordingly, there is no problem of this sort with his true belief at T2 either.

was overly susceptible to peer-pressure from two of her friends who belonged to a religious cult. After repeatedly hearing them rant and rave about the corrupt minds and souls of non-believers, she eventually became convinced that the testimony of atheists is nearly completely unreliable.[14] During this time, Nora had several conversations with Calvin, a fellow student in one of her classes who, as a matter of fact, was an extremely reliable source of information and whom she had every reason to believe was both competent and sincere with respect to his reports. Yet Nora also knew that Calvin was an atheist, and so she believed him to be a highly unreliable epistemic source. One day after class, they were discussing World War II and Calvin told Nora, much to her surprise, that Hitler was raised a Christian. Being momentarily caught off guard, Nora found herself believing this proposition on the basis of Calvin's epistemically flawless testimony.

Now, several years after graduating from college, Nora is no longer in touch with her friends who were members of the religious cult and she has ceased believing that the majority of the testimony offered by atheists is highly unreliable—such a belief has simply faded from her memory. At the same time, however, she still believes on the basis of memory dating back solely to Calvin's testimony that Hitler was raised a Christian.

The first point to notice is that when Nora originally acquired her belief that Hitler was raised a Christian (at T1), she had an undefeated psychological defeater for this belief and, accordingly, cannot be said to have had the knowledge in question at this time. Specifically, by virtue of believing both that the testimony of atheists is highly unreliable and that Calvin is an atheist, she has a belief that indicates that the source of her belief about Hitler is epistemically problematic. In this way, whatever justification she might have acquired from the reliability of Calvin's testimony is defeated by the irrationality of simultaneously holding a belief on the basis of Calvin's testimony and believing that he is an unreliable epistemic source. At T1, therefore, Nora does not rationally believe, justifiedly believe, or know that Hitler was raised a Christian.

At the present time (at T2), however, it is not irrational for Nora to believe that Hitler was raised a Christian on the basis of memory that is traced back solely to the testimony offered by Calvin because she no longer believes that the testimony of atheists is highly unreliable. Nora, then, does not have an undefeated psychological defeater for her current belief about Hitler and, accordingly, the justification conferred on her belief by Calvin's testimony being in fact reliable is not defeated. Given that the only factor preventing Nora's belief from being an instance of

---

[14] I say "nearly completely unreliable" because it is rather implausible to suppose that Nora believed that an atheist's mundane testimony—e.g., reports about her name, what she had for breakfast, the time of day, and so on—are also highly unreliable.

knowledge at T1 was the presence of an undefeated psychological defeater, the absence of this factor renders her current belief an instance of knowledge at T2. Thus, Nora rationally believes, justifiedly believes, and knows at T2 that Hitler was raised a Christian without rationally believing, justifiedly believing, or knowing this proposition when it was originally acquired at T1. So, condition (1) of the PVM is not necessary for memorial knowledge, justification, or rationality and, *a fortiori*, condition (2) is not necessary. Hence, memory can function as a generative source with respect to each of these epistemic properties.

The general point exploited by CULT FRIENDS—which closely parallels that exploited by PERSISTENT BELIEVER in Chapter 2—is that *undefeated psychological defeaters are not necessarily retained with their defeatees via memory*. For, as we saw with Nora, a subject may simply forget the belief that did the defeating work in question while retaining the belief that was originally defeated. In this way, psychological defeaters do not simply "come along for the ride" when their defeatees are remembered over time. Rather, such beliefs themselves need to be independently remembered. So, just as a subject's relation to normative defeaters can change over time because of developments in the external environment, a subject's relation to psychological defeaters can change over time as the subject's doxastic system evolves. Because of this, if the presence of an undefeated psychological defeater is the only factor preventing a belief from being an instance of knowledge (justified belief/rational belief), then such a belief can become knowledge (justified belief/rational belief) via memory when the defeater itself is forgotten at a later time.[15]

---

[15] There is a second type of case involving psychological defeaters that shows the PVM to be false, which parallels SERIOUS STUDENT from Chapter 2. Consider the following:

SKEPTICAL STUDENT: During her Introduction to Philosophy class last semester, Claire was introduced to the evil demon argument in Descartes's *Meditations*. Through the course of the lecture and discussion, she became increasingly plagued by skeptical worries, so much so that by the end of the class period, she was utterly convinced that she could be the victim of an evil demon's deceptive ways and, accordingly, was not justified in holding the vast majority of her beliefs. As a matter of fact, however, Claire was not being so deceived, and her perceptual faculties were a highly reliable means of acquiring true beliefs. At this time, Claire momentarily drifted out of the discussion, glanced out the classroom window, and saw a red-tailed hawk fly across the quad. Despite her skeptical doubts, she found herself falling into her old epistemic ways by forming the corresponding true belief that a red-tailed hawk just flew across the quad.

At the present time, Claire is no longer taking any philosophy classes and she has ceased entertaining skeptical worries—indeed, since becoming a business major, philosophical thoughts couldn't be further from her mind. Today, the topic of regional wild birds came up while Claire was talking to a friend and she remembered her experience of seeing a red-tailed hawk fly across the quad last semester.

Now, when Claire originally acquired her belief that a red-tailed hawk flew across the quad (at T1), she had an undefeated psychological defeater for this belief and, accordingly, cannot be said to have had the knowledge in question at this time. In particular, while in the grips of deep skeptical worries, her belief that she could be the victim of an evil demon prevented her from rationally trusting her senses

Against CULT FRIENDS, however, it may be argued that Nora does in fact know at T1 that Hitler was raised a Christian. In particular, it may be doubted whether an unjustified belief, such as Nora's belief about the unreliability of atheists at T1, can really do the defeating work in question. For, one might ask, how can a belief that is false, unreliably produced, and unreasonable (i.e., not supported by good epistemic reasons) prevent a belief that is true, reliably produced, and otherwise reasonable from being an instance of knowledge?

By way of response to this objection, it is important to notice that what makes an undefeated psychological defeater epistemically problematic is that it is *held in conjunction with another belief*. The defeater itself need not be true, justifiedly believed, or rationally believed to have the power to defeat other beliefs precisely because it need not be true, justifiedly believed, or rationally believed to render it irrational to hold certain other beliefs. For instance, *given* that Nora in the envisaged case above believes that the testimony of atheists is very unreliable, it is highly irrational for her to accept the testimony of someone whom she knows to be an atheist. That is, it is irrational for her to hold *both* of these beliefs. So, even if the psychological defeater in question is itself epistemically problematic, this does not prevent it from having the capacity to defeat other beliefs.

A second way to reject the force of CULT FRIENDS is to grant that Nora does not know at T1 that Hitler was raised a Christian, but to argue that neither does she know this at T2. Specifically, one might claim that unless Nora acquires some reason to reject her earlier belief that the testimony of atheists is highly unreliable, she still has an undefeated psychological defeater at this time—that is to say, the defeater is still capable of doing the defeating work at T2 even though she does not then believe it.

---

and, therewith, from being epistemically justified in forming the corresponding beliefs. However, since Claire is not in the grips of skeptical worries at the present time (at T2), she does not have an undefeated psychological defeater for her current belief that she previously saw a red-tailed hawk fly across the quad, and thus it is not irrational for her to hold this belief. Because of this, the justification that was conferred on her belief by the fact that it was reliably produced is no longer defeated. Given that the only factor preventing Claire's belief from being an instance of knowledge at T1 was the presence of an undefeated psychological defeater, the absence of this factor renders her current belief an instance of knowledge at T2. Thus, Claire rationally believes, justifiedly believes, and knows that a red-tailed hawk flew across the quad at T2 without rationally believing, justifiedly believing, and knowing this proposition when it was originally acquired at T1.

Although CULT FRIENDS and SKEPTICAL STUDENT are structurally similar examples, i.e., they both exploit the failure of undefeated psychological defeaters being retained with their defeatees, they may appeal to slightly different intuitions. For instance, while SKEPTICAL STUDENT can be read as drawing on skeptical and contextualist or subject-sensitive invariantist intuitions, CULT FRIENDS focuses more directly on the incompatibility of knowledge and irrationality. (See Cohen (1986, 1988, and 1998), DeRose (1992, 1995, and 1999), and Lewis (1996) for some of the most prominent defenses of contextualism and Hawthorne (2004) for subject-sensitive invariantism.)

The most straightforward response to offer here is to point out that psychological defeaters are, by definition, propositions that are *believed*[16] by the subject in question to be true. Given that it is stipulated in the example that Nora no longer believes at T2 that the testimony of atheists is highly unreliable, it is true by definition that she does not have the undefeated psychological defeater in question at this time.

A more promising line of argument, however, is to argue, not that Nora has an undefeated *psychological* defeater but, rather, that she has an undefeated *normative* defeater at T2 that prevents her from knowing that Hitler was raised a Christian. For recall that a normative defeater is a proposition that a subject should believe (whether or not she does believe it) given the evidence that is available to her. One might argue, then, that in the absence of any reason to reject her earlier belief that the testimony of atheists is highly unreliable, Nora *should* hold this belief at T2 even if, as a matter of fact, she does not.

It is, no doubt, true that there are cases in which a subject's undefeated psychological defeater, so to speak, "turns into" an undefeated normative defeater when it is merely forgotten rather than itself defeated. For instance, suppose that Gordon comes to truly believe that Wendy is a compulsive liar on the basis of an extremely reliable epistemic source whom he has very good reason to trust. Years later he bumps into Wendy and, having forgotten his earlier belief about her reporting habits, he comes to believe that she was just awarded a Mellon Fellowship on the basis of her testimony. Here, one might rightly argue that there is an important sense in which Gordon's undefeated psychological defeater becomes an undefeated normative defeater when it is forgotten, thereby still preventing Wendy's testimony from imparting knowledge (or justified belief/rational belief) to him. For Gordon's earlier belief that Wendy is a compulsive liar is, from an epistemic point of view, quite impeccable: it is true, reliably produced, and supported by good reasons. Given this, one might claim that merely forgetting such a belief does not prevent it from continuing to defeat beliefs that Gordon forms on the basis of Wendy's testimony. More precisely, if a subject *justifiedly* holds an undefeated psychological defeater, then such a belief may "turn into" an undefeated normative defeater if it is merely forgotten rather than itself defeated.[17]

---

[16] As was noted in Chapter 2, psychological defeaters can also be doubts, but this is not relevant here.

[17] It should be emphasized that such a justified undefeated psychological defeater *may* turn into an undefeated normative defeater, but it need not. In SKEPTICAL STUDENT from note 15 above, for instance, Claire merely forgot at T2 the justified skeptical worries that defeated her red-tailed hawk belief at T1, and yet there I claimed that Claire could still have the knowledge in question at T2. Why? Well, skeptical doubts are a very unique kind of psychological defeater, in large part because it is questionable whether there can be a genuine defeater-defeater for such a defeater. Thus, as noted earlier, we must either agree that forgotten skeptical worries need not turn into undefeated normative

Nora's epistemic situation, however, is importantly different from Gordon's. For Nora's belief about the testimony of atheists was never epistemically justified to begin with—quite the contrary. She formed this belief because she repeatedly heard a couple of her friends who belong to a religious cult rant and rave about the corrupt minds and souls of non-believers. To claim that Nora's undefeated psychological defeater turned into an undefeated normative defeater, then, is to claim that Nora should hold a belief at T2 that she never should have held in the first place (at T1). For recall that the precise characterization of a normative defeater is that it is a proposition that a subject ought to believe to be true, yet indicates that a further belief of this subject's is either false or unreliably formed or sustained. This characterization of a normative defeater is often, in turn, fleshed out in terms of being a proposition that a subject is justified in believing to be true. But in what sense could it correctly be said that Nora is justified in believing at T2 that the testimony of atheists is highly unreliable? Such a proposition, were she to believe it at T2, would be neither externally justified (e.g., it wouldn't be reliably produced) nor internally justified (e.g., it wouldn't be held on the basis of good epistemic reasons).[18] So, Nora has neither an undefeated psychological nor a normative defeater at T2 and, therefore, can be said to have the knowledge in question at this time.

The third strategy for defending the PVM from CULT FRIENDS is to argue that even if Nora can properly be said to know at T2 that Hitler was raised a Christian, the knowledge in question is not purely memorial. For the most natural interpretation of the situation is that Nora no longer believes at T2 that the testimony of atheists is highly unreliable because she acquired a defeater-defeater for this belief after graduating from college. That is, through the acquisition of further relevant information, the undefeated psychological defeater from T1 is itself defeated at T2. The knowledge in question at T2, then, is a hybrid case, consisting of contributions made by memory, inference, and whatever the source of the further information is. Thus, so long as the PVM is restricted to cases of pure memorial knowledge, one may argue that (1) and (2) are indeed necessary conditions.

While it is true that Nora *might* have ceased holding the psychological defeater in question by virtue of acquiring a defeater-defeater at T2, it is by no means necessary

defeaters or conclude that nearly everyone who has been convinced by skeptical doubts knows very little thereafter.

[18] Because Nora's belief about the testimony of atheists is highly irrational itself, it may be said that she has a normative defeater for the undefeated psychological defeater in question. What is important to recognize, however, is that the relationship between a normative defeater and a psychological defeater differs from the relationship between a defeater-defeater and a defeater. In particular, while a defeater-defeater can restore knowledge that had been undermined by the presence of a defeater, thereby making the doxastic system in question *less* epistemically problematic, the conjunction of a normative and a psychological defeater makes the doxastic system in question *more* epistemically problematic.

that this is the case. Indeed, in the way that CULT FRIENDS is constructed, such a belief is said to have "simply faded from her memory." So, even if the PVM applies only to cases of pure memorial knowledge, there is no reason to suppose that Nora's knowledge that Hitler was raised a Christian fails to qualify as such at T2.

One final question that may be lingering with respect to both CORRUPT MAYOR and CULT FRIENDS, however, is this: in what sense precisely is memory functioning as a generative source in the above cases? For, in both cases, testimony produced the original belief in question and memory preserved it over time. What, then, is memory generating?

By way of response to this question, it is important to notice that in both CORRUPT MAYOR and CULT FRIENDS, a belief that was not known (or, in CULT FRIENDS, justified or rational) when originally acquired became known (and, in CULT FRIENDS, justified/rational) at a later time *without input or assistance from any other epistemic source besides memory.* Thus, even though memory did not generate the belief in question, it generated *the epistemic status* of the belief in question.[19] And this is sufficient not only to falsify the PVM, but also to conclude that memory has the capacity to function as a generative epistemic source.

A.4 Lack of Belief

In this section, I shall present one further case against the Preservation View of Memory. Unlike those found in the previous sections, however, this example does not depend on features about either undefeated normative or psychological defeaters. Instead, this case shows that, through certain changes in a subject's cognitive system over time, memory has the capacity not only to generate the epistemic status of the item in question, but also to generate the belief itself.

To begin, consider the following:

OVERLOADED DRIVER: Yesterday morning was like most others for Clifford: he spent it drinking coffee, listening to the radio, and driving in his car during his hour-and-a-half commute to work. As was typical for these commutes, Clifford's attention was divided between the other cars on the road, the surrounding environment, the discussion and music on the radio, and his thoughts about the day's work. Because of this perceptual and cognitive overload, Clifford found

---

[19] Of course, there is a difference in the way that the epistemic status is generated in CORRUPT MAYOR and CULT FRIENDS. In CORRUPT MAYOR, knowledge is generated at T2 by virtue of memory operating in a different epistemic environment than at T1, while in CULT FRIENDS, knowledge (justification/rationality) is generated by virtue of a subject forgetting information at T2 that functioned as a psychological defeater at T1.

himself, as he often did on these drives, taking in more pieces of information than he actually processed at that time.

Indeed, this was made apparent earlier this morning, when Clifford bumped into his friend, Phoebe, at the bakery and started talking about his commute. During this conversation, Phoebe asked him whether construction had begun on I55. Though this is not the freeway that Clifford takes to work, he does pass it every day and, moreover, it is the route that he occasionally takes to a nearby shopping center. Upon being asked this question by Phoebe, Clifford paused, called to mind passing I55 on his drive to work yesterday, and correctly remembered seeing construction work being done on this freeway. He, therefore, responded affirmatively to Phoebe's question, adding that he will be sure to map some alternate routes so as to avoid the traffic delays inevitably brought by construction. Prior to the recollection of the visual image triggered by this question, however, Clifford would have continued taking I55 to the shopping center and wouldn't have made even minor efforts to avoid this freeway.

The first point to notice about this case is that before the conversation with Phoebe in the bakery (at T1), it would not be correct to say that Clifford believed that there was construction work being done on I55. For, though he had reliably taken in the visual image of the construction workers on this freeway and had properly registered this information in his cognitive system, he had not actually formed the corresponding belief. And since it does not make sense to say that a subject rationally believes, justifiedly believes, or has knowledge of a proposition that is not even believed by this subject, Clifford fails to satisfy both (1) and (2) of the PVM at T1.

Once Phoebe's question prompts the recollection of the relevant visual image (at T2), however, the raw materials from Clifford's original perceptual experience are turned into a belief state. In particular, by virtue of calling to mind and processing the information that he had taken in at T1, he forms the corresponding belief at T2 that construction work was being done on I55. Moreover, because this information had been both reliably produced and reliably registered in Clifford's cognitive system, there is nothing to prevent this newly formed memorial belief from being rational, justified, and known at T2. Thus, Clifford rationally believes, justifiedly believes, and knows at T2 that construction work was being done on I55 without rationally believing, justifiedly believing, or knowing this proposition when it was originally acquired at T1.[20]

---

[20] It was suggested to me by an anonymous referee that, although this example does falsify the PVM, it does not undermine a weaker version of this thesis requiring only that the subject be *justified*

I suspect that a proponent of the PVM is most likely to reject the force of OVERLOADED DRIVER by arguing that Clifford does, in fact, have the belief in question at T1. Specifically, one might claim that the changes in Clifford's cognitive system between T1 and T2 do not take him from the absence of belief to belief but, rather, from a tacit or merely dispositional belief to an explicit or conscious belief state. This, of course, is a common epistemic occurrence: you ask me whether I believe that oranges don't grow on kangaroos and, even though I had never consciously formed this belief prior to your question, I readily assent—your question, that is, merely prompts me to explicitly believe something that I tacitly believed all along.

Despite the fact that it is not uncommon for a tacit or merely dispositional belief to become a conscious belief, however, this is not what is taking place in Clifford's cognitive system in OVERLOADED DRIVER. For notice that everything about Clifford's behavior prior to his conversation with Phoebe supports the thesis that he does not have any sort of belief about the construction in question. He would, for instance, have taken I55 to the shopping center, he wouldn't have made even minor efforts to avoid this freeway, and so on. Notice further that after speaking with Phoebe, Clifford vows to change his behavior by taking steps to avoid I55 because of the likely traffic delays. Now compare this with the example of my tacit or dispositional belief that oranges don't grow on kangaroos. It is reasonable to think that my behavior prior to and after your question would be strikingly similar: at both times, for instance, I would not turn to a kangaroo to quench my thirst, I would be surprised to learn that our oranges at home were from Australia, and so on. What these considerations suggest is that there is an intimate connection between beliefs and actions, even when the former are tacit or merely dispositional. Given that all of Clifford's actions at T1 are consistent with him not believing that construction is being done on I55, it seems clear that he fails to even tacitly or dispositionally hold this belief at this time.[21]

Nevertheless, a proponent of the PVM may pursue a different line of defense by arguing that the knowledge (justification/rationality) in question at T2 is not, in fact, generated by the faculty of memory; instead, it is generated by reason,

---

in believing the proposition in question at T1. While this is true, CORRUPT MAYOR and CULT FRIENDS do undermine even this weaker version of the PVM. Thus, this sort of modification will not render the spirit of the PVM defensible.

[21] Of course, being manifested in Clifford's behavior is not a *criterion* of his believing that construction is being done on I55; rather, it is *good evidence* for thinking that he holds such a belief. Moreover, it is not my intention here to be offering necessary and/or sufficient conditions for belief but, rather, to be working with an intuitive distinction (one that is recognized by many philosophers and cognitive scientists) between belief-states and states that are merely informational.

with the resulting knowledge (justification/rationality) being inferential rather than memorial in character. For instance, Ernie asks Tammy whether it is cold outside today. Tammy pauses, calls to mind having seen people wearing coats and hats this morning when she looked out the window, forms the belief that it is cold outside today, and responds affirmatively to Ernie's question. Now, though the resulting knowledge prompted by Ernie's question is newly acquired and owes much to the visual image that had been stored by memory in Tammy's cognitive system, one might argue that it is not itself generated by memory. For, the raw materials from Tammy's original perceptual experience of seeing the people out the window were used to infer that it is cold outside today, thereby making the knowledge in question inferential. And, one might ask, isn't this very similar to how Clifford's knowledge about the construction work on I55 is generated in OVERLOADED DRIVER?

Even if we grant both that Tammy's knowledge of the weather is inferential rather than memorial and that there are similarities between her cognitive situation and Clifford's in OVERLOADED DRIVER, there is nonetheless a crucial difference; namely, that while the content of Tammy's belief about it being cold outside goes beyond the content of the information that had been stored in her memory, the content of Clifford's belief simply mirrors the information that had been stored in his. To see this, notice that the two cases *would* be analogous in this respect if, for instance, Tammy merely came to know that people were wearing coats and hats this morning or, alternatively, if Clifford came to know that there would be traffic delays on I55 (because of the construction work). But, as OVERLOADED DRIVER is described, there is simply no relevant inference taking place in the formation of Clifford's belief about the construction work[22]—at least none that isn't also found in nearly every other case of belief formation.

A further strategy for resisting OVERLOADED DRIVER is to argue that while it is correct to say that Clifford fails to believe that construction work is being done on I55 at T1, it is on the basis of delayed perception rather than memory that Clifford comes to know this proposition at T2. For instance, consider the following: a split second after Harriet perceives that she has fallen

---

[22] It was brought to my attention by Dean Zimmerman that since it doesn't make sense to say that Clifford literally *saw* construction work taking place on I55 at T1—rather, he saw, for instance, workers in hardhats drilling with jackhammers—he is inferring that construction work is taking place on I55 at T2. Because of this, isn't it correct to say that Clifford's knowledge of the construction work at T2 is inferential? I am inclined to say that seeing workers in hardhats drilling on the freeway with jackhammers *just is* to see construction work being done. Nevertheless, those who resist this can simply modify OVERLOADED DRIVER so that Clifford's belief *that construction work is being done on I55* is replaced with the belief *that workers in hardhats were drilling on I55 with jackhammers*.

into a vat of liquid nitrogen, she freezes completely, and all of her cognitive activities cease. She remains frozen until the year 2525, when she is instantaneously thawed. At that moment, Harriet's cognitive activities pick up where they left off: she processes the information that she acquired through perception 5 centuries earlier, and thereby comes to believe and know that she has fallen into a vat of liquid nitrogen. Now, this, one might claim, is clearly a case of delayed perceptual knowledge—not memorial knowledge. So, why can't the same thing be said with respect to OVERLOADED DRIVER?[23]

To my mind, what the case of Harriet reveals is not that Clifford's knowledge is perceptual instead of memorial but, rather, that the sheer amount of time that passes between the acquisition of information and the formation of the corresponding belief has nothing of importance to do with what kind of knowledge is at issue. For what really matters for individuating kinds of knowledge are differences in the kinds of cognitive processing that are operative in a subject's system. For instance, the typical case of memorial knowledge involves information—usually in the form of a belief—having been *stored* at an earlier time and then *recalled* or *retrieved* at a later time. No such cognitive processes take place either in the case of Harriet or in the standard case of perceptual knowledge. Thus, to show that Clifford's knowledge at T2 in OVERLOADED DRIVER can plausibly be regarded as perceptual, more needs to be done than revealing that a great deal of time can pass between the reception of information and the formation of a perceptual belief. It also needs to be shown that the very same cognitive processing that we standardly attribute to memory can occur with the resulting knowledge being perceptual rather than memorial. Moreover, notice that the cognitive processing that is operative in Clifford's system—the storing and retrieving of information—is identical to standard cases of memorial knowledge. Indeed, the only difference between Clifford's knowledge at T2 and typical cases of memorial knowledge is that the psychological item that is stored in and then retrieved from his cognitive system is merely an informational state rather than a belief. And in the absence of an argument showing why *this* fact should render the resulting knowledge perceptual, it must either be conceded that Clifford's knowledge at T2 is indeed memorial or the very distinction between perceptual and memorial knowledge is in danger of collapsing.

Memory, therefore, does not merely have the capacity to preserve epistemic features generated by other sources. For, as we have seen, there are two different ways in which memory can function generatively: first, memory can generate the epistemic status of an already held belief and, second, memory can generate the

---

[23] I owe this objection to Cody Gilmore.

belief itself. Thus, contrary to the standard view in contemporary epistemology, memory can indeed function as a generative epistemic source.

A.5 Changes in Environments, Consumer and Epistemic

In a recent paper, Thomas D. Senor attempts to undermine my argument that the PVM is false. To this end, he begins by offering responses that the proponent of such a view can provide to CORRUPT MAYOR and CULT FRIENDS. He then argues that even if my counterexamples are granted, they are irrelevant to a "carefully construed" version of the PVM or, what Senor calls, *preservationism*. In what follows, I take up each of Senor's points in turn, showing that none of his arguments succeed in challenging my original conclusion that memory can function as a generative epistemic source.

Let us begin with Senor's discussion of CORRUPT MAYOR. According to Senor, the normative defeater Arthur had at T1 can continue to defeat his belief about the mayor at T2—despite the fact that it no longer exists—and hence Arthur lacks the knowledge in question at both times. His central argument in support of this conclusion is to appeal to the following analogy:

Suppose Smith wants to buy a car for $25,000. His available cash is exactly equal to the price of the car. However, the local sales tax is 10% so Smith is $2,500 short of what he needs. Smith notices in the fine print of the contract for the car that the buyer may choose to pay the tax directly to the local tax assessor as long as this is done within a week of the purchase. Seeing a way of getting the car for the money he has, Smith exercises this option with no intention of paying the tax …. On the assumption that the tax is legitimate, he is culpable for buying the car as he did. Now suppose that two months after his purchase, the sales tax is repealed. If Smith were to buy the same car with the same resources today, his purchase would be legitimate. But the truth of this counterfactual doesn't alter the fact that Smith *is* culpable for having purchased the car as he did and for continuing to enjoy owning it without having paid the tax due. (Senor 2007: 205)

According to Senor, then, just as changes in the "consumer environment" do not affect the status of illegitimate purchases made prior to such alterations, so, too, changes in the epistemic environment do not affect the status of defeated beliefs formed prior to such alterations. Because of this, the fact that at T2 all of the major newspapers and television stations ceased reporting the false information about the mayor does not alter the defeated status of Arthur's acquired belief at T1. Hence, contrary to what I concluded in CORRUPT MAYOR, Senor maintains that Arthur fails to justifiedly believe or know that the mayor had accepted bribes in exchange for political favors at *both* T1 and T2.

There is, however, a crucial difference between Senor's above example of Smith's car purchase and CORRUPT MAYOR: namely, that while the local sales tax at the time of Smith's car purchase is *legitimate*, the relevant defeating evidence at the time Arthur forms his belief about the mayor is *misleading*. For in CORRUPT MAYOR, the counterevidence that functions as a normative defeater is brought about by a vast conspiracy on the part of the mayor's allies to protect his political reputation by covering up his indiscretions. In particular, his allies convince all of the major newspapers and television stations to report that the mayor's political opponents had orchestrated a plan to win the upcoming election by *falsely* presenting him as having been the recipient of bribes. The fact that the counterevidence in question is false and, therefore, misleading is crucial to the case's ability to function as a counterexample to the PVM. Indeed, it is in large part because of its misleading nature that I argue that Arthur can come to have justified belief and knowledge of the mayor's bribes once the changes in his epistemic environment obtain.

To make this point clearer, let us consider a modified case of Senor's Smith example that would be more analogous to CORRUPT MAYOR. Suppose that everything is the same as described in Senor's Smith case with the following exception: the reason why the sales tax is repealed two months after Smith's car purchase is because the state has since become aware that its citizens are being overtaxed. So, rather than lowering taxes across the board, the state decides to eliminate sales tax on car purchases. Now, even if Smith's behavior is illegitimate at the time of the car purchase, it seems clear that this is not the case at the later time when the tax is repealed. For there is a very good reason why the state repealed the tax at the later time—they came to realize that it shouldn't have been imposed in the first place. Similarly, even if false, fabricated media reports can function as a normative defeater for Arthur's belief about the mayor when present in his immediate environment, they should no longer do so when they have been replaced with true, genuine reports. For there is a very good reason why the media discounted the original reports at the later time—they came to realize that they shouldn't have been presented in the first place. Contrary to Senor's conclusion, then, just as changes in the consumer environment *can* affect the status of illegitimate purchases made prior to such alterations, so, too, changes in the epistemic environment *can* affect the status of defeated beliefs formed prior to such alterations. Hence, Senor has given us no reason to deny my original conclusion: while Arthur fails to justifiedly believe or know that the mayor accepted bribes at

T1, he justifiedly believes and knows that this is the case at T2 without having acquired any additional evidence between T1 and T2 that is relevant to this belief.

A.6 Forgotten Evidence and Forgotten Defeaters

Let us now turn to Senor's response to CULT FRIENDS, the initial part of which can be found in the following passage:

the preservationist can offer an explanation for why he thinks, *pace* Lackey, that Nora fails to know in both instances: Nora doesn't know *now* because she didn't know *then*; since she lacked knowledge (and even justification) at the time the belief was formed, and since there has been no additional positive epistemic change...her potential knowledge remains defeated despite the fact that the [psychological] defeater has faded from her memory.

Lackey is...assuming that the belief is defeated at t only if there is a [psychological] or normative defeater at t. But this assumption is [to] be rejected by the preservationist. For it is part and parcel of the preservationist claim that, without the addition of an epistemic boost, the epistemic status of a memory belief cannot be greater than its status at the time the belief was formed. (Senor 2007: 203)

As far as I can tell, this response does little more than reiterate the very view that is being targeted by my counterexamples—the PVM or preservationism. It is much like a proponent of a justified true belief account of knowledge responding to Gettier cases by saying, "Well, it is part and parcel of the JTB account of knowledge that justified true beliefs are instances of knowledge. Hence the subjects in your purported counterexamples do have the knowledge in question." Obviously, this response will not do. In CULT FRIENDS, I present a case in which it is *intuitively plausible* that the subject fails to know at T1 but knows merely on the basis of memory at T2, just as Gettier counterexamples present cases in which it is intuitively plausible that justified true beliefs fall short of knowledge. It is then incumbent upon the proponent of the targeted view *to explain away these intuitions, not to merely reiterate the theory under attack.*

Senor does, however, provide a more substantive response to CULT FRIENDS; namely, he argues that since it is clear that evidence that has been forgotten can continue to *justify* a remembered belief, evidence that has been forgotten should be able to similarly continue to *defeat* a remembered belief. He writes:

I believe that Abraham Lincoln was killed in Ford's Theater. Undoubtedly, when I first formed this belief, I had another belief or beliefs I could cite as its ground (i.e., that my teacher, who is reliable, said it or that I read it in a history text).

But the passage of time and the limitations of memory have conspired to rid me of my earlier, justifying beliefs. Nevertheless, I take it that my memory belief about Lincoln's assassination is justified and likely counts as knowledge. (Senor 2007: 204)

According to Senor, then, despite the fact that at T2 he no longer remembers the evidence that justified his belief at T1 about Lincoln's assassination, this does not prevent him from justifiedly believing and indeed knowing at T2 that this fact obtained. For the original evidence that justified the belief about Lincoln's assassination at T1 can continue to justify this belief at T2 even after it has been forgotten. But, since there is purportedly no reason why forgotten evidence can function only positively, Senor argues that evidence that defeats a belief when it was originally formed at T1 should similarly continue to defeat this belief at T2 even after it has been forgotten. Given this, Senor claims that, contrary to the conclusion drawn by me, Nora fails to justifiedly believe and know that Hitler was raised a Christian at *both* T1 and at T2 since the relevant undefeated defeater can function negatively even after it no longer exists.

By way of response to this line of argumentation, I shall make three central points. First, the example of Lincoln's assassination at Ford's Theater has the potential to be slightly misleading. For when one remembers a very famous historical event, such as Lincoln's assassination, it is very likely that the justification of such a belief involves countless pieces of evidence accumulated from a multitude of different sources, including teachers, books, news reports, documentaries, and so on. Hence, even if one forgets at T2 the evidence that *originally* justified one's belief about Lincoln's assassination at T1, one most likely has acquired a great deal of *additional* evidence between T1 and T2 that supports this belief. And this additional support may be at least partially responsible for the intuition that many of us have that we clearly know that Lincoln was assassinated at Ford's Theater, despite having forgotten the original evidence supporting such a belief.

Of course, this worry can easily be avoided by simply choosing an example that clearly parallels the structure of CULT FRIENDS. To this end, the following three features are of particular importance to this case:

(i) Q is the only thing defeating S's belief that *p* at T1,
(ii) no additional evidence of any kind has been acquired between T1 and T2 that is relevant to S's belief that *p*, and
(iii) Q is completely forgotten at T2.

So, in order to be properly analogous, Senor's forgotten evidence case should clearly include the following features:

(i) R is the only thing justifying S's belief that *p* at T1,

(ii) no additional evidence of any kind has been acquired between T1 and T2 that is relevant to S's belief that p, and

(iii) R is completely forgotten at T2.

In particular, the case should be constructed so as to ensure that, unlike, e.g., an adult's belief about Lincoln's assassination, (ii) can plausibly be satisfied.

Here is where the second point I should like to make against Senor's argument emerges: once the case is formulated so as to be clearly analogous to my CULT FRIENDS, Senor's appeal to forgotten evidence no longer does the work he intends. For instance, consider the following:

CLOSET SMOKER: When Louise was 2 years old, her mother was diagnosed with a serious heart condition that severely limited her physical activity until she was healthy enough to undergo heart surgery. This placed a great deal of stress on Louise's father, who struggled to maintain the house and care for their three children during this difficult time. One morning, Louise walked into the living room of their home and was the only person to see her father smoking his first and last cigarette, a failed attempt on her father's part to relieve some of the anxiety of the situation. Now, as a 25-year-old adult, Louise believes that her father smoked earlier in his lifetime. Nevertheless, she has absolutely no recollection of ever seeing her father smoking, nor has she acquired additional evidence of any kind between her 2-year-old self and her 25-year-old self that is relevant to this belief.

Now, CLOSET SMOKER satisfies (i)–(iii) and thus appropriately parallels CULT FRIENDS. But does Louise at 25 years old know that her father smoked earlier in his lifetime? Clearly not. If the only evidence for this belief is the forgotten perceptual experience of her 2-year-old self, with absolutely no additional evidence of any kind having been accumulated since then, it is hard to see how she could know that this is the case when she is 25.[24]

What CLOSET SMOKER reveals, then, is that there are *at least some cases in which forgotten evidence fails to continue to justify a given belief.* So, in order to legitimately appeal to this phenomenon to argue against CULT FRIENDS, Senor needs to, first, provide a principled distinction between those forgotten evidence cases that result in knowledge and those that do not and, second, show why CULT FRIENDS is analogous to the former but not the latter. In the absence of this, there is nothing to prevent the conclusion that Nora's relation to her defeater at T2 parallels Louise's relation to her positive evidence at T2. Otherwise put, there

---

[24] If one doubts whether Louise in fact knows that her father smoked at T1 because one doubts whether a 2-year-old could know such a thing in the first place, change the age of the child to 3 or 4. All I need for my example to clearly work is for the subject to have acquired the original evidence when she was quite young.

is nothing to undermine the original conclusion drawn: while Nora fails to know that Hitler was raised a Christian at T1, she knows this on the basis of memory at T2 without having received any additional evidence relevant to this belief between T1 and T2.

This leads to the third point I wish to make here. If there are cases in which a belief at T2 seems to be justified or known despite the fact that the original evidence acquired at T1 for such a belief has since been *completely* forgotten, I suspect that what would do the justificatory or epistemic work—at least much of the time—is something like *earned self-trust* in ourselves as epistemic agents. For instance, if nearly every time I find myself with a given belief—even when I cannot recall why I believe it or where it came from—it turns out to be true, then I may accumulate very good reasons for believing myself to be a reliable source of beliefs. This trust that I acquire in myself as a believer can provide at least some epistemic support for those beliefs that I hold in the face of forgotten evidence. But there is simply no analogue of earned self-trust in cases involving defeaters that could explain why justification and knowledge would continue to be absent long after a given defeater has been forgotten. This provides further reason for doubting that forgotten evidence and defeaters are analogous in the way that Senor suggests.

A.7 *Prima Facie* and *Ultima Facie* Justification

The final argument Senor makes against my view of memory is that even if CORRUPT MAYOR and CULT FRIENDS are granted, I have "failed to appreciate the essence of the preservationist's view." Because of this, Senor claims that my counterexamples turn out to be irrelevant to the PVM or preservationism "carefully construed" (Senor 2007: 205).

This carefully construed version of the PVM is one that appeals to the *prima facie/ultima facie* distinction. According to Senor, a belief is *prima facie* justified (epistemized) if it attains the level of justification (epistemization) which, in the absence of undefeated defeaters, is sufficient for its being *ultima facie* justified (epistemized).[25] Senor then argues that the PVM should be understood in the following way: a source is epistemically generative only if it produces *prima facie* justification and epistemization; memory is incapable of producing *prima facie* justification and epistemization; therefore, memory is not a generative epistemic source. Because both CORRUPT MAYOR and CULT FRIENDS rely on the

---

[25] Following Senor, who follows Alston, "epistemization" picks out that feature or property enough of which converts true belief into knowledge. In this sense, it is equivalent to Plantinga's specific use of "warrant" (see Plantinga (1993a and 1993b)).

relevance of defeaters, they do not show that memory is capable of producing *prima facie* justification and epistemization; thus, they do not succeed as counterexamples to this carefully construed version of the PVM.

In response to this final argument against my view of memory, I shall make two main points. First, even if this is what the preservationist *should* say, it is not what the preservationists in the literature *do* say, nor is it even compatible with what many proponents of the PVM actually say. For instance, the sense in which memory is not a generative epistemic source is most frequently discussed in connection with knowledge. So, for instance, recall Robert Audi's claim that "[j]ust as we cannot know that *p* from memory unless we have *come* to know it in another way, say through perception, we cannot know that *p* on the basis of testimony unless the attester... has come to know it (at least in part) in another way... Memory and testimony... are not generative with respect to knowledge: characteristically, the former is preservative, the latter transmissive" (Audi 1997: 410). Similarly, recall that Michael Dummett says, "Memory is not a *source*, still less a *ground*, of knowledge: it is the maintenance of knowledge formerly acquired by whatever means" (Dummett 1994: 262, original emphasis). Obviously, there is no distinction between *prima facie* knowledge and *ultima facie* knowledge; accordingly, there is no clear sense in which Senor's distinction can be applied so as to subsume preservationism about knowledge.[26] Given this, Senor's suggestion at best represents *a substantive revision to preservationism about memory*, one that significantly modifies the sense in which memory fails to be a generative epistemic source in ways that are most likely not even welcome to many of its proponents.

Second, and perhaps more importantly, even if the proponent of the PVM accepts this substantive revision suggested by Senor, and we grant that the distinction between *prima facie* and *ultima facie* justification and epistemization can do the work in question, OVERLOADED DRIVER—which Senor does not discuss[27]—shows that *memory can generate even* prima facie *justification and*

---

[26] It is also questionable whether there is an interesting distinction—if one at all—between *prima facie* rationality and *ultima facie* rationality. This makes it equally doubtful whether Senor's suggestion can be applied to preservationist views of rationality, such as David Owen's: "If a belief is irrational when adopted, it remains just as irrational while laid up in memory" (Owens 2000: 156).

[27] Curiously, Senor writes: "Before evaluating Lackey's examples, I should mention that there is a section of Lackey's [appendix] that I will not be addressing. In section [A.4], she argues that memory can be epistemically generative because it can produce new beliefs... There is an obvious sense in which memory functions generatively here, and I have no wish to deny the obvious. However, since such examples are also instances of *belief* generation, they are very much unlike the main examples in her [appendix]. The main sections of her [appendix], and the ones with which I shall be taking issue, are intended to show that memory can be epistemically generative even when it is not doxastically generative. And it is her argument for this that I take to be mistaken" (Senor 2007: 199). This passage is curious because I include three counterexamples to the PVM, two that appeal to defeaters and one that involves belief formation. I do not regard two out of three of these cases as the "main examples" in my

epistemization. In this case, memory is generating not only the belief in question at T2, but also *both prima facie* and *ultima facie* justification and epistemization. For, even though the information about the construction work on I55 was originally placed in Clifford's cognitive framework via perception, the belief itself, along with all of the epistemic properties it possesses, was generated by the faculty of memory. Specifically, Clifford's faculty of memory reliably stored the raw materials from his perceptual experience and then worked these materials into a belief state that is both *prima facie* and *ultima facie* justified and epistemized. Moreover, since the belief in question is true, it also qualifies as an instance of knowledge. Hence, even if we accept Senor's substantive revision to preservationism—that proponents of such a view are committed only to the thesis that memory is incapable of generating *prima facie* justification and epistemization—OVERLOADED DRIVER shows that this significantly weaker version of the view is false as well.

I conclude, then, that Senor has failed to provide a compelling reason to doubt my original conclusion: memory is not a merely preservative epistemic source but, rather, it can generate epistemic features in its own right.

A.8 Concluding Remarks

In this final section, I shall briefly sketch an alternative conception of memory, one that avoids the objections afflicting the PVM and adequately captures the capacities of memory as an epistemic source.

There are two central insights underlying the Preservation View of Memory that are both true and important. The first is that memory, unlike sources such as sense perception and reason, must ultimately depend on resources produced by another epistemic source. For instance, while I may come to know that there is currently an owl in my backyard merely on the basis of sense perception, my remembering that there was an owl in my backyard yesterday ultimately depends both on memory *and* the source responsible for the original production of this information.[28] The second insight is that in order for this information to be capable

---

appendix, nor do I think that it is legitimate to argue against only two of the cases while suggesting that a general defense of preservationism is being offered, especially when the counterexample not discussed poses a problem for the proffered defense.

[28] "Ultimately" is key here. For notice that in OVERLOADED DRIVER, Clifford depends only on resources provided by memory at the time that he is forming the belief about construction on I55. Nevertheless, the information that he accesses via memory was originally stored by a non-memorial source; namely, sense perception. So, it is true that Clifford's remembering that there is construction being done on I55 *ultimately* depends both on memory and the source responsible for the original production of this information.

of later qualifying as justified belief or knowledge, it needs to be stored and accessed by memory in a reliable or otherwise truth-conducive way.

These insights, however, are accompanied by some widespread errors in the epistemology of memory—errors that were made apparent in the preceding sections. For instance, it is thought that the information stored in memory must always be in the form of belief, a thesis shown to be false by OVERLOADED DRIVER. Moreover, it is assumed that the only way for this information to be stored and accessed in a reliable way is for it to enter a subject's cognitive framework as justified belief or knowledge, an assumption shown to be false by CORRUPT MAYOR and CULT FRIENDS. And, finally, it is believed that the sort of dependence that memory has on other sources leads to the conclusion that memory cannot function as a generative epistemic source—a conclusion that has been argued against throughout this appendix.

What we need, then, is a view of memory that captures the important insights mentioned above yet avoids the errors found in the PVM. To this end, I propose the following *Non-Preservative View of Memory*:

> NPVM: S knows (justifiedly believes/rationally believes)[29] that p on the basis of memory at T2 only if: (1) the information that p was reliably registered in S's cognitive system at an earlier time, T1,[30] (2) the information that p was registered in S's cognitive system at T1 via a source other than memory, (3) the information that p is reliably retrieved by S at T2, and (4) S does not have any undefeated defeaters for the belief that p at T2.[31]

The notion of reliability found in conditions (1) and (3) is intended to be unspecific—it can be fleshed out in terms of a general externalist conception of epistemic justification. For instance, in order for the information that p to be reliably registered, it may need to be *sensitive* in Nozick's sense or *safe* in Sosa's sense—i.e., p would be not be registered in S's cognitive system if p were false, or p would

---

[29] It should be noted that there are wildly different conceptions of rationality, ranging from highly internalist and subjective views to entirely externalist and objective ones. Thus, these necessary conditions should be read as applying to only one kind of rationality.

[30] Note that this condition merely requires that the information that p be reliably registered in S's cognitive system at an *earlier time* rather than when the information was *originally acquired*. This is to accommodate cases such as the following: at T1, Flora acquires the information that whales are mammals from an unreliable classmate, at T2 she receives this same information from a reliable biologist, and at T3 she reliably retrieves this information with no undefeated defeaters. Now, while the information in question was reliably registered at an earlier time (T2), it was not reliably registered when it was originally acquired (at T1). Yet, it seems clear that Flora can have memorial knowledge that whales are mammals at T3. (I owe this point to Tomis Kapitan.)

[31] A condition requiring the truth of the information will need to be included to distinguish memorial knowledge from memorial justification.

not be registered in S's cognitive system without it being so that p.[32] Or, in order for the information that p to be reliably retrieved, it may need to be formed by a virtuous or properly functioning cognitive agent in an appropriate environment.[33] But no matter how the details of these conditions are worked out, the point that is of import here is that neither justified belief nor knowledge is required in order for information to be reliably stored and retrieved by the faculty of memory.[34]

The notion of information found in conditions (1)–(3) is also intended to be fairly unspecific so as to be compatible with various theories.[35] Informational states may, for instance, have propositional content, conceptual content, non-conceptual content, and so on. The crucial point for our purposes, however, is that informational states need not be in the form of beliefs in order to be properly registered in cognitive systems.

Finally, as with the PVM, the NPVM does not specify sufficient conditions. Other necessary conditions may need to be added as well—for example, one that rules out Gettier cases—but these will most likely be conditions that figure in a general epistemology. For, in the NPVM, we find what is distinctive about memorial justification and knowledge. And what we find is that memory not only has the capacity to preserve justified belief and knowledge, but also the capacity to generate these epistemic features in its own right, a view importantly different from that currently dominating the epistemology of memory.

[32] See Nozick (1981) and Sosa (1996, 1999, 2000, and 2002), respectively. For additional endorsements of safety, see Williamson (2000) and Pritchard (2005).

[33] See, for instance, Sosa (1991) and Plantinga (1993b), respectively.

[34] It should be noted that a consequence of requiring condition (1) for memorial justification is that subjects inhabiting a world under the influence of a Cartesian demon would be justified in holding very few, if any, of their memorial beliefs. As indicated in the Introduction, however, I am assuming that justification is a necessary condition for knowledge. In *this* sense of justification, it seems reasonable to deny such subjects memorial justification. In the sense of justification having to do with being epistemically responsible in one's believings (which may or may not be necessary for knowledge, depending on how this notion is cashed out), such subjects can be said to be justified in holding their memorial beliefs.

[35] See, for instance, Grice (1957), Dennett (1969), and Dretske (1981).

References

Achinstein, Peter (1978), "Concepts of Evidence," *Mind* 87: 22–45.

—— (1983), *The Nature of Explanation* (Oxford: Oxford University Press).

Adler, Jonathan E. (1994), "Testimony, Trust, Knowing," *The Journal of Philosophy* 91: 264–75.

—— (1996), "Transmitting Knowledge," *Noûs* 30: 99–111.

—— (2002), *Belief's Own Ethics* (Cambridge, MA: The MIT Press).

—— (2006), "Epistemological Problems of Testimony," *The Stanford Encyclopedia of Philosophy (Winter 2006 Edition)*, Edward N. Zalta (ed.), URL = <http://plato.stanford. edu/archives/win2006/entries/testimony–episprob/>.

Alston, William P. (1989), *Epistemic Justification: Essays in the Theory of Knowledge* (Ithaca: Cornell University Press).

Anscombe, Elizabeth (1979), "What Is It to Believe Someone?," in C. F. Delaney (ed.), *Rationality and Religious Belief* (Notre Dame: University of Notre Dame Press), 141–51.

Audi, Robert (1995), "Memorial Justification," *Philosophical Topics* 23: 31–45.

—— (1997), "The Place of Testimony in the Fabric of Knowledge and Justification," *American Philosophical Quarterly* 34: 405–22.

—— (1998), *Epistemology: A Contemporary Introduction to the Theory of Knowledge* (London: Routledge).

—— (2004), "The A Priori Authority of Testimony" in Ernest Sosa and Enrique Villanueva (eds.), *Philosophical Issues* 14: 18–34.

—— (2006), "Testimony, Credulity, and Veracity," in Jennifer Lackey and Ernest Sosa (eds.), *The Epistemology of Testimony* (Oxford: Oxford University Press), 25–49.

—— (2007), "Justifying Grounds, Justified Beliefs, and Rational Acceptance," in Mark Timmons, John Greco, and Alfred R. Mele (eds.), *Rationality and the Good* (Oxford: Oxford University Press), 222–47.

Austin, J. L. (1979), "Other Minds," in his *Philosophical Papers*, 3rd edn. (Oxford: Oxford University Press).

Bach, Kent and Harnish, Robert (1979), *Linguistic Communication and Speech Acts* (Cambridge, MA: The MIT Press).

Baier, Annette (1986), "Trust and Antitrust," *Ethics* 96: 231–60.

Bergmann, Michael (1997), "Internalism, Externalism and the No-Defeater Condition," *Synthese* 110: 399–417.

Bergmann, Michael (2004), "Epistemic Circularity: Malignant and Benign," *Philosophy and Phenomenological Research* 69: 709–27.

____(2006), *Justification without Awareness* (Oxford: Oxford University Press).

BonJour, Laurence (1980), "Externalist Theories of Epistemic Justification," *Midwest Studies in Philosophy* 5: 53–73.

____(1985), *The Structure of Empirical Knowledge* (Cambridge, MA: Harvard University Press).

____(2002), *Epistemology: Classic Problems and Contemporary Responses* (Lanham, MD: Rowman and Littlefield).

____and Sosa, Ernest (2003), *Epistemic Justification: Internalism vs. Externalism, Foundations vs. Virtues* (Oxford: Blackwell).

Brandom, Robert (1983), "Asserting," *Noûs* 17: 637–50.

____(1994), *Making It Explicit* (Cambridge, MA: Harvard University Press).

Buenting, Joel (2006), "Re-Thinking the Duplication of Speaker/Hearer Belief in the Epistemology of Testimony," *Episteme* 2: 129–34.

Burge, Tyler (1993), "Content Preservation," *The Philosophical Review* 102: 457–88.

____(1997), "Interlocution, Perception, and Memory," *Philosophical Studies* 86: 21–47.

Chakrabarti, Arindam (1994), "Telling as Letting Know," in Bimal Krishna Matilal and Arindam Chakrabarti (eds.), *Knowing from Words* (Dordrecht: Kluwer Academic Publishers), 99–124.

Chisholm, Roderick M. (1989), *Theory of Knowledge*, 3rd edn. (Englewood Cliffs, NJ: Prentice-Hall).

Clément, Fabrice, Koenig, Melissa A., and Harris, Paul L. (2004), "The Ontogenesis of Trust," *Mind and Language* 19: 360–79.

Coady, C. A. J. (1992), *Testimony: A Philosophical Study* (Oxford: Clarendon Press).

____(1994), "Testimony, Observation and 'Autonomous Knowledge'," in Bimal Krishna Matilal and Arindam Chakrabarti (eds.), *Knowing from Words* (Dordrecht: Kluwer Academic Publishers), 225–50.

Cohen, Stewart (1986), "Knowledge and Context," *The Journal of Philosophy* 83: 574–83.

____(1988), "How to Be a Fallibilist," *Philosophical Perspectives* 2: 91–123.

____(1998), "Contextualist Solutions to Epistemological Problems: Skepticism, Gettier, and the Lottery," *Australasian Journal of Philosophy* 76: 289–306.

____(2004), "Knowledge, Assertion, and Practical Reasoning," in Ernest Sosa and Enrique Villanueva (eds.), *Philosophical Issues* 14: 482–91.

____and Lehrer, Keith (1983), "Justification, Truth, and Coherence," *Synthese* 55: 191–207.

Conee, Earl and Feldman, Richard (1985), "Evidentialism," *Philosophical Studies* 48: 15–34.

———(2004), *Evidentialism: Essays in Epistemology* (Oxford: Oxford University Press).

Dennett, Daniel C. (1969), *Content and Consciousness* (London: Routledge and Kegan Paul).

DeRose, Keith (1992), "Contextualism and Knowledge Attributions," *Philosophy and Phenomenological Research* 52: 913–29.

———(1995), "Solving the Skeptical Puzzle," *The Philosophical Review* 104: 1–52.

———(1999), "Contextualism: An Explanation and Defense," in John Greco and Ernest Sosa (eds.), *The Blackwell Guide to Epistemology* (Oxford: Blackwell), 187–205.

———(2002), "Assertion, Knowledge, and Context," *The Philosophical Review* 111: 167–203.

Dretske, Frederick (1981), *Knowledge and the Flow of Information* (Cambridge, MA: MIT Press).

———(1982), "A Cognitive Cul-de-Sac," *Mind* 91: 109–11.

Dummett, Michael (1994), "Testimony and Memory," in Bimal Krishna Matilal and Arindam Chakrabarti (eds.), *Knowing from Words* (Dordrecht: Kluwer Academic Publishers), 251–72.

Dunn, Judith and Kendrick, Carol (1982), "The Speech of Two- and Three-Year-Olds to Infant Siblings: 'Baby Talk' and the Context of Communication," *Journal of Child Language* 9: 579–95.

Elgin, Catherine Z. (2002), "Take It from Me: The Epistemological Status of Testimony," *Philosophy and Phenomenological Research* 65: 291–308.

Evans, Gareth (1982), *The Varieties of Reference* (Oxford: Clarendon Press).

Faulkner, Paul (1998), "David Hume's Reductionist Epistemology of Testimony," *Pacific Philosophical Quarterly* 79: 302–13.

———(2000), "The Social Character of Testimonial Knowledge," *The Journal of Philosophy* 97: 581–601.

———(2002), "On the Rationality of our Response to Testimony," *Synthese* 131: 353–70.

———(2006), "On Dreaming and Being Lied To," *Episteme* 3: 149–59.

———(2007), "What Is Wrong with Lying?" *Philosophy and Phenomenological Research.* 75: 535–57.

———(forthcoming), "Cooperation and Trust in Conversational Exchanges." *Theoria.*

Foley, Richard (1994), "Egoism in Epistemology," in Frederick Schmitt (ed.), *Socializing Epistemology: The Social Dimensions of Knowledge* (Lanham, MD: Rowman & Littlefield), 53–73.

Fricker, Elizabeth (1987), "The Epistemology of Testimony," *Proceedings of the Aristotelian Society,* supp. vol. 61: 57–83.

——(1994), "Against Gullibility," in Bimal Krishna Matilal and Arindam Chakrabarti (eds.), *Knowing from Words* (Dordrecht: Kluwer Academic Publishers), 125–61.

——(1995), "Telling and Trusting: Reductionism and Anti-Reductionism in the Epistemology of Testimony," *Mind* 104: 393–411.

——(2002), "Trusting Others in the Sciences: *A Priori* or Empirical Warrant?," *Studies in History and Philosophy of Science* 33: 373–83.

——(2006a), "Testimony and Epistemic Autonomy," in Jennifer Lackey and Ernest Sosa (eds.), *The Epistemology of Testimony* (Oxford: Oxford University Press), 225–50.

——(2006b), "Second-Hand Knowledge," *Philosophy and Phenomenological Research.* 73: 592–618.

——(2007), "Audi on Testimony," in Mark Timmons, John Greco, and Alfred R. Mele (eds.), *Rationality and the Good* (Oxford: Oxford University Press), 100–05.

Gambetta, Diego (1988), "Can We Trust Trust?," in Diego Gambetta (ed.), *Trust: Making and Breaking Cooperative Relations* (Oxford: Blackwell), 213–37.

Gettier, Edmund (1963), "Is Justified True Belief Knowledge?" *Analysis* 23: 121–3.

Goldberg, Sanford C. (2005), "Testimonial Knowledge through Unsafe Testimony," *Analysis* 65: 302–11.

——(2006), "Reductionism and the Distinctiveness of Testimonial Knowledge," in Jennifer Lackey and Ernest Sosa (eds.), *The Epistemology of Testimony* (Oxford: Oxford University Press), 127–44.

——(2008), "Testimonial Knowledge in Early Childhood, Revisited," *Philosophy and Phenomenological Research* 76: 1–36.

Goldberg, Sanford and Henderson, David (2006), "Monitoring and Anti-Reductionism in the Epistemology of Testimony," *Philosophy and Phenomenological Research* 72: 600–17.

Goldman, Alvin I. (1976), "Discrimination and Perceptual Knowledge," *The Journal of Philosophy* 73: 771–91.

——(1986), *Epistemology and Cognition* (Cambridge, MA: Harvard University Press).

——(1992), *Liaisons: Philosophy Meets the Cognitive and Social Sciences* (Cambridge, MA: MIT Press).

——(1999), *Knowledge in a Social World* (Oxford: Clarendon Press).

Graham, Peter J. (1997), "What is Testimony?," *The Philosophical Quarterly* 47: 227–32.

Graham, Peter J. (2000a), "Transferring Knowledge," *Noûs* 34: 131–52.

Graham, Peter J. (2000b), "Conveying Information," *Synthese* 123: 365–92.

—— (2006), "Liberal Fundamentalism and Its Rivals," in Jennifer Lackey and Ernest Sosa (eds.), *The Epistemology of Testimony* (Oxford: Oxford University Press), 93–115.

Greco, John and Sosa, Ernest (eds.) (1999), *The Blackwell Guide to Epistemology* (Oxford: Blackwell).

Grice, H. P. (1957), "Meaning," *The Philosophical Review* 66: 377–88.

—— (1989), *Studies in the Way of Words* (Cambridge, MA: Harvard University Press).

Hardwig, John (1985), "Epistemic Dependence," *The Journal of Philosophy* 82: 335–49.

—— (1991), "The Role of Trust in Knowledge," *The Journal of Philosophy* 88: 693–708.

Harman, Gilbert (1968), "Knowledge, Inference, and Explanation," *American Philosophical Quarterly* 5: 164–73.

—— (1973), *Thought* (Princeton: Princeton University Press).

—— (1980), "Reasoning and Explanatory Coherence," *American Philosophical Quarterly* 17: 151–8.

Hawthorne, John (2004), *Knowledge and Lotteries* (Oxford: Oxford University Press).

Hendricks, Scott (2005), "Demons and the Isolation Argument," *The Philosophical Quarterly* 55: 403–18.

Hinchman, Edward S. (2005), "Telling as Inviting to Trust," *Philosophy and Phenomenological Research* 70: 562–87.

Holton, Richard (1994), "Deciding to Trust, Coming to Believe," *Australasian Journal of Philosophy* 72: 63–76.

Hume, David (1977), *An Enquiry Concerning Human Understanding*, Eric Steinberg (ed.), (Indianapolis: Hackett).

Insole, Christopher J. (2000), "Seeing Off the Local Threat to Irreducible Knowledge by Testimony," *The Philosophical Quarterly* 50: 44–56.

Klein, Peter (1971), "A Proposed Definition of Propositional Knowledge," *The Journal of Philosophy* 68: 471–82.

—— (1976), "Knowledge, Causality, and Defeasibility," *The Journal of Philosophy* 73: 792–812.

—— (1979), "Misleading 'Misleading Defeaters'," *The Journal of Philosophy* 76: 382–6.

—— (1980), "Misleading Evidence and the Restoration of Justification," *Philosophical Studies* 37: 81–9.

Koenig, Melissa A., Clément, Fabrice, and Harris, Paul L. (2004), "Trust in Testimony: Children's Use of True and False Statements," *Psychological Science* 15: 694–8.

Koenig, Melissa A. and Echols, Catharine H. (2003), "Infants' Understanding of False Labeling Events: The Referential Roles of Words and the Speakers who Use them," *Cognition* 87: 179–208.

Koenig, Melissa A. and Harris, Paul L. (2005), "Preschoolers Mistrust Ignorant and Inaccurate Speakers," *Child Development* 76: 1261–77.

Kusch, Martin (2002), *Knowledge by Agreement: The Programme of Communitarian Epistemology* (Oxford: Oxford University Press).

Kvanvig, Jonathan (forthcoming), "Assertion, Knowledge, and Lotteries," in Patrick Greenough and Duncan Pritchard (eds.), *Williamson on Knowledge* (Oxford: Oxford University Press).

Lackey, Jennifer (1999), "Testimonial Knowledge and Transmission," *The Philosophical Quarterly* 49: 471–90.

———(2003), "A Minimal Expression of Non–Reductionism in the Epistemology of Testimony," *Noûs* 37: 706–23.

———(2004), "Review of Michael DePaul and Linda Zagzebski (eds.), *Intellectual Virtue: Perspectives from Ethics and Epistemology*," *Notre Dame Philosophical Reviews*.

———(2005a), "Testimony and the Infant/Child Objection," *Philosophical Studies* 126: 163–90.

———(2005b), "Memory as a Generative Epistemic Source," *Philosophy and Phenomenological Research* 70: 636–58.

———(2006a), "The Nature of Testimony," *Pacific Philosophical Quarterly* 87: 177–97.

———(2006b), "Introduction," in Jennifer Lackey and Ernest Sosa (eds.), *The Epistemology of Testimony* (Oxford: Oxford University Press), 1–21.

———(2006c), "It Takes Two to Tango: Beyond Reductionism and Non-Reductionism in the Epistemology of Testimony," in Jennifer Lackey and Ernest Sosa (eds.), *The Epistemology of Testimony* (Oxford: Oxford University Press), 160–89.

———(2006d), "Knowing from Testimony," *Philosophy Compass* 1: 432–48.

———(2006e), "Review of Martin Kusch, *Knowledge by Agreement: The Programme of Communitarian Epistemology*," *Philosophy and Phenomenological Research* 72: 235–8.

———(2006f), "Learning from Words," *Philosophy and Phenomenological Research* 73: 77–101.

———(2007a), "Why Memory Really *Is* a Generative Epistemic Source: A Reply to Senor," *Philosophy and Phenomenological Research* 74: 211–21.

———(2007b), "Norms of Assertion," *Noûs*. 41: 594–626.

Lackey, Jennifer and Sosa, Ernest (eds.), (2006), *The Epistemology of Testimony* (Oxford: Oxford University Press).

Lehrer, Keith (1965), "Knowledge, Truth, and Evidence," *Analysis* 25: 168–75.

—— (1974), *Knowledge* (Oxford: Oxford University Press).

—— (2006), "Testimony and Trustworthiness," in Jennifer Lackey and Ernest Sosa (eds.), *The Epistemology of Testimony* (Oxford: Oxford University Press), 145–59.

Lehrer, Keith and Paxson, Thomas (1969), "Knowledge: Undefeated Justified True Belief," *The Journal of Philosophy* 66: 225–37.

Lewis, David (1996), "Elusive Knowledge," *Australasian Journal of Philosophy* 74: 549–67.

Lipton, Peter (1998), "The Epistemology of Testimony," *Studies in History and Philosophy of Science* 29: 1–31.

Lutz, Donna J. and Keil, Frank C. (2002), "Early Understanding of the Division of Cognitive Labor," *Child Development* 73: 1073–84.

Lyons, Jack (1997), "Testimony, Induction and Folk Psychology," *Australasian Journal of Philosophy* 75: 163–78.

McDowell, John (1994), "Knowledge by Hearsay," in Bimal Krishna Matilal and Arindam Chakrabarti (eds.), *Knowing from Words* (Dordrecht: Kluwer Academic Publishers), 195–224.

MacFarlane, John (2005), "Knowledge Laundering: Testimony and Sensitive Invariantism," *Analysis* 65: 132–8.

Mackie, J. L. (1970), "The Possibility of Innate Knowledge," *Proceedings of the Aristotelian Society* 70: 181–96.

Matilal, Bimal Krishna and Chakrabarti, Arindam (eds.), (1994), *Knowing From Words* (Dordrecht: Kluwer Academic Publishers).

Millgram, Elijah (1997), *Practical Induction* (Cambridge, MA: Harvard University Press).

Moore, G. E. (1962), *Commonplace Book: 1919–1953* (London: Allen & Unwin).

Moran, Richard (2005), "Problems of Sincerity," *Proceedings of the Aristotelian Society* 105: 341–61.

—— (2006), "Getting Told and Being Believed," in Jennifer Lackey and Ernest Sosa (eds.), *The Epistemology of Testimony* (Oxford: Oxford University Press), 272–306.

Nozick, Robert (1981), *Philosophical Explanations* (Cambridge, MA: The Belknap Press).

Owens, David (2000), *Reason without Freedom: The Problem of Epistemic Normativity* (London: Routledge).

—— (2006), "Testimony and Assertion," *Philosophical Studies* 130: 105–29.

Pea, Roy D. (1982), "Origins of Verbal Logic: Spontaneous Denials by Two- and Three-year-olds. *Journal of Child Language* 9: 597–626.

Pettit, Phillip (1995), "The Cunning of Trust," *Philosophy and Public Affairs* 24: 202–25.

Plantinga, Alvin (1993*a*), *Warrant: The Current Debate* (Oxford: Oxford University Press).

____(1993*b*), *Warrant and Proper Function* (Oxford: Oxford University Press).

____(2000), *Warranted Christian Belief* (Oxford: Oxford University Press).

Pollock, John (1986), *Contemporary Theories of Knowledge* (Totowa, NJ: Rowman & Littlefield).

Pritchard, Duncan (2004), "The Epistemology of Testimony," *Philosophical Issues* 14: 326–48.

____(2005), *Epistemic Luck* (Oxford: Oxford University Press).

Recanati, François (1987), *Meaning and Force: The Pragmatics of Performative Utterances* (Cambridge: Cambridge University Press).

Reed, Baron (2000), "Accidental Truth and Accidental Justification," *The Philosophical Quarterly* 50: 57–67.

____(2001), "Epistemic Agency and the Intellectual Virtues," *The Southern Journal of Philosophy* 39: 507–26.

____(2006), "Epistemic Circularity Squared? Skepticism about Common Sense," *Philosophy and Phenomenological Research* 73: 186–97.

____(2007), "The Long Road to Skepticism," *The Journal of Philosophy.* 104: 236–62.

____(forthcoming), "In Defense of Stable Invariantism," *Noûs*.

Reid, Thomas (1983), *Essay on the Intellectual Powers of Man* in Ronald E. Beanblossom and Keith Lehrer (eds.), *Thomas Reid's Inquiry and Essays* (Indianapolis: Hackett).

Reynolds, Steven L. (2002), "Testimony, Knowledge, and Epistemic Goals," *Philosophical Studies* 110: 139–61.

Root, Michael (2001), "Hume on the Virtues of Testimony," *American Philosophical Quarterly* 38: 19–35.

Ross, Angus (1986), "Why Do We Believe What We Are Told?," *Ratio* 28: 69–88.

Ross, James (1975), "Testimonial Evidence," in Keith Lehrer (ed.), *Analysis and Metaphysics: Essays in Honor of R. M. Chisholm* (Dordrecht: Reidel), 35–55.

Rysiew, Patrick (2002), "Testimony, Simulation, and the Limits of Inductivism," *Australasian Journal of Philosophy* 78: 269–74.

Schmitt, Frederick F. (1987), "Justification, Sociality, and Autonomy," *Synthese* 73: 43–85.

Schmitt, Frederick F. (ed.), (1994), *Socializing Epistemology: The Social Dimensions of Knowledge* (Lanham, MD: Rowman & Littlefield).

—— (1999), "Social Epistemology," in John Greco and Ernest Sosa (eds.), *The Blackwell Guide to Epistemology* (Oxford: Blackwell), 354–82.

—— (2006), "Testimonial Justification and Transindividual Reasons," in Jennifer Lackey and Ernest Sosa (eds.), *The Epistemology of Testimony* (Oxford: Oxford University Press), 193–224.

Senor, Thomas D. (1993), "Internalistic Foundationalism and the Justification of Memory Belief," *Synthese* 94: 453–76.

—— (2007), "Preserving Preservationism: A Reply to Lackey," *Philosophy and Phenomenological Research*. 74: 199–208.

Shatz, Marilyn and Gelman, Rochel (1973), "The Development of Communication Skills: Modifications in the Speech of Young Children as a Function of Listener," *Monographs of the Society for Research in Child Development* 38: 1–37.

Shogenji, Tomoji (2006), "A Defense of Reductionism about Testimonial Justification of Beliefs," *Noûs* 40: 331–46.

Shope, Robert (1983), *The Analysis of Knowing* (Princeton: Princeton University Press).

Sosa, Ernest (1974), "How Do You Know?," *American Philosophical Quarterly* 11: 113–22.

—— (1979), "Epistemic Presupposition," in George S. Pappas (ed.), *Justification and Knowledge: New Studies in Epistemology* (Dordrecht: Reidel), 79–92.

—— (1991), *Knowledge in Perspective: Selected Essays in Epistemology* (Cambridge: Cambridge University Press).

—— (1996), "Postscript to 'Proper Functionalism and Virtue Epistemology'," in John L. Kvanvig (ed.), *Warrant in Contemporary Epistemology* (Lanham, MD: Rowman & Littlefield), 271–81.

—— (1999), "How Must Knowledge Be Modally Related to What Is Known?," *Philosophical Topics* 26: 373–84.

—— (2000), "Contextualim and Skepticism," in J. Tomberlin (ed.), *Philosophical Issues*, suppl. to *Noûs* 34: 94–107.

—— (2002), "Tracking, Competence, and Knowledge," in Paul Moser (ed.), *The Oxford Handbook of Epistemology* (Oxford: Oxford University Press), 264–87.

—— (2006), "Knowledge: Instrumental and Testimonial," in Jennifer Lackey and Ernest Sosa (eds.), *The Epistemology of Testimony* (Oxford: Oxford University Press), 116–23.

Stalnaker, Robert (1978), "Assertion," *Syntax and Semantics* 9: 315–32.

Stanley, Jason (2005), *Knowledge and Practical Interests* (Oxford: Oxford University Press).

Stevenson, Leslie (1993), "Why Believe What People Say?," *Synthese* 94: 429–51.

Strawson, P. F. (1994), "Knowing From Words," in Bimal Krishna Matilal and Arindam Chakrabarti (eds.), *Knowing from Words* (Dordrecht: Kluwer Academic Publishers), 23–7.

Swain, Marshall (1981), *Reasons and Knowledge* (Ithaca, NY: Cornell University Press).

Taylor, Marjorie, Cartwright, Bridget S., and Bowden, Thomas (1991), "Perspective Taking and Theory of Mind: Do Children Predict Interpretive Diversity as a Function of Differences in Observers' Knowledge?," *Child Development* 62: 1334–51.

Taylor, Marjorie, Esbensen Bonnie M., and Bennett, Robert T. (1994), "Children's Understanding of Knowledge Acquisition: The Tendency for Children to Report That They Have Always Known What They Have Just Learned," *Child Development* 65: 1581–1604.

Traiger, Saul (1993), "Humean Testimony," *Pacific Philosophical Quarterly* 74: 135–49.

Unger, Peter (1975), *Ignorance: A Case for Scepticism* (Oxford: Oxford University Press).

Van Cleve, James (2006), "Reid on the Credit of Human Testimony," in Jennifer Lackey and Ernest Sosa (eds.), *The Epistemology of Testimony* (Oxford: Oxford University Press), 50–74.

Wanderer, Jeremy (unpublished), "Defending Defensibility."

Webb, Mark Owen (1993), "Why I Know About As Much As You: A Reply to Hardwig," *The Journal of Philosophy* 90: 260–70.

Weiner, Matthew (2003), "Accepting Testimony," *The Philosophical Quarterly* 53: 256–64.

——(2005), "Must We Know What We Say?," *The Philosophical Review* 114: 227–51.

Welbourne, Michael (1979), "The Transmission of Knowledge," *The Philosophical Quarterly* 29: 1–9.

——(1981), "The Community of Knowledge," *The Philosophical Quarterly* 31: 302–14.

——(1986), *The Community of Knowledge* (Aberdeen: Aberdeen University Press).

——(1994), "Testimony, Knowledge and Belief," in Bimal Krishna Matilal and Arindam Chakrabarti (eds.), *Knowing from Words* (Dordrecht: Kluwer Academic Publishers), 297–313.

Williams, Bernard (2002), *Truth and Truthfulness* (Princeton: Princeton University Press).

Williams, Michael (1999), *Groundless Belief: An Essay on the Possibility of Epistemology*, 2nd edn. (Princeton: Princeton University Press).

Williamson, Timothy (1996), "Knowing and Asserting," *The Philosophical Review* 105: 489–523.

——— (2000), *Knowledge and its Limits* (Oxford: Oxford University Press).

Wolterstorff, Nicholas (2001), *Thomas Reid and the Story of Epistemology* (Cambridge: Cambridge University Press).

Index